# CONTENTS ■

# ACKNOWLEDGEMENTS

The books in this series are a departure from traditional law texts and represent one view of a type of learning resource that we feel is particularly useful to students. The series editors would therefore like to thank the publishers for their support in making the project a reality. In particular we would also like to thank Alexia Chan for her continued faith in the project from its first conception and Tessa Heath for all her hard work well above and beyond the call of duty.

Jacqueline Martin and Chris Turner

I would like to thank Chris Gale for his work in ensuring that the book is as accurate and readable as possible and I would like to dedicate the book to my husband Richard, who, over the last few months, has burnt almost as much midnight oil as myself and provided constant support and invaluable advice.

Judith Bray

The authors and publishers would like to thank the following for permission to reproduce copyright material: Sweet & Maxwell for extracts on pp 49, 180-181, 374-375 and 436; Oxford University Press for extracts on pp 1, 39–40, 49–50 and 94; LexisNexisUK for extracts on pp 43, 124, 136, 139, 178, 202, 203–204, 234, 372 and 439. © Crown copyright material is reproduced with permission of the Controller of HMSO.

The publishers apologise if inadvertently any sources remain unacknowledged and will be glad to make the necessary arrangements at the earliest opportunity.

# PREFACE ■

The *Unlocking the Law* series is an entirely new style of undergraduate law textbooks. Many student texts are very prose dense and have little in the way of interactive materials to help a student feel his or her way through the course of study on a given module.

The purpose of this series, then, is to try to make learning each subject area more accessible by focusing on actual learning needs, and by providing a range of different supporting materials and features.

All topic areas are broken up into 'bite size' sections with a logical progression and extensive use of headings and numerous sub-headings. Each book in the series will also contain a variety of charts, diagrams and key fact summaries to reinforce the information in the body of the text. Diagrams and flow charts are particularly useful because they can provide a quick and easy understanding of the key points, especially when revising for examinations. Key facts charts not only provide a quick visual guide through the subject but are useful for revision purposes also.

The books have a number of common features in the layout. Important cases are separated out for easy access and have full citation in the text as well as the table of cases for ease of reference. The emphasis of the series is on depth of understanding much more than breadth. For this reason each text also includes key extracts from judgments where appropriate. Extracts from academic comment from journal articles and leading texts are also included to give some insight into the academic debate on complex or controversial areas. In both cases these are indented to make them clear from the body of the text.

Finally, the books also include much formative 'self-testing', with a variety of activities ranging through subject specific comprehension, application of the law, and a range of other activities to help the student gain a good idea of his or her progress in the course.

Symbols used in this series:

 This is a small extract from a judgment in a case. It may follow a case example or the case may be identified immediately above.

 This is a section from an Act.

 This is an Article of the EC Treaty or of the European Convention on Human Rights.

This is a clause from the Draft Criminal Code.

Where a paragraph is indented, this is an extract from an academic source such as an article or a leading textbook.

Note also that all incidental references to 'he', 'him', his, etc are intended to be gender neutral.

Land law is not a dry academic subject; it covers issues that affect all our lives such as the buying and selling of houses, the letting or renting of flats, disputes between neighbours and the inheritance of property under a will. It even covers the finding of treasure in the ground. I hope you will find the layout of this book helpful and stimulating. The aim is to combine explanations of the law with short summaries of cases and some practical exercises. The law is as stated on 29th December 2003 and covers all recent developments such as the Land Registration Act 2002 and the introduction of Commonhold.

Judith Bray

# TABLE OF CASES

# TABLE OF STATUTES AND OTHER INSTRUMENTS

## Statutes

# Statutory instruments

# European legislation

# LIST OF FIGURES

# chapter 1 INTRODUCTION

## 1.1 Introduction

Land is central to everyone's lives. We all have to live somewhere, even if it is not a permanent home. Land law is the study of the relationship between land and the owner of that land. However, when we speak of owners of land we include not only the owner in law, who has the right to buy and sell the land, but also others who have lesser rights, such as the right to walk on the land. So, many different people can be said to be owners of rights in respect of the same piece of land. These rights may also extend to having rights of control over your neighbour's land: if they try to develop their garden and build another house or build an extension, you may be able to stop them. It is the way all these rights overlap that causes some of the problems in land law.

> 'The name "land law" suggests a simple contextual category: all the law about land
> . . . Every business needs premises, every factory needs a site. For most of us as
> private individuals our home is the centre of our lives. Functionally, this core of
> land law has the task of providing the structure within which people and businesses
> can safely acquire and exploit land for daily use, to live and to work. To discharge
> that function, it has to have its own conceptual apparatus. . . . There is a recurrent
> problem. Property rights in land have roots a millennium deep in a pre-commercial
> society in which land and wealth were virtually synonymous. The structuring of
> land and the power that went with it was then land law's principal mission . . .'
>
> P Birks, 'Before We Begin: Five Keys to Land Law'
> in S Bright and J Dewar (eds), *Land Law: Themes and Perspectives* (Oxford University Press, 1998), p 457.

## 1.2 The definition of 'land'

The definition of 'land' has long troubled lawyers. We can start by looking at the statutory definition. 'Land' is defined in the Law of Property Act 1925 at s 205(1)(ix):

**S** 's 205(1)(ix) Land includes land of any tenure, and mines and minerals, whether or not held apart from the surface, buildings or parts of buildings (whether the division is horizontal, vertical or made in any other way) and other corporeal hereditaments also a manor, an advowson, a rent and other incorporeal hereditaments; and an easement, right, privilege, or benefit in, over or derived from land . . . And mines and minerals include any strata or seam of minerals or substances in or under any land, and power of working and getting the same'.

It is a long and complex definition and shows that land can include many different aspects and rights.

## 1.2.1 Corporeal and incorporeal hereditaments

Within the definition in s 205, two types of rights are identified: corporeal and incorporeal hereditaments.

**1. Corporeal hereditaments**: these are rights that have some real or tangible quality. They would include anything growing on the land, such as shrubs and trees, or anything which is found under the ground, such as minerals. These will be as much part of the land as the physical plot of land itself.

**2. Incorporeal hereditaments**: these are rights in land that are intangible. They cannot be physically seen but their effect can be felt. An example would be the right to use your neighbour's garden as a short cut. This will affect your neighbour's enjoyment of his land. These rights, which also include mortgages and leases, will also affect the exact nature of your neighbour's rights over his plot of land.

## ACTIVITY

Consider the following rights over land: are they corporeal or incorporeal hereditaments?

1. You have agreed with your neighbour that he will not use his land for business purposes.

2. You plant several rose bushes in your garden.

3. You allow your friend to rent your garage.

4. You find some gold in the stream which runs through your garden.

5. The property that you agree to buy has a large stable block.

Land also has a three-dimensional quality – a surface area, the airspace above it and the ground below – and also a possible fourth dimension which is made up of rights and interests in the land and, more importantly, the length of time that you can enjoy the land. We shall start by looking at the way these rights and interests have developed over hundreds of years to leave us with the system that we know today.

## 1.3 Tenures and estates in land

### 1.3.1 Tenure

After 1066 all land was held to be owned by the king, and his subjects were then granted rights in that land. The rights that they held were really as tenants of the king. In return for the land the tenants agreed to carry out certain duties for the king. This was called **tenure**. It was a bit like paying rent but instead of paying money the tenants agreed to do something that the king wanted to be done. Tenure took several different forms – spiritual, military or agricultural.

Examples of tenure: agreement by the tenant to pray for the soul of the grantor (frankalmoign); provision of armed horsemen for battle (knight service); and performance of agricultural services (socage).

## 1.3.2 Estates

An estate was a right of possession. Historically, it was referred to as a right of **seisin**. When we speak of 'estates' we are talking about how long a person is allowed to enjoy the plot of land.

'The land itself is one thing, and the estate in the land is another thing, for an estate in the land is a time in the land, or land for a time, and there are diversities of estates, which are no more than diversities of time.'

*Walsingham's Case* (1573) 75 ER 80

The law would protect the tenant's right to the land against anyone unless they could prove that they had a better right to the land than the tenant.

Today there are only **two ways** that you can be said to own land in law:

1. either you have a **freehold estate** which is regarded as absolute ownership

2. or you can have a **leasehold estate** which is absolute ownership but only for a defined period of time, for example you could rent a flat for two years.

## 1.3.3 Legal estates in land before 1925

The position was very different in 1066. There were several legal estates in land which were regarded as absolute ownership.

1. **Fee simple**: this could last as long as the original grantee or his heirs survived. In practical terms this meant that it could last indefinitely. Until the fourteenth century the land had to pass through the family and could not be sold to someone out of the family. This rule was changed gradually until eventually it could be sold in your lifetime or left by will.

2. **Fee tail**: this is not recognised as a legal estate today. It was a grant of land that could only pass to a certain class of descendant, usually the descendants of the original grantee. It could last for as long as the original grantee or his descendants survived. Eventually, when the line of direct descendants ran out, the Crown could claim the land and it passed out of the family.

3. **Life estate**: this was recognised as a freehold estate although it was limited in length. It would come to an end on the death of the holder of the life estate. It could be transferred to someone else but only during the original owner's lifetime and they knew it would end when the original owner died.

Now a few useful legal definitions:

- **grantor** means the person who owns the land but is passing it to someone else. This would have been the person who had received it from the king. He became grantor of the land when he passed it on to someone else

- **grantee** means the person who receives the land from the grantor.

Today, only the first of the three legal estates in land is recognised. The others will be less than a legal estate. They take effect **in equity**, which means rights in the land where the owner has only limited control over decision-making over the land itself, for example he has no right to sell the legal estate.

## 1.3.4 Estates in land from and after 1925

After 1925 the number of legal estates in land was reduced to two:

**1.** an estate in fee simple absolute in possession (the freehold estate)

**2.** an estate for a term of years absolute (the leasehold estate).

So the freehold estate in land is also called a **fee simple absolute in possession**. This can be broken down into three different parts:

**1. fee simple**: meaning freehold ownership giving absolute rights over the property during someone's lifetime but also the chance to leave it to anyone you wish on your death. (If you remember from above, the life estate was a legal estate but the property would revert back to the grantor when the grantee died.)

**2. absolute**: meaning no limits on ownership, for example to Y until he leaves school, would not give Y absolute ownership and control over the property.

**3. in possession**: meaning immediate occupation and enjoyment of the land. There would be no question of anyone else having a prior claim.

## 1.3.5 Limitations on ownership

What if there are potential limits on ownership?

There may be terms imposed on ownership which will affect the nature of ownership. These generally take one of two forms:

**1.** a conditional fee simple

**2.** a determinable fee simple.

## A conditional fee simple

Property may be given to someone but a condition may be attached which imposes conditions on the enjoyment of the land, for example 'to X provided that he does not become a lawyer'. This does not prevent the gift from taking effect in law. If the condition is carried out then the gift does not automatically return to the grantor but he has the choice of whether or not to reclaim it. The grantor could ignore the condition and it will remain with the grantee. Some conditions are void because they are seen to be contrary to public policy. A condition which is uncertain or a condition which encourages divorce or separation would be void on these grounds. The grantee would then be able to take the land free from the condition.

# CASE EXAMPLE

### *Blathwayt v Baron Cawley* **[1976] AC 397**

A testator drew up his will leaving his estate to a number of persons in succession, but under Clause 6 it was held that the interest of any person entitled would determine if he became a Roman Catholic. Sometime after the testator died the life tenant became a Roman Catholic and the interest determined and passed to the next person entitled. The court considered whether the clause was void for uncertainty.

'On the question whether the forfeiture clause, in so far as it relates to being or becoming a Roman Catholic is void for uncertainty. I am clearly of the opinion that it is not. Clauses relating in one way or another to the Roman Catholic Church, or faith have been known and recognised for too many years both in acts of Parliament . . . and in wills and settlements for it now to be possible to avoid them on this ground.'

Lord Wilberforce

# CASE EXAMPLE

### *Re Moore* **(1888) 39 Ch D 116**

Money was to be paid to the testator's sister 'while so living apart from her husband'. This was held to be void as it was contrary to public policy. It appeared to encourage separation of the parties.

## A determinable fee simple

In some cases the gift may give rise to a determinable fee simple in which case the grantee does not receive a legal estate with all the consequences of ownership but instead receives an estate in equity. These rights will last until the determining event occurs.

Consider the following examples:

**1.** 'to A until he marries'

**2.** 'to B provided that he remains a barrister'.

In **1**. A has a determinable estate which will not take effect in law and if A marries the land will revert to the grantor automatically.

In **2**. B has a conditional fee simple which takes effect as a legal estate unless B leaves the Bar, in which case the grantor can reclaim the land.

The difference between the two rests largely on the words used. Words such as 'unless', 'on condition that', 'if' and 'provided that' suggest a conditional fee simple, but words such as 'until', 'so long as', 'whilst' or 'during' suggest a determinable fee simple.

## ACTIVITY

Look at the following examples and decide whether they suggest a determinable or conditional fee simple and what the consequence will be if the condition is held to be void:

**1.** 'to Robert until he becomes a judge'

**2.** 'to Susie during her years at university'

**3.** 'to my children unless they start smoking'

**4.** 'to Flora unless she marries someone not of Jewish parentage'

**5.** 'to David provided that he has no more contact with his ex-wife Davina'.

# 1.4 Ownership of the surface of the land: boundaries

'Whoever owns the soil owns everything up to the heavens and down to the depth of the Earth.'

Attributed to Accursius of Bologna in *Glossa Ordinaria* on *Corpus Iuris* (13th C.)

Any landowner wants to be quite clear about the extent of rights that he may have over the plot of land that he has purchased. He will start by finding out where the boundaries are. This will depend on the site of the land; in particular, does it border the sea or a river?

# 1.4.1 Land bordering the coast or a river

Land is often seen as permanent and unchanging but the processes of coastal erosion and deposition challenge this. Over a period of time, where land borders a river or the sea, soil may be removed by erosion and it appears to cease to belong to the owner and will transfer to the land of another. The effect of this is that one person's land will increase at the expense of the other. The law has to deal with this.

# 1.4.2 The doctrines of accretion and diluvion

The doctrines of **accretion** and **diluvion** are the legal mechanisms employed to resolve disputes arising through changes in land bordering water.

**1.** The doctrine of **accretion** says that any naturally occurring additions of soil to the waterside land become the property of the owner of the land which is increased.

**2.** The doctrine of **diluvion** is the reduction in an area of land by naturally occurring movements of soil.

According to Lord Wilberforce in *Southern Centre of Theosophy Inc v State of South Australia* [1982] 1 All ER 283 the changes must take place very slowly, gradually and by imperceptible movements. He added: 'In the lottery of life the land owner may lose as well as gain from changes in the water boundary or level'.

This case concerned an inland lake in Australia which was reduced in size by 20 acres through deposits of sand over 60 years. The lake was owned by the Crown but it was held that it lost title to the 20 acres. This was added to the title held by the owners of the area gaining the land.

If there are any sudden changes as a result of flooding then the rules do not apply and the boundaries remain the same. For example, X and Y both own land on either side of a river. Suppose there is a storm which results in X's land losing considerable amounts of soil and so Y's land is considerably increased. Y cannot then claim the change in boundary under the doctrine of accretion and X's boundary will be changed to adapt to the sudden change.

Compare the situation where X is convinced that his land is receding. He measures the boundary and after five years there is a change of one third of a metre – the doctrine will probably apply and X cannot do anything about the loss to his land.

## When will the doctrine be applied?

The modern law stops short of applying the doctrine of accretion to all cases. It has to be decided whether the interest in land which is the subject of **accretion** is fixed or moveable and this is only made clear by looking at the wording of the conveyance. So if you know that the boundaries are subject to change and the conveyance refers to this then the landowner with an increased area of land cannot claim that for himself.

Case law shows that you can exclude the operation of the doctrine of accretion by clear words in the conveyance.

The Land Registration Act 2002, s 61 expressly states that a registered estate in land as shown in the register as having a particular boundary does not affect the operation of **accretion** and **diluvion**.

The doctrine of accretion shows us that not only does land extend upwards and downwards, it can grow or shrink in surface area.

## 1.4.3 Other boundaries

Even where boundaries do not border the sea and inland waterways, there may be uncertainty. The Land Registration Rules accept that maps and plans are imprecise and a filed plan or general map relevant to any registered title is normally 'deemed to indicate the general boundaries only' and the exact line of the boundary is left undetermined. This general principle has been preserved in the Land Registration Act 2002. There is provision under s 60 for rules to make provision for boundaries to be fixed exactly.

 's 60(3) Rules may make provision enabling or requiring the exact line of the boundary of a registered estate to be determined and may, in particular, make provision about –

    (a) the circumstances in which the exact line of a boundary may or must be determined;

    (b) how the exact line of a boundary may be determined;

    (c) procedure in relation to applications for determination.'

Unless such an application is made then older, more general, rules will apply.

These are some of the presumptions which can be used to decide the issue.

### The 'hedge and ditch' rule

*Wibberley (Alan) Building Ltd v Insley* [1999] 1 WLR 894 applied this rule which suggests that where land is bounded by a hedge and ditch then the boundary lies along the edge of the ditch on the far side of the hedge. This assumes that the ditch builder deposited the earth on his own land rather than the land of his neighbour.

### The '*ad medium filum*' rule

This applies to land which abuts a highway or non-tidal river. The rule says that the boundary between properties on opposite sides of the road is a line drawn down the middle of the road. The owners of land adjoining the highway are presumed to own the sub-soil as far as the middle of the road and the airspace above the soil. The owner cannot use the sub-soil so as to interfere with the use of the highway, for example if the sub-soil contained a mineral such as fuller's earth, you could not extract it in such a way as to cause subsidence to the road.

## 1.4.4 Natural rights of support for the land

Landowners have certain rights which are incidental to ownership and could give rise to an action in tort if they are interfered with. It is accepted that every landowner has the right to enjoy his land in its natural state and this means it must not be put at risk by a neighbour who undermines the foundations.

---

### APPLYING THE LAW

A landowner may be able to sue if his neighbour starts extensive mining operations and as a result his house is affected by subsidence. In order to be successful he would have to prove that his land has been affected. No case would succeed in court if the owner merely had proof that mining operations were going on and could affect his house.

---

It is important to note that the right only affects the land itself and not the buildings on the land. This can be criticised. It should extend to buildings. A landowner cannot expect to be compensated if the buildings on his land were undermined by the activities of his neighbour. However, the landowner may have a remedy because the right of support for buildings may be recognised as an easement. The problem is that the claimant must satisfy the rules relevant to easements rather than have the chance of claiming the right automatically.

## CASE EXAMPLE

### *Dalton v Henry Angus & Co* (1861) 6 App Cas 740

The court upheld an easement of support to be enjoyed by one landowner as against another. There was disagreement in court as to whether this was a negative or positive easement. The House of Lords held it to be a positive easement.

# 1.5 Ownership of the surface of the land: items found in or on the surface of the land, including minerals

## 1.5.1 Fixtures and fittings

Section 205 of the Law of Property Act 1925 specifically mentions buildings and parts of buildings as forming part of the land. This is further developed because any item affixed to the land becomes

land itself. There is an old maxim '*quicquid plantatur solo, solo cedit*' which, translated, means 'whatever is attached to the soil becomes part of it'. The word 'fixture' means anything that has become so attached to the land that it forms part of the land.

If the item has not become a fixture then it will be a mere chattel and so will not pass with the property to the purchaser and the seller can legally take it as his own on the sale of the property, for example the clothes of the seller will always remain chattels and will not pass to the purchaser, but what of the fitted wardrobe that they are in? Some fitted wardrobes are attached to the wall but some can be free-standing. The law has to resolve the question of whether the purchaser can claim the fitted wardrobe and any other item that is not clearly a fixture or a chattel.

The law applies two tests:

**1.** the degree of annexation

**2.** the purpose of annexation.

# CASE EXAMPLE

### *Holland v Hodgson* (1872) LR 7 CP 328

Blackburn J said:

> 'There is no doubt that the general maxim of the law is, that what is annexed to the land becomes part of the land; but it is very difficult, if not impossible to say with precision what constitutes annexation sufficient for this purpose. It is a question which must depend on the circumstances of each case, and mainly on two circumstances, as indicating the intention viz. the degree of annexation and the object of the annexation. When the article in question is no further attached to the land, than by its own weight it is generally to be considered a mere chattel . . . but even in such a case, if the intention is apparent to make the articles part of the land, they do become part of the land . . . Thus blocks of stone placed one on top of another without any mortar or cement for the purpose of forming a dry stone wall would become part of the land, though the same stones, if deposited in a builder's yard and for convenience sake stacked on the top of each other in the form of a wall, would remain chattels'.

Blackburn J is highlighting the importance of the method of annexation of the object to the land. He suggests that even if an object is very heavy, if it never becomes fixed to the land then it remains a chattel, whereas an item that is firmly fixed will become a fixture.

He then goes on to introduce the idea that what matters is the intention when the item is fixed. This becomes more significant than the practical question of how the item was attached to the ground.

'On the other hand, an article may be very firmly fixed to the land, and yet the circumstances may be such as to shew that it was never intended to be part of the land, and then it does not become part of the land . . . Perhaps the true rule is, that articles not otherwise attached to the land than by their own weight are not to be considered as part of the land, unless the circumstances are such that they were intended to be part of the land, the onus of showing that they were so intended lying on those who assert that they have ceased to be chattels, and that, on the contrary, an article which is affixed to the land even slightly is to be considered as part of the land, unless the circumstances are such as to shew that it was intended all along to continue a chattel, the onus lying on those who contend that it is a chattel'.

## The degree of annexation

This depends on whether the item is resting on the land by its own weight or whether it has been fixed. Traditionally, if an object rested on the ground by its own weight it was regarded as a chattel. So a Dutch barn resting on timber on the ground would be a chattel and could be removed by the seller.

# CASE EXAMPLE

### *Hamp v Bygrave* (1983) 266 EG 720

A number of items were removed by the seller and the purchasers argued that they were fixtures and should remain at the property. The items included patio lights fixed to the wall with screws, six urns resting on their own weight, a stone Chinese ornament resting on its own weight, several statues and their plinths and a lead trough.

J 'The first question is, therefore, were the items or any of them, fixtures? It is accepted that the answer to that question depends upon the application of two tests. First what was the degree of annexation? There is no doubt that none of the items was fixed or attached to the land or to any structure which was itself attached to the land. Each rested by its own weight either on the land itself or on some sort of plinth, and only in the case of the Chinese figure was the plinth fixed or attached to the land. Judged by this test therefore they were all prima facie chattels'.

Boreham J

However, it is clear that the way the item is fixed is not conclusive, particularly today when technological advances have allowed items to be removed easily, even after semi-permanent fixing.

In *Holland v Hodgson* (1872) it was held that there were two questions to ask:

**1.** whether the annexation was intended to increase the value or enjoyment of the property

**2.** was it for the better enjoyment of the item?

What happens if there is no annexation at all? This may be because the item is very heavy and so rests on its own weight.

# CASE EXAMPLE

*Eliteson Ltd v Morris* **[1997] 1 WLR 687**

A wooden bungalow rested on its own weight on concrete pillars. As pointed out in the judgment, the materials used to construct the building, such as the chipboard ceilings, had all started life as chattels.

> 'A house which is constructed in such a way so as to be removable, whether as a unit, or in sections, may well remain a chattel, even though it is connected temporarily to mains services such as water and electricity. But a house which is constructed in such a way that it cannot be removed at all, save by destruction, cannot have been intended to remain as a chattel. It must have been intended to form part of the realty . . . Applying the dry stone wall analogy to the present case, I do not doubt that when Mr Morris's bungalow was built, and as each of the timber frame walls were placed in position, they all became part of the structure, which was itself part and parcel of the land'.

Lloyd LJ

The issue in this case was whether the occupiers of the bungalow occupied as tenants, which depended on the property being found to be a fixture. If it was a chattel then they would have been mere licensees and would have been unprotected when the owner of the land tried to evict them. The court found that the bungalow was a fixture.

In *D'Eyncourt v Gregory* (1866) LR 3 Eq 382 a number of statues were arranged in the garden and the purchaser argued that they were fixtures and should be left with the property. The court looked to the second test (the purpose of annexation) and concluded that the statues were intended to become an integral part of the garden and so could not be removed by the sellers. You could say that they were not just arranged in the garden: they had become part of the garden itself.

Compare this decision with the later case of *Leigh v Taylor* [1902] AC 157 where a different result was achieved. The owner of a large house had hung tapestries on the walls in the main drawing room. They were attached by tacking them to strips of wood which were then fixed to the wall. The House of Lords held that, unlike in *D'Eyncourt v Gregory* (1866), the tapestries had never been intended to become part of the property. The degree of annexation was all that was necessary to display the tapestries and for the owner to enjoy them. It was commented by Lord Halsbury that fashions had now changed and that attitudes to ornamentation had also changed.

Lord Scarman pointed out in *Berkley v Poulett* (1977) 241 EG 911, a later case, that a degree of annexation which in earlier times the law could have treated as conclusive may now prove nothing. So the degree of annexation is less important today although it will show where the burden of proof lies if an item is **securely** fixed. In these cases the burden shifts to those arguing that it is not a fixture. In other words, the burden of proof will shift to the seller as he will want to prove that the items are chattels, so enabling him to take items away after sale. For example, if a wardrobe has been fastened to the wall then the burden will shift to the seller to argue that this was for convenience only and that the wardrobe remained a chattel even after annexation.

## The purpose of annexation

This test is far more decisive in deciding whether an item is a fixture. This is principally because the technical skills of affixing and removing objects to land or buildings have improved significantly over the years.

Even where items have been attached to the land, making them appear to be part of that land, the question of whether they are fixtures or not will depend on whether they were put there for the better enjoyment of the property or for the better enjoyment of the item.

Consider these cases: in *Re Whaley* [1908] 1 Ch 615 tapestries and portraits had all been fixed to the wall to form an Elizabethan room. They were held to be part of the general architectural design of the room and were held to be fixtures. In *Berkley v Poulett* (1977) the seller had taken a number of items from the premises including statues, a sundial and some pictures fixed into recesses in the walls of the property. The purchaser claimed that they were fixtures. The Court of Appeal held that none of the items could be fixtures; they were all chattels.

Scarman J looked at each in turn:

1. He found that the statue and the sundial had never been fixed to the property. They had not become fixtures because they had never formed part of an architectural design. The plinth was a fixture but the owner of the property had changed the item which went on it from time to time. This meant that the actual location of the plinth was important but the items which were fixed to it were not part of some grand design for the garden.

2. The pictures were in recesses in a panelled room. However, they were not considered to be a part of a composite design. In other words, it was a matter of choice which particular pictures were put there.

## 1.5.2 Everyday objects in a house

When property is sold, certain items which are found in most people's homes are presumed to be fixtures and certain items will be presumed to be chattels.

# CASE EXAMPLE

**TSB v Botham [1996] EGCS 149**

Mr Botham had failed to keep up with mortgage repayments and the bank sold his flat. Any fixtures would pass to the purchaser but chattels would have to be passed back to Mr Botham. The case concerned such items as fitted cupboards in the kitchen, 'white goods' consisting of the main electrical appliances in the kitchen, light fittings throughout the house, fitted carpets and also curtains.

The judge at first instance held most of the items to be fixtures.

The Court of Appeal held:

1. The bathroom fittings and kitchen units, work surfaces and the fitted sink were all fixtures. The court thought it was misleading to apply the same tests to domestic dwellings as were applied to ornamental items or machinery in factories.

2. The light fittings were chattels, except those that had been specially fitted in recesses.

3. The carpets, curtains and blinds were chattels and could all be removed because, although they had been cut to fit the rooms and the windows, they were attached to the building in an insubstantial way. 'The methods of keeping fitted carpets in place and keeping curtains hung are no more than is required for enjoyment of those items as curtains and carpets' (Roch LJ).

4. The white goods, ie the washing machine, dishwasher and refrigerator, were all chattels. Roch LJ distinguished the reasoning of the judge at first instance who had held these items to be fixtures. He based his judgment on the fact that the items probably remained in position by their own weight and not by virtue of the links between them and the building. He found that they were designed to last for a limited period of years. The degree of annexation was slight and they could be removed without damage to the fabric of the building and normally without difficulty.

## 1.5.3 Items bought under hire purchase

The court in *TSB v Botham* (1996) also looked at items being purchased under a hire purchase agreement and which continued to be owned by the hire purchase company. The existence of the agreement will not prevent the item from becoming a fixture. In *Botham* some of the items had been purchased under hire purchase but the court held that this did not influence the decision as to whether they were fixtures or fittings. However, the owner under the agreement may have a right to enter and remove the item even when it has become a fixture.

The right of the former owner to enter and take the item away is a form of equitable interest giving the right to enter the premises and sever and remove chattels under the hire purchase agreement which have become fixtures.

## 1.5.4 Intention of the parties

The intention of the parties is only relevant to the extent that it can be part of the tests which look at the degree and object of the annexation. The subjective intention of the parties cannot affect the question whether the chattel has in law become part of the freehold.

ASE EXAMPLE

**Melluish (Inspector of Taxes) v BMI (No. 3) Ltd [1996] 1 AC 454**

A number of items including central heating installed in council flats, lifts in car parks and the filtration system in swimming pools were recorded as remaining in the ownership of the suppliers. However, the court held that simply to include a provision in the contract that these items remained in the ownership of the suppliers did not prevent them from taking effect as fixtures.

If the seller says 'I thought the fitted wardrobes were always chattels' then the court will look at how they were fixed to the wall and the purpose of fixing them. This is similar to the approach the courts might take in other areas of law, such as contract, where a condition of a contract cannot become a warranty merely because the parties call it a warranty. A lease of land will not become a licence in land just because the agreement says it is a licence.

 'The terms expressly or implicitly agreed between the fixer of the chattel and the owner of the land cannot affect the determination of the question whether, in law, the chattel has become a fixture and therefore in law belongs to the owner of the soil . . . such an agreement cannot prevent the chattel, once fixed, becoming in law part of the land and as such owned by the owner of the land so long as it remains fixed'.

*Melluish (Inspector of Taxes) v BMI (No. 3) Ltd* (1996) (Lord Browne-Wilkinson LJ).

The issue will always depend on the two tests laid down in *Holland v Hodgson* (1872):

**1.** degree of annexation and

**2.** purpose of annexation.

## ACTIVITY

Consider the following items and decide whether they are fixtures or chattels and can be removed by the seller:

1. Long velvet curtains and pelmets.

2. A fitted stair carpet.

3. A fridge in the kitchen.

4. Pine kitchen cupboards which have been designed for the kitchen by a local builder.

5. Four recessed lights which have been attached to the dining room ceiling.

6. A greenhouse and a garden shed. The garden shed was put up two years ago by the seller but the greenhouse was there when he arrived.

7. A statue of Persephone which is firmly attached to a concrete pillar which is placed in the middle of the garden.

8. A car bought a year ago which has not passed its MOT and is sitting in the garage.

9. A gas fire in the living room in regular use in the winter.

10. A freezer which is in the utility room.

## KEY FACTS

| Annexation | | Fixture or chattel | Case |
|---|---|---|---|
| Degree of annexation. | Resting on its own weight. | Fixture | Eliteson v Morris (1997) |
| How firmly was the object fixed? | Insubstantially fixed. | Chattel | Leigh v Taylor (1902) |
| | Substantially fixed. | Fixture | TSB v Botham (1996) (fitted kitchen) |
| Purpose of annexation. | For the improvement of the land. | Fixture | TSB v Botham (1966) (light fittings) |
| | For the use and enjoyment of the item. | Chattel | Berkley v Poulett (1977) |
| | Part of an architectural design. | Fixture | Re Whaley (1908) D'Eyncourt v Gregory (1866) |

## 1.5.5 The tenant's right to remove fixtures

The general rule was that the tenant had to leave any fixture that he had affixed to the premises during the tenancy. However, there are several exceptions:

### Trade fixtures

A tenant has always been able to remove trade fixtures that he has installed during the term of his lease. He must show that they were necessary for his trade or business.

> **Mancetter Developments v Garmanson Ltd [1986] QB 1212**
>
> Tenants who ran a chemical business were allowed to remove an extractor fan from the wall of their premises after their lease had expired.

Even where, under the ordinary rules, items have become fixtures, the law will allow tenants of business premises to remove them.

> **Young v Dalgety plc [1987] 1 EGLR 116**
>
> Tenants were allowed to remove light fittings and a carpet which they had fitted during their tenancy. This right carries over to a new tenancy.

### Ornamental and domestic fixtures

Any item added to the premises purely for ornamental or domestic purposes can always be removed by the tenant. It will depend on the way that it has been attached. If an item can be removed without substantial damage to the structure of the building then it will be seen as a chattel.

> **Spyer v Phillipson [1929] 2 Ch 183**
>
> A tenant of domestic premises had installed valuable antique wood panelling and other ornamental items. It was held that these were domestic or ornamental fixtures and he was entitled to remove them. They did not belong to the landlord.

## Agricultural fixtures

The general law prevented the agricultural tenant from removing articles from premises that he had rented. However, under the Agricultural Holdings Act 1986, some items can be removed by an agricultural tenant if certain conditions apply:

**1.** the tenant must give one month's notice to the landlord

**2.** all rent due must have been paid and

**3.** there must be no damage to the premises when the item is removed, unless this is unavoidable.
   If the landlord offers to buy the items and the price is fair then he is entitled to keep them.

Under all these exceptions the tenant must normally remove the items **during the tenancy** but he continues to have the right even after it has ended if either:

**1.** he has the right to remain in possession or

**2.** if he did not have time to remove these items (in which case he must be given a reasonable time to remove them).

The tenant must make good any damage which occurs when he removes the items from the property. In *Mancetter v Garmanson* (1986) the large hole left by the extractor fan had to be filled in by the tenant.

# 1.5.6 The loss of the right to remove fixtures

## The seller and the purchaser

Where items are expressly referred to in the contract then the rules concerning fixtures and fittings are displaced. So, if the seller tells the purchaser that the items are going to be removed, even if they are firmly fixed to the property the purchaser cannot challenge their removal.

Any other fixture is assumed to pass with the land, even if the contract does not mention an item, and the purchaser can challenge their removal.

ASE EXAMPLE

---

*Taylor v Hamer* **[2002] EWCA Civ 1130**

A seller removed a large quantity of old stone flagstones and took them from a property in Worcestershire to the Isle of Wight. The particulars of sale had not mentioned them. The Court of Appeal held that they must be returned. The purchaser relied on two clauses in the conditions of sale which said:

**1.** the buyer accepts the property in the physical state as it is in at the date of the contract

**2.** the seller will transfer the property in the same condition as it was at the date of contract.

The important issue here was: what was 'the property'? The court held that it meant 'what a reasonable person who knows what the parties know when they contracted would have taken it to mean'. In this case the facts indicated that they would have meant a garden with flagstones unless it was specifically mentioned that they were going to be removed.

### The mortgagor and the mortgagee

Since fixtures are assumed to be part of the land then they will become part of the property subject to the mortgage. In *TSB v Botham* (1996) the mortgagee argued that many expensive items had become part of the land and so would pass with the land when it was repossessed.

## 1.6 Chattels found in or on the surface of the land

If an object is found in or attached to the ground then the owner of the land has the best claim to it after the true owner of the object. The position will be different where the object is resting on the ground because the finder of the object then has a good claim. Everyone is familiar with the saying 'finders keepers'. It has some truth in land law, but only in some cases.

For example, if you are out walking and you find a gold ring resting on the ground then you may have a claim as the finder, but if the ring is buried in the soil and you have to dig it up then the claim will be between the owner of the land and the owner of the ring.

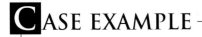
# CASE EXAMPLE

**Armory v Delamirie (1722) 1 Strange 505**

A jewel was found by a chimney sweeper's boy who claimed ownership as finder of the item. A dishonest employee of a jeweller took the jewel and the finder claimed ownership: 'the finder of a jewel, though he does not by such finding acquire an absolute property or ownership, yet he has such a property as will enable him to keep it against all but the true rightful owner'.

In these cases there are several different people who may have a good claim:

1. the true owner of the object
2. the finder of the object
3. the owner of the land
4. an employee of the owner of the land.

The claim to ownership depends on where the object was found and the extent to which the object was attached to the ground.

## 1.6.1 Objects found in the ground

At common law, where an item is found in the ground, the landowner in possession of the land is entitled to it if the true owner cannot be found.

**CASE EXAMPLE**

**Elwes v Brigg Gas Company (1886) 33 Ch D 562**

A long leaseholder could claim possession of a pre-historic boat found partially buried in the ground of his property. The finder of the item could not claim it for himself. It was held to belong to the landowner.

'He was in possession of the ground, not merely of the surface, but of everything that lay beneath the surface down to the centre of the Earth, and consequently in possession of the boat . . . The plaintiff then, being thus in possession of the chattel, it follows that the property in the chattel was vested in him. Obviously the right of the original owner could not be established.'

Chitty J

**CASE EXAMPLE**

**South Staffordshire Water Co v Sharman [1896] 2 QB 44**

It was held that employees of the landowner could not keep rings found in the mud of an old pond. They were the property of the landowner. The finders were employed by the landowner to remove the mud and they had a clear right to direct how the mud and anything in it should be dealt with.

## 1.6.2 Minerals found in the ground

Minerals found in the ground are part of the land and as a general principle belong to the landowner. Over the years many exceptions have developed. Ownership of all coal and natural gas is vested exclusively in various privatised corporations under statute, for example the Coal Industry Act 1994 and the Gas Act 1986. The Petroleum Act 1998 gives to the Crown the exclusive right of 'searching and boring for' and getting petroleum. 'Petroleum' is defined as 'any mineral oil or relative hydrocarbon and natural gas existing in its natural condition'. The Crown has had a prerogative right to gold and silver for centuries.

**CASE EXAMPLE**

**The Case of Mines (1567) 1 Plowd 310**

It was stated that any mine, whether of gold, silver or other metals containing in them gold or silver of even the smallest of quantities, was a Royal mine.

The ownership of mines under land can be severed from the ownership of the surface. The presumption that the landowner of the surface owns the land beneath can be rebutted by proof of long and continuous use of the mine or land beneath. In this way, land really does become three-dimensional.

## 1.6.3. Objects found on the surface of the ground

In *Elwes v Brigg Gas Company* (1886) if the item had been found resting on the ground then the finder may have had a good claim. However, the owner of the land may also have a good claim if he could prove that he intended to exercise manifest control over the land and anything found on it.

**CASE EXAMPLE**

**Parker v British Airways Board [1982] QB 1004**

A passenger found a gold bracelet on the floor of an executive airport lounge at Heathrow Airport. He handed it to the owners of the land (British Airways Board) in order for them to attempt to find the true owner. He challenged their claim to keep the bracelet for themselves. The court upheld the finder's claim.

'The plaintiff's claim is founded on the ancient common law rule that the act of finding a chattel which has been lost and taking control of it gives the finder rights with respect to that chattel . . . The common law right asserted by the plaintiff has been recognised for centuries . . . Some qualification has to be made in the case of finder who is trespassing. The person vis à vis whom he is a trespasser has a better title. The fundamental basis of this is clearly public policy. Wrongdoers should not benefit from their wrongdoing.'

Donaldson LJ

Donaldson LJ laid down the following rules on the rights and obligations of the finder:

1. The finder of a chattel acquires no rights unless (a) it has been abandoned or lost and (b) he takes it into his care.

2. If the finder is trespassing or acting with dishonest intent then he acquires very few rights.

3. The finder of a chattel acquires ownership against all but the true owner if he was on the land lawfully.

4. An employee working in the course of his employment who finds an item finds that item on behalf of his employer.

5. The finder is under an obligation to take measures to find the owner of the object.

Donaldson LJ then discussed the rights of the occupier, which he said depended on whether the occupier had manifested a desire to control the property.

Several questions must be addressed:

## Where was the object found? Was it in a public or private place?

If the object is in a **public place** then the finder has a good claim.

ASE EXAMPLE

### Bridges v Hawkesworth (1851) 21 LJQB 75

A commercial traveller found a parcel which contained some bank notes when he was in the defendant's shop. He claimed them for himself. It was held that if he had found them in the street he could have claimed them. Since the shop was open to the public and they were invited to come there then the reasoning was that the notes, being dropped in the public part of the shop, were never in the custody of the shopkeeper.

## Did the owner of the land manifest control over the land?

The general principle is that where a person has possession of a house or land he must show that he intends to control it if he is to claim any lost items found on the land. If it can be proved that he does control the land in this way then there is a presumption that anything found either by an employee of the owner or a stranger will be the property of the landowner.

So the issue all depends on what the law views as 'control'.

## What constitutes 'control'?

Donaldson LJ held in *Parker v British Airways Board* (1982) that a bank would exercise sufficient control over a bank vault if an item was found there. This would be because it would be closed to the general public and only limited people would have access. He contrasted areas such as a park where the public has unlimited access during the day. Between these two extremes he highlighted those areas where the public have limited rights of access, such as a petrol filling station forecourt.

In *Parker*, British Airways exercised some control over the airport lounge by checking tickets and allowing only certain people to enter but it was held that this was not sufficient to allow them to argue that they had superior rights to items found there.

### What if the finder was trespassing?

 **ASE EXAMPLE**

**Waverley BC v Fletcher [1996] QB 334**

The defendant used a metal detector in a public park owned by the claimants, Waverley Borough Council. He found a medieval brooch nine inches below the surface. It was held that the council had a better claim than the finder. The object was beneath the surface and the finder became a trespasser when he began to dig the ground. He had permission to walk in the public park but he did not have permission to use a metal detector and dig in the ground.

### Rights of the true owner

If the finder or the landowner claims the object then he is under a duty to take reasonable steps to trace the true owner who will still own the goods. The finder will have a duty to advertise the find and follow up any advertisements about lost items. It is only when the owner cannot be found that the finder can exert his rights.

 **ASE EXAMPLE**

**Moffat v Kazana [1969] 2 QB 152**

A now-deceased man (Mr Russell) had hidden a biscuit tin containing cash in the roof of his house. The house was sold to the defendant, who discovered the tin three years later. The deceased had simply forgotten about the money. It was held that although it is implied that the true owner of a chattel found on the land has a title superior to that of anybody else, it would not affect items that had been abandoned.

'If Mr Russell never got rid of the notes, that is to say, never got rid of the ownership of the notes, he continued to be owner of them and, if he continued to be the owner of them, he had a title to those notes which nobody else, whether the owner of the land in which they were found, or the finders, or anybody else would have.'

Wrangham J

## KEY FACTS

1. Objects found in or on the ground *prima facie* belong to the true owner of the object.

2. If the true owner cannot be found then ownership lies with the owner of the land if the object is found buried in the land (*Elwes v Brigg Gas Company* (1886)).

3. If the true owner cannot be found and the object is resting on the surface, the object is the property of either the finder or the landowner.

4. Ownership then depends on whether the landowner has shown that he intends to exercise a sufficient degree of control over the land (*Parker v British Airways* (1982)).

5. If the landowner has sufficient control over the land then he can claim any objects found.

6. If the finder is trespassing then objects found belong to the landowner (*Waverley B C v Fletcher* (1996)).

7. The finder can be trespassing either because he has no right to be on the land or because he is using the land in a way not permitted by the landowner (*Waverley B C v Fletcher*).

# ACTIVITY

Mrs Turner enjoyed visiting National Trust houses. One hot summer's day, she went to see a famous garden. She took her lunch and ate it in the garden. She was interested in the plants and when no one was looking she used the spoon that she had been using for her lunch and dug up one of the plants. She then noticed something in the ground, shining brightly. She put it into her pocket and looked at it when she got home. It was a gold bracelet.

Mrs Turner would like to keep the bracelet but she does not know what to do about it. Advise her whether or not she can keep it for herself.

Would it make any difference if the bracelet was resting on the ground when she found it?

## 1.7 Treasure

If an item is found that comes within the definition of 'treasure' then it will be the property of the Crown. The definition of what 'treasure' is can be found in the Treasure Act 1996. This Act was passed to replace the common law of treasure trove which had a number of difficulties, not least a very narrow definition of what treasure could be. The old law excluded many ancient items which had little or no gold or silver content but were often far more valuable. The new Act allows antiquities without a high metal content to come within the definition and so be preserved for the national heritage. There is provision for rewards to be paid to anyone who finds an object that comes within the definition of 'treasure'. It is now a criminal offence to fail to report a relevant find to the Coroner within 14 days.

### 1.7.1 The Treasure Act 1996

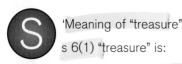

'Meaning of "treasure"

s 6(1) "treasure" is:

    (a) Any object at least 300 years old when found which –

        (i)  is not a coin but has metallic content of which at least 10 per cent by weight is precious metal;

        (ii)  when found, is one of at least two coins in the same find which are at least 300 years old at that time and have that percentage of precious metal; or

        (iii) when found, is one of at least ten coins in the same find which are at least 300 years old at that time;

    (b) Any object at least 200 years old when found which belongs to a class designated under section 2(1);

(c) Any object which would have been treasure trove if found before the commencement of section 4;

(d) Any object which when found, is part of the same find as –

    (i) An object within paragraph (a) (b) or (c) found at the same time or earlier; or

    (ii) An object found earlier which would be within paragraph (a) or (b) if it had been found at the same time.

(2) Treasure does not include objects which are –

    (a) unworked natural objects, or

    (b) minerals as extracted from a natural deposit, or which belong to a class designated under section 2(2).

. . .

s 2 The Secretary of State may by order, for the purposes of section 1(1)(b) designate any class of object which he considers to be of outstanding historical, archaeological or cultural importance.

. . .

s 3(3) "Precious metal" means gold or silver.

. . .

s 8(1) A person who finds an object which he believes or has reasonable grounds for believing is treasure must notify the Coroner for the district in which the object was found before the end of the notice period . . .

(3) Any person who fails to comply with subsection (1) is guilty of an offence.'

A Code of Practice accompanied the Treasure Act, giving guidelines for the payment of rewards (Treasure Act 1996: Code of Practice) which depends on whether the finder is deliberately searching for artefacts.

If the finder is **deliberately** searching for artefacts then a reward will be payable where:

**1.** he has valid permission from the occupier to be on the premises and

**2.** he has complied with the obligation to report a find to the Coroner and

**3.** there has been no damage to the premises.

If an artefact is found **by chance** then a reward is payable where:

**1.** the finder has permission to be on the premises and

**2.** the finder has reported his find to the Coroner.

He will generally receive half of whatever reward is paid by the Coroner and the landowner will receive the other half. Even if he did not have permission to be on the premises then the guidelines allow for a possible reward to be divided between the occupier, the landowner and the finder.

'Of course, objects of recent vintage may be treasure by virtue of having been found in circumstances which clearly associate them with objects which are otherwise treasure within section 1. Always assuming that the true owner cannot be ascertained, suppose a hoard of 18th century coins contains say, two or more gold coins which are at least 300 years old. The two or more gold coins aged 300 years or more will be treasure (section 1(1)(a)(ii)). Section 1(1)(d) of the Act will operate so as to engage the balance of coins, and their container together with any other contents such as books or papers, and transform them into treasure irrespective of the proof of an *animus recuperandi* or their precious metal content, if any. The point may well be of practical significance, not only for the purposes of the grant of a reward, but also because, were the coins or other objects not to be treasure then the ordinary law of "finders keepers" would fall to be applied.'

J Marston and L Ross, 'Treasure and Portable Antiquities in the 1990s still chained to the Ghosts Of Past: The Treasure Act 1996' [1997] 61 Conv 273.

# ACTIVITY

Your friend Terence is walking one summer's afternoon with his dog Fedora and she starts digging furiously in the ground. Fedora uncovers what looks to Terence like a number of coins and a pottery vase which looks very old and valuable to him. He takes them home and shows them to his wife who is a history teacher and she recognises that the coins are Roman. He wants to keep them in his own coin collection but is unsure whether he can do so. He would like to give the vase to his mother as a present.

Terence comes to you for your advice.

# 1.8 Ownership of airspace above the land

'He who owns the land owns everything reaching up to the very heavens and down to the depth of the Earth.'

Attributed to Accursius of Bologna in *Glossa Ordinaria* on *Corpus Iuris* (13th C.)

Land must include part of the airspace above the ground, otherwise building above ground level would be a trespass. However, it cannot be an unlimited part of that airspace; it cannot be 'to the heavens above' as otherwise every time an aircraft flew over a house it would be trespassing.

The law has tried to define how much of the airspace is owned by a landowner. Airspace has been split into two levels: the higher stratum and the lower stratum.

## 1.8.1 The higher stratum

Until the advent of air travel, no one could pass through the higher part of the atmosphere so ownership was never an issue. It was assumed that the landowner had ownership of the airspace. Air travel transformed the idea of ownership of the higher stratum of airspace. Planes now regularly fly through that part of the airspace above people's houses and gardens. However, the courts are unwilling to allow ownership in the higher stratum.

**CASE EXAMPLE**

**Re the Queen in Right of Manitoba and Air Canada** (1978) 86 DLR (3d) 631

Attempts by Manitoba to argue that sales of goods on board aircraft flying over the province could be taxed failed, on the basis that no one could claim ownership of that part of the airspace.

**CASE EXAMPLE**

**Bernstein v Skyviews and General Ltd** [1978] QB 479

The claimant claimed trespass because the defendant flew over his land without permission and took aerial photographs. The claim was unsuccessful.

'The [claimant] claims that as owner of the land he is also owner of the airspace above the land, or at least has the right to exclude any entry into the air space above his land.

. . . That an owner has certain rights in the air space above his land is well established by authority. He has the right to lop the branches of trees that may overhang his boundary, although this right seems to be founded in nuisance rather than trespass . . . In *Wandsworth Board of Works v United Telephone Company* (1884) 13 QBD 904 the Court of Appeal did not doubt that the owner of land would have the right to cut a wire placed over his land . . . I can find no support in authority for the view that a landowner's rights in the air space above his property extend to an unlimited height. In the same case Bowen LJ described the maxim, *usque ad coelum*, as a fanciful phrase, to which I would add that if applied literally it is a fanciful notion leading to the absurdity of a trespass at common law being committed by a satellite every time it passes over a suburban garden

. . . The problem is to balance the rights of an owner to enjoy the use of his land against the rights of the general public to take advantage of all that best struck in

> our present society by restricting the rights of an owner in the air space above his land to such a height as is necessary for the ordinary use and enjoyment of his land and the structures upon it, and declaring that above that height he has no greater rights in the air space than any other member of the public.'
>
> Griffiths J

The main principles to consider from this judgment are:

**1.** the owner has rights in airspace above his property.

**2.** the owner does not own unlimited rights over airspace, otherwise there would be a trespass every time a satellite flew over someone's garden.

**3.** the owner owns as much of the airspace as he needs for the ordinary use and enjoyment of his land.

This area of law is now largely governed by legislation such as the Civil Aviation Act 1982.

 's 76(1) No action shall lie in respect of trespass or in respect of nuisance, by reason only of the flight of an aircraft over any property at a height above the ground which, having regard to wind, weather and all circumstances of the case is reasonable . . .'.

So this Act prevents actions in nuisance or trespass against aircraft flying over houses unless the aircraft fails to comply with any relevant regulations.

## 1.8.2 The lower stratum

The law accepts that the landowner has rights over the airspace immediately above his property. 'You own as much as is necessary for the reasonable enjoyment of your property' (Griffiths J in *Bernstein v Skyviews and General Ltd* (1978)). So this will vary according to the type of property that you own. However it probably stops short of the altitude over which aircraft can legally fly. Under the Rules of the Air Regulations 1996 it is held to be no lower than 200 metres above roof level. There are a number of exceptions to this, including where an aircraft is taking off and landing and also where it is necessary to fly lower in order to save life.

One of the first cases on this issue was *Pickering v Rudd* (1815) Camp 219 where the judge, Lord Ellenborough, did not think that there would an invasion of airspace by a balloon passing over one's property and no action for trespass could be taken.

This view was criticised and overturned in a number of following cases including *Gifford v Dent* [1926] WN 336 where an overhead sign which was erected on the wall above the ground-floor premises which had been bought by the claimant was held to constitute a trespass.

In *Wandsworth District Board of Works v United Telephone Co Ltd* (1884) 13 QBD 904 a telephone line running across a street could constitute a trespass, although not on the particular facts of that case.

In *Kelsen v Imperial Tobacco* [1957] 2 QB 334 the claimant was seeking an injunction to stop the defendants from using an advertising sign. The sign projected into the airspace immediately above the claimant's shop. However, although it projected over the land it did not interfere with his enjoyment of the airspace so an action in nuisance would not be successful. If he hit his head every time he left his premises then an action in nuisance would succeed. For an action in trespass to succeed the owner must show that he owned that portion of airspace. The judge found that the sign did amount to a trespass to the airspace above the land and awarded damages to the claimant.

Several cases have been brought where property developers have used cranes which have swung through the airspace above adjoining buildings. If you apply the principles from *Bernstein v Skyviews and General Ltd* (1978) that a landowner is entitled to as much airspace as is necessary for the ordinary use and enjoyment of his land and the structures upon it, then the owner of a high-rise block may be able to claim a much more extensive ownership of airspace than someone who lives in a bungalow or low-rise building. So an injunction was granted against the use of a crane which swung over the claimant's land in *Woollerton and Wilson Ltd v Richard Costain Ltd* [1970] 1 WLR 411 (although the defendant offered substantial sums in compensation which led to the suspension of the injunction) and again later in *Anchor Brewhouse Developments Ltd v Berkeley House (Docklands Developments) Ltd* [1987] 38 BLR 82.

## KEY FACTS

**Rights over airspace**

1. Airspace is split between the upper stratum and the lower stratum.

2. There can never be ownership of the upper stratum (Civil Aviation Act 1949 and *Bernstein v Skyviews and General Ltd* (1978)).

3. Ownership of the lower stratum depends on what can be said is reasonable for the use and enjoyment of the property (*Kelsen v Imperial Tobacco* Co (1957)).

4. 'Reasonable for use and enjoyment of the property' will vary according to the height and type of the building.

# Further reading

Birks, P, 'Before We Begin: Five Keys to Land Law' in S Bright and J Dewar (eds), *Land Law: Themes and Perspectives*, (Oxford University Press, 1998) pp 457–460.

Bridge, S, 'Part and Parcel: Fixtures in the House of Lords' (1997) CLJ 498.

Haley, M, 'The Law of Fixtures: An Unprincipled Metamorphosis' [1998] Conv 137.

Macmillan, C, 'Finders Keepers, Losers Weepers – But who are the losers?' [1995] 58 MLR 101.

Stevens, J, 'Finders Weepers – Landowners Keepers' [1996] Conv 216.

Wilkinson, H W, 'Chattels, Fixtures and Land' [1997] NLJ (July) 1031.

Wu, Tang Hang, 'The Right of Lateral Support of Buildings from Adjoining Land' [2002] Conv 237.

# chapter 2 COMMON LAW AND EQUITY ■

## 2.1 Common law and equity

Historically, England had two systems of law. Initially, there was common law. This arose from a combination of law initiated centrally and local laws but when this was shown to be defective a new system called equity grew to supplement the common law.

### The growth of common law

Before 1066, local law had been the main source of law but it varied from region to region and people could be treated differently according to which area they came from. After 1066 there was a move to create a system of law that was uniform to all of England and Wales. This system became known as the common law and it was administered by the Royal courts. At first it was welcomed as a fair system but it soon became clear that it had a number of defects.

## 2.1.1 Defects in the common law system

1. An action in court could only be started by a writ and there were only a certain number of writs available. After 1215 and the passage of the Provisions of Oxford in 1258 it was not possible for the courts to extend the circumstances for new writs and so a claimant had to bring his action within the narrow circumstances of the existing writs. If there was no writ suitable for his claim, he had no right to bring an action to the courts.

2. The common law had only a limited number and range of remedies available.

3. The common law did not recognise certain types of right such as the rights of the mortgagee or the rights of a beneficiary behind a trust.

The dissatisfied litigant had nowhere to go except to take his case directly to the king and to ask the king to exercise his discretion in the litigant's favour.

## 2.1.2 The growth of equity

So it was recognised that there were many defects in common law. Some of the litigants appealed directly to the king. The cases were decided individually and the king was not bound by the narrow constraints of common law so some found that they were successful in their claim. Others followed suit, hoping the king would also find in their favour. Eventually, the king found that there were too many appeals for him to deal with on his own and cases were passed to his adviser, the Lord Chancellor. He was a man of the Church and so came to his decisions through applying principles of fairness and conscience. This contrasted with common law where the law was strictly applied.

Eventually, a separate court grew up called the Court of Chancery, which was recognised as a court of conscience and which later developed its own principles and rights.

The differences between the courts were significant:

1. The Court of Chancery would decide cases according to what seemed **just** and **equitable** whereas the common law courts were concerned with the strict enforcement of legal rights.

2. The Court of Chancery was prepared to grant **a range of remedies** including injunctions to restrain actions and specific performance of a contract. These were often more appropriate in the circumstances. The remedies available in the common law courts consisted only of damages.

3. The Court of Chancery was willing to recognise **new rights** such as the mortgage and the trust, which the common law courts refused to recognise.

By the sixteenth century, the position of Lord Chancellor was no longer given to a religious person but always to a lawyer. The court gradually became bound by rules and cases were no longer decided according to their particular circumstances and facts.

Problems arose in the administration of both the courts and there grew considerable rivalry as to which court was superior. It was also possible to bring an action on the same facts in both courts if the claimant sought different remedies. So if he were seeking damages then he would pursue the case in the common law courts but if he were seeking an injunction then he would pursue his case in the courts of equity. Pursuing two actions in two different courts was costly and time-consuming.

## APPLYING THE LAW

Edmund has promised to supply 50 sheep to Edward on the first Tuesday in March. He fails to do so. Edward wants the sheep and no one else can supply them. He can sue at common law for the breach of contract and also bring an action in equity in the Chancery court for specific performance of the contract. There would be two separate actions and two sets of lawyers.

## 2.1.3 The Judicature Acts 1873–75

Two separate courts and two systems of law were wasteful and ineffective. Litigants had to wait months, even years, for a judgment. There was also conflict between the two systems. Reform came in the shape of the Judicature Acts in 1873–75 which combined the two systems of law and equity. It also combined the two courts, forming the Supreme Court which could hear cases both in common law and in equity. There was now effectively one system to govern all cases. However, the

law expressly laid down that where there was any conflict between the rules of common law and the rules of equity then the rules of equity were to prevail: now s 49(1) Supreme Court Act 1981.

## 2.1.4 Have common law and equity totally fused?

Some lawyers are not convinced that the two systems ever fused. It is true that in some ways equity and common law do remain distinct although they are both administered in the same court.

The two arguments:

1. 'The two streams of jurisdiction though they run in the same channel run side by side and do not mingle their waters' (Ashburner, *Principles of Equity* (2nd edn, 1933). Ashburner was arguing here that although the systems run side by side, they have not combined.

2. Others disagree and Lord Diplock in *United Scientific Holdings Ltd v Burnley Borough Council* [1978] AC 904 said: 'The innate conservatism of English lawyers may have made them slow to recognise that by the Judicature Act 1873 the two systems of substantive and adjectival law formerly administered by Courts of Law and Courts of Chancery were fused.'

What we have to look at here is how the two systems affect our study of land law. Although the systems of law and equity have merged, there are still both legal and equitable rights in land. These can exist over the same piece of property.

If you own the land at law or have legal rights in the land then you can claim a legal remedy which takes effect in common law and, most importantly, your claims are good against the whole world. Your rights cannot be defeated by anyone. If you have an equitable right which takes effect in equity then your rights do not bind the world. They are good against everyone unless they can prove that they have a better title than you. So they will never defeat legal rights but as they may affect the legal title so the legal owner takes the land subject to your rights. Equitable rights strictly give rise to an equitable remedy but legislation has now expressly allowed damages to be granted instead of the equitable remedy (s 50 Supreme Court Act 1981).

## 2.2 The development of the trust

We have seen that equity contributed to the law in several different ways. Possibly the most significant contribution of equity was the recognition of new rights and in particular the trust.

### 2.2.1 The historical development of the trust

Trusts were first used at the time of the Crusades. Picture the scene:

Many landowners were recruited to fight in the crusades. This involved leaving their lands and family for months, probably years. Someone needed to be in charge while they were away. The solution was to ask a friend to take over. The friend needed some control over the land and this

was achieved by transferring the land to the friend while the crusader was away, but on the strict understanding that all income was to be for the benefit of their family and the property would be returned when they returned from fighting.

So Thomas leaves for the Crusades, leaving Edward in charge of his land on behalf of his two sons, Adam and Ben. For two years, Edward runs the property and makes a considerable sum of money but he keeps it for himself. Thomas returns and Edward refuses to hand over the money or return the property which is now in his name.

Thomas goes to the common law courts and it is held that he has no right to bring the claim since, in common law, Edward is now the owner. What does Thomas do? The only path left open is to go to the king and to ask him to intervene and to force Edward to return his land and to give all the profits to Adam and Ben, recognising that the transfer to Edward was only temporary. The king is prepared to act. This is the first recognition of a trust by the courts. You may read that at first it was not called a trust but a 'use'. The reason for this was that the land was conveyed 'for the use of the third party'. This distinguished the transfer from being one for his own benefit. The development of the use into the trust was a result of refusal by the Crown to recognise uses, so a second use was employed to allow the same effect and the second use was the forerunner of the trust today.

The reason why the common law courts were so reluctant to recognise the trust was because the property was put into the name of the trustee. They were the owners at law. Legally, they had control over the property. The rights of the beneficiaries were based on conscience and were recognised because the Lord Chancellor thought it would be unconscionable to ignore their rights.

## APPLYING THE LAW

Hereward creates a trust in favour of Edmund and transfers his property to Harold. Harold holds the property in his name and decides to give it to his friend, John, and not to preserve it for Edmund. What could Edmund do? He would be able to force Harold to transfer the property to him in the first example, but what about John? John had not paid for the land. The law later allowed Edmund to enforce against John because he received the land as a gift.

## 2.2.2 The trust today

The trust involves three sets of interests. It has been called the 'magic triangle' by Alastair Hudson in his book *Equity and Trusts* (2nd edn, Cavendish, 2003). (See Figure 2.1.)

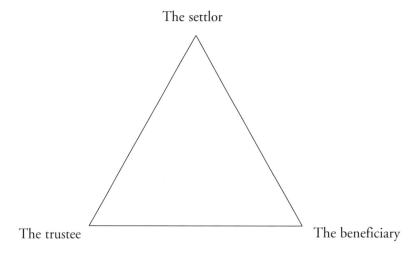

*Figure 2.1 The 'magic triangle' in trusts*

**1.** Initially the **settlor** has absolute ownership of his property. He decides that he wants someone to benefit eventually from all or some of his property, but not immediately, so he transfers his property to another called the trustee who gets absolute ownership of the property, but not to enjoy for himself. He owns it on behalf of the beneficiaries.

**2.** The **trustee** receives the property but holds it on trust for the benefit of the beneficiaries. The trustee holds the legal title to the property. So if the trust property comprised land and included a house he would have the title in his name and be registered at the Land Registry as the owner. However, the trustee cannot claim the land for himself. He must keep the trust property separately from his other property.

**3.** The **beneficiary** has a personal right to force the trustees to act on his behalf if they refuse to act. He does not own a legal interest in the property but only an equitable interest. He cannot deal with the legal title so he cannot create a lease or mortgage the property; only the trustees can do this.

Once the trust has been created or constituted, the settlor loses all control over the property unless he is also a beneficiary or he acts as trustee himself. The important fact to remember is that once the trust is constituted, the settlor cannot change his mind and try to recover his property. In many cases in land law the settlor may be the same person as the trustee but he fulfils different roles and owes different duties.

Some trusts arise **expressly** because the settlor wants to create a trust over his property but some trusts arise by **implication**.

## 2.2.3 The express trust

These trusts arise by deliberate act of the owner of the property. The settlor may appoint as a trustee either himself or a third party known to the settlor who agrees to act as trustee. Whenever there is an express declaration of trust in land *inter vivos* it must be evidenced in writing, according to s 53(1)(b) of the Law of Property Act 1925: 'a declaration of trust respecting land or any interest therein must be manifested and proved by some writing signed by some person who is able to declare such trust or by his will.'

NB '*Inter vivos*' means a trust created during a lifetime, as opposed to one created in a will, taking effect on death.

## 2.2.4 Resulting and constructive trusts

These trusts are not deliberately imposed by the settlor but arise by implication of law. The parties may not even be aware that a trust has been created.

- **Resulting trusts** are trusts imposed because of the circumstances, such as where a partner to a relationship contributes to the purchase of property but is not registered as joint owner; the law will give that person a share in equity. The owner of the legal estate is said to own on trust for them both. Unlike express trusts, there is no requirement for a formal record of the trust.

- **Constructive trusts** are trusts that are imposed by the court because it would be 'unconscionable' for the owner of the property to hold that property for themselves.

### APPLYING THE LAW  ☐ ☐ ☐

Janet and John both contribute to the purchase of Windy Hollow, a cottage in Malvern. Janet contributes £5,000 from her savings and John contributes £25,000 from his savings and the rest is raised by a mortgage. The property is registered in John's name. He owns the legal estate and he is said to hold Windy Hollow on resulting trust for himself and Janet. He could decide to try to raise some extra cash by taking out a second mortgage and he would be able to do this without consulting Janet. He could also put the house on the market without consulting her but any sale would be subject to her rights in the property.

☐ ☐ ☐

### APPLYING THE LAW  ☐ ☐ ☐

Mary and Mark move into Windy Hollow and the house is registered in Mark's name. Mark has provided most of the purchase money while the rest has been raised on mortgage. The house is in a very poor state. Mark tells Mary that he is holding the house as trustee on trust for them both. Mary carries out work on the property and supervises the builders while Mark is at work. Mark will hold the title on constructive trust for himself and Mary.

☐ ☐ ☐

Under the trust we see the possibility of property being owned by one or more persons on behalf of themselves and/or several different people. They will all have rights but the nature of the rights will vary according to whether the rights are legal or equitable in nature. Trusts are often used where the beneficiary is unable to hold property because of a disability. No one can own land at law until they reach the age of 18. The land must be held under a trust until their eighteenth birthday.

## ACTIVITY

Consider this example and decide who is the settlor, who is the trustee and who is the beneficiary.

Frank wants to give his seaside holiday house, Cliff View, to his grandson Ben, aged 12, but Ben is not old enough to own property yet so Frank asks his old friend Graham to look after it for him until Ben is old enough to hold it in his own name.

What would happen if Graham refused to hand over the house when Ben reaches 18?

## 2.3 The difference between legal and equitable interests in property

Within the trust of the property Cliff View the trustee (Graham) owns the legal estate and the beneficiary (Ben) owns the equitable estate. So, in a single piece of property there are two sets of interests shared between the trustee and the beneficiary. Whenever property is shared between two or more persons a trust is said to arise, splitting the legal and equitable ownership.

In many cases the trustees and beneficiaries are the same people. This is because the law will always impose a trust where property is co-owned.

## APPLYING THE LAW

Fred purchases 14 London Road for himself and his girlfriend, Clare. Clare contributes £20,000 and Fred contributes £40,000. Fred owns the legal estate absolutely and he is trustee of the equitable estate which is shared between himself and Clare. He is both trustee of the equitable estate and also beneficiary of the trust because he shares the equitable estate with Clare.

Traditionally, equitable rights arose because they were rights in property not recognised by common law. Sometimes equitable rights arose because formalities had not been complied with when rights in property had been either transferred or created. Equity would still recognise the interest and would enforce the rights of the claimant.

Today, legal rights are distinguishable from equitable rights because the owner of a legal estate can deal with the estate at law and the owner of an equitable estate only has rights to deal in the equitable estate.

## 2.3.1 Rights *in rem* and rights *in personam*

The law draws an important distinction between rights which are said to be proprietary in nature and rights which are said to be purely personal. If you have a proprietary right then you can claim rights in the property itself. These rights will endure when the property passes into the hands of a third party. By way of contrast, a personal right is only good against another individual. The right cannot be enforced against anyone else.

If you have a proprietary right then the right will be good against the property even if it is later sold to someone else since the right is not against the owner but a right in the property itself. This difference can be traced back to the first division between legal and equitable rights.

Historically, legal rights were enforceable only in the common law courts of the king. Equitable rights were only enforceable in the Courts of Chancery but at the discretion of the king and later the Lord Chancellor.

Another difference lay in the fact that legal rights are rights *in rem* giving rise to real actions and equitable rights are rights *in personam* giving rise to personal actions'.

### 'Realty and Personalty

. . . There is an almost perfect match between the category of real property and land. If a lay person hears "real property", or "real estate", or "realty", what will come to mind will be an image of land. For most lawyers the effect will be the same. Some lawyers may just manage to remind themselves that they should be thinking more abstractly, not of the land itself, but of interests in land. "Personal property" or "personalty" similarly evoke cars, cows, televisions, crockery, pictures, money, and a host of other moveable things. In fact the correlation is not quite perfect. A lease of land, however long, is technically personalty, and some moveable things are heirlooms and fall within the category of realty . . . A judgment in money can be called personal because it gives the victorious plaintiff no right in or to any particular thing but merely a right that a person, the defeated defendant, pay the sum in question, a right backed by the law's machinery for executing judgments. . . . In some actions you could recover the thing itself. Those actions

came to be called "real actions", "real" meaning "thing-related" in the simple sense that the person claiming would recover the very thing claimed. The subject matter of real actions then became real actions then became real property or realty, the especial thing-relatedness of such assets being their specific recoverability: if it came to litigation, you would get back the thing itself.'

P Birks, 'Before We Begin: Five Keys to Land Law' in S Bright and J Dewar (eds),
*Land Law: Themes and Perspectives* (Oxford University Press, 1998), pp 470–471

Birks is highlighting the difficulties in trying to put all property into categories. In particular, the lease was considered to be personal property which could only give rise to a personal action. It did not give rise to a right *in rem* and so was not a claim to the land itself but only a personal claim against the landlord.

## APPLYING THE LAW

Two brothers were left property by their grandfather. John was left all the realty and James was left all the personalty. The grandfather had a lease of a large farmhouse and even if the lease was of 100 years it was still regarded as a personal right and not a right in realty so James would inherit the lease and not John.

Leases are still classified as personalty but it makes little difference and under s 1 of the Law of Property Act 1925 they give rise to a legal estate in land.

## 2.3.2 The effect of equitable rights on third parties

Another important difference between legal and equitable rights is the way such rights are enforceable against a third party. It used to depend on whether the land was **unregistered**, meaning it involved the proof of a good root of title of at least 15 years, or **registered** land, meaning it involved registration at the Land Registry.

If you had a legal interest in unregistered land then that would be a right in the land itself and anyone who acquired the land would be bound by that right even if they did not know about it. If you had a legal interest in registered land then that had to be registered at the Land Registry if it was to be a right binding on the land.

Equity would only enforce rights against certain persons. When the trust was first recognised by equity, the beneficiary could only enforce the trust against the trustee. Later the trust was enforceable against third parties who purchased the land knowing that there were third party rights in that land.

As we will see below, only the *bona fide* purchaser without notice of rights will be able to take land without being subject to rights in equity.

## 2.3.3 The *bona fide* purchaser for value without notice

A purchaser could acquire land without being subject to equitable rights in the land if he could claim to be a *bona fide* purchaser without notice of the rights.

NB '*Bona fide*' means 'in good faith'. It is said of someone who takes the property honestly, not knowing that there are any other rights in the land. Once the purchaser could establish that he was a *bona fide* purchaser for value then he had what James LJ described in *Pilcher v Rawlins* (1872) 7 Ch App 259 as an 'absolute, unqualified, unanswerable defence' against an equitable right. This was because the effect of the claim was that it destroyed the equitable interest involved and it could not be revived. It makes no difference that a later purchaser does have notice of these rights.

Consider the earlier example where Hereward creates the trust in favour of Edmund and transfers it to Harold as trustee. Harold holds the property in his name and then gives it to his friend, John. John will take subject to Edmund's rights.

Contrast the situation where John pays Harold £200 for the land instead of receiving it as a gift. Then it would be treated differently and the law would have allowed John to keep the land.

In the second example, John is called a '*bona fide* purchaser for value of a legal interest without notice'. The *bona fide* purchaser is also called 'equity's darling' because the courts of equity were prepared to look more favourably on someone who had paid for property. However, he could only take free of someone's rights if he was unaware of them. If John had been told by Harold that he had the right to transfer the property to him and John did not know of Edmund's rights then John would be 'without notice of Edmund's rights'. Suppose that John was told by a neighbour that Edmund had rights, then he would lose the protection and he would be bound by his rights.

## CASE EXAMPLE

### *Wilkes v Spooner* [1911] 2 KB 473

The landlord granted two leases of two properties to Spooner. Spooner assigned one lease to Wilkes and Spooner covenanted within the lease not to compete with Wilkes' own business as a butcher. When Spooner surrendered his lease to the landlord he granted a fresh lease to Spooner's son who started a business as a butcher, knowing of the covenant. The landlord did not have notice of the covenant and so it was destroyed when the lease was surrendered to the landlord and therefore Spooner's son was not bound by the covenant.

## 2.3.4 What does 'bona fide purchaser for value' mean?

**1.** *Bona fide*: this means 'to act in good faith'.

**2.** Purchaser for value: this means that something of value must have been given. It does not have to be money, it could be 'in kind' and it does not have to be what the property is worth. The word 'purchaser' goes beyond the purchaser of the fee simple and includes mortgagees and also lessees.

**3.** Of a legal estate: the purchaser must have purchased a legal estate in the land rather than an equitable estate.

## 2.3.5 Notice

The *bona fide* purchase must be without notice of the equitable rights: There were three different forms of notice:

**1. Actual notice**: a purchaser had actual notice if he knew of any rights affecting the land because he had been told of the rights or had found out for himself. Later, when rights were capable of registration, it meant rights which the purchaser knows about because they were registered and the purchaser has checked and found out about them. There is a duty to check and below we will see that it is no excuse to say you have not had time to check the register for rights.

**2. Constructive notice**: a purchaser had constructive notice if he would have been aware of the estate if he had checked for himself. Checking would include all those inquiries and inspections which he ought reasonably to have made. This would be either by visiting the property or by checking whether registrable rights had been registered. The purchaser should always visit the property because he may be bound by rights that can only be discovered by physical inspection of the property. Under s 199 of the Law of Property Act 1925 the purchaser is prejudicially affected by notice of those matters which would have come to his knowledge if such inquiries and inspections had been made as ought reasonably to have been made by him. The main questions are 'knowing something' that would have stimulated inquiry or 'wilfully abstaining from inquiry to avoid notice', as considered by Purchas LJ in *Kemmis v Kemmis* [1988] 1 WLR 1307.

> **J** 'If the party asserting that he takes free of the earlier rights of another knows of certain facts which put him on inquiry as to the possible existence of the rights of that other and he fails to make inquiry or take such other steps as are reasonable to verify whether such earlier right does or does not exist, he will have constructive notice of the earlier right and take subject to it.'
>
> Browne-Wilkinson LJ in *Barclays Bank v O'Brien* [1994] 1 AC 180

**3. Imputed notice**: a purchaser would have imputed notice if his legal agent (usually his solicitor or his adviser) had made investigations. They would check on his behalf and even if they had not told him of the rights, the law would say he had notice of the rights.

> 'Although forming a fundamental stratum of English land law, the doctrine of notice has been heavily overlaid by various regimes for the registration of land interests and by the statutory mechanism for "overreaching" prior equitable rights. It was indeed a large part of the strategy of the property legislation of 1925 to eliminate the uncertainty generated by the notice doctrine. Accordingly the operation of the doctrine is nowadays marginal: it applies only to unregistered land and, even here, its role is severely limited.'

Gray and Gray, *Elements of Land Law* (3rd edn, Butterworths, 2001), p 1115

# ACTIVITY

Hereward owns a large property in Warwickshire called Windy Heath. He transfers it to his friend Harold on trust for his three grandchildren, Edmund, William and Gerald, who are all students. Consider the effect of Harold's actions in each of the following situations:

1. Harold decides to give Windy Heath to his friend John.

2. Harold decides to sell Windy Heath to his friend James.

3. Harold decides to sell Windy Heath to James but he knows about the three grandchildren because he has been told that they were staying there for the summer.

4. Harold decides to sell Windy Heath to Joan who never visits the property but her solicitor Frank does and he finds the three children have been staying there.

# 2.3.6 Overreaching

## Definition

Overreaching arises on the sale of property which is held under a trust. So it can apply to any jointly held property. The principle of overreaching is that rights arising under equity which attach to the land can be transferred from the land to the capital money. It allows land under a trust to be sold free of certain rights. The purchaser may have notice of the rights of the beneficiaries but will still be held to take free of these rights. The rights may have been entered on the register against the title of the property. Overreaching can apply to all land held in trust, whether it has registered or unregistered title.

## Purpose of overreaching

Overreaching allows land to be disposed of free of rights affecting the land. It allows the rights of the beneficiaries to be safeguarded by making the trustee statutorily obliged to transfer the capital money to them.

## Conditions for overreaching

Under s 27(2) of the Law of Property Act 1925, overreaching will apply where there are two or more trustees or a trust corporation and the purchase money is paid over to both of them. (See Figure 2.2.)

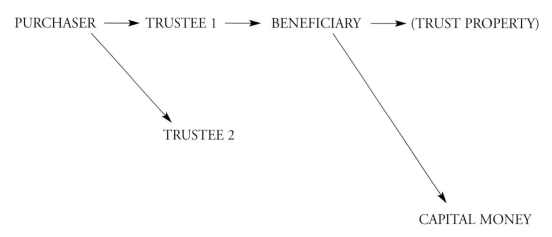

 *Figure 2.2 Overreaching*

Overreaching will not apply where the capital money is only paid over to a single trustee.

# CASE EXAMPLE

**Williams & Glyn's Bank v Boland [1981] AC 487**

A husband owned the legal title to the matrimonial home. The wife had an equitable estate in the land because she had made contributions to the purchase. The husband had taken out a loan with Williams & Glyn's Bank who had executed a charge over the property. The wife was not aware of the loan and did not have to be consulted. When the husband failed to make the agreed repayments the bank claimed the right to sell the property. The rights of the wife were not overreached because the 'sale', i.e. the loan from the bank, had been made to a sole trustee, i.e. the husband. The wife's right to remain in the property was upheld.

Overreaching will only apply where the purchase money is paid over to two trustees.

# CASE EXAMPLE

### City of London Building Society v Flegg [1988] AC 54

A son, his wife and his parents joined together to purchase property. The son and daughter-in-law were registered as owners. They owned the legal estate as trustees for themselves and their parents-in-law. The son took out a second mortgage with his wife and the money was paid over to them by the building society. The parents-in-law were in occupation of the property but when the loan was not repaid and the building society decided to exercise its power of sale it was held that their rights were overreached.

The rights of the parents-in-law should have been protected because their rights were transferred to the capital money. However, on the sale of the property the building society had first claim on the purchase money and there was nothing left after the loan had been repaid. It suggests that overreaching will not necessarily protect the beneficiaries of the trust and much will depend on whether there are two trustees of the land. Where the trustees exceed their powers then overreaching will not apply. However it must be an *ultra vires* transaction.

# CASE EXAMPLE

### First National Securities Ltd v Hegerty [1984] 3 WLR 769

Here it was held that where the transaction was fraudulent because the husband had forged his wife's signature then there could be no overreaching of the wife's share.

Compare:

# CASE EXAMPLE

### State Bank of India v Sood [1997] Ch 276

In this case the two trustees mortgaged trust land which they owned. They did not receive the capital money because the complicated transaction meant the purchase money was not paid over to them (the mortgage being taken out to back an earlier loan). The claimants argued that their rights in the property were not overreached because the purchase money had not been advanced to the two trustees. The Court of Appeal held that their rights had been overreached.

# CASE EXAMPLE

**Birmingham Midshires Mortgage Services Ltd v Sabherwal (2000) 80 P & CR 256**

It was held that even an interest that took effect under proprietary estoppel can be subject to overreaching. This was a right in land that arose because the party had been led to believe that they had a right in land and they had acted on it. However, this right could transfer to the purchase money because the property was sold and the purchase money was handed over to two trustees.

# ACTIVITY

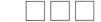

Consider the following examples and decide whether the rights of the beneficiaries are capable of being overreached or not:

1. Carrie and Susan and their parents Freda and Simon decide to buy a country cottage together. The two girls contribute £10,000 and their mother Freda contributes £20,000. The rest is provided by Simon. The legal estate is registered in Simon's name alone. Simon takes out a second loan with the Doubtful Bank Ltd. He fails to repay the money and runs away with Flora, the local barmaid. The daughters and their mother want to remain in the house.

2. Henry and Margaret buy a country cottage in Kent. They both contribute towards the purchase money and are registered as owners. Henry takes out a second loan by fraudulently using Margaret's signature on the form which the building society did not check.

3. Jean and Peter live together in Number 4 Magnificent Mansions. Peter purchased the property in his sole name with a contribution of £15,000 from Jean. He takes out a second loan on the property when he runs into financial difficulties in his new business. He appoints his brother as a second trustee. He is unable to repay the loan and the bank wants to sell the property to recover the money.

# 2.4 The historical background to the property legislation of 1925

Before 1925 there were a number of pitfalls for the potential purchaser of land. There could be equitable rights affecting his land which could be binding and he might not have had an opportunity to find out about them. Purchasers of land would buy land subject to an equitable

estate if they had notice of the estate. As seen above, notice could take three different forms and much would depend on actual knowledge. This created further pitfalls for the purchaser. The purchaser could find himself bound by unknown rights of third parties if he was held to have constructive notice.

The purchase itself was also a lengthy and difficult procedure because the title required proof that the seller owned the property and initially there were several legal estates in land. As you had to investigate each seller's right to sell the land, this could be time-consuming, expensive and prone to mistakes. If there was another sale within a relatively short space of time then the whole procedure had to be repeated; you could not rely on the investigations of the earlier sale.

So the two main problems in the transfer of land were:

**1.** the complication of proving title to the land you were buying

**2.** finding out whether other people had rights in the land you were buying.

Under 1. the purchaser had to check that each owner of a legal estate in the land he was purchasing had rights. Since there could be several legal estates in any land purchased, this involved proof for each separate estate. Also, the purchaser had to check that no one else had hidden rights in the legal estate.

Under 2. the purchaser had to check whether anyone had a right in equity that could affect his enjoyment of the land. These would not be immediately obvious.

These were just two of the problems for the purchaser of property in the nineteenth and early twentieth centuries. The problems prompted the passage of a whole range of property legislation in 1925, the most significant in land law being the Law of Property Act, the Land Registration Act and the Land Charges Act. These have all been supplemented and replaced by subsequent legislation but the main principles behind the legislation remain the same. The Land Registration Act 1925 has now been repealed by the Land Registration Act 2002.

## 2.4.1 Legal estates under the Law of Property Act 1925

Under s 1(1) of the Law of Property Act 1925 the only legal estates that could exist in land were reduced to two:

**1.** the term of years absolute and

**2.** the fee simple absolute.

However, apart from the two legal estates, there were lesser rights which could be created and were enforceable at law.

## 2.4.2 Legal interests under the Law of Property Act 1925

Under s 1(2) of the Law of Property Act 1925 the following interests could exist at law:

- an easement, right or privilege in or over land for an interest equivalent to an estate in the fee simple absolute in possession or a term of years absolute (s 1(2)(a))

- a rentcharge in possession issuing out of or charged on land being either perpetual or for a term of years absolute (s 1(2)(b))

- a charge by way of legal mortgage (s 1(2)(c))

- and any other similar charge on land which is not created by an instrument (of very little importance today) (s 1(2)(d))

- rights of re-entry exercisable over a legal term of years absolute (this right reserved to the owner of the rentcharge to enter the land if the owner of the estate fails to pay the sum due) (s 1 (2)(e)).

Under the Law of Property Act 1925 all other estates and interests were therefore equitable.

## 2.4.3 Equitable interests

Other proprietary rights in land therefore are said to be equitable only under s 1(3) of the 1925 Act. These include:

**1.** the rights of a beneficiary under a trust of land

**2.** an interest under a contract to create a legal estate or interest in land. The purchaser is treated as owning an equitable estate from the date the contract is exchanged. The legal estate continues to vest in the owner

**3.** restrictive covenants

**4.** interests that become equitable as a result of statutory reform. These would include any interest that is not within s 1(1) or s 1(2) of the Law of Property Act 1925, eg life estates will only exist in equity

**5.** interests that have not conformed with the requisite formalities in their creation, eg a deed to convey an interest in land which must be signed, witnessed and delivered. If these are not complied with then the interest conveyed will be equitable only. This list would include leases, easements and profits à prendre and also mortgage charges. They are capable of existing at law.

## 2.4.4 The 1925 property legislation

As noted above, there were some real problems with the transfer of rights and estates in land. As a result, six Acts were passed in 1925 which fundamentally changed the shape of land law in England and Wales.

'the structure of modern land law was put in place by the 1925 legislation, whose dominant policy was to facilitate the transfer of land by easing the burden on purchasers without defeating the interests of others unfairly. A fundamental principle underlying the legislation, but nowhere explicitly stated in it, was to distinguish between commercial interests and family interests. Examples of commercial interest are leases, rights of way and mortgages; such rights are almost invariably created for money or money's worth. Examples of family interest are rights of beneficiaries under a trust or settlement (this includes the beneficial rights of co-owners of land); such rights are not usually created for money or money's worth. Broadly speaking, with some exceptions intentionally created in 1925 and a few further exceptions not envisaged by the 1925 legislation which have been created subsequently by both the courts and the legislature, it was intended that:

**(1)** commercial interests should bind the successors in title of the person who created them; and

**(2)** family interests should upon sale or other disposition giving rise to the payment of a capital sum be overreached, that is to say transferred from the land to that capital sum, and so should not bind the successors in title of the person who created them.'

*Megarry's Manual of the Law of Real Property* (Sweet & Maxwell, 2002),
Chapter 4: 'The structure put in place by the 1925 legislation', p 73

The Land Registration Act 1925 (LRA 1925) introduced a system of registration of title to replace the unregistered system of conveyancing. There had been a limited system of registration of title prior to 1925 but the LRA 1925 was far more ambitious. This would go some way towards eliminating the problems that were created by making it necessary to prove title on each sale of the property.

The Acts passed in 1925 established a completely different approach to property law although many of their main objectives have still not been fulfilled today, over 75 years later.

The main principle that was established was the idea that title should be registered – so there would be no need to actually 'prove' good title each time the property changed hands. Registration of title, however, was not entirely new.

### 'The Emergence of Registration

. . . In retrospect, the value of registration of title seems irresistibly obvious. Instead of having a system of archaeological proof, in which the task of the conveyancer was to sift through many layers of paper title, establishing which interests were still relevant or effective, and ensuring that there was no danger of hidden documents surfacing in the future, one would have a much simpler scheme of tabular proof,

in which all effective interests would be visible at a glance. The idea of registration, and the sort of administrative framework which it implied, had been familiar for many decades before the first effective scheme of registration of title was introduced by the Land Transfer Act 1897. During that period there were various attempts to implement a system of registration, and many inquiries into the failure of these tentative schemes. These moves were played out against the background of progress in other areas of property law . . . There are a number of reasons why it took so long for these strands to be bound into an effective scheme of registration of title. First, a good deal of time was wasted on experiments with deeds registration. Secondly, there were some outstanding technological problems to be overcome, not least that of finding an effective method of identifying and indexing landholdings. Most contentious and most important there is the question of economic self interest. The question is whether, or to what extent, the slow evolution and final configuration of registration should be attributed to the success of a campaign of resistance to reform, mounted by the conveyancing profession in the defence of its monopoly.'

A Pottage, 'Evidencing Ownership' in S Bright and J Dewar (eds),<br>
Land Law: Themes and Perspectives (Oxford University Press, 1998), pp 142–144

## 2.5 The Land Charges Act 1925

Where title remained unregistered because it was outside the area of compulsory registration, a system of registration of equitable interests in land was introduced in the Land Charges Act 1925. This replaced the different types of notice.

The Land Charges Act 1925 was replaced by the Land Charges Act 1972 but the same list of charges introduced under the 1925 Act remains.

### 2.5.1 Classes of land charges

Land charges are divided into six classes (Classes A–F) with some further sub-division. Classes C, D and F are the most important:

- **Class A:** Charges that arise under statute but come into operation when the owner applies for registration, for example a landlord's right to receive compensation under the Agricultural Holdings Act 1986. They are very rare.

- **Class B:** Similarly, these are rights under statute which come into operation directly from the statute rather than on the application.

- **Class C:** These land charges are sub-divided into four groups:

1. The **puisne mortgage** which is a legal mortgage not protected by title deeds. In unregistered land this will always be a second mortgage. This is unusual because it is the only legal interest capable of being registered as a land charge under the Land Charges Act 1925. The Act was intended to cover equitable interests only.

2. The **limited owner's charge**. This is a right in equity which can be registered against the estate, for example Gordon is a tenant for life in an existing settlement and from his own resources he pays for the inheritance tax on the whole estate under the settlement. He is entitled to register the charge and will be able to claim to have the sum discharged out of the estate and paid to him.

3. The **general equitable owner's charge**. This covers a number of rights which are not registrable under any other heading. A number of rights are excluded from this group, for example interests under trusts.

4. **Estate contracts.** These are important in conveyancing. An estate contract consists of any contract to convey or create a legal estate in land or any option to purchase a legal estate or any right of pre-emption in respect of a legal estate (this is a right of first refusal). When a purchaser of land exchanges contracts with the seller, the purchaser gets an equitable estate in the land. This estate is capable of registration. Once registered it attaches to the land. If the seller tries to sell to anyone else the second purchaser will be bound by the rights of the first purchaser because he bought subject to their rights. In view of the relatively short period between exchange of contracts and completion, solicitors rarely registered an estate contract for the purchaser, which was potentially taking a grave risk. In *Midland Bank Trust Co Ltd v Green* [1981] 2 WLR 28, discussed below, the consequences of failure to register become apparent. Note that only the option to purchase was registrable under the 1925 legislation and the right of pre-emption could not be registered.

- **Class D**: This group is further sub-divided into three sub-headings:

1. **Inland Revenue charges** for inheritance tax payable on death.

2. **Restrictive covenants.** This class covers any restrictive covenant created after 1926 but excluding any covenant that was created between lessor and lessee. Once the interest is registered then the purchaser is bound by the covenant. If the holder of the right fails to register the right then the fact that the purchaser knows about the right is irrelevant.

3. **Equitable easements.** Any easement that has been created on or after 1st January 1926 and which is equitable only. A legal easement in unregistered land would not be registrable under this category since it would take effect in law and be binding on the world, irrespective of registration.

- **Class E:** This class comprises annuities created before 1926, which are very rare indeed.

- **Class F:** This is an important group which are referred to as 'matrimonial home rights'. They were first created by the Matrimonial Homes Act 1967. They are now contained in the Family Law Act 1996, much of which was repealed but those sections covering rights to occupy the matrimonial home were preserved. The right can only be claimed by a spouse who is not a co-owner of the matrimonial home. Once registered the spouse has the right to occupy the home which is owned by the other spouse. The significant fact is that the right is dependent on status and not on contributions made towards the purchase.

Kathy's right under the Family Law Act 1996 is quite separate from any property rights which may arise under the divorce legislation. It is also irrelevant that she has not contributed to the

purchase of the property. If she had failed to register the right then she could not rely on it even if she later registers it, as it must be in place when Anthony Crook exchanges contracts with Keith.

## 2.5.2 Registration of land charges

Registration under the Land Charges Act 1925 is made by the person claiming the right. Registration is made against the name of the owner of the property and not the name of the property. This has caused a number of problems in the past:

**1.** There may have been defective registration of the charge because the name used was wrong.

**2.** There may have been a defective search because the purchaser searched against the wrong name.

**3.** The purchaser may not know the full names of all the previous owners of the property because the seller has only to prove title for the previous 15 years.

**Each of these problems is discussed below:**

**1. Registration in the wrong name.** If the registration was made in an incorrect name then the court is presented with a problem because a later purchaser may be given a clear certificate showing no land charges against the land itself. In *Oak Co-operative Building Society v Blackburn* [1968] Ch 730 the charge was registered against the name of 'Frank David Blackburn'. A search was made by a subsequent purchaser against the name of 'Francis Davis Blackburn'. The court upheld the earlier registered charge as it was made against a recognised form of 'Francis'. The court concluded that there should have been searches in all forms of the purchaser's name as the defendants would then have found the earlier charge.

**2. Search against incorrect name**. The general rule is that a purchaser who claims a search against an incorrect name will be bound by any charges that are registered against the correct version of the owner's name. Under s 198 of the Law of Property Act 1925 'the registration of any instrument or matter . . . shall be deemed to constitute actual notice of such instrument or matter and of the fact of registration to all persons and for all purposes connected with the land affected as from the date of registration'.

**3. The purchaser may not know the names of all previous owners of the land**. On any sale of property with unregistered land all charges properly registered will continue to affect the land. The problem for the purchaser is that if they do not know the names of all the previous owners then they have no way of discovering all the potential charges that have been registered against their names and could therefore be binding on the land.

Wade described the use of a name-based register as the equivalent of creating Frankenstein's monster, which, with the passing years, would become not only more dangerous but also more difficult to kill. He pointed out that as the years went by it would become impossible successfully to convert the register from 'name-based' into 'title-based'. The time and costs involved would make it impossible. (H W R Wade, 'Land Charges Required' [1956] CLJ 216.)

The problem has not been solved within the land charges system itself but by the introduction of compulsory registration of title which itself is title-based. Charges in the registered land system are registered against the name of the property.

## 2.5.3 The effect of registration

After 1925 all registrable interests were either registered, in which case the purchaser took subject to them, or were not registered, in which case the purchaser took free of them. The effect of non-registration of a charge depends on which class of charge was involved. In Classes C(iv) and D(i)–(iii) the purchaser of a legal estate in the land charged for money or money's worth can take free of the unregistered charge. It means that whereas under the other land charges a purchaser of an equitable estate can take free of the charge, only the purchaser of a legal estate can take free of the unregistered charge under Class C(iv) and D(i)–(iii). The purchaser of an equitable estate will therefore be bound by an unregistered estate contract in the land.

## APPLYING THE LAW

Barbara exchanges contracts with Loveday to purchase a large house in Surrey. Barbara fails to register an estate contract under C(iv). Loveday later exchanges contracts with Aynia. Aynia will not be bound by the unregistered contract with Barbara. However, she would be bound if Loveday had given her the property by way of gift.

Once a search had been made at the Land Charges Registry a certificate would be produced and if a charge against the land had not been made, for whatever reason, then the charge would not be binding on the land.

It no longer mattered whether or not the purchaser actually knew about the existence of equitable rights in land. These rules could have very dramatic results because the court had no right to intervene, however unfair the result might seem.

CASE EXAMPLE

### *Midland Bank Trust Co Ltd v Green* **[1981] 2 WLR 28**

A father owned land with unregistered title. He granted his son a 10-year option to purchase the land at an agreed price but the son failed to register the option against the father's name. Later, the father sold the farm to his wife at undervalue, in order, principally, to avoid the option after a quarrel with the son. The son tried to register the option but it was held to be too late. Even though the mother was aware that the son had rights in the land, she still took free of his rights. She had purchased the farm for £500 when it was worth about £40,000.

1. Oliver J at first instance held that the option was not binding because it had not been registered before the 'purchase' by the wife.

2. The Court of Appeal reversed the finding of Oliver J. Lord Denning drew attention to the fact that the statutory immunity could only be claimed for unregistered options where payment had been for a fair and reasonable value in money and money's worth and not at undervalue. Lord Denning regarded the payment of £500 as a gross undervalue.

3. The House of Lords reversed the finding of the Court of Appeal. Lord Wilberforce held that the wife need only show that payment had been for 'money or money's worth'. He relied on the contractual rule which said that the court will not enquire into the adequacy of consideration as long as the consideration is real. She had paid £500 which was held to be valuable consideration. The House of Lords unanimously held that the unregistered land charge was unenforceable against the purchaser. The House of Lords held that good faith was irrelevant in this transaction. The wife had known that the transaction would affect the son's right to exercise the option but this did not affect the transaction.

An option to purchase can be very valuable. It gives a right to demand the transfer of property at the agreed price at any time during the period of the option. Once registered, it will be binding on the land. It does not prevent a later sale to someone else but the person with the option has the right to claim the property at the agreed price, even from the third-party purchaser. Where property is rising in value it can be a very valuable right to own. In commercial transactions the option is usually granted for valuable consideration.

## 2.5.4 Rights that are incapable of registration under the Land Charges Acts 1925–72

Under unregistered conveyancing there are still some equitable rights that are incapable of registration. Even after the passage of the Land Registration Act 2002, they will continue to be relevant because there are still substantial numbers of properties with unregistered title.

There is no requirement compulsorily to register your land unless you carry out a transaction that acts as an 'event' which triggers registration.

One of the most important rights in unregistered land that cannot be registered is the right of a beneficiary under a trust of land. These are the rights of someone who has contributed to the purchase of land but does not have rights in law. These rights cannot be entered on the Land Charges Register. The old rules concerning the doctrine of notice govern whether these rights are binding on a purchaser.

# CASE EXAMPLE

**Kingsnorth Finance Co Ltd v Tizard [1986] 1 WLR 783**

The husband held the legal title to land on trust for himself and his wife. The wife had an interest in the property because of contributions she had made towards the purchase. The wife lived apart form the husband who remained in the matrimonial home with the two children of the marriage. The wife continued to return to the property, often twice a day, to cook for the children and to carry out domestic chores. The husband secretly took out a loan with a finance company. It then obtained a charge over the house giving it rights over the property if the husband defaulted on the repayments. He later left to go to America with one of the children. An agent from the finance company had visited the premises but the husband had arranged the visit when the wife was not visiting and had eliminated all traces of her existence, hiding photographs and all her remaining possessions in the house. The agent of the finance company failed to make sufficient enquiries. It was held that the finance company did not take free of the wife's rights as it had constructive notice of her rights.

This case suggests that any bank or building society would be bound in unregistered land by the rights of a wife or any holder of an equitable interest where there had **not** been proper enquiry. 'Proper enquiry' includes failure to ask questions about others who may have potential rights in the property. Mr Tizard had put 'single' as his status on his application for a loan. However, there were clearly children in the property and this should have alerted the agent to ask further questions about their mother and whether she had any potential rights in the property.

# ACTIVITY

**1.** List the problems with unregistered conveyancing prior to 1925.

**2.** Explain why so many properties with unregistered title remain today.

# Further reading

Harpum, C, 'Purchasers with Notice of Unregistered Land Charges' [1981] CLJ 213.

Harpum, C, 'Overreaching, Trustees' Powers and the Reform of the 1925 legislation' [1990] CLJ 277.

Howell, J, 'Notice: A Broad view and a Narrow view' [1996] Conv 34.

Howell, J, 'The Doctrine of Notice: An Historical Perspective' [1997] Conv 341.

Thompson, M P, 'The Purchaser as Private Detective' [1986] Conv 283.

# chapter 3

# REGISTERED LAND ■

In view of the significance of land it is important to have some reliable system of recording transactions involving land ownership.

## 3.1 Introduction to registration of title

The traditional system of unregistered conveyancing had no record of the ownership of the property other than the deeds themselves. It was open to fraud and misuse. Documentation could always become lost or damaged. These problems were soon recognised and over a period of 300 years attempts were made to regulate the system of recording ownership of land in the UK. The first successful Act was passed in 1862 but the first meaningful Act was the Land Transfer Act of 1875 which introduced the idea of a single Land Registry. The Land Registry would be used to record ownership of land and those records could be relied on by subsequent purchasers. The idea was to have a system of registering title to land which had two features:

**1.** the title to land would be guaranteed by the state and

**2.** it could be relied on by all prospective purchasers as proof of ownership of property.

The old system of unregistered land was based on the purchaser investigating the title deeds. This had to be repeated on each sale of the property. It was wasteful and repetitive and there was always the risk that undiscovered rights attaching to the land would bind the purchaser.

The Land Registry Act 1862 and Land Transfer Act 1875 introduced the principle of registration but the system was voluntary and most titles remained unregistered. In 1897 compulsory registration was introduced on the sale of property in London. This was the beginning of a system which now affects all dealings in land.

### 3.1.1 Features of the land registration system

The scheme of registration of title aims to create a system in which one register will disclose who owns any piece of land and all the rights and interests that bind that land.

Registration allows registered estates in land, both freehold and leasehold, to be separately registered. Each has its own title on the Register. The Register guarantees the title once it has been registered and the purchaser can accept the state of that title without making his own separate investigation of the title.

The Register is divided into separate sections which cover different aspects of ownership: the property itself; rights affecting the property; and ownership of the property.

## 3.1.2 The aims behind the Land Registration Acts

The Land Registration Act 1925 intended to introduce a system of land registration which would eventually extend to all land. Indeed, the aim was for the system to extend to all areas within 30 years. There were two ways of extending the registration system:

1. **Voluntary registration**: the owner had the option of whether or not to register the title; as the advantages were not necessarily clear and it cost the owner to register, few took this option up.

2. **Compulsory registration**: the purchaser had to register as soon as an event triggering registration took place. Initially this was only on the sale of the property but it gradually extended to cover most dealings in property. Under the Land Registration Act 2002 it includes the transfer by gift and a transfer under a court order. There is no option for the purchaser but to register because otherwise they lose the property.

## APPLYING THE LAW

Valentine owns Cedar Grange which has unregistered title. He lives in an area of compulsory registration. He does not have to register his title until he deals in the land in a particular way. While he lives there, enjoying his property, the title remains unregistered. He sells the land to Asif. The sale will act as a trigger for compulsory registration. The sale will be under the rules governing unregistered conveyancing. However, after the completion of the sale, Asif will have to take steps to register the title.

Gradually, areas of compulsory registration were extended to more and more of England and Wales. The last areas of voluntary registration were brought into the system in 1990. However, even in 2004, over 10 per cent of all titles to land remain unregistered.

## 3.1.3 The key features of the registration system

1. The mirror principle.
2. The insurance principle.
3. The curtain principle.

1. Under the **mirror principle** it is held that the Register is an accurate and conclusive reflection of ownership of title and also relevant interests affecting the land in question. The mirror principle relies on registration of all rights. If rights can exist in land that cannot or need not be registered then the Register does not give an accurate picture of the title to the land.

2. Under the **insurance principle** the accuracy of the Register is guaranteed and, if the Register is found to be inaccurate it will be altered or rectified. Any persons affected by alteration/rectification are entitled to be paid a sum in compensation.

3. Under the **curtain principle** the purchaser of land is not concerned with matters behind the entries on the Register, for example trusts affecting the land. The purchaser is not concerned with whether the beneficiaries' interests in the land are satisfied after sale.

## 3.1.4 The Land Registry

The Land Registry consists of three registers:

1. the **Property Register** which describes the property and will refer to a filed plan prepared from the Ordnance Survey map; this part of the Register may include details of any benefits attached to the land, such as easements and restrictive covenants. It also describes the status of the property, whether it is held with freehold or leasehold title

2. the **Charges Register** which shows details of any incumbrances or third-party rights registered against the estate. These are usually negative rights which exist in equity and restrict the rights of the owner, for example restrictive covenants enjoyed over the land or mortgages and charges secured over the property

3. the **Proprietorship Register** which shows the name and address of the registered proprietor of the relevant title, the date of registration and the nature of the title; it will also record any restrictions on the power of the proprietor to deal with the land, for example he is a trustee or has been declared bankrupt; there may be entries preventing any disposition of the land without the approval of the lender.

NB An incumbrance means a right that attaches to the title of land.

For an example of a register, see Figure 3.1.

**OFFICIAL COPY OF REGISTER ENTRIES**
This official copy shows the entries subsisting on the register on **9 December 2003** at **11:44:12**.
This date **must be quoted as the search from date in any official search** application based on this copy.
Under s.67 of the Land Registration Act 2002, this copy is admissible in evidence to the same extent as the original.
Issued on 9 December 2003.
This title is dealt with by **Land Registry, Maradon Office**.

# Land Registry

**Title Number: CS72510**

Edition Date: 3 December 2003

## A: Property Register

*This register describes the land and estate comprised in the title.*

CORNSHIRE : MARADON

1. (19 December 1989) The **Freehold** land shown edged with red on the plan of the above title filed at Land Registry and being 13 Augustine Way, Kerwick (PL14 3JP).

2. (19 December 1989) The mines and minerals are excluded.

3. (19 December 1989) The land has the benefit of a right of way on foot only over the passageway at the rear leading into Monks Mead.

4. (3 December 2003) The exact line of the boundary of the land in this title (between the points A — B in blue on the title plan) is determined under section 60 of the Land Registration Act 2002 as shown on the plan lodged with the application to determine the boundary dated 3 December 2003.

   Note: Plan filed.

## B: Proprietorship Register

*This register specifies the class of title and identifies the owner. It contains any entries that affect the right of disposal.*

**Title Absolute**

1. (10 July 2000) **PROPRIETOR:** PAUL JOHN DAWKINS and ANGELA MARY DAWKINS both of 28 Nelson Way, Kerwick, Maradon, Cornshire PL14 5PQ and of pjdawkins662@ail.com

2. (10 July 2000) The price stated to have been paid on 2 June 2000 was £78,000.

3. (10 July 2000) **RESTRICTION:** No disposition by a sole proprietor of the land (not being a trust corporation) under which capital money arises is to be registered except under an order of the registrar or of the Court.

4. (5 October 2002) Caution in favour of Mary Gertrude Shelley of 18 Cambourne Street, Kerwick, Maradon, Cornshire, PL14 7AR and care of Messrs Swan & Co of 25 Trevisick Street, Kerwick, Maradon, Cornshire PL14 6RE.

5. (28 November 2003) RESTRICTION: No disposition of the registered estate by the proprietor of the registered estate is to be registered without a written consent signed by the proprietor for the time being of the charge dated 12 November 2003 in favour of Fast and Furious Building Society referred to in the charges register.

## Specimen Register

## C: Charges Register

*This register contains any changes and other matters that affect the land.*

1. (19 December 1989) The passageway at the side included in the title is subject to rights of way on foot only.

2. (10 July 2000) A Transfer of the land in this title dated 2 June 2000 made between (1) John Charles Brown and (2) Paul John Dawkins and Angela Mary Dawkins contains restrictive covenants.

   NOTE: Original filed.

3. (1 August 2002) **REGISTERED CHARGE** dated 15 July 2002 to secure the moneys including the further advances therein mentioned.

4. (1 August 2002) **PROPRIETOR:** WEYFORD BUILDING SOCIETY of Society House, The Avenue, Weyford, Cornshire CN12 4BD.

5. (28 November 2003) **REGISTERED CHARGE** dated 12 November 2003.

6. (28 November 2003) **PROPRIETOR:** FAST AND FURIOUS BUILDING SOCIETY of Fast Plaza, The Quadrangle, Weyford, Cornshire CN14 3NW.

7. (3 December 2003) The parts of the land affected thereby are subject to the leases set out in the schedule of leases hereto.

************************

## Schedule of Notices of Leases

| | Registration date and Plan ref. | Property description | Date of lease and Term | Lessee's Title |
|---|---|---|---|---|
| 1. | 3.12.2003 | 13 Augustine Way, Kerwick | 12.11.2003 999 years from 10.10.2003 | CS385372 |

### END OF REGISTER

*NOTE: A date at the beginning of an entry is the date on which the entry was made in the Register.*

■ *Figure 3.1 Example of a register*

There is a central Land Registry which can be found in London. However, for practical purposes there are district land registries around the country. They each have an extensive geographical catchment area. The registration rules are common to all. The district land registries all deal in land in the same way.

## 3.1.5 How land registration works: key facts

### First registration

1. If land has not been registered before, the purchaser buys the land subject to the old rules of unregistered conveyancing. Title is investigated under the traditional rules and the seller must show a 15-year good root of title.

2. The purchaser then has a duty to register his legal estate. Failure to do so within a time limit will result in the purchaser losing his legal estate in land.

3. The Registry is responsible for investigating title before first registration; it will check the accuracy of all the documents of title and, if satisfied, it will then register the new owner as Proprietor on the Proprietorship Register.

4. Once registered, the Land Registry guarantees the accuracy of the registration of title.

5. Before the Land Registration Act 2002 the Land Registry issued a document called a land certificate. These replaced the documents of title used in unregistered conveyancing. The 2002 Act has abolished land certificates and they are no longer issued. Today, a title information document is issued with an official copy of the Register and an official copy of the title plan. These documents have no legal significance.

6. Where land was subject to a mortgage then the Land Registry would issue a document called a charge certificate to the lenders. These have also been abolished under the 2002 Act.

7. However, registration is not simultaneous with the purchase. This takes place some weeks later and for a time the seller's name is on the Register although the purchaser has moved into the property and is now living there. This is called the 'registration gap' and can cause difficulties if new rights arise in the 'gap' between the conveyance and the registration of the new owner.

8. If the land was subject to third-party rights these would be recorded in the Charges Register. Some rights were not capable of registration. This meant that it would not be possible to find out about them by checking with the Land Registry. The only way that they could be discovered was by visiting the land itself. In this way the system of land registration is not completely accurate as to the state of the land.

## Steps in first registration of title

| | COMMENTS |
|---|---|
| **Step One:** Purchaser buys land subject to unregistered conveyancing rules. | The seller must show a good root of title of at least 15 years. The property is conveyed to the purchaser by deed. |
| **Step Two:** The purchaser seeks registration of the title at the Land Registry. Failure to register within a time limit results in loss of property. | The Land Registry is responsible for checking the accuracy of all the documents and investigating the title. |
| **Step Three:** The Land Registry issues a title information document and official copies of the title and the plan. | The Land Registry once issued a land certificate on registration, which replaced documents of title, but these have now been abolished. |

## Subsequent registration

**1.** If registered land is sold then the new purchaser would apply to the Land Registry to be registered as the new proprietor of the land.

**2.** Prior to sale, the purchaser investigates the land by visiting the land itself to find out if there are any rights not capable of registration and also by checking the Charges Register.

**3.** The title has already been investigated so this part would be straightforward; there does not have to be a fresh investigation into the state of the title. Any new incumbrances affecting title would have been added as they came into existence. The Land Registry would have checked these before adding them to the title.

**4.** Prior to 2002, a new land certificate would be issued to the new owner; today, a title information document is issued which has no significance in law.

Under the Land Registration Act 2002, land and charge certificates have been abolished. The Register itself represents proof of ownership. Land certificates will gradually be removed from circulation. When land is sold they must be submitted to the Land Registry with any application for registration and the Land Registry will not issue a replacement.

**Steps in subsequent registration of title**

| | | |
|---|---|---|
| **Step One:** Buyer decides to purchase property. The purchase is completed. | The buyer checks the Register for information about the property. | The Land Registry guarantees the accuracy of the original registration. |
| **Step Two:** Buyer applies to be registered as the new proprietor of the land. | The Land Registry does not have to carry out checks of the title as this has already been done. | Registration must be carried out within two months. New proprietor is registered as owner. |
| **Step Three:** The existing land certificate must be submitted to the Registry. | A title information document will be issued. | No fresh land certificate is issued. |

# 3.2. The reform of the law on land registration

## 3.2.1. The need for reform

This aim of land registration for all under the Land Registration Act 1925 was not fulfilled and certainly not within the 30-year period it had envisaged. Compulsory registration was not introduced universally until 1990. The land registration system itself was found to have a number of problems. These were disclosed in the Report of the Law Commission called *Land Registration for the 21st Century: a Conveyancing Revolution*.

**1.** There had been considerable litigation over the status of overriding interests and it was agreed that they should be reduced in number or possibly abolished.

**2.** The legislation was very complicated, with too many rules affecting the registration of interests.

**3.** The gap between transfer and registration often gave rise to uncertainty and should be closed by using modern technology.

**4.** There was no provision for the advance in modern technology in the system of conveyancing.

**5.** The rules relating to adverse possession of land should be reformed.

The Land Registration Act 2002 now aims to achieve the original objective outlined in the Land Registration Act 1925, of converting every title in land to registered title. However, the Land Registry admits that there are still millions of unregistered titles in existence.

The 2002 Act repeals the entire 1925 Act. However, many of the original principles and ideals are included in the 2002 Act, as well as a number of major changes and reforms.

## 3.2.2 The objectives of the 2002 Act

**1.** The Register should be a complete and accurate reflection of the state of title of the land at any given time.

**2.** The number of overriding interests in land should be reduced.

**3.** The Act should reflect the advances in modern technology.

# 3.3 Registration under the Land Registration Act 2002

Only legal estates are capable of registration.

Under s 1 of the Law of Property Act 1925 there are two legal estates in land:

**1.** the fee simple absolute (the freehold estate) and

**2.** the term of years absolute (the leasehold estate).

The 2002 Act has extended the type of leasehold estate capable of registration from any lease in excess of 21 years to any lease in excess of seven years. Any lease which is to take effect more than three months after the grant of the lease (known as a 'future lease') must be registered. They cannot take effect as overriding interests because they would not be visible to the purchaser when visiting the property, so the purchaser would have no way of knowing that they were in existence.

There are three separate provisions for registration under the 2002 Act:

**1.** Under **s 3**, which covers **first** registration of title, a title may be **voluntarily** registered. The owner takes the initiative for registration; it is not triggered by some event such as purchase. This incurs a lower fee so it only applies in limited circumstances; it does not apply where there is a transfer of title. It would be tempting to use the cheaper fees for voluntary registration before a sale has been finalised.

**2.** Under **s 4**, which also covers **first** registration, there is provision for **compulsory** registration of title when an event triggers the need to register. These include a wide variety of circumstances such as a transfer for valuable consideration and a gift.

**3.** Under **s 27**, where there is a **disposition** of an estate or charge which is **already registered** then that must be registered before it can take effect.

## 3.3.1 Voluntary registration under s 3

It is now also possible voluntarily to register legal estates as well as the following with their own titles:

**1. profits à prendre:** these are rights to take something from another's land, for example the right to take fish from a river or the right to take wood for fuel. This is quite independent of ownership of the land but is dependent on having a right to enter the other's land

**2. franchises:** these are rights or privileges which are granted by the Crown, for example the right to hold a market or a fair in their own right

**3. rentcharges:** this is a right to receive a periodic sum of money from the owner of land charged with that payment. It excludes rent payable under a lease or tenancy and any sum payable as interest.

's 3(1) This section applies to any unregistered legal estate which is an interest of the following kinds –

(a) an estate in land,

(b) a rentcharge,

(c) a franchise, and

(d) a profit à prendre.

(2) Subject to the following provisions, a person may apply to the registrar to be registered as the proprietor of an unregistered legal estate to which this section applies if –

(a) the estate is vested in him, or

(b) he is entitled to require the estate to be vested in him.'

So the person registering the right must show that it is held for an interest equivalent to a legal estate, either a fee simple absolute or, under s 3(3), a term of years absolute where the lease has at least seven years to run. The person cannot apply to be voluntarily registered if he has purchased the property. This is because he will be compelled to register the title under the compulsory provisions of s 4.

There is also a new provision for Crown land to be voluntarily registered. There are problems with this, discussed in Chapter 1. The Crown is the feudal landlord of all property held in the United Kingdom. It does not hold the land as freehold or under a fee simple absolute in possession, so the first step is for the Crown to grant itself a freehold estate.

Section 79 allows the Queen to grant a fee simple absolute to herself and then allows her to register this. The main advantage of this will be to prevent adverse possessory rights running against the Crown.

## APPLYING THE LAW ☐☐☐

The Queen owns the large estate of Windsor Great Park. It is possible for the Queen to grant herself a freehold estate of a part of it. She can then approach the Registrar to register the title of the land. If squatters took possession of the land under the reform of the rights of squatters to acquire adverse possessory rights, the Queen would have to be informed if any attempt was made for the squatters to register title.

☐☐☐

# 3.3.2 Events which trigger compulsory registration under s 4

Today, any dealing in a legal estate which has an unregistered title will make it subject to compulsory registration. The 2002 Act refers to 'events' triggering compulsory registration. The only estates which can continue to have unregistered title are those estates which are not subject to any dealing at all in the title. However, the registration of a land charge in unregistered land will not trigger registration of title.

's 4(1) The requirement of registration applies on the occurrence of any of the following events –

(a) the transfer of a qualifying estate –

(i) for valuable or other consideration, by way of gift or in pursuance of an order of any court, or

(ii) by means of an assent (including a vesting assent); . . .'

Consideration can be money but it can include the exchange for assets or exchange for land. Gifts were included in compulsory registration in 1997 and cover both *inter vivos* gifts as well as assents giving effect to a gift under a will or on intestacy.

's 4(1) (c) the grant out of a qualifying estate of an estate in land –

(i) for a term of years absolute of more than seven years from the date of the grant

(ii) for valuable consideration, by way of gift or in pursuance of an order of any court

. . .

(g) the creation of a protected first legal mortgage of a qualifying estate'.

The Land Registration Act 1997 included all first mortgages of an unregistered title as triggers for registration. Mortgages that escape registration are second mortgages of unregistered land.

In the 2002 Act:

's 4(2) For the purposes of subsection (1) a qualifying estate is an unregistered legal estate which is:

(a) a freehold estate in land, or

(b) a leasehold estate in land which, at the time of the transfer, grant or creation, has more than seven years to run

. . .

(7) In subsection (1)(a) and (c) references to transfer or grant by way of gift include transfer or grant for the purpose of –

(a) constituting a trust under which the settlor does not retain the whole of the beneficial interest

(b) uniting the bare title and the beneficial interest in property held under a trust under which the settlor did not, on constitution, retain the whole of the beneficial interest.

(8) For the purposes of subsection (1) (g)

(a) a legal mortgage is protected if it takes effect on its creation as a mortgage to be protected by the deposit of documents relating to the mortgaged estate, and

(b) a first legal mortgage is one which, on its creation ranks in priority ahead of any other mortgages then affecting the mortgaged estate.'

The 1925 Act made registration compulsory on **dispositions** of the estate. By way of contrast, the 2002 Act makes registration compulsory on any **event** concerning the estate. These include:

**1.** the transfer for valuable consideration of a freehold or leasehold estate in unregistered land

**2.** a gift of an unregistered estate

**3.** a transfer in pursuance of an order of the court

**4.** the grant of a lease in excess of seven years to take effect immediately or to take effect in the future

**5.** the creation of the protected first legal mortgage of a qualifying estate.

### 3.3.3 Events which do not require compulsory registration under the 2002 Act

Certain events specifically do not induce compulsory registration:

**1.** where land is transferred to trustees to hold the estate 'as nominees for [S]' will not induce compulsory registration

**2.** the transfer of the legal estate by the operation of law which includes the transfer on death of someone's estate to his personal representatives

**3.** a merger of a lease by assignment or surrender of a lease to the owner of the immediate reversion.

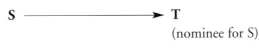

**(S)**

■ *Figure 3.2 Transfer with no element of gift*

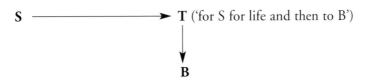

■ *Figure 3.3 Transfer with gift as a triggering event*

In Figure 3.2 there is no element of gift, whereas in Figure 3.3 there is a gift of the property which will pass eventually to B. In Figure 3.3 there is a triggering event.

Since the aim of the 2002 Act is for 100 per cent compulsory registration of title to all land in the UK there is provision in the Act under s 5 to permit the Lord Chancellor to add new events that will themselves trigger compulsory registration.

# ACTIVITY

> Consider the following examples and decide whether they are capable of registration in their own right:
>
> 1. Rachael buys fishing rights over a stretch of the River Test which runs through her neighbour Rory's land.
>
> 2. Eleanor is granted a five-year lease of a flat in Newcastle.
>
> 3. Patrick is given a lifetime right to take wood from his neighbour Edward's land.
>
> 4. Anna sells the right to hold a mid-summer fair on her land to a friend, Barry. Anna's family were granted this right in 1386.
>
> 5. Zoe takes an eight-year lease over a large house in Dulwich.
>
> 6. Phoebe has a large garden which leads down to the River Yealm. She grants her neighbour a right of way to the river over her land.
>
> Will the registration be compulsory or can it be made voluntarily?

## 3.3.4 The effect of the duty to register under the 2002 Act

When unregistered land is dealt with in such a way as to give rise to an event which triggers compulsory registration, the time starts to run in which registration must take place. Registration must take place within two months of the relevant period (s 6(4) of the 2002 Act). The period can be extended by the Registrar if he is satisfied that there is good reason to do so.

### Failure to register the fee simple absolute

Failure to register a fee simple absolute or freehold estate within the time limit will result in the transfer becoming void, which means that the transferor will hold the legal estate on bare trust for the transferee. The transferor is the seller of the land and the transferee is the purchaser.

### Failure to register the term of years absolute

Failure to register a term of years absolute or leasehold estate or a protected mortgage of property will result in the interest becoming void and the transfer will take effect as a contract for valuable consideration to grant or create a lease or mortgage.

If the transferee wants the property, which is likely since valuable consideration will normally have been paid, then steps must again be taken to ensure that the property can be registered. It will be necessary to attempt to transfer the interest a second time. This will result in additional costs. The 2002 Act lays down that these should be borne by the transferee or grantee or possibly the mortgagor. They will also be liable for any other liability which has been reasonably incurred because the interest has not been registered.

 's 8 If a legal estate is retransferred, granted or recreated because of a failure to comply with the requirement of registration, the transferee, grantee or, as the case may be, the mortgagor –

(a) is liable to the other party for all the proper costs of and incidental to the retransfer, regrant or recreation of the legal estate, and

(b) is liable to indemnify the other party in respect of any other liability reasonably incurred by him because of the failure to comply with the requirement of registration.'

## APPLYING THE LAW

Thomas purchases Greenacre Cottage, which had an unregistered title, from Phillip on 1st June. He leaves for a long holiday in South America in mid-June. He did not register the title before he left. He stays away until late September because he loves the life in Argentina and cannot bear to leave. He has now lost his chance to register the title and Phillip is now holding the title to Greenacre Cottage as bare trustee. The original transfer is now void and there must be a fresh transfer to Thomas. Any extra costs accruing to Phillip must be borne by Thomas.

Under s 11(2) of the 2002 Act, once registration has taken place, the estate is vested in the proprietor.

Section 11(3) states that the estate is vested in the proprietor, together with all interests subsisting for the benefit of the estate.

## 3.3.5 Different classes of title

The Land Registry has a choice of classes of title to grant to a registered estate. The Land Registration Act 1925 laid down the following classes of title which may be registered:

1. **absolute freehold**: an absolute title guarantees that the estate registered is vested in the registered owner named in the Proprietorship Register, subject only to entries in the Register and any overriding interests that may affect it. In practice this is most likely to be the type of title registered and it is very unusual for the Registrar to register a freehold estate with any other title

2. **absolute leasehold**: this guarantees not only that the lease under which the land is held is vested in the owner but also that the lease itself was validly granted, so the Registrar can grant an absolute leasehold title once he is satisfied that there is good title to both the freehold and the lease itself

3. **qualified freehold**: in very rare cases where the Registrar thinks that either the title of the applicant has limitations in time or the title itself is not good, then a qualified title will be granted. An example might be that the title is subject to rights arising because the title has only been investigated for less than the required 15 years for good root of title, for example only 12 years. There may be practical reasons why the full 15 years were not covered but the title granted will still be less than absolute, to take account of the fact that someone with rights arising in the three years not investigated may claim rights to the property

**4. qualified leasehold**: these are similar to qualified freehold

**5. possessory freehold**: this type of title is granted when the claim is based on adverse possession or the title deeds have been either lost or destroyed. The practical effect of a possessory title is that you can deal in it in the same way as the owner of an absolute title but the land is subject to any right including overriding interests that were in existence prior to registration of title. The guarantee on a possessory title will cover only errors or omissions in the title occurring since the date of registration

**6. possessory leasehold**: these have the same qualifications as possessory freehold title

**7. good leasehold**: where there is no evidence of the quality of the superior title of the landlord then the Registrar cannot grant absolute leasehold but can only grant good leasehold. There may be no evidence to confirm that the lessor was entitled to grant the lease. The Land Registry will only guarantee the title from the date of the lease itself.

All seven classes of title can still be registered under the 2002 Act although in practice the absolute freehold and the absolute leasehold will continue to be the most frequently used.

## 3.3.6 The transfer of a registered title

The transfer of the legal estate in **unregistered** land took place on completion of the sale. The law then immediately regarded the purchaser as the new owner. In **registered** land the position is slightly different. The transfer of the legal estate in the land does not take place until the name of the purchaser has been placed on the Register.

 's 27(1) If a disposition of a registered estate or registered charge is required to be completed by registration, it does not operate at law until the relevant registration requirements are met.'

The section continues by listing all the types of disposition which require registration to take place.

 's 27(2) In the case of a registered estate, the following are the dispositions which are required to be completed by registration –

(a) a transfer

(b) where the registered estate is an estate in land, the grant of a term of years absolute –

(i) for a term of more than seven years from the date of the grant,

(ii) to take effect in possession after the end of the period of three months beginning with the date of the grant,

(iii) under which the right to possession is discontinuous.'

Section 27 firstly covers the transfer of the freehold estate. In the case of the transfer of a leasehold estate it depends whether the freehold estate is already registered. If the landlord's title is unregistered then, on the creation of a lease, registration should take place under s 4 (see above). This covers first registration of title. If the title is registered then registration takes place under s 27.

Other dealings with title which require registration in order to take effect include:

1. **legal easements**: they cannot be registered with separate title but must instead be registered on the Property Register of the land benefiting from the easement

2. **legal charges (mortgages)**: again, they cannot be registered with their own title but must be entered on the Charges Register of the land which carries the charge.

### Registration of registrable interests under the Land Registration Act 2002

| | **Voluntary registration under s 3 LRA 2002** | **Compulsory registration under s 4 LRA 2002** | **Registration under s 27 LRA 2002** |
|---|---|---|---|
| When the section applies | The applicant can decide to register where certain conditions apply. | Applies where a triggering event occurs. | Applies on a disposition requiring registration. |
| An estate in land: freehold or leasehold estate in land | Where the estate is vested in the applicant or he is **entitled** to have the estate vested in him. | The transfer of a qualifying estate either as a gift or through sale or any event triggering registration. | A disposition of a registered estate. |
| A rentcharge | Where an estate is vested in the applicant or he is **entitled** to have the estate vested in him. | | The express grant or reservation of an interest under s 1(2)(b). |
| A franchise | Where the estate is vested in the applicant or the applicant is **entitled** to have the estate vested in him. | | The grant of a lease of a franchise or manor which is itself a registered estate. |
| A profit à prendre | Where the estate is vested in the applicant or the applicant is **entitled** to have the estate vested in him. | | The express grant or reservation of an interest under s 1(2)(a) LPA 1925. |

# 3.4 Interests in registered land protected by Land Registry notice

There are three types of rights that can exist over registered land:

1. **registrable estates and interests**: these include the two legal estates in land that are listed under s 1 of the Law of Property Act 1925 as well as other legal interests such as legal mortgages and legal easements

2. **registered incumbrances**: this is a residual category of interests which were referred to as minor interests under the 1925 legislation and do not fall into either of the other two categories. They include any interest which affects the registered title which cannot take effect as an overriding interest

3. **overriding interests**: these are interests which exist over a registered title but which are not protected by an entry on the register but which still bind the land. They have been retained by the Land Registration Act 2002 in spite of the problems they present. They are not protected by an entry on the Register so the only way that a purchaser can discover their existence is by making enquiries and visiting the property.

## 3.4.1 Methods of protection for registered burdens on registered land

Under the 2002 Act there are now only two methods of protection for registered incumbrances or burdens on registered land:

1. the notice and

2. the restriction.

Two of the previous four methods of protection – the caution and the inhibition – have been abolished. They may be referred to in earlier case law and remain on the Register during the transition to the new system and will therefore be briefly mentioned here. Cautions are now used in a different context as cautions against first registration of title.

## 3.4.2 Old methods of protecting burdens on registered land

1. The **notice**: this was an entry entered in the Charges Register and was dependent on production of the relevant land certificate and so relied on the co-operation of the landowner and was not generally hostile in nature when used to register interests.

2. The **caution**: by way of contrast, this was a hostile entry and did not require the production of the land certificate. A caution would restrict the way that the proprietor dealt with the land. The proprietor had the right to challenge the entry. The cautioner had the right to be notified of any dealing in the land. The entry was temporary in nature and was either converted into a notice by the Registrar or removed from the Register.

**3.** The **restriction**: this was an entry entered on the Proprietorship Register and had the effect of limiting the proprietor's power to dispose of the property, for example in a trust of land there may have been a restriction on dealing with a sole trustee.

**4.** The **inhibition**: an inhibition would be entered on the Proprietorship Register. It prevented any registered dealing in the land. It would be used in such cases as where a bankruptcy order had been made in respect of a registered proprietor.

# 3.4.3 New methods of protecting burdens on registered land

There are now only **two** ways of protecting a minor interest under the 2002 Act:

## Notices

Under s 32 of the Land Registration Act 2002 these are described as an entry in the Register in respect of the burden of an interest affecting a registered estate or charge. These replace notices and cautions under the Land Registration Act 1925. Once a notice is entered in the Charges Register then a purchaser will be bound by the interest. Most interests can be protected by notice but some interests are expressly excluded by the 2002 Act:

's 33 **Excluded interests**

No notice may be entered in the register in respect of any of the following:

(i) a trust of land; or

(ii) a settlement under the Settled Land Act 1925;

(iii) a lease granted for a term of years of three years or less from the date of the grant, and which is not required to be registered;

(iv) a restrictive covenant made between lessor and lessee, so far as related to the property leased;

(v) an interest which is capable of being registered under the Commons Registration Act 1965; and

(vi) an interest in coal or any coal mine and any rights attaching under the Coal Industry Act 1994; . . .'

Interests under a trust cannot be entered as a notice on the Register; they are far better protected by the use of a restriction. This list also includes leases of less than three years, leaving leases of between three and seven years capable of being entered on the Register by way of notice. Leases over seven years are registrable interests and are entered with their own title. You could criticise the reforms for leaving leases treated in three different ways according to the length of the lease.

A notice can be either:

**a** agreed or

**b** unilateral.

**a** An **agreed notice**: this must fall within one of three types listed in the 2002 Act under s 34:

    **1.** the applicant must be either the registered proprietor or the person entitled to be registered as proprietor of the estate or charge that is burdened by the interest to be noted

    **2.** consent is given by the registered proprietor of the estate or charge who consents to the entry of the notice and

    **3.** the Registrar is satisfied as to the validity of the applicant's claim.

In the first two situations the parties are agreed about the entry of the notice and there will be no disagreement. In the last situation the entry of the notice will be with the Registrar's consent. The last category will include the right of a non-property-owning spouse to enter a notice under the Family Law Act 1996. This was allowed under the law pre-2002 and continues although the property-owning spouse will now be notified of the entry.

**b** A **unilateral notice** can be entered without the consent of the proprietor of the legal estate. It is used where there is hostility between the parties. If the Registrar enters a unilateral notice in the Register, the proprietor of the registered legal title or charge to which the entry relates must be notified of the entry.

When the notice is entered on the Register, two key features must be shown; it must identify itself as a unilateral notice and it must also indicate who is the beneficiary of the notice. The unilateral notice is similar to the old caution but is more effective as protecting the rights of the person making the entry.

It is more effective because it actually protects the interest lodged on the Register. It differs from the old caution because the caution only allowed the cautioner the right to be informed of any dealings in the title. Today, it provides priority for the right it protects.

Once the notice is entered, the proprietor has the right to be informed and under s 36 can apply to the Registrar to have the notice cancelled, this is called 'warning-off'. If a dispute arises then this must be referred to the adjudicator for settlement. Of course, if the proprietor applies for cancellation and the beneficiary of the notice does not object, then the notice will be cancelled. If the proprietor can prove that the right protected does not exist, then removal will be ordered.

## Restrictions

These replace inhibitions and old restrictions. They are defined under s 40 of the 2002 Act as 'an entry in the register regulating the circumstances in which a disposition of a registered estate or charge may be the subject of an entry in the register'. They will restrict any dealing with the registered estate or charge.

The most common situation for their use is when the land sold is held under a trust. If there is a restriction on the Register then the purchaser will insist on compliance with the restriction. The terms of the restriction will be that the purchase money is paid to two trustees, so overreaching the equitable interest arising under the trust.

## APPLYING THE LAW

Peter has split up with his girlfriend Josie. He decides to sell his house in London so that he can work in the country. Josie made contributions to the purchase of the London property but was never registered as co-owner of the property. However, on advice from a friend who was a lawyer, she registered a restriction to protect her interest in the property. Max visits the house and decides he wants to buy it immediately. When his solicitor makes a search at the Land Registry she discovers that there is a restriction on the title. Max will now be advised to insist that a second trustee is appointed. If Max buys from Peter alone, Josie's rights will not be overreached and will remain in the land rather than being transferred to the purchase money.

Another situation when the use of restrictions is appropriate is where land is managed by a management company and there is a restriction in the Register which indicates that no registration of a transfer may be made without the consent of an officer of the management company.

Restrictions can be registered without the consent of the registered proprietor, for example where a right is claimed under an implied trust but the registered proprietor denies the existence of the right.

## 3.4.4 Removal of old forms of entry on the Register

1. **Inhibitions** have been abolished by the 2002 Act and have been replaced by restrictions. They were comparatively rare as their effect was fairly draconian. However, existing inhibitions will remain on the Register during the transitional arrangements

2. **Cautions** against interests on subsequent registration have been abolished by the 2002 Act. However, existing cautions will remain on the Register during the transitional period. Cautions can still be entered against first registration and these will be held in a new Cautions Register. The effect of such a caution will be that the cautioner will be notified of any application to register the property.

### The Cautions Register

Cautions will be recorded in the new Cautions Register. Any person having an interest in unregistered land can lodge a caution against first registration. This is to ensure that the registration will take account of the rights claimed in the land.

There are special rules which prevent registration of a caution against one's own estate where it is registrable. This is to prevent someone from using the system of cautions as a substitute for first registration. It is also intended to try to persuade people who own unregistered title to register their land voluntarily. This is not the first time that the legislation has tried to encourage voluntary registration of title but the incentives are greater under the 2002 Act.

## Making an application

**1.** An application to lodge a caution is made to the Registrar.

**2.** The grounds for making such an application are given.

**3.** Objections can be made to the Registrar.

**4.** Unless the objection is thought to be groundless, the matter must be referred to the adjudicator.

**5.** Some objections can be dealt with by agreement between the parties and will not be referred to the adjudicator.

## Effect of a caution against first registration

Under s 16(1) of the Land Registration Act 1925:

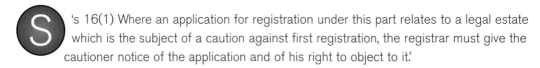

's 16(1) Where an application for registration under this part relates to a legal estate which is the subject of a caution against first registration, the registrar must give the cautioner notice of the application and of his right to object to it.'

The registration of this type of caution does not give priority but merely gives the cautioner the right to be notified of a later transaction.

## Cancellations

Certain persons can apply to the Registrar to cancel a caution against first registration.

## Who can apply for cancellation of a caution against first registration?

**1.** The owner of the legal estate to which the caution applies.

**2.** A mortgagee of the land.

**3.** A receiver appointed to deal with the estate of the legal estate owner.

On receipt of the application for cancellation the Registrar must then notify the cautioner and notify him that he will cancel the caution unless the cautioner objects within a specified time, and only the cautioner has the power to object to the application to cancel.

The matter must be referred to the adjudicator unless agreement can be reached or it is shown that the objection is groundless.

Where the estate owner has consented to the lodging of the caution, it is unlikely that he will then be allowed to object to it. There is a duty to act reasonably when entering a caution, so damages can be awarded for any loss caused by an entry which is groundless.

**The steps in the registration of a caution against first registration**

| | |
|---|---|
| A person cannot lodge a caution against his or her own estate where that estate is registrable. | s 15(3) LRA 2002 |
| Anyone can object to the application for the caution against first registration. | s 73(1) LRA 2002 |
| If the objection is groundless or can be disposed of by agreement, the objection is ignored. | s 73(6) LRA 2002 |
| If the objection is not groundless and cannot be disposed of by agreement, it is then referred to an adjudicator. | s 73(7) LRA 2002 |
| The cautioner will receive notification of any subsequent application for first registration and the cautioner will be told of their right to object to it. | s 16(1) LRA 2002 |
| Certain persons, such as the legal estate owner and mortgagees and receivers, can apply to cancel a caution against first registration: the warning-off procedure. | s 18(1) LRA 2002 |
| Only the cautioner can object to the application to cancel the caution. | s 73(2) LRA 2002 |
| Unless agreement can be reached or the application is groundless, the matter must be referred to the adjudicator. | s 73(7) LRA 2002 |

# 3.4.5 The effect of registration of a burden on registered land

If the burden or incumbrance is not registered then a purchaser will take free of the third-party interest and the question of notice is quite irrelevant.

 's 29(1) If a registrable disposition of a registered estate is made for valuable consideration, completion of the disposition by registration has the effect of postponing to the interest under the disposition any interest affecting the estate immediately before the disposition whose priority is not protected at the time of registration.'

# APPLYING THE LAW

Annie and Stuart have seen a beautiful house in Somerset which they decide to buy. They visit the house and a neighbour tells them that there is a covenant attached to the land that prevents them from using the property for the purposes of running a business. Annie wants to start an organic jam business which she intends to run from home. The Charges Register does not show a covenant relating to use of the premises.

Annie will not be bound by the covenant even though she is aware of its existence. A covenant must be entered on the Register for it to take effect as a binding interest.

**J** | 'It is vital to the working of the Land Registration system that notice of something which is not on the register should not affect a transferee unless it is an overriding interest'.

*Strand Securities v Caswell* [1965] Ch 958

Where a disposition is made without valuable consideration then an unprotected burden will remain binding on the transferee.

# 3.5 Overriding interests

Overriding interests are interests which are binding on the registered proprietor despite not being on the Register. The categories of right were laid down in s 70 of the Land Registration Act 1925. There were many different classes of right covering many different aspects of land ownership.

These have caused considerable problems in the system of registration of land. Since the Register does not reflect the existence of overriding interests, the only way that the purchaser can find out about their existence is by visiting the property. The purchaser must inspect the property and of course this can create problems if he misses the overriding interest when he visits, as in most cases he will still be bound by it.

Under s 70(1) of the Land Registration Act 1925 there was a long list of overriding interests. The list included easements, and rights of squatters under the Limitation Acts, but the most significant group of all were rights of a person in actual occupation of property, under s 70(1)(g). There was considerable litigation covering this subsection alone.

# 3.5.1 Rights of persons in actual occupation under s 70(1)(g)

Section 70(1)(g) required proof of two elements:

**1.** an interest in the land

**2.** actual occupation of the land.

> **Williams & Glyn's Bank v Boland [1981] AC 487**
>
> A husband and wife purchased property together. It had registered title. They both made
> contributions but it was registered in the husband's sole name. The husband held the legal
> estate on trust for himself and his wife in equal shares. The husband then mortgaged the
> property to Williams & Glyn's Bank by way of legal mortgage. He could do this on his own
> without consulting the wife because she did not have an interest in the legal estate. He
> defaulted on the repayments and Williams & Glyn's Bank sought possession of the property.
> The issue was whether they were subject to Mrs Boland's interest. She had the right to
> register the equitable interest as a minor interest but she had failed to do so. She was in
> occupation of the property and was found to have an overriding interest under s 70(1)(g) of
> the 1925 Act. Her husband was the sole trustee so her rights were not transferred to the
> property but were rights in the land and were good even against a legal mortgage.
>
> One aspect of the decision that caused unease was the fact that her rights were capable
> of registration but she still had an overriding interest. She was therefore protected in two
> ways. She could register but if she failed to do so she could also claim an overriding
> interest. Usually the system would give only one type of protection.

## An interest in land

The claimant must show that he has an interest in land and not a purely personal right to be on
the property.

> **National Provincial Bank Ltd v Ainsworth [1965] AC 1175**
>
> The right claimed was the right of the wife to occupy property because she was a wife.
> This claim was based on status and not on contributions as in the case of *Williams & Glyn's
> Bank v Boland* (1981). Lord Denning argued strongly that the wife should be protected in

this case. He argued that she had 'a deserted wife's equity', but his argument was rejected. The House of Lords held that her right was purely personal and could not constitute an overriding interest. However, Lord Denning was later vindicated when legislation was passed giving a wife the right to register her rights based on her status under the Matrimonial Homes Act 1967; this is now incorporated into the Family Law Act 1996.

## Actual occupation

The concept of what constitutes 'actual occupation' has troubled the courts over the years. At one extreme, it is obvious that it includes someone living in property as their sole residence. Mrs Boland is an example of someone clearly in actual occupation. At the other extreme, there are cases where someone may live away from home and so will not be in actual occupation for all of the time.

It has been held that 'actual occupation' should be determined according to the ordinary meaning of the term. There is no definition in the 1925 Act. This is not surprising, since it can vary on the facts.

Consider the following examples:

1. Alice has bought a new flat. She is allowed into the flat one day early, to put up some curtains. She decides to sleep there overnight.

2. Tom and Henry are twin boys aged 16. Both their parents travel in their work so the boys often live in their family home on their own.

3. Annie and Ian buy a dilapidated barn. They fall in love with it but it is not habitable and they cannot live there, however Annie visits daily, to oversee the builders.

4. Paul and Paula have recently split up. Paul and the children, aged 10 and 12, continue to live in the property and Paula returns every day to make them a meal and do household chores.

5. Carmel, who is pregnant, has recently split up with her husband, Gerry. While she is in hospital having the baby, Gerry comes into the property and changes all the locks.

6. Mr Singh owns a large area of land which could be used for development. He used the land for storage of his goods and he boarded it up, changing the locks. The title was fraudulently transferred to Mr Tan by a third party and Mr Tan subsequently registered it.

The facts of all the above situations have been the subject of decided cases:

# CASE EXAMPLE

### 1. *Abbey National Building Society v Cann* [1991] 1 AC 56

An aunt acquired rights in property owned by her nephew, through her rights under the 'right to buy' legislation. She was on holiday on the actual date of moving. However, her belongings were moved in by removal men. The actual move started some 35 minutes before completion and some of her furniture was moved into the premises. The courts decided that this was insufficient for her to claim that she was in actual occupation.

# CASE EXAMPLE

### 2. *Hypo-Mortgage Service v Robinson* [1997] 2 FLR 71

It was held that infant children could not be in actual occupation of property. 'The minor children are there because their parent is there. They have no right of occupation of their own. As Templeman J put it in *Bird v Syme-Thomson* [1979] 1 WLR 440 '... they are there as shadows of occupation of their parent ...' (Nourse LJ). It makes no difference that they are often in the property on their own.

# CASE EXAMPLE

### 3. *Lloyds Bank v Rosset* [1989] Ch 350

A husband and wife, recently married, decided to purchase a semi-derelict property. They could not move in until a certain amount of renovation work had been done and much of it was supervised by the wife. The work was still in progress after the transfer but the issue was whether the wife could be in actual occupation when she was not in permanent occupation. She had spent a considerable amount of time at the property but could not be said to be in permanent occupation. The builders were working at the premises permanently. Although the court accepted that it was not necessary for the wife to be living there, it drew a distinction between intending to move in and actually living in the premises. The builders were held not to be in actual occupation on behalf of Mrs Rosset.

# CASE EXAMPLE

### 4. *Kingsnorth Trust v Tizard* [1986] 1 WLR 783

This was an unregistered land case but the principles can be applied in registered land cases. A married couple split up. They had lived in property owned by the husband but the wife had made contributions towards the purchase. Mrs Tizard continued to return to the property to care for the children and to carry out household chores. She also stayed in the property when her husband was away. The property was mortgaged by Mr Tizard and he did not disclose that his wife had rights in the property. It was held that the mortgagees took subject to her rights.

# CASE EXAMPLE

### 5. *Chhokar v Chhokar* [1984] FLR 313

A married couple split up. The wife remained in the property but had to leave when she had to go into hospital to have a baby. It was held that this did not constitute a break in actual occupation. The case suggests that brief absences will not interfere with actual occupation of land.

# CASE EXAMPLE

### 6. *Malory Enterprises v Cheshire Homes (UK)* [2002] Ch 216

Malory was the registered proprietor of land. A third party had forged a transfer to Cheshire Homes. As Malory had remained in actual occupation by virtue of storage of goods, the changing of locks on the land and fencing of the property, the Court of Appeal held that he had an overriding interest which was binding on Cheshire Homes. 'What constitutes actual occupation of property depends on the nature and state of the property in question, and the judge adopted that approach. If a site is uninhabitable, as the rear land was, residence is not required, but there must be some physical presence, with some degree of permanence and continuity … Moreover no-one visiting the rear land at the time of the sale to Cheshire could have drawn the conclusion that the land and buildings on the rear land had been abandoned; the evidence of activity on the site clearly indicated that someone claimed to be entitled to it.' (Arden LJ).

**What constitutes actual occupation?**

| | |
|---|---|
| Occupation of the property preparatory to moving in cannot be held to be actual occupation. | *Abbey National v Cann* (1991) |
| Children cannot be said to be in actual occupation on their own behalf in property owned by their parents. | *Hypo-Mortgage Service v Robinson* (1997) |
| Occupation by builders working on property cannot constitute actual occupation. | *Lloyds Bank v Rosset* (1989) |
| Occupational rights in unregistered land are subject to the doctrine of notice. | *Kingsnorth Trust v Tizard* (1986) |
| A short visit away from the property, eg a visit to hospital, will not prevent actual occupation from continuing. | *Chhokar v Chhokar* (1984) |
| There will be actual occupation where the owner uses the property for storage, keeps it locked and ensures it is securely fenced, although the title has been registered in the name of another. | *Malory Enterprises v Cheshire Homes* (2002) |

# 3.5.2 Reform of overriding interests under the Land Registration Act 2002

The Law Commission wanted to reform this aspect of land registration but had to accept that there were reasons why overriding interests could not be abolished altogether.

> 'The way in which the law on overriding interests has developed over the last seventy two years has demonstrated that overriding interests are by no means only "minor liabilities" ... Most overriding interests do appear to have one shared characteristic, however, that is related to the orthodox explanation of them, namely that it is unreasonable to expect the person who has the benefit of the right to register it as a means of securing its protection.'

Law Commission, *Land Registration for the 21st Century: A Conveyancing Revolution* (Law Com No 271)

Some of the reasons why overriding interests should be retained are as follows:

**1.** overriding interests provide a means of accommodating rights which can be created informally and where it is unrealistic to register at the time of creation, for example rights of persons in actual occupation

**2.** some rights are either pointless or inconvenient to register. The Law Commission specifically mentioned leases and also rights in coal

**3.** there are some rights which are otherwise protected and it would therefore be unrealistic to expect them to be registered. An example of such rights would be local land charges which are registered at a Local Land Charges Register.

> 'Thus the rationale that underpins the informal acquisition of interests in land would be defeated by a prescriptive method of ensuring their priority against a purchaser. Accordingly, the 2002 Act retains the idea that certain interests should be given priority over the estate of a subsequent registered proprietor even though that interest has not been entered on the land register. However the principal means by which the 2002 Act aims to improve the accuracy of the register is to narrow the scope for unregistered interests to have overriding effect.'
>
> N Jackson, 'Title by Registration and Concealed Overriding Interests: the Cause and Effect of antipathy to Documentary Proof' (2003) 119 LQR 660

However, there are many who continue to criticise the retention of overriding interests. If a purchaser makes an attempt to discover whether there are overriding interests but continues to be unaware of their existence, he will still be bound by them and there is no provision for compensation to be paid.

The Land Registration Act 2002 has affected overriding interests in a number of different ways:

**1.** the number of rights have been **reduced in number**, for example liability to repair the chancel of a church and the rights acquired by squatters under adverse possession

**2.** a number of overriding interests which existed under the Land Registration Act 1925 will be **phased out after 10 years**, for example the ancient right of franchises, manorial rights, Crown rents and rights concerning embankments and sea walls and payments in lieu of tithe also called corn rents

**3.** some rights have retained their status as overriding interests but their **scope has been narrowed down and clarified**, for example easements and profits under s 70(1)(a) of the 1925 Act and also rights of persons in actual occupation under s 70(1)(g) of the 1925 Act

**4.** a requirement that when an overriding interest is discovered it will be entered on the Register; any person applying for registration now has a **duty to disclose any overriding interests** known to him.

## 3.5.3 Overriding interests under the Land Registration Act 2002

The 2002 Act distinguishes between those overriding rights which come within **Schedule 1** (interests which override a first disposition) and **Schedule 3** (interests which override registered

dispositions). The law gives greater recognition to those rights coming within Schedule 1 as opposed to those rights coming within Schedule 3.

The 2002 Act allows **15** overriding interests to continue, although **five** will disappear after 10 years

## Overriding interests which have been abolished by the 2002 Act

One of the intentions of the 2002 Act was to reduce overriding interests. The following categories of right have been abolished:

**1.** rights acquired or in the course of being acquired under the Limitation Act 1980. These were overriding under s 70(1)(f) of the Land Registration Act 1925. These are squatters' rights. There are transitional arrangements which will apply for three years after the 2002 Act has come into force. The squatter who had already extinguished the owner's title before the 2002 Act came into force will continue to have an overriding interest even if he or she is not in actual occupation. The squatter will have three years to protect his or her position by registering title. (These rights will be considered in detail in Chapter 14.)

**2.** rights of persons in receipt of rent and profits, save where enquiry is made of such persons and the rights are not disclosed. This allowed someone who was a landlord but not in occupation to claim an overriding right

**3.** rights excepted from the effect of registration with possessory, qualified or good leasehold title. These were dealt with under s 70(1)(h) of the 1925 Act and as they are binding under ss 11 and 12 of the 2002 Act it is considered to be unnecessary for them to take effect as overriding interests.

## Rights taking effect under Schedule 1

When any person becomes the first registered proprietor of a freehold estate in land on first registration, they take the legal estate subject to certain interests.

Section 11(4):

**a** interests which are the subject of an entry in the register in relation to the estate

**b** unregistered interests which fall within any of the paragraphs of Schedule 1.

Schedule 1 includes the following:

**1.** leasehold estates not exceeding seven years

**2.** interests of persons in actual occupation

**3.** easements and profits à prendre

**4.** customary rights

**5.** public rights

**6.** local land charges

**7.** mines and minerals.

Interests of persons under a settlement under the Settled Land Act 1925 are excluded. The 2002 Act has been far more generous in relation to overriding interests under Schedule 1 on first registration. There are significant differences between the provisions of Schedule 1 and Schedule 3.

## Schedule 3

There are limits in this Schedule on rights that can be overriding:

**1.** Under paragraph 1 leases which should have been registered with their own titles even though they are seven years or less cannot be overriding.

**2.** Interests of persons in actual occupation, with the exception of:

   (i)   an interest under a settlement under the Settled Land Act 1925

   (ii)  an interest of a person of whom inquiry was made before the disposition and who failed to disclose the right when he could reasonably have been expected to do so

   (iii) also an interest belonging to a person whose occupation would not have been obvious on reasonably careful inspection of the land at the time of the disposition and of which the person to whom the disposition is made does not have actual knowledge at that time

   (iv)  a leasehold estate in land to take effect in possession after the end of the period of three months beginning with the date of the grant and which has not taken effect in possession at the time of the disposition.

These are all rights which depend on actual occupation. There is a similarity with s 70(1)(g) of the 1925 Act as that section holds that the right will be overriding except when inquiry has been made and the person has not disclosed the right when they could reasonably have been expected to do so.

However, the provision for the exclusion of rights that are not apparent and not actually known is new and will have the effect of restricting rights that can be binding. This increases the need for inspection of the property and protects the purchaser who takes adequate steps to visit the property and inspect.

The final difference is that future leases, of whatever length, which are registrable will not be overriding.

There are quite significant differences between the treatment of easements and profits à prendre under Schedule 1 and Schedule 3.

Under Schedule 1 an existing legal easement will override on first registration. This clearly excludes equitable easements. Both implied and express easements appear to be covered under this Schedule. However, Schedule 3 restricts the number of legal easements. Under s 27(2) of the 2002 Act the disposition of a legal interest including an easement requires completion by registration. It seems that the only easements which can be overriding under Schedule 3 are those that arise under prescription or implied grant.

## ACTIVITY

Consider the facts of this problem:

Leah purchased the freehold title to a property called Runaway House. Sometime later, Tom married Leah and he moved into the house. Tom was often away and she had to deal in the affairs of the house on her own. Her neighbour Joan asked to enter into a restrictive covenant, with her, not to use the house for any business purposes. She paid Leah for this. Leah granted David a legal lease for six years, over a cottage attached to the house. Tom has met someone else and Leah now thinks she would like to sell the property but is concerned as to the status of the rights that she has granted over the property. Advise Leah what these rights are and whether they are binding on the property.

# 3.6 Alteration and indemnity

Under the Land Registration Act 1925 there was provision for rectification of the Register in cases where there was an error on the face of the Register. There is still provision for changes to the Register in the 2002 Act but it is called 'alteration'. Rectification continues, but as just one way of altering the Register.

The change in terminology was made as a result of recommendations of the Law Commission. They thought it was misleading to describe all changes as rectification and that it would be better if they were described as alterations, saving the term 'rectification' for those entries which required to be actually rectified. They gave examples of minor changes which are often made such as the removal of obsolete entries which differ vastly from errors on the Register. 'Alteration' is the term used to describe any abnormal change in the Register which did not proceed from an application.

Alteration can now be made under s 65 of the 2002 Act but the details are contained in Schedule 4.

## 3.6.1 Alteration of the Register under the Land Registration Act 2002

'Schedule 4

1. In this Schedule, references to rectification, in relation to alteration of the register, are to alteration which −

   (a) involves the correction of a mistake, and

   (b) prejudicially affects the title of a registered proprietor.

2. (1) The court may make an order for alteration of the register for the purpose of –

(a) correcting a mistake,

(b) bringing the register up to date, or

(c) giving effect to any estate, right or interest excepted from the effect of registration.

3. (2) If alteration affects the title of the proprietor of a registered estate in land, no order may be made under paragraph 2 without the proprietor's consent in relation to land in his possession unless –

(a) he has by fraud or lack of proper care caused or substantially contributed to the mistake, or

(b) it would for any other reason be unjust for the alteration not to be made.'

There is also provision for altering the Register without a court order in certain cases under Schedule 5. The 2002 Act is governed by principle rather than covering specific circumstances when the Register can be altered.

'5. The registrar may alter the register for the purpose of –

(a) correcting a mistake,

(b) bringing the register up to date,

(c) giving effect to any estate, right or interest excepted from the effect of registration, or

(d) removing a superfluous entry.'

The 2002 Act envisages administrative alterations where no one is prejudiced by the change in the Register as well as a prejudicial alteration which is referred to as 'rectification of the Register'. In the second category the problem for the Registrar is that there may be two claimants over one piece of property. Special rules apply where the registered proprietor is in possession of the property.

# CASE EXAMPLE

### *Kingsalton v Thames Water Developments* [2002] 1 P & CR 184

The Court of Appeal overturned the judgment of the judge at first instance who had found against a registered proprietor who was in possession of a disputed strip of land. The court did not order rectification in favour of the claimant, however an indemnity payment was ordered.

Although the 2002 Act laid down that the Register will not be rectified against an innocent proprietor, the court will order rectification against a proprietor in possession where

**1.** the proprietor has caused or substantially contributed to the mistake by fraud or lack of proper care;

**2.** it would be unjust not to make the alteration

## 3.6.2 Human rights

It could be argued that refusal to register in favour of someone who has lost his title to land as a result of an error in the registration process may lead to a claim under the Human Rights Act 1998. Their argument would be founded on contravention of Article 1 of the First Protocol of the European Convention on Human Rights. This issue was argued unsuccessfully in *Kingsalton v Thames Water Developments Ltd* (2002). The court rejected the human rights claim and held that it was a legitimate aim in the public interest to enhance the security of the land registration system. The court also felt that the payment of an indemnity under Schedule 8 to the 2002 Act would ensure that the unsuccessful claimant would be compensated.

## 3.6.3 The payment of an indemnity

The Land Registration Act 1925 provided for the payment of an indemnity where loss had been caused by rectification or refusal to rectify.

There is provision under Schedule 8 to the 2002 Act for the payment of an indemnity by the Registrar in a number of situations, including:

**1.** to anyone who suffers loss by reason of rectification of the Register

**2.** refusal to correct a mistake

**3.** removal of title from an innocent victim of forgery

**4.** a mistake in an official search.

This mirrors the circumstances for payment of compensation under the old rules. The grounds for the payment of compensation had been extended under the Land Registration Act 1997. An indemnity is not payable where the Register is merely altered.

A claim for indemnity must be brought within six years from the time that the claimant knows or ought to have known of his claim.

How much will be paid? In cases of rectification an indemnity representing the full value of the estate or interest then lost will be paid. Where rectification is refused, the amount paid will be the equivalent of the value of the interest at the time of the error. This can be unfair where the error occurred at a time when the value of the property was much lower.

## ACTIVITY

> Consider the following situations and decide whether the Register should be altered:
>
> Sam was registered proprietor of a large house, Briardale. He and his wife had run it as a guest house for some years on their own and later with their son Tom and daughter-in-law Ursula. When Sam's wife died he took a less active part in running the guest house. One day, Tom persuaded Sam to transfer the property to his two younger brothers, Bruce and Ben, to hold Briardale on trust for Tom and his wife for life with remainder for their three sons. Tom and Ursula decide to take a six-week holiday to Australia while Briardale was being refurbished. When they return they find that Bruce and Ben have charged the guest house to the Littlehaven Building Society and have absconded with the mortgage monies.
>
> Advise Sam whether he can get the Register altered in his favour and whether he is entitled to an indemnity payable in his favour.

## 3.7 Removal of the registration gap

Under s 93 of the 2002 Act, when entries are made under the system of e-conveyancing discussed in Chapter 4 there will no longer be any risk that rights will arise in the gap between completion and registration because there will be no gap. Dispositions will not have effect at all unless they are carried out electronically. This means that only those interests which are created electronically will be binding on the land. It will, however, be some years before e-conveyancing is introduced for all.

> 'However while much attention is rightly given to the considerable impact it will have on those every day principles of land registration that currently regulate over £2000 billion worth of property. As has been said already, most of these substantive changes are designed to facilitate the new conveyancing processes and to ensure that we move from registration of title to a system where it "will be the fact of registration and registration alone that confers title".'

M Dixon, 'The Reform of Property Law and the Land Registration Act 2002:
A Risk Assessment' [2003] 67 Conv 136

The new legislation is still in the early days and the impact will not be clear until it has been tested in the courts. However, it has been much welcomed by practitioners and once e-conveyancing has been introduced it should reduce much of the litigation over rights arising in the registration gap.

# Further reading

Cooke, E, 'The Land Registration Bill 2001' [2002] Conv 11.

Dixon, M, 'The Reform of Property Law and the Land Registration Act 2002: A Risk Assessment' [2003] 67 Conv 136.

Ferris, G and Battersby, G 'The general principles of overreaching and the modern legislative reforms 1996-2002' (2003) 119 LQR 94.

Jackson, N, 'Title by Registration and Concealed overriding interests: the Cause and Effect of Antipathy to documentary Proof' (2003) 119 LQR 660.

Land Registry e-Conveyancing website: www.land registry.gov.uk/e-conveyancing

Law Commission, Land Registration for the 21st Century: A Conveyancing Revolution (Law Com Report No 271, 2001).

Tee, L, 'The Rights of every person in Actual Occupation: an Enquiry into section 70(1)(g) Land Registration Act 1925' [1998] CLJ 328.

# chapter 4 THE TRANSFER AND CREATION OF PROPERTY INTERESTS ■

## 4.1 The importance of formalities in the transfer and creation of property interests

Land has always been treated differently from other interests and rights. Land has a special significance and so special formalities are required for a transfer of an interest in land. If you transfer personalty – a piece of jewellery or a car – then the law allows a purely oral transfer but if you transfer land then the law insists that it must be in a special written form. This is called a **deed** and it is a particularly formal document. Deeds can be used to transfer other interests and are compulsory in some circumstances but a deed must be used for the transfer of an interest in land. Formalities are also important when contracts are drawn up to sell land. There are many reasons for imposing strict formalities for the sale of land. The principal reason is to ensure that there is evidence of the sale so there can be no later dispute about who owns the land.

> 'Quite apart from the evidentiary benefit to third parties the parties to the transaction may themselves need evidence of the existence of terms of the transaction, to forestall or settle disputes at some future point, when memories have become unreliable. This is important for transactions involving property rights, since they tend to be of longer duration than purely personal rights . . . and it is particularly important relating to land, because one of the notable features of real (as compared with personal) property is its sheer durability. The most effective type of formality for this purpose is one requiring some permanent record – writing, registering, and the like – which in fact all current English land law formalities prescribe. However, even a requirement that a transaction be completed in front of witnesses is better in this respect than total informality, since it increases the stock of (impartial) oral evidence and thus the chance that the transaction can be reconstructed accurately'.

> P Critchley, 'Taking Formalities Seriously' in S Bright and J Dewar (eds), *Land Law: Themes and Perspectives* (Oxford University Press, 1998), p 515–516

### 4.1.1 Reasons for formalities being used for the sale of land

We can point to the following reasons for formalities having been relied on for the sale and disposition of interests in land:

1. it provides **written evidence** of a transaction. There is an element of risk in relying on purely oral evidence

2. it gives those entering a transaction **a warning that the transaction will have a legal effect**. The parties will treat such transactions with more care than a transaction which they do not believe is enforceable in the courts

3. it means that the **terms themselves will be clear**. In a purely oral transaction there could be some dispute about the exact terms of sale, for example the cost of the property, the date for completion.

There are **disadvantages** in the use of formalities:

1. the cost of forms or registration and possibly the cost of legal advice. This can unjustly penalise some people and force them to withdraw from the transaction

2. making formalities compulsory results in any informal transaction becoming unenforceable, which seems unjust where non-compliance is as a result of ignorance.

However, most people would argue that the advantages in the use of formalities far outweigh the disadvantages.

## 4.2 Contracts for sale and dispositions of interests in land: the steps leading to a conveyance of property

The purchase of land takes certain **defined steps** before the legal estate passes from one person to another. When land is sold from one person to another there are three distinct stages.

**Stage one**: the **preliminary negotiations**. These will not have any effect in law. If someone views a house and likes it enough to make an offer which is accepted by the seller this will not be enforceable until contracts have been exchanged.

## APPLYING THE LAW

Ellen decides to sell her house. She puts it on the market and several people visit her. Gerald offers her the full purchase price if she agrees to a quick sale. They have a cup of tea to celebrate, and they shake hands. He writes a letter to her, saying 'I love your house and I am contacting my solicitor immediately'. Ellen hears nothing more from him. Their agreement is not binding because it is not regarded as a binding contract. Ellen cannot go to court and seek an order forcing Gerald to pursue the sale.

**Stage two:** the **exchange of contracts** between the seller and the purchaser. This is the stage after preliminary negotiations where the parties sign contracts which have been drawn up, usually by their legal advisers. The contract constitutes a binding agreement to sell and transfer the land in return for the payment of an agreed price. The contract will become binding once it has been exchanged with the other side. If the transaction is not pursued then either side can go to court for a remedy.

**Stage three**: this involves the **transfer of ownership** from the seller to the purchaser. It used to be done by the transfer of the documents of ownership (called the deeds) to the purchaser. Under the system of registration of title it is done by transferring the title from one party to the other and then that is entered on the Register of title.

The exchange of contracts does not give effect to the transfer of the land from the seller to the purchaser; this depends on a further stage. Up until contracts are exchanged, the parties are free to withdraw from the agreement without fear of legal action being taken against them. The agreement may be made 'subject to contract' which is often interpreted as leading to legal consequences but in spite of attempts over the years to argue that this is binding, such an agreement will not be legally binding.

# 4.3 Stage one: pre-contract stage

At this stage the parties are still negotiating the sale of the property. The negotiations may reach the stage where the purchaser makes an offer to the seller who accepts the offer. The agreement may be made 'subject to contract'. However, they are not contractually bound.

The preliminary negotiations have the effect of a 'gentleman's agreement' which is not binding in law. In the words of Sachs LJ, in reality, both parties act in the mutual hope that 'the other will act like a gentleman' in circumstances where neither 'intends to act if it is against his material interests' (*Goding v Frazer* [1967] 1 WLR 286).

The fact that there is no legally binding agreement at this stage can cause problems for the purchaser who then finds that the seller has sold to someone else, as he is legally entitled to do.

# 4.3.1 'Gazumping' and 'gazundering'

There have been attempts to try to make the early stage of negotiations enforceable in the courts. The buyer of property is always at risk that another buyer will come along and offer more money and that this will be accepted by the seller and the would-be purchaser will have no remedy in the courts. The acceptance of the higher price is called 'gazumping' and in a rising property market such as was experienced in the UK in the 1980s, hundreds of buyers of property were affected by it. The alternative – 'gazundering' – will affect sellers in a falling property market. They agree a sale with a buyer and then, as the property market falls, the buyer decides to reduce his offer or withdraw altogether.

Gazumping has a far greater impact than gazundering because the purchaser may have incurred costs over the property which will then be lost.

> J 'For very many people their first and closest contact with the law is when they come to buy or sell a house. They frequently find it a profoundly depressing and frustrating experience. The vendor puts his house on the market. He receives an offer which is probably less than the asking price. He agonises over whether to accept or hold out for more. He decides to accept, perhaps after negotiating some increase. A deal is struck. Hands are shaken. The vendor celebrates, relaxes, makes plans for his own move and takes his house off the market. Then he hears that the purchaser who was formerly pleading with him to accept the offer has withdrawn. No explanation is given, no apology made. The vendor has to embark on the whole dreary process of putting his house on the market all over again'.
>
> *Pitt v PHH Asset Management Ltd* [1994] 1 WLR 327 (Sir Thomas Bingham)

The main reason why there is no legally binding agreement until the exchange of contracts is to give the parties a chance to make enquiries and searches before committing themselves to the sale or purchase. However, other systems (eg the Scottish system of conveyancing) build in commitment at a much earlier stage.

As suggested below, the use of compulsory seller's packs should reduce the threat of gazumping.

# 4.3.2 Seller's packs

Over the years, the fact that preliminary agreements can never take effect in law has been criticised. In many cases there may be expenditure of time and money on the negotiations, particularly by the purchaser. If the sale does not go ahead then this is lost and cannot be recovered.

The government has introduced a number of proposals for compulsory seller's packs. These would be information packs about the property, provided by the seller. Their use would accelerate the whole process of home buying and reduce costs for the purchaser.

It has been envisaged that the seller's pack would contain the following:

**1.** title documents

**2.** answers to standard pre-contract enquiries

**3.** planning and Building Regulations consents

**4.** warranties and guarantees for any work that has been carried out

**5.** a draft sale contract

**6.** a surveyor's report on the condition of the property and its energy efficiency and

**7.** if the property is leasehold, information about the lease, service charges, insurance and the management arrangements.

Other information may also be made available. One of the main advantages is that it would reduce the threat of gazumping and encourage faster sales of property.

There have been a number of pilot schemes, including one in Bristol. A government press notice issued in March 2000 comments as follows:

> 'Emerging findings from the Bristol home buying and selling pilot scheme suggest that having a seller's pack improves confidence in the process. Three quarters of sellers are confident that the sale will proceed to completion and nine out of ten sellers believe the seller's pack will make their sale quicker than normal'.

There are problems associated with the packs, in particular the **surveyor's report**. The timing of such a report will be important as the state of a property varies all the time. Surveys also vary in detail and cost. The seller will be tempted to get the least expensive type, which may not answer all the significant questions that the purchaser may want answered. For example, a detailed survey of the roof may take time but without such a report the purchaser is at risk of buying a property which may need considerable work and expenditure at a later date.

## 4.3.3 The lock-out agreement

In *Pitt v Asset Management Ltd* (1984) it was held that it is possible to overcome the limitations of the 'subject to contract' rule by drawing up a 'lock-out' agreement or 'exclusivity' agreement. A lock-out agreement is a prior collateral contract for valuable consideration that, during a stipulated period, the vendor will not negotiate with anyone else. It is important to see that this agreement does not give the purchaser the right to require that the land be sold to him but merely entitles the purchaser to recover damages for breach of the agreement.

Such an agreement is not a contract for the sale of land, so it is not subject to the same formalities. It need not be in writing, although it generally will be put in writing. It goes some way towards solving the problems of gazumping as it prevents the seller for a period of time from negotiating with third parties. The purchaser has time to get the necessary enquiries dealt with, so at the end of the lock-out period he is ready to proceed.

> **J** 'B, by agreeing not to negotiate for this fixed period with a third party, locks himself out of such negotiations. He has in no legal sense locked himself into such negotiations with A. What A has achieved is an exclusive opportunity, for a fixed period, to try and come to terms with B, an opportunity for which he has, unless he makes his agreement under seal, to give good consideration.'
>
> *Walford v Miles* [1992] 2 AC 128 (Lord Ackner)

# 4.4 Stage two: the exchange of contracts

The **contract for a sale of land** today is in a standard form which has been drawn up by the Law Society but which can be varied by the parties themselves. In theory, the parties could draw up their own contract but this is rarely done.

## 4.4.1 The Law of Property (Miscellaneous Provisions) Act 1989

Any contract for the sale or other disposition of an interest in land created after 27th September 1989 must comply with the Law of Property (Miscellaneous Provisions) Act 1989:

 's 2(1) A contract for sale or other disposition of an interest in land can only be made in writing and only by incorporating all the terms which the parties have expressly agreed in one document or, where contracts are exchanged, in each.

(2) The terms may be incorporated in a document either by being set out in it or by reference to some other document.

(3) The documents incorporating the terms or, where contracts are exchanged, one of the documents incorporating them (but not necessarily the same one) must be signed by or on behalf of each party to the contract.'

An 'interest' in land means any estate, interest or charge in or over land.

Essentials for the contract for sale:

**1.** the contract for sale of land must be in writing

**2.** it must contain all the terms of the agreement

**3.** it must be signed by both the parties. Note that under s 2(3) **both** parties must sign, not just the party to be charged. Where contracts are exchanged then both copies must be signed – one by the seller and the other by the buyer.

## 4.4.2 What is the position if any of these provisions is not complied with?

The contract is void. The law does not regard it as an unenforceable contract but as a void contract.

Compare s 40 of the Law of Property Act 1925: under this section a contract merely had to be **evidenced** in writing so the law was less stringent with regard to formalities of contract. If there was no evidence in writing then the contract could still be saved if there were sufficient acts of part-performance. An example would be allowing the purchaser into possession as soon as there was an agreement to sell. This would be seen as a sufficient act of part-performance relying on the previously agreed terms. This doctrine was abolished under the 1989 Act. Contracts for the sale of land made before 1989 were still governed by the old law.

# ACTIVITY

Consider these examples and decide whether the contracts will be enforceable under the 1989 Act:

1. Alex wants to sell some land. A contract for the sale of land is drawn up between Alex and Max. The contract is in writing.

2. Alex wants to sell some land to Max. A contract is drawn up in writing but only Max signs. Alex changes his mind and wants to withdraw from the sale.

3. Alex wants to sell some land but he wants the date of sale to be delayed for two months. The contract is in writing but this term is not put into the contract. Again, he changes his mind and no longer wants to sell.

4. Alex wants to sell the same land but does not put the contract into writing but merely shakes hands with Max who is allowed to move some possessions into the barn on the land. He terminates a lease on a lock-up garage where he has been storing the possessions. Later, Alex decides not to sell to Max.

In all but the first example, the contracts will be unenforceable under the 1989 Act.

However, under s 40 of the 1925 Act all the contracts would have been enforceable and Max could have insisted on Alex going ahead with the sale.

The document incorporating the terms of the contract agreed by the parties must be signed not simply by 'the party to be charged' but by or on behalf of all the parties to the contract. Further, the signature itself must be a signature by hand and not merely a stamp or a typed name.

# CASE EXAMPLE

**_Firstpost Homes Ltd v Johnson_ [1995] 1 WLR 1567**

In this case the buyer had prepared a letter for the seller to sign: the buyer's name was typed at the top of the letter. The buyer had signed the plan mentioned in the letter but not the actual letter itself and it was held that there was no contract because the plan did not refer to the letter. If two documents are to be used then the first must refer to the second document. It was held that the contract must be contained in one document or two documents joined together. All the terms of the contract must be signed by all the parties to the contract. A signature must be a real signature by hand and is not constituted by the printing or typing of a party's name as the addressee of a supposedly contractual undertaking.

The rules are applied slightly differently according to the type of right in property that is involved.

## 4.4.3 Options to purchase

An option to purchase is a right given to a purchaser to call on the seller to sell the land within the stipulated period at a pre-agreed price. Usually, the holder of the option will have given consideration. The buyer may wait until the value of the property goes up and then they may exercise the option. The seller must sell to them and if they sell to anyone else, the right of the buyer is binding on the new purchaser so long as he has notice of the existence of the option.

The rules concerning formalities for options to purchase land are slightly different from formalities generally concerning the disposition of an interest in land.

The agreement conferring the option must conform to s 2(1) of the Law of Property (Miscellaneous Provisions) Act 1989.

# CASE EXAMPLE

**_Spiro v Glencrown Properties Ltd_ [1991] Ch 537**

It was held that the notice given by the parties exercising the option does not have to comply with the requirement for writing under s 2 of the 1989 Act. So it will still be an effective notice even if it has been signed by only one of two option holders.

'Apart from authority, it seems plain enough that section 2 was intended to apply
to the agreement which created the option and not to the notice by which it was
exercised. Section 2, which replaced section 40 of the Law of Property Act
1925, was intended to prevent disputes over terms they had agreed. It
prescribes the formalities for recording their mutual consent. But only the grant of
the option depends upon consent. The exercise of the option is a unilateral act. It
would destroy the very purpose of the option if the purchaser had to obtain the
vendor's countersignature to the notice by which it was exercised'.

Hoffmann J

## 4.4.4 Collateral contracts

If the parties agree other conditions in a separate agreement then that is a **collateral contract** and
that is enforceable as a separate agreement so long as the terms are not at the heart of the contract.
The collateral contract does not need be evidenced in writing if it can be interpreted as not being
one for the disposition of an interest in land.

 ASE EXAMPLE

### Record v Bell [1991] 1 WLR 853

In this case the collateral contract was a promise by the seller to the purchaser as to the
state of the seller's title. There was no writing to support this promise which would satisfy
the requirements of s 2(1) of the 1989 Act. This was held to be collateral to the main
contract and did not require writing. It was held that the term did not comprise part of the
main contract and it did not undermine the validity of the main contract.

## 4.4.5 The contract: 'one document' rule

Section 2(1) of the 1989 Act envisages that there will be one document rather than two, meaning
that one single document will contain all the terms of the contract. However, under s 2(2) there
can be limited joinder of documents. This had been allowed under pre-1989 law. This means that
some of the terms could be in another document but they must be expressly referred to in the
primary contractual document, which must be signed.

Exchange of contracts will always involve two contracts and each party will sign one copy. The next
stage is for the contracts to be 'exchanged' so that each party sends the copy that they have signed
to the other and then the contracts are effective.

The 1989 Act specifically deals with this under s 2(3):

's 2(3) The document incorporating the terms or, where contracts are exchanged, one of the documents incorporating them (but not necessarily the same one) must be signed by or on behalf of each party to the contract'.

## Can letters represent two documents?

The courts have considered whether the two documents mentioned in s 2(3) of the 1989 Act can be two letters exchanged by the parties.

# CASE EXAMPLE

### Commission for New Towns v Cooper (Great Britain) Ltd [1995] Ch 259

It was concluded that the exchange of letters cannot usually constitute a contract although if the letters expressly refer to an agreement that is already in existence then the letters will be enforceable.

'the authorities show that, even if the expression "exchange of contracts" is not a term of art, it is a well-recognised concept understood both by lawyers and laymen which has the following features.

1. Each party draws up or is given a document which incorporates all the terms which they have agreed, and which is intended to record their proposed contract. The terms that have been agreed may have been agreed either orally or in writing or partly orally or partly in writing.

2. The documents are referred to as "contracts" or "parts of contracts," although they need not be so entitled. They are intended to take effect as formal documents of title and must be capable on their face of being fairly described as contracts having that effect.

3. Each party signs his part in the expectation that the other party has also executed or will execute a corresponding part incorporating the same terms.

4. At the time of execution neither party is bound by the terms of the document which he has executed, it being their mutual intention that neither will be bound until the executed parts are exchanged.

**5.** The act of exchange is a formal delivery by each party of its parts into the actual or constructive possession of the other with the intention that the parties will become actually bound when exchange occurs, but not before.

**6.** The manner of exchange may be agreed and determined by the parties. The traditional method was by mutual exchange across the table, either parties or their solicitors being present. It also commonly takes place by post, especially where the parties or their solicitors are at a distance'.

Stuart-Smith LJ

The postal exchange has been superseded by telephone exchange.

## CASE EXAMPLE

### *Domb v Isoz* [1980] Ch 548

In the first case to accept the concept of telephone exchange, the Court of Appeal held that there was exchange as soon as the other side had both parts of the contract in his possession which had been signed by each party. Exchange was effected by a telephone call to the other solicitor authorising exchange without physical exchange, ie 'once a contract . . . is in the physical possession of his own solicitor or in the possession of the solicitor on the other side who has agreed to hold that part to the other order of the despatching solicitor . . . '

Templeman LJ

## 4.4.6 A variation in the terms of the contract

Where the terms are subsequently varied then they will not be effective unless both parties sign them.

To conform with s 2 of the 1989 Act, the contract must be in writing and all the terms must be included in the contract. This is subject to the possibility that a term has been omitted by a genuine mistake, in which case the court may rectify the agreement. This means that the contract will take effect with the omitted term included. The rectified document must be signed by both parties or the earlier signatures must be acknowledged. However, it does not give the parties the chance to include fresh terms which they had not previously discussed.

If the parties informally vary the terms of the contract then the informal variation will not take effect and the original contract will stand in these cases.

# CASE EXAMPLE

**McCausland v Duncan Lawrie [1997] 1 WLR 38**

It was held that an informal variation to the terms of the contract will not affect the previous formally agreed contract. In this case the completion date, a Sunday, had been stipulated in the original enforceable contract. The parties informally rearranged the completion date for another day The solicitors for the two parties exchanged letters varying the completion date.

The Court of Appeal held that this did not amount to an effective variation of contract because it did not satisfy s 2 and the requirement that both parties had to sign the contract. In this case the court enforced the original contract and upheld the date agreed in the formal contract.

If the parties had failed to stipulate a completion date at all then the contract would have been rendered void as all the terms were not in the contract as laid down in the 1989 Act. Here, there was a completion date in the formal contract, so that contract was enforceable.

## 4.4.7 Exceptions to the requirements of s 2 of the Law of Property (Miscellaneous Provisions) Act 1989

1. The 1989 Act expressly excludes contracts to **grant leases of less than three years** in length at full market rent (s 2(5)(a)) – these can be created orally.

2. The 1989 Act also expressly excludes a contract made in the course of a **public auction** (s 2(5)(b)) and a contract regulated under the **Financial Services Act 1986** (s 2(5)(c)).

3. It will not apply to **collateral contracts** if they are not considered to be a disposition of an interest in land (*Record v Bell* (1991)).

4. **Proprietary estoppel**. The Law Commission anticipated that the doctrine of part-performance might be replaced by proprietary estoppel. Once part-performance had been abolished, its role in the enforcement of rights rendered unenforceable by the lack of formalities would be taken over by the doctrine of proprietary estoppel. In *Lim Teng Huan v Ang Swee Chuan* [1992] 1 WLR 113, a case decided by the Privy Council, an agreement that did not comply with s 2 was upheld on the basis of proprietary estoppel. They held that it would be unconscionable for the plaintiff to go back on an agreement made with the defendant that he could go into occupation of property that he had built on jointly owned land. The doctrine of estoppel was expressly endorsed by Robert Walker LJ in *Yaxley v Gotts* [2000] 1 All ER 711: 'The circumstances in which s 2 has to be complied with are so various, and the scope of the doctrine of estoppel is so flexible, that any general assertion of s 2 as a "no-go area" for estoppel would be unsustainable'.

**5. Constructive trusts**. A constructive trust may be imposed by the courts where they believe that conduct has been unconscionable. The 1989 Act expressly preserves the operation of constructive trusts in connection with contracts which do not comply with the need for writing under s 2(5)(c) and nothing in the section affects the creation or operation of resulting, implied or constructive trusts. It was held expressly in *Yaxley v Gotts* (2000) that where a constructive trust can be pleaded then the non-compliance with s 2 will not be fatal. In this case the courts upheld an oral agreement by an estate owner to grant a builder the ground floor of premises in exchange for labour, materials and services supplied for work on other parts of the property. This decision raises one significant difficulty as it allows contracts to be upheld which would otherwise be void for lack of formality and can cause uncertainty.

> 'Before 1989 even if there was no valid memorandum within the meaning of section 40 of the LPA 1925 equity might still decree specific performance of a contract for the sale of land if certain requirements were met. It would do so if there was a sufficient act of part performance . . . this had to be done by the plaintiff . . . It is generally accepted . . . that part performance was unsatisfactory in its application and was abolished by the Law of Property (Miscellaneous Provisions) Act 1989. Attention then moves to possible alternatives to the doctrine . . . An examination of section 2 of the Act and the Law Commission's report reveals the possible alternatives as being rectification, collateral contract, estoppel and constructive trusts. The majority of the judicial pronouncements since the Act have been in relation to these last two concepts'.

G L H Griffiths, 'Part Performance – Still Trying to Replace the Irreplaceable?' [2002] Conv 216

Griffiths shows us in his article that there are problems in using constructive trusts and also estoppel because they are both unclear as to what will be the remedy granted if the court finds in favour of the claimant. This is true particularly in cases of estoppel.

> 'The finding of a constructive trust will mean that the claimant has a right which in addition to being undoubtedly proprietary in nature is, according to a considerable body of authority, capable of binding third parties. In these respects, it is, at the very least a comparable alternative to part performance. Furthermore, as with the latter, there is no discretion as to the remedy awarded'.

G L H Griffiths

Griffiths continues his article by considering whether or not estoppel goes some way towards replacing the old doctrine of part-performance.

'The position in estoppel – and indeed its case for replacing part performance – may be much less clear cut for although there are strong indications that a right so based may bind a third party acquiring land to which it relates, this cannot at present be regarded as being beyond doubt . . . However, it is clear that ... the courts have one clear aim. This is as Scarman LJ observed in *Crabb v Arun DC* to give the "minimum equity to do justice" to the claimant, a task approached "in a cautious way".

What form this minimum justice will take may be greatly influenced by whether estoppel is seen as satisfying only the claimant's reliance upon the representation or the legitimate expectations engendered by it . . . The two approaches produce markedly different results and in theoretical terms only if the expectation analysis is correct can estoppel be said to provide a satisfactory substitute for part performance'.

Griffiths highlights how the law has adapted since the passage of the 1989 Act removing the doctrine of part-performance and shows that the result achieved may not be as predictable but the contract, which fails to conform to the necessary formalities may still be enforceable either under proprietary estoppel or under a constructive trust.

## KEY FACTS

### The contract

1. The parties are not bound until there has been exchange of contracts.

2. The seller may be bound before exchange not to negotiate with anyone else for a limited period of time by a lock-out agreement.

3. The contract must conform with s 2(1) of the Law of Property (Miscellaneous Provisions) Act 1989. It must be in writing and signed by both the parties. It must incorporate all the terms which the parties have expressly agreed.

4. Two documents can make up the contract but must be joined by each expressly referring to the other.

5. A collateral contract does not have to conform with the requirements of s 2 of the 1989 Act.

6. Any variation in the terms of the contract will not be effective unless both parties sign them.

7. A contract which does not comply with s 2 of the 1989 Act may still be upheld on the grounds of either estoppel or a constructive trust.

# 4.5 Enforcement of agreements for sale of land

Once contracts have been exchanged there is a binding contract between the parties. This means that neither party can then withdraw from the sale without committing a breach of contract. If one party does breach the contract, the other will be able to seek a remedy from the courts. Since the property involved is land, which is regarded in law as unique, an order for specific performance is available.

Specific performance is an equitable remedy and so, like all equitable remedies, it is discretionary and may be unavailable in the following circumstances:

**1.** if the party seeking it has acted **unconscionably**

**2.** if the award would **prejudice the interests of third parties** or

**3.** if it would cause **hardship** amounting to an injustice.

If specific performance is refused or not sought by the parties then damages can be claimed for the loss of the bargain if either party refuses to perform the contract.

Rescission may be available if it is possible to return the parties to the position they were in before contracts were exchanged. Where this is impossible then damages will be the appropriate remedy.

If there has been an error in the contract then rectification can be claimed. The contracts can then be relied on in their altered state and the sale can proceed.

The contract itself is regarded as a type of interest in land, which is known as an **estate contract**. Since it does not fall within either of the legal estates mentioned in s 1(2) of the Law of Property Act 1925 it is only capable of being an equitable interest. If the land is wrongly conveyed to someone other than the purchaser by the vendor before the purchaser completes the sale, it is possible that the third person will be bound by the purchaser's estate contract.

This will depend on whether it has been properly protected by registration. In the case of registered land this will be by the entry of a burden on the Charges Register. Registration is essential in case the seller accepts a further offer for the property. The second purchaser will realise that there has been another earlier agreement when he sees the registered estate contract.

If no estate contract is entered then the second purchaser has no way of knowing about the earlier negotiations.

# ACTIVITY

Consider these situations. In each case, is there an enforceable contract?

1. Mark decides to sell his house. He immediately puts it on the market and Sally offers him the full asking price. Contracts are prepared by both solicitors. Sally's signature is typed in by the secretary because Sally is away at the time. When she comes back Sally initials the signature.

2. Tim has agreed to sell his house to Jane. His solicitor writes to say that Tim wants to delay the completion date. Jane's solicitor writes back to agree.

3. Anne sells her house to Neil. Contracts are exchanged. Neil registers his estate contract. Les offers Anne £30,000 more and behind Neil's back she agrees to sell to Les. How does that affect Neil's rights? Would it make any difference if Neil's rights were not registered and Les simply knew that Neil had offered to buy the house?

The entering into a binding contract does not transfer the legal title to the purchaser. However, because 'equity treats as done that which ought to be done' and the contract to transfer the land is specifically enforceable, the equitable ownership of the land passes to the purchaser as soon as the contract is entered. This has the consequence that from the moment of exchange of contracts the vendor becomes a trustee and holds the property **on trust for the purchaser**.

# CASE EXAMPLE

### *Lysaght v Edwards* (1876) Ch D 499

'the moment you have a valid contract for sale the vendor becomes in equity a trustee for the purchaser of the estate sold'.

Jessel M R

One of the consequences of this is that from the moment of contract the purchaser is required to insure the land, since under common law the risk passes to him when he obtains the equitable ownership of the land. So if there is a fire which destroys the house between contract and completion, the purchaser must still pay the full asking price as the risk has now passed to the purchaser. The purchaser must insure the property as soon as possible after exchange of contracts.

The Law Commission has criticised this because 'it is fundamentally unsatisfactory and unfair'. It thought it was unfair because it imposed a responsibility on the purchaser to protect his property at a time when he has no physical control over it.

The Standard Conditions of Sale used in the purchase of property allow for the vendor to retain the risk until completion; he will not be under an obligation to insure the property. The purchaser

may have the right to rescind the contract if the physical state of the property has made it unsuitable for its purpose at the date of the contract as a result of damage which is outside the purchaser's insurance contract. These conditions of sale go some way towards redressing the imbalance between the position of the purchaser and the seller after the exchange of contracts.

# 4.6 Transfer of interests in land and other property

## 4.6.1 Stage three: completion of the sale

The final stage in the transfer of land is completion. This is the formal transfer of the legal title from the vendor to the purchaser. It was traditionally six weeks after exchange of contracts but it is now far shorter and can be on the same day but is most likely to be about three weeks afterwards.

In order to convey, transfer or create a legal estate or interest in land it has traditionally been necessary to use a deed.

 's 52(1) of the Law of Property Act 1925 ... All conveyances of land or any other interest therein are void for the purpose of conveying or creating a legal estate unless made by deed.'

### What is a deed?

'the most solemn act that a person can perform with respect to a particular piece of property or other right'.

A deed is a document which has been executed to accord with certain prescribed formalities. These formalities depend on the date at which the deed was executed.

### Deeds prior to July 1990

All deeds had to be signed, sealed and delivered. There was no express requirement for the deed to be witnessed, although it was usual practice to do so. The most important factor was the seal, which was once a genuine sealing wax seal melted on to the paper and then impressed with a special mark. Long before 1990 this had ceased to be usual practice and a standard seal was stuck on to the deed.

### Deeds after July 1990

 's 1 Law of Property (Miscellaneous Provisions) Act 1989

(1) Any rule of law which:

(a) restricts the substances on which a deed may be written;

(b) requires a seal for the valid execution of an instrument as a deed by an individual; or

(c) requires authority by one person to another to deliver an instrument as a deed on his behalf to be given by deed,

is abolished.

(2) An instrument shall not be a deed unless:

(a) it makes it clear on its face it is intended to be a deed by the person making it or, as the case may be, by the parties to it (whether by describing itself as a deed or expressing itself to be executed or signed as a deed or otherwise); and

(b) it is validly executed as a deed by that person or, as the case may be, one or more of those parties.

(3) An instrument is validly executed as a deed by an individual if and only if:

(a) it is signed:

(i) by him in the presence of a witness who attests the signature; or

(ii) at his discretion and in his presence and the presence of two witnesses who each attest the signature; and

(b) it is delivered as a deed by him or a person authorised to do so on his behalf.'

## KEY FACTS

### What is a deed?

- A deed must make it clear on its face that it is intended to be a deed.
- It must be signed by the grantor or by both of them if there is more than one.
- The signature must be witnessed.
- It must be delivered as a deed by the grantor or someone authorised to do so on his behalf.

The purchaser has the responsibility of drawing up the draft transfer of sale. Completion differs between unregistered and registered land.

The eventual introduction of e-conveyancing will result in the demise of the deed. It will no longer be necessary because the documents will be created on line and signed with an electronic signature.

## 4.6.2 Completion of sale in unregistered land

In unregistered land the interest vests as soon as the formalities have been completed. There must be a formal conveyance using a deed and the title deeds of the property must be handed over to the purchaser.

Once the purchase monies have been paid then the purchaser is deemed to be owner of the property. However, since 1990 any sale of land will act as one of the 'triggers' for registration of title and the property will then need to be registered. All new owners of property acquired under the unregistered system of conveyancing have to apply to the Land Registry for first registration as registered proprietor.

Registration must be made within two months of purchase (s 6 of the Land Registration Act 2002). If registration is not made within two months then the conveyance is void and the legal estate reverts back to the seller who will hold it on a bare trust for the purchaser in the case of a freehold estate (s 7(2)(a) LRA 2002) or in the case of a lease of more than seven years in duration, as a contract to grant or create a lease (s 7(2)(6) LRA 2002).

In some cases of non-registration of a disposition, for example the grant of a new estate such as a new lease, the grant will become void and the disposition will take effect simply as an estate contract. Increasingly, it will become rarer and rarer for there to be an unregistered conveyance of property.

## 4.6.3 Registered land

In registered land there are no documents of title to transfer so on receipt of the purchase monies the seller's solicitor will complete the transaction by sending the form of transfer to the purchaser's solicitors. The transfer is by a Land Registry Form which takes effect as a deed (but it differs from the deed of conveyance in unregistered land). It must be 'signed and delivered' to the other party's solicitors. It must also be witnessed.

The transfer is not final until the title has been registered in the Proprietorship Register at the Land Registry. That is the moment when legal title passes. Traditionally, this has taken several weeks to complete so there has arisen what is known as a 'registration gap'.

### 'The defects in the present system

*The "registration gap"*

. . . The fact that there is a period of time between the execution of a transfer or other disposition and its subsequent registration gives rise to a number of difficulties. We have mentioned one of these above, namely that it is necessary to have in place a system of official searches which offer priority protection. It is in practice not uncommon for applications to register a disposition to be made long after the period of protection has passed thereby placing the transferee at risk. In any event, the official search procedure applies only to a purchaser, who is defined as "any person (including a lessee or chargee) who in good faith and for valuable consideration acquires or intends to acquire a legal estate in land". There is no equivalent protection available, at least at present, for those who are intending to acquire some lesser interest in the property, such as an equitable chargee or the grantee of an option'.

Law Commission and HM Land Registry, *Land Registration for the Twenty-First Century: A Consultation Document* (Law Com 254, 1998)

This will be removed under e-conveyancing as completion and registration will all be one computerised process which will be carried out at the Land Registry. Transfer still involves the transfer of paper-based written deeds. Transfer of title will be simply a matter of updating the Register with the new owner's name and details. This will then be instantly accessible electronically to the general public. The new owner will not receive a land certificate noting the change in ownership. One of the advantages is that it will avoid duplication of effort and also the risk of error. However, it also risks new types of crime in the transfer of property. The problems will arise with electronic signatures. They will have to be kept safe and public registers will have to be under sufficient degree of security. It could always be possible that someone could steal the key giving access to the signature and then misuse it in some way, using the signature to sign documents fraudulently.

## Stages in the conveyancing process in registered land

| | | |
|---|---|---|
| Property visited and liked, offer made to the seller. Seller accepts offer. Lock-out agreement may be negotiated. | Effect not binding in law. | *Pitt v PHH Asset Management Ltd* (1994) |
| Contracts exchanged. Must comply with the requirements of the LP (MP) Act 1989: writing; all terms included; signed by both parties. | Parties now bound, cannot change mind without incurring penalties. | *Firstpost Homes Ltd v Johnson* (1995); *Spiro v Glencrown Properties* (1991) |
| Completion, mortgage finalised and money paid. | The seller holds as trustee for the purchaser who has an equitable estate but the seller's name is still registered at the Land Registry. | |
| Registration of the purchaser's name at the Land Registry. | The purchaser is now the owner at law of the property. | s 27 LRA 2002 |

> Mercia agrees to buy 55 Grange Road from Vivien. She particularly likes the way that Vivien has decorated the property. They draw up an agreement which they both sign but it does not mention the carpets and curtains that Mercia had agreed to buy and which were to be included in the sale at a price to be agreed. The agreement also omits other important points such as the date when the sale will be completed and the exact amount to be paid by way of deposit. Mercia later has second thoughts about the property and wants to withdraw from the purchase.
>
> Advise Mercia whether she is bound by the purchase and what remedy would be appropriate if she is so bound.

## 4.7 E-conveyancing

Much of the law on exchange of contracts and completion will be transformed by the advent of electronic conveyancing or 'e-conveyancing'. One of the reasons for the passage of the 2002 Act was to facilitate electronic conveyancing. It has long been recognised that computerisation of conveyancing will have several advantages. It will speed up the whole process of house purchase and also minimise mistakes. There are provisions in the 2002 Act and also in the Electronic Communications Act 2000 for the introduction of e-conveyancing.

Under s 93 of the 2002 Act the Lord Chancellor has the power to make the system compulsory. It will be available to both legal practitioners and members of the general public who wish to carry out their own conveyancing.

> 'The aims of electronic conveyancing are quite clear, namely to remove the traditional paper requirements normally associated with the conveyancing transactions and replace them with a system allowing the transfer of property interests between parties to be conducted via a computer. This will include not only the final stages of conveyancing such as the exchange and completion of land transactions but all associated communications beforehand, including those concerned with the drafting of contracts and the exchange of the lists of fixtures and fittings'.

> D Capps, 'Conveyancing in the 21st Century: An Outline of Electronic
> Conveyancing and Electronic Signatures' [2002] Conv 443

### 4.7.1 How will the system work?

Conveyancers will have to use specific software which, once installed, will give them access to a secure system. It will not be accessible through the Internet. The secure system will give conveyancers the right to access each other and exchange all relevant information and documentation. When the buyer and seller have agreed the terms of the contract they will send a copy in electronic form to the Land Registry where it will be checked electronically, to find any inconsistencies. The buyer and seller will have first agreed the terms of the contract in an on-line secure deal room. The contract will then be made in electronic form and signed using a digital signature which will be carried out electronically. The electronic signature will have the same force of law as a signature on a paper conveyance.

's 91(4) A document to which this system applies is to be regarded as –

    (a) in writing, and

    (b) signed by each individual, and sealed by each corporation, whose
       electronic signature it has.'

One of the main advantages with such a system will be the ease with which searches can be made into the land. There is often considerable delay for the purchaser of property before these are all completed. The new system will allow all of these to be carried out electronically. The rules will allow an electronic contract to replace a paper contract.

The contracts will then be binding but must be registered in the same way as before if they are to bind the land in the event of another sale.

Completion and registration will be done electronically. The same process will be carried out for the completion of sale and for registration. The main advantage at this stage will be the removal of the 'registration gap' between completion and the entry on the Register of the new owner, so minimising any risk of rights arising in that gap. The registration gap arises because at the time of sale of registered land the seller remains registered as owner of the property and it is often several weeks before the buyer's name appears at the Registry. This will not happen with electronic conveyancing because the registration of the new owner will take place at the same time as completion.

## 4.7.2 The electronic document

Under s 91(3) of the 2002 Act, the documents must satisfy certain conditions:

**1.** the date and time of the transaction must be included in the document

**2.** the electronic signatures of all the parties involved must be added to the document

**3.** authentication of the electronic signatures

**4.** such other conditions as rules may provide are met.

## 4.7.3 The effect of e-conveyancing

At the moment it is not clear which rights will be subject to the system of e-conveyancing. It is clear that not all rights will be subject to the system. However, there are several likely effects on the transfer and nature of rights of such a system:

**1.** it will no longer be relevant whether the transfer of the legal estate has been by deed

**2.** it will also no longer be relevant whether the right is equitable or legal in nature.

## 4.7.4 Comment

It is anticipated that only those who are authorised to do so will be able to use the system of e-conveyancing so some could argue that it will now be subject to state control.

There are some risks involved with digital signatures because they can be misused. The risks of fraud if interested parties gain access to the Register are great and although the system may become more certain, it will not be without potential problems.

> 'The secrecy of the signature key, and the nature of the assurance that it is accessible only to its owner, is critical to the usefulness of digital signatures. The verification procedure can say no more than that the text was signed with a specified signature key. It cannot say who made or authorised the running of the signature algorithm and the supply to it of the necessary inputs, namely the text to be signed and the signature key. The security of the signature key, and the trustworthiness of the computer on which the signature algorithm is run, are the basis for inferring from a successful signature verification that the apparent signatory is bound by what was signed'.
>
> S Mason and N Bohm, 'The Signature in Electronic Conveyancing: an Unresolved Issue?' [2003] 67 Conv 460

Mason and Bohm discuss the insecurity of computers, citing a number of examples of how computers can be insecure, for example the user fails to log off and leaves the computer unattended; the user uses a password that is easy to guess. More sophisticated possibilities lie in the installation of software which can record the user's keystrokes which would include a password and these can be subsequently retrieved. They also point out that the possibilities are enhanced where the user's computer is connected to the Internet.

The main problem that could arise is a possible fraudulent sale by someone who has access to the electronic signature key, eg Jon purports to be the vendor, Ken, and sells Ken's property to an innocent purchaser, Les. Will this sale be upheld by the Land Registry, since it has used a valid electronic signature? There is no means of deciphering whether the signature is forged where it is signed electronically.

The recent case of *Malory Enterprises Ltd v Cheshire Homes (UK) Ltd* [2002] Ch 216 suggests that where a conveyance is based on a forgery then this cannot be a disposition giving legal rights to the innocent purchaser. The subsequent registration can be rectified by the Registrar since the true owner had sufficient standing to sue for trespass. Perhaps this reasoning will be applied to electronic signatures where they are used illegally.

The proposed system is not without its critics and many think that the provisions will bring with them a number of problems.

> 'An unfortunate side effect of the apparent consensus surrounding the proposed changes has been a lack of any real scrutiny of both the technical aspects of e-conveyancing (and its core technology of digital signatures) and the way in which these will affect the practical implementation of any new system. There has been an assumption that the technical aspects of the proposed reforms are workable'.

R Perry, 'E-Conveyancing: Problems Ahead?' [2003] 67 Conv 215

The article highlights how many major IT projects have failed in recent years, giving an alarming figure of 31 per cent of a group of 3,500 abandoned in recent years, many of them government-funded projects. Perry also looks at the advantages that the system will offer. There is a likelihood of a saving in costs because two transactions will be combined together but Perry suggests that the costs in trying to keep the electronic signatures secure will itself be costly so that saving may be less than is currently envisaged.

Provision for e-conveyancing is made in the Land Registration Act 2002 but it will not be in force until there has been extensive consultation and it will then be introduced under Land Registration Rules laid down by the Lord Chancellor. The introduction will be gradual and it is also likely that the two systems will run side by side for some period of time.

# Further reading

Capps, D, Conveyancing in the 21st Century: An Outline of Electronic Conveyancing and Electronic Signatures [2002] Conv 443.

Griffiths, G L H, 'Part Performance – Still Trying to Replace the Irreplaceable?' [2002] Conv 216.

Mason, S and Bohm, N 'The Signature in Electronic Conveyancing: an Unresolved Issue?' [2003] 67 Conv 460.

Moore, I, 'Proprietary Estoppel, Constructive Trusts and s.2 of the Law of Property (Miscellaneous Provisions) Act 1989' [2000] MLR 912.

Perry, R, 'E-Conveyancing: Problems ahead?' [2003] 67 Conv 215.

Spiro, D E, 'The Easy Option' [1991] NLJ 124.

Swann, S J A, 'Part performance back from the dead?' (1997) Conv 293.

Thompson, M P, 'New Wine from Old Bottles' Case Note on *Morritt v Wonham* [1994] Conv 233.

Thompson, M P, 'Oral Agreements for the Sale of Land' [2000] 64 Conv 245.

Thornton, R, 'How to Lock Out a Gazumper' [1993] CLJ 392.

# chapter 5 EQUITABLE RIGHTS IN LAND ■

## 5.1 The nature of equitable rights in land

The creation and transfer of rights in land is subject to certain formalities. If these are not complied with, equity may step in and recognise rights which, although not recognised in law, will be recognised as equitable rights. These will affect the legal owner's enjoyment of the property and also his right to transfer the property.

In some situations the law may also impose a trust because of the circumstances, and then equitable interests and rights will also be created.

We have already considered the fact that wherever there are two or more owners of property the law will automatically impose a trust.

The legal owner is said to own as **trustee**.

### 5.1.1 The definition of a 'trust'

A trust allows ownership in property to be split between legal and equitable ownership:

- the **legal title** to property is held by one or more persons (the trustee)
- the **equitable title** is owned by the beneficiaries.

The trustee holds the legal title on behalf of the beneficiaries who take the benefit of the trust. In land, where a trust is frequently implied, the trustees and beneficiaries are often the same people.

### 5.1.2 Types of trust

Trusts are split into two categories:

**1.** the **express trust** based on the declared intentions of the parties, and

**2.** the **implied trust**, generally based on the presumed intentions of the parties.

## 5.2 The express trust

In an express trust the settlor **either** asks the trustees expressly to hold on trust for the beneficiaries on the terms named by the settlor **or** the owner of the property declares himself to be trustee of the land on behalf of the beneficiary.

An express trust can also arise under a will. The main point is that a will takes effect on death, which distinguishes wills from *inter vivos* transfers.

Under the Wills Act 1837, no will shall be valid unless –

's 9(a) it is in writing, and signed by the testator, or by some other person in his
presence and by his direction; and

(b) it appears that the testator intended by his signature to give effect to the will; and

(c) the signature is made or acknowledged by the testator in the presence of two
or more witnesses present at the same time; and

(d) each witness either –

(i) attests and signs the will; or

(ii) acknowledges his signature,

in the presence of the testator (but not necessarily in the presence of any other
witness), but no form of attestation shall be necessary.'

Unless a will complies with this section, it shall not take effect and any provision under the will
cannot take effect.

The creation of an express trust in land *inter vivos* must comply with s 53(1)(b) of the Law of
Property Act 1925 which requires evidence in writing. The trust will be unenforceable unless there
is written evidence. This does not mean that it will be void. The effect of this is that the beneficiary
can seek to enforce the trust but if the action is defended by those who will be entitled if the trusts
fails and the claim is based on the fact that there is no written evidence, this will make it
unenforceable.

## APPLYING THE LAW

Flora tells her nephew, Donald, that she will hold her flat in London on trust for him.
He is pleased about this but she does not put it into writing. She gives him the rent she
receives from the property every year. He can challenge her promise but if she says that
she never put it into writing then Donald cannot force her to transfer the flat to him.

There are exceptions:

**1.** resulting, implied or constructive trusts are expressly excluded under s 53(2) of the 1925
Act. No writing is necessary for these types of trust to come into existence

**2.** the court makes an exception in cases of fraud. It was laid down in *Rochefoucauld v
Boustead* [1897] 1 Ch 196 that where someone receives property knowing that they are to
hold as a trustee then they cannot deny the existence of the trust: 'It is fraud on the part of
a person to whom land is conveyed as a trustee, and who knows it was so conveyed, to
deny the trust and claim the land for himself. Consequently, notwithstanding the statute,

119

it is competent for a person claiming land conveyed to another to prove by parol evidence that it was so conveyed upon trust for the claimant, and that the grantee, knowing the facts, is denying the trust and relying upon the form of conveyance and the statute, in order to keep the land for himself.' (Lindley J).

This means that although in law the property has been transferred to someone else but with no interest in writing, if they know that the transfer is not a gift for them, equity will say they do not enjoy it for themselves but for the person named as beneficiary.

## APPLYING THE LAW  □□□

Tim transfers his house to his brother, Chris, telling him he is to hold as trustee for Tim's twin boys until they are 18. Tim should put this into writing but because the boys are members of the family he may not think to do so. In law, Chris owns for himself absolutely but the boys can force Chris to convey the house to them when they are 18 because it would be a fraud for him to refuse to do so as he knows he holds as trustee.

□□□

The trustees of an express trust of land are under a duty under the common law and also under the Trustee Acts 1925 and 2000 to act in the best interests of the beneficiaries and according to the settlor's instructions. The beneficiaries have the right to compel the trustees to carry out the terms of the trust. If the court finds the trustee to be in breach of his duties then he must compensate the trust.

## 5.3 Implied trusts

Trusts can arise where the parties involved have not thought about creating a trust and have not taken any express steps to do so. The law simply imposes a trust because it is appropriate to do so.

Where one person owns land but two or more persons own equitable interests in the land, the law will imply a trust of land. The rights in equity may arise because there have been contributions to the purchase. These rights will take effect in the form of an implied, a resulting or a constructive trust. For the lawyer and the courts, it is quite difficult to distinguish between these types of trust.

> **J** 'A resulting, implied or constructive trust – and it is unnecessary for the present purposes to distinguish between these three classes of trust – is created by a transaction between the trustee and the *cestui que trust* in connection with the acquisition by the trustee of a legal estate in land, whenever the trustee has so conducted himself that it would be inequitable to allow him to deny to the *cestui que trust* a beneficial interest in

> the land acquired. And he will be held so to have conducted himself if by his words or conduct he has induced the cestui que trust to act to his own detriment in the reasonable belief that by so acting he was acquiring a beneficial interest in the land'.
>
> Lord Diplock in *Gissing v Gissing* [1971] AC 886

The *'cestui que trust'* is just another name for a beneficiary under a trust.

Although Lord Diplock is here referring to three types of trust, conventionally, today, there is no discernible difference between a resulting trust and an implied trust but there remains a difference between a resulting and constructive trust.

# 5.4 Resulting trusts

## 5.4.1 The definition of 'resulting trusts'

A resulting trust gives effect to the presumed intentions of the parties. They arise where the parties have not declared any express intention to create a trust but the law will imply a trust because of particular circumstances. The law looks at the circumstances and concludes that the owner of the land does not own absolutely for themselves but owns on behalf of another or others. The ownership then is said to 'result' back to the person providing the money, rather than remaining with the person who owned the property at law.

The best example is where property is bought in the name of someone but the purchase money is provided by another.

## APPLYING THE LAW

John buys Windy Ridge. Janet provides £5,000 towards the purchase price but John is registered as owner. The law says that Janet would assume that she would get an interest in Windy Ridge. This is because the law does not think that people intend to make gifts to each other. John owns the property absolutely in law but he owns as trustee of the equitable interest in Windy Ridge for himself and Janet.

If Janet had provided **all** the purchase money then John will hold as trustee for Janet absolutely.

There will be a resulting trust where there has been a purchase in two names, for example in both Janet's and John's names but the money has been provided by one person, for example Janet.

## 5.4.2 Presumed intention

The resulting trust then depends upon presumed intention for its operation.

> **J** 'A trust of a legal estate . . . results to the man who advances the purchase money'.
>
> Eyre CB in *Dyer v Dyer* (1788) 2 Cox Eq Cas 92

If both parties make contributions then the courts will presume a resulting trust for both. This is because it would be **unconscionable** for the owner to keep the property for himself absolutely. This is a presumed intention because, unlike an express trust, the parties do not have to intend that a trust be created. It is also irrelevant whether or not they know that a trust has arisen. NB the key word here is 'unconscionable'.

# ACTIVITY

Consider the following situations and decide whether there is a resulting trust and, if so, for whom.

1. Alex purchases a flat in his name, with money provided by himself and Alice.

2. John purchases a farm in his name, with money provided solely by his Aunt Jemima.

3. Hanna purchases a bungalow in her name and that of her friend Polly, with money provided solely by Polly.

The resulting trust depends on the intentions of the parties at the time of the purchase of the property. If money is provided at a later date then it cannot give rise to a resulting trust but it can give rise to another type of implied trust. The theory is based on the presumed intentions of the parties at the time the property was purchased. If the intention does not arise until after the acquisition of the legal title, there should be no resulting trust.

## 5.4.3 Rebuttal of the presumption of resulting trust

### Gifts

The resulting trust is based on the presumed intentions of the parties and this presumption is **rebuttable**. The parties are both free to come to court with evidence to show that they intended to make a gift or perhaps a loan.

In the example at section 5.4.1, John can always come to court and say that as Janet intended to make him an outright gift towards the purchase of Windy Ridge, there is no resulting trust in Janet's favour. Then the law says that the presumption of a resulting trust in Janet's favour is **rebutted**.

## Loans

A resulting trust will not be inferred where there is proof that the money advanced was by way of a loan. In this case the money is not referable to acquiring as a purchaser and so the lender cannot argue that they can take an interest in the property. The loan is personal to the borrower.

 ASE EXAMPLE

**Re Sharpe (a bankrupt) [1980] 1 WLR 219**

The purchaser's great-aunt had contributed towards the purchase of a house. The purchaser was declared bankrupt and the great-aunt tried to argue that her nephew held the property on resulting trust for her. This would give her rights in the property which would be satisfied in full. The court held that she had made him a loan and the property therefore was not held on resulting trust for her. Although here the court did not find evidence of a resulting trust, the great-aunt was given the right to remain in the property under another type of implied trust.

## Presumption of advancement

There is also another presumption that can rebut the presumption of a resulting trust and that is the presumption of advancement. It arises in certain relationships, usually where the donor has an obligation to provide for the donee, for example father and child; husband and wife. It also arises where someone acts *in loco parentis*. This means that someone has taken on the responsibility of maintaining another. It does **not** arise between mother and child or between wife and husband.

 ASE EXAMPLE

**Sekhon v Alissa [1989] 2 FLR 94**

A mother had transferred the whole of her savings to her daughter in order that she could purchase property. It was shown that this was done in order to gain a tax advantage but it was still held to be a resulting trust since there was no presumption of advancement.

However, in a case like this, where the presumption of advancement does not apply, it does not prevent the presumption of resulting trust from being rebutted by evidence of a gift.

## APPLYING THE LAW

Chris is 18 years old. After his 'gap year' he went to university in London. His father bought him a flat in Clapham. The flat was registered in Chris's name. Under any other circumstances the flat would be held for Chris's father by Chris on resulting trust because one person provided all the purchase money but the property was registered in the name of another.

**But** as this was a purchase by a father for his son, there is a **presumption of advancement** and this rebuts the presumption of resulting trust. It is important here that Chris is already 18, as the property would be held on trust in any circumstances if he were under 18 as children cannot hold property in their own name until the age of 18.

The presumption of advancement is not without its critics, as it seems to be curiously out of date in the world today.

'The stark truth is that the concept of presumed advancement has a distinctly patriarchal resonance which causes many to question today whether it properly has any substantial role in the ascertainment of beneficial intentions'

Gray and Gray, *Elements of Land Law* (3rd edn, Butterworths, 2001), p 682

This presumption can itself be rebutted. In the example above, if Chris's father wanted to retain an interest in the flat then he can rebut the presumption of advancement by showing that he did not intend to make an outright gift of the flat.

## ASE EXAMPLE

### *Warren v Gurney* [1944] 2 All ER 472

A father purchased a house and put it into his daughter's name but the presumption of advancement was rebutted because it was clear that he did not intend a gift but always intended to loan the money to his daughter. The father retained the title deeds until his death. In this case the daughter held on resulting trust for her father.

## 5.4.4 Improper motive in transfer of property

In some cases there may be an improper motive for the transfer of the property. The transfer may be done purely to defeat creditors, in which case the court will look carefully at the motive of the party making the transfer.

If a husband puts the title to a house in his wife's name then the presumption of resulting trust is rebutted by the presumption of advancement. The court will not allow the husband to come to court and try to rebut the presumption of advancement by evidence that the only reason that he put the title into the name of his wife was because he wanted to avoid his creditors in the event of bankruptcy.

 **CASE EXAMPLE**

> ### *Gascoigne v Gascoigne* [1918] 1 KB 223
>
> A husband put the title to a house into the name of his wife. It was done purely to avoid creditors from taking his house. It was held that he could not come to court to say that the house belonged to him because he would be using his own dishonesty to support his own case.

**CASE EXAMPLE**

> ### *Tinker v Tinker* [1970] P 136
>
> 'I am quite clear that the husband cannot have it both ways. So he is on the horns of a dilemma. He cannot say that the house is his own and, at one and the same time, say that it is his wife's. As against his wife, he wants to say that it belongs to him. As against the creditors, that it belongs to her. That simply will not do. Either it was conveyed to her for her own use absolutely: or it was conveyed to her as trustee for her husband. It must be one or the other. The presumption is that it was conveyed to her for her own use: and he does not rebut that presumption by saying that he only did it to defeat his creditors. I think that it belongs to her'.
>
> Lord Denning

In cases where there has been an illegal motive but it has not been put into effect, the law will allow the ordinary presumptions to apply.

# CASE EXAMPLE

### *Tinsley v Milligan* [1994] 1 AC 340

Miss Milligan and her lover, Miss Tinsley, bought a house jointly, both providing purchase money, but it was put into Miss Tinsley's name for the sole reason that Miss Milligan wanted to claim social security benefits. Miss Tinsley claimed that the property was held by her absolutely because of the illegal motive but the court held that it was held on resulting trust for Miss Milligan. The illegal motive was irrelevant and was not relied on by Miss Milligan in support of her claim. Miss Tinsley argued that the illegal motive tainted the entire claim but this was rejected by the court. The court found that Miss Milligan could rely on the presumption of a resulting trust to support her claim.

# CASE EXAMPLE

### *Tribe v Tribe* [1996] Ch 107

The above principle was supported in this case, where a father had transferred his house into his son's name on the basis that it would be out of the hands of his creditors. The creditors were not deceived, as he had sufficient funds to pay them all. The son then refused to return the property, relying on the presumption of advancement. The court upheld the claim of the father as he was not relying on an illegal motive that had been carried out but merely on a reason to rebut the presumption of advancement. If the creditors had been wrongly deprived of their money then the father would not have been able to reclaim his property from his son.

## Rebuttal of presumption of resulting trust

| | | |
|---|---|---|
| Gifts | Based on evidence that a gift was intended | |
| Loans | No resulting trust where it is proved that a loan was made as a loan and is not referable to rights in the property | *Re Sharpe (a bankrupt)* (1980) |
| Advancement to members of one's family, either father to child or husband to wife | Outright gift presumed on basis of presumption of advancement | *Warren v Gurney* (1944); *Sekhon v Alissa* (1989) |
| Improper motive for transfer of property | Will not rebut presumption of resulting trust unless improper motive was not carried out | *Tinker v Tinker* (1970); *Tribe v Tribe* (1996); *Gascoigne v Gascoigne* (1918); *Tinsley v Milligan* (1994) |

## KEY FACTS

**Presumptions of resulting trusts and advancement**

1. A resulting trust will be presumed where property is transferred into the name of one person but all or part of the purchase money has been provided by another.

2. The presumption of a resulting trust can be rebutted by the presumption of advancement. This arises in certain relationships, for example father and child; husband and wife.

3. Both presumptions can be rebutted by evidence of a gift or a loan.

4. An illegal motive cannot normally be relied on to rebut either presumption.

5. Where it can be shown that the illegal purpose has not been carried into effect, the illegal purpose can be used as evidence in court.

## 5.4.5 The effect of s 60(3) of the Law of Property Act 1925

The operation of a resulting trust rests on the fact that the legal title to land is purchased in the name of A but the capital is provided by B or by A and B together. If property is simply transferred voluntarily from B to A, a gift is assumed and A will be able to claim absolute ownership without the inference of a resulting trust.

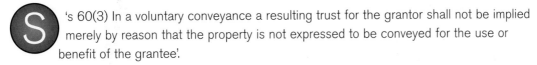

's 60(3) In a voluntary conveyance a resulting trust for the grantor shall not be implied merely by reason that the property is not expressed to be conveyed for the use or benefit of the grantee'.

This does not mean that you could never have a resulting trust where land is subject to a voluntary transfer. It depends on whether there is evidence that the transferee was to hold on resulting trust for the transferor.

# ASE EXAMPLE

### *Hodgson v Marks* [1971] Ch 892

The claimant transferred property into the name of her lodger in circumstances where it was clearly not intended that the lodger should be the beneficial owner. The court looked at the effect of s 60(3) of the 1925 Act and concluded that it was 'a debatable question' whether a resulting trust arose on a voluntary transfer by A to stranger B. This was revisited in the later case of *Lohia v Lohia* [2001] WTLR 10 (see below).

# CASE EXAMPLE

**Lohia v Lohia [2001] WTLR 10**

The Court of Appeal considered whether the presumption of resulting trust applies on a voluntary transfer of land and concluded that s 60(3) abolished the presumption of a resulting trust and there would have to be evidence that a resulting trust was to apply on a voluntary conveyance of property. However, this subsection remains confusing as normally when there is a change in the law it is expressly referred to as a change to existing rules but the wording of s 60(3) does not expressly refer to such a change.

## APPLYING THE LAW

Uncle Bill decides to transfer his two-bedroom cottage into his nephew Ben's name. He executes a transfer in Ben's name and Ben registers his title. There is no presumption of resulting trust in Uncle Bill's favour.

## APPLYING THE LAW

Uncle Bill decides to transfer his four-bedroom house to his nephew, Ben. Bill says that he intends to continue to receive the rent from the student who rents a ground-floor self-contained flat. This raises the presumption of a resulting trust because it suggests that he did not intend to convey to Ben absolutely.

In the second case there is evidence that suggests that the property is to be held on resulting trust for Uncle Bill.

## 5.4.6 Types of contributions that give rise to a resulting trust

A resulting trust will arise on the basis of different types of contributions towards the purchase of property. The key feature of them all is whether they are referable to the purchase of the property.

## Direct contributions to the purchase price

### APPLYING THE LAW □□□

If Gillian gives her boyfriend, Jack, a cheque for £30,000 towards the purchase of a flat costing £90,000 which is put into Jack's name, then Gillian will be presumed to have a share in the property. Her contribution was one-third of the purchase price, so she can claim a one-third share in the property. It is irrelevant that there is no written evidence of the transaction as it is an implied trust (s 53(2) of the Law of Property 1925).

□□□

According to *Burns v Burns* [1984] Ch 317, a direct cash payment is sufficiently referable to the acquisition of title to generate a trust and the contributor will be presumed to have intended that they should acquire a beneficial share in the property.

## Contribution to the deposit or legal expenses

### APPLYING THE LAW □□□

If Gillian gives her boyfriend a cheque for £3,000 towards the deposit, or even the legal expenses of the purchase of a flat put into Jack's name, there is a presumption that the property is held on resulting trust for Gillian.

□□□

# CASE EXAMPLE

### *Midland Bank v Cooke* [1995] 4 All ER 562

Property was purchased by a husband and wife. It was partly financed by a cheque for £1,100 given to the parties as a wedding gift from the husband's parents. This gave the wife a share in the property. Her share by way of resulting trust should have amounted to the same fraction as her contribution to the purchase price (approximately 6.74 per cent). The courts actually found that she was entitled to more, by imposing a constructive trust on the proceeds of sale.

## Contribution to mortgage repayments

These are treated as the equivalent to a contribution to the purchase price and will give rise to a resulting trust. There is a problem if a resulting trust is defined as arising at the time of the purchase to give effect to the presumed intentions of the parties at the time of the acquisition of the property because contributions towards the mortgage do not arise until the property has already been purchased. However, if Gillian has not got sufficient savings to pay towards the initial deposit and purchase price but instead says she will pay £150 every month from her salary, starting with the first instalment after sale, then this should be enough to establish a resulting trust. If one party does not initially contribute to the purchase but later takes on the responsibility of discharging the mortgage, strictly this cannot take effect as a resulting trust.

In *Gissing v Gissing* (1971) Lord Diplock related the payment of the mortgage instalments to the acquisition of the property in this way:

> J 'The economic reality which lies behind the conveyance of the fee simple to a purchaser in return for a purchase price the greater part of which is advanced to the purchaser upon a mortgage repayable by instalments over a number of years, is that the new freeholder is purchasing the matrimonial home upon credit and that the purchase price is represented by instalments by which the mortgage is repaid in addition to the initial payment in cash. The conduct of the spouses in relation to the payment of the mortgage instalments may be no less relevant to their common intention as to the beneficial interests in a matrimonial home acquired in this way than their conduct in relation to the payment of the cash deposit'.

# CASE EXAMPLE

### *Bernard v Josephs* [1982] Ch 391

It was recognised that the economic reality of most couples' finances is that resources are often pooled and so it is difficult to work out which party was responsible for the payment of the mortgage. 'But often where a couple are living together and both are working and pooling their resources, which one of them pays the mortgage may be no more than a matter of internal accounting between them. In such a case the judge must look at the contributions of each to the family finances and determine as best he may what contribution each was making towards the purchase of the house' (Griffiths LJ).

## Household expenses

There have been attempts to argue in a number of cases that the contributions to the general household expenses can give rise to a resulting trust. A particularly forceful argument is that these contributions will release funds from the other party to pay the mortgage. However, unless there is an express agreement that this kind of arrangement will give rise to rights in the property, the courts have taken a particularly harsh approach to this type of contribution. The problem is that they cannot automatically be linked to the acquisition of the property itself.

 **CASE EXAMPLE**

### Burns v Burns [1984] Ch 317

The parties had a long relationship amounting to some 19 years and they had two children. The woman stayed at home for much of the marriage, caring for the children. When the relationship broke down, the woman claimed a share of the property, based on her indirect contributions towards living expenses. This case was not decided on principles of matrimonial law because the parties were never married. It was decided purely on property law principles and so the courts were not entitled to take domestic duties and later contributions to household expenses into account when assessing shares in the property.

It can seem unfair to a party to a relationship that contributions in kind or through domestic services do not lead to rights in property, especially in circumstances such as *Burns v Burns* (1984) where they take place over a long period of time. Such contributions may influence financial decisions in divorce proceedings but if the parties in a relationship are not married and that relationship breaks down then they cannot be used in support of a claim based on a resulting trust.

> 'It is virtually impossible to infer a *quid pro quo* agreement or common intention where the claimant has merely commenced cohabitation with the proprietor or paid housekeeping expenses of an everyday "revenue" nature or has had a baby, such conduct being almost certainly referable to the mutual love of the parties rather than to some understanding relating such conduct to the acquisition of a beneficial interest in the home'.

D J Hayton, 'Equitable Rights of Cohabitees' [1990] Conv 370

## The right to buy under the Housing Act 1985

The court recognises that a tenant's right to buy under the Housing Act 1985 can represent a contribution to the purchase of property and so give the tenant rights even where they have not contributed in cash.

It is difficult to quantify the contribution but it is best seen in terms of the actual reduction in the purchase price. If there were two joint occupiers then they may both have a right to buy the property and the courts have to decide how to quantify the shares in the property. This could be apportioned between the parties.

If there is a separate agreement as to how much each person is to receive, that will govern the apportionment. In *Savill v Goodall* [1993] 1 FLR 755 it was held that as the parties had agreed that they should share the beneficial interest equally, that agreement would govern the actual apportionment.

**Types of contributions that may give rise to a resulting trust**

| | |
|---|---|
| Direct contributions to purchase price | |
| Contributions to the deposit or legal expenses | *Midland Bank v Cooke* (1995) |
| Contributions to mortgage repayments | *Gissing v Gissing* (1971) (Lord Diplock's judgment: no resulting trust found); *Bernard v Josephs* (1982) |
| Household expenses | *Burns v Burns* (1984): no resulting trust |
| Right to buy under Housing Act 1985 | *Savill v Goodall* (1993) |

## 5.4.7 Assessing the shares of the parties in a resulting trust

Where the property is held on resulting trust it is assumed that the shares will be proportionate to the contribution that has been made. These are said to crystallise at the date of acquisition.

If at the date of acquisition of the property A pays one-third of the purchase price, B will hold one-third of the value of the property on resulting trust for A.

## APPLYING THE LAW

Robert and Penny decide to buy a new house together. It is registered in Robert's name but Penny makes a contribution of £15,000 from her savings. The house is purchased for £150,000. Robert will hold the house on resulting trust for Penny and when it is sold she will be entitled to claim one-tenth of the value. So if, in five years' time, it is sold for £300,000 she will be able to claim £30,000.

'In *Midland Bank v Cooke* [1995] 4 All ER 562 the Court of Appeal has examined whether, in the absence of any actual "agreement" as to the extent of the beneficial interest, the resulting interest must be proportional to the contribution to the purchase of the property by the non-legal title holder. In giving sole judgment of the court, Waite L.J. held that once Jane Cooke had shown some direct contribution it was open to the court to calculate the extent of her beneficial interest otherwise than in proportion to that direct initial contribution. In such a case the court must scrutinise the whole course of dealings between the parties . . . The preponderance of previous English authority had indicated that the resulting trust is proportional to the cash sum contributed, as any other way would require the court to give an opinion as to what the property interest should be in all the circumstances rather than to make a finding on the evidence as to what it was. This limitation is one factor which has caused a shift in argument to the more flexible constructive trust, which permits the ultimate interest to differ from the money value contributed'.

P O'Hagan, 'Quantifying Interests under Resulting Trusts' (1997) 60 MLR

What we learn from this analysis of *Midland v Cooke* is that where there is an initial contribution to the purchase price, however small, by the claimant then a resulting trust is presumed. If there is no further evidence of intention with regards to the property then it will be apportioned according to the size of the contributions. If there is evidence of a common intention to share the property between the contributing parties then the court has the power to review other issues in assessing the relevant shares. The important point to remember is that these other matters would have been ignored in assessing whether a resulting trust had arisen at all.

# ACTIVITY

Consider the following and decide whether in each case the property is held on resulting trust:

1. Jilly and Alf live together in Alf's house, purchased before they began to live together, for £80,000 with a mortgage of £40,000. Jilly gave up work when their first child was born. After three years she decided to return to work and agreed that she would pay the mortgage instalments; she has now made repayments of over £2,500.

2. Hilly and Ron live together in a house purchased by Ron for £40,000 in his name, with £10,000 provided by Hilly.

**3.** Tilly and Fred had been living together. They decided to get married and Tilly's parents gave them a cheque for £2,000 as a wedding present. They used the money as a deposit for the purchase of their house, valued at £120,000 which is registered in Fred's name.

**4.** Dilly and Don live together in a run down house purchased for £60,000 in Don's name. Dilly loves renovating old houses and she works continuously on the house for two years. She assesses the cost of her labour and materials at £20,000.

If you find evidence of a resulting trust in the above situations then calculate the shares that each party can claim.

## KEY FACTS

**1.** Where direct contributions in money are made towards the purchase of property then this will raise the presumption of a resulting trust.

**2.** A contribution to the deposit will also raise the presumption of a resulting trust.

**3.** A contribution to mortgage instalments or even the release of money from the payment of household expenses for one party in order that they may pay the mortgage repayments may raise the inference of a resulting trust.

**4.** The payment of household expenses and contributions in kind cannot raise the inference of a resulting trust.

**5.** The right to buy under the Housing Act 1985 is seen as a direct contribution towards payment towards the purchase of property and can also infer a resulting trust.

# 5.5 Constructive trusts

## 5.5.1 The definition of a 'constructive trust'

It has long been recognised that it is difficult to define a constructive trust clearly, because it can arise in such a large number of diverse situations:

> J  'English Law provides no clear and all-embracing definition of a constructive trust. Its boundaries have been left perhaps deliberately vague, so as not to restrict the court by technicalities in deciding what the justice of a particular case may demand'.
>
> *Carl Zeiss-Stiftung v Herbert Smith & Co (No. 2)* [1969] 2 Ch 276

## Constructive trusts arise by operation of law

Constructive trust arises in circumstances outlined by Lord Millett in *Paragon Finance plc v D B Thakerar & Co* [1999] 1 All ER 400 where it would be 'unconscionable for the owner of property (usually but not necessarily the legal estate) to assert his own beneficial interest in the property and deny the beneficial interest of another'.

Such trusts are imposed because it would be **unconscionable** for the owner at law to claim the legal estate wholly or in part for himself. They arise in many situations both in land law and also the law of trusts.

## APPLYING THE LAW

If an express trustee of a trust fund takes part of the property for himself then the courts will impose a constructive trust over that property and the trustee will hold the property and any profit he makes from it as constructive trustee.

## APPLYING THE LAW

If two people, X and Y, join together to buy property and Y says he has no money to put towards the purchase but he will renovate the property and X agrees that they will share the property between them, a trust will arise. If the owner X tries to deny any rights in the property to Y then the courts will impose a constructive trust and X will hold on constructive trust for Y.

Constructive trusts are similar to resulting trusts but there are also significant differences.

## The similarities

**1.** They are informal in nature.

**2.** They do not require written evidence for their operation (s 53(2) of the Law of Property Act 1925).

**3.** They both rely on intention, although the role of intention in constructive trusts is far more positive. The court must be satisfied that it was intended that the non-legal owner would acquire an equitable interest in the property or it must be inferred from their conduct before they can impose a constructive trust. In a resulting trust the intention is presumed and need not be express. The intention that the non-legal owner is to own a share can always be rebutted by evidence, for example that it was a gift.

## The differences

**1.** Constructive trusts rely on a bargain between the parties, whereas the resulting trust relies on contributions of the parties.

**2.** The shares awarded under a constructive trust do not depend on the exact contributions of the parties, whereas in a resulting trust the shares are usually the equivalent of the amount contributed to the initial purchase.

> 'Whilst resulting trusts focus on **contributions** towards the purchase of realty, constructive trusts are more heavily concerned with **bargains** relating to beneficial ownership. Consistently with its disfavour of informal mechanisms of rights creation, English law generally denies effect to mere oral gifts, agreements or transactions relating to land. But once the repudiation of an informally promised beneficial entitlement crosses the threshold of unconscionable behaviour, equity is ultimately prepared to impose a special form of trust liability on the errant estate owner, thereby safeguarding the bargained interest notwithstanding its informality of origin'.

> Gray and Gray, *Elements of Land Law* (3rd edn, Butterworths, 2001), p 702

The recent law on constructive trusts starts with the important decision of the House of Lords in *Gissing v Gissing*. The case concerned a claim by a former wife to a proprietary interest in the house owned by her husband and subject to a mortgage. The wife claimed that she had contributed substantially, though indirectly, to the payment by her husband of the original deposit and the subsequent instalments payable under the mortgage which enabled him to acquire the house. The husband had paid for the house and had paid for all the mortgage payments. The wife had made indirect payments; she had purchased clothes for herself and their child; she had contributed towards the housekeeping; and had spent money on the garden and buying furniture.

Lord Diplock considered all these contributions and found that they were not referable to the house and held that the husband was absolutely entitled to the house and that the wife had no interest in it by way of trust. It was also significant that the House of Lords could find no conduct from which it could be inferred that the parties had a common intention that the wife was to be entitled to a share of the house.

> **J** 'The picture presented by the evidence is one of husband and wife retaining their separate proprietary interests in the property whether real or personal purchased with their separate savings and is inconsistent with any common intention at the time of the purchase of the matrimonial home that the wife, who neither then nor thereafter contributed anything to its purchase price or assumed any liability for it, should nevertheless be entitled to a beneficial interest in it'
>
> Lord Diplock

## 5.5.2 Types of constructive trust

Here are some situations where the courts have been prepared to impose a constructive trust:

1. Xanthe and William agree that when Xanthe sells her house to Zelda, William will be able to retain an interest in the property. The courts will then hold that it would be unconscionable for Zelda to deny William any rights in the property if Zelda buys subject to William's rights.

2. If Xanthe and William agree that Amy shall have rights in the property when Xanthe sells to William then the courts will impose a constructive trust in Amy's favour.

3. If Xanthe and William agree that William will now have rights in Xanthe's house.

Under 1. there is a problem because the agreement is not in writing so the formalities necessary for a transfer of land have not been complied with. It can only be enforceable if the courts are willing to impose a constructive trust which does not require writing.

### Bannister v Bannister [1948] 2 All ER 133

The purchaser of property orally agreed that the seller would be able to live there for the rest of her life. This was not recorded in writing and the purchaser sought to rely on this when he tried to evict the seller. However, the court held that the right for the purchaser to live in the property must be upheld.

Under 2. a third party cannot generally enforce an agreement in his favour unless the Contracts (Rights of Third Parties) Act 1999 applies or a constructive trust can be imposed. So Amy cannot claim that she can remain in the property unless she can raise evidence that William holds the property on constructive trust for her.

### Binions v Evans [1972] Ch 359

A widow was given the right to live in a cottage for her lifetime. She agreed that she would carry out certain duties such as keeping the cottage in good repair. The cottage was then sold on to purchasers who tried to evict her. The court was agreed that the widow should remain in the cottage but the judges differed about the reason why she should have the right to remain.

Lord Denning found that she had a contractual licence since she had furnished some consideration and that since the purchasers bought the property knowing of her rights then they bought as constructive trustees and could not seek to evict her. The reasoning in this case has been questioned in later cases but it is clear that where the purchasers buy property and a constructive trust can be upheld then the rights of the beneficiary of such a trust cannot be denied.

## CASE EXAMPLE

### Lyus v Prowsa Developments Ltd [1982] 1 WLR 1044

A plot of land was owned by a company which subsequently went into liquidation. The claimants entered into a contract with the company to buy a plot on the land as well as a house to be built on it. The defendants purchased the entire plot including the claimant's estate and later sold on to the second defendants. They were held to buy subject to the claimant's interest as they bought expressly subject to the claimant's rights.

It is important to note that the court will not impose a constructive trust unless it is satisfied that the conscience of the estate owner is affected. If land is simply expressed to be conveyed 'subject to contract' it does not necessarily mean that the purchaser will be bound. It is important that in *Lyus v Prowsa Developments* the purchaser bought the land at a reduced price. It would then be unconscionable for them to refuse the claimant rights in the property.

In 3. above, a resulting trust is dependent on rights that can be identified on the acquisition of the property but a constructive trust can arise after the property has been purchased. If William moves into Xanthe's house and they live together for a year, in which time he decorates the house and renovates the loft, turning it into an extra bedroom, William may get rights even though these rights arise after Xanthe first purchased the property. William must show evidence of an agreement that before he started work on the house he is to have an interest in the property. If they have a row and Xanthe decides to sell the house it would be unconscionable for her to deny his rights in the house.

The courts are reluctant to uphold rights in these circumstances unless there is very clear evidence of an agreement and also some detriment suffered by the party who attempts to enforce it.

So in *Bernard v Josephs* Griffiths LJ held that the mere fact that one party 'has spent time and money on improving the property' would not normally be sufficient ground to justify an inference of a constructive trust.

# 5.5.3 Elements in a constructive trust

A constructive trust depends on proof of THREE elements:

**1.** the common intention or a bargain between the parties

**2.** a change of position by the claimant or the fact that he can show that he relied on the bargain and suffered to his detriment

**3.** the fact that the legal owner has denied the rights of the claimant.

## 1. The common intention

A constructive trust of land depends on proof that both parties were to have an interest in the land.

> 'For present purposes every constructive trust derives from some bargain which affects the conscience of the party who is eventually made liable as constructive trustee'.

> Gray and Gray, *Elements of Land Law* (3rd edn, Butterworths, 2001), p 713

There are two alternatives:

**a  evidence of an agreement** between the parties that they are both to have a share in the property. This must be supported by evidence that the claimant relied on this and acted to his detriment

**b  no evidence of an agreement** between the legal owner and the claimant to share the equitable interest. Only direct contributions to the purchase price will be enough to infer a constructive trust in these circumstances.

## (a) Evidence of an agreement or arrangement

The party seeking to establish rights in the land has to point to some agreement made between the parties prior to the purchase of the property. This was identified in *Lloyds Bank v Rosset* [1991] 1 AC 107 by Lord Bridge. He said that there must be proof of an 'agreement, arrangement or understanding reached between them that the property is to be shared beneficially'. He went on to accept that such an arrangement might be imperfectly remembered and the discussion itself may be imperfect in terms. The problem in this area is that people in a relationship rarely have detailed discussions about property rights. It is only the very cynical or perhaps two lawyers who would sit and discuss such things at the start of a relationship.

> **J** 'Spouses living in amity do not normally think it necessary to formulate or define their respective interests in property in any precise way. The expectation of parties to every happy marriage is that they will share the practical benefits of occupying the matrimonial home whoever owns it. But this is something quite distinct from sharing the beneficial interest in the property asset which the matrimonial home represents'.
>
> Lord Bridge in *Lloyds Bank v Rosset*

# CASE EXAMPLE

### *Lloyds Bank v Rosset* [1991] 1 AC 107

This case concerned a couple who purchased a house in a state of disrepair, in Mr Rosset's sole name, with funds wholly supplied by Mr Rosset through a mortgage with the bank. The house was uninhabitable, so Mrs Rosset took over the job of supervising the building work and carrying out much of the decorating herself. She had considerable expertise in this area and had undertaken such work professionally. The marriage broke down and Mr Rosset defaulted on repayments to the bank who sought possession of the property. The wife claimed that she had a beneficial interest in the house based on a constructive trust. Her claim was unsuccessful.

Lord Bridge was reluctant to find in Mrs Rosset's favour because he felt that the kind of work that she carried out was work that any wife would carry out in similar circumstances: 'It would seem the most natural thing in the world for any wife, in the absence of her husband abroad, to spend all the time she could spare and to employ any skills she might have, such as the ability to decorate a room, in doing all she could to accelerate progress of the work quite irrespective of any expectation she might have of enjoying a beneficial interest in the property'.

It is possible that there is a genuine discussion when property is purchased, particularly where it is in one name only.

The courts have sometimes found the necessary **common intention** to infer a constructive trust.

Two cases were cited by Lord Bridge in *Lloyds Bank v Rosset*: *Eves v Eves* [1975] 1 WLR 1338 and *Grant v Edwards* [1986] Ch 638. In both these cases the courts were able to point to discussion of interest which led them to find a common intention that the beneficial interest was to be shared between the parties.

### Eves v Eves [1975] 1 WLR 1338

A couple lived together in property vested in the man's name. The woman made no
financial contribution but there was evidence that she had contributed towards the
renovation of the property. The fact that distinguishes this case from *Rosset* is that the
parties had discussed the possibility of the woman getting a share in the property, and
the man had told her that she was too young to have a legal estate in property, which was
incorrect but it was sufficient to show that she was intended to have some rights.

### Grant v Edwards [1986] Ch 638

The facts here were similar to those of *Eves v Eves* because in this case there was a
discussion between the parties about the woman getting a beneficial interest in the
property. Since she was in the middle of divorce proceedings and her new partner
thought it would have an effect on the amount that she would be entitled to, he decided
not to enter her name on the Register. Nourse LJ held that she would be entitled to a
share since there was a clear inference from the conversation about why the woman's
name was not on the title that she was to get an interest in the property.

## (b) Implied common intention inferred from the conduct of the parties

Where there is no evidence of an express common intention, the court then needs to establish that
the claimant has made direct contributions towards the purchase price. These contributions could
either be to the initial purchase price or to the payment of mortgage instalments.

Here, the parties can bring evidence to court that they had discussed the ownership of the property,
however informal these discussions might be. The courts look at the overall circumstances of the
case.

In *Lloyds Bank v Rosset* Lord Bridge said that he doubted 'anything falling short of direct
contributions would suffice'. These direct contributions could either be towards the purchase itself
or towards the mortgage instalments. In these cases indirect contributions will never be sufficient.

This is very similar to a resulting trust since the contributions arise at the initial purchase. The real
difference lies in the role of intention. In a resulting trust intention is only relevant to rebut the
existence of the trust but in a constructive trust intention is the significant indicator of the fact that
a trust has arisen.

## KEY FACTS

### Finding a constructive trust

**1.** There must be evidence of an agreement from conversations between the parties in the past that the claimant is to have a share in the property.

**2.** This must be supported by evidence of detrimental reliance.

**3.** If there is no evidence of an express common intention then a common intention can be implied by the courts but the evidence needed in support must be contributions in money towards the purchase. Anything less will not be sufficient to infer a constructive trust.

## 2. Detrimental reliance

According to Lord Bridge in *Lloyds Bank v Rosset*, it is not merely enough to show that there has been a common agreement but there must also be evidence that this has been relied on.
It is necessary to show that you have altered your position in reliance on the agreement made.

## APPLYING THE LAW

Flora is promised by Sandy that she will get a share in the three-bedroomed house owned by him. She gives up her rent-protected tenancy to move in with him. She then starts to renovate the property and pays towards the mortgage instalments. These can all be taken together to infer rights under a constructive trust.

Some behaviour stops short of coming within the definition of 'detrimental behaviour' as there has not been sufficient sacrifice or detriment in the real sense.

If the claimant has simply relied on behaviour that has given him a benefit either because it is something he likes to do anyway or because he has saved money or he has been compensated in some other way then this will not support a claim for a constructive trust.

## **C**ASE EXAMPLE

### *Hannaford v Selby* (1976) 239 EG 811

The claimant cultivated vegetables in his son-in-law's garden but this could not be relied on as 'detriment' in any relevant sense, since he was regarded as merely indulging his 'one absorbing hobby'.

## **C**ASE EXAMPLE

### *Layton v Martin* [1986] 2 FLR 227

The claimant had provided housekeeping and other services. These were then relied on as acting to her detriment but the court held that she had already been compensated at least in part by the award of a regular salary.

## **C**ASE EXAMPLE

### *Wayling v Jones* (1993) 69 P & CR 170

The claimant gave evidence that he would have acted in the same way even if he had not been promised a share in the property. This put the court in a difficult position because it had to decide whether the issue should be considered objectively or subjectively. If it was a subjective test then the claimant must fail even though the court thought it was the type of behaviour that was capable of giving rights in the property. In the event, the court found that there had been detriment.

'During the course of such relationships, the parties will inevitably change their positions in all sorts of ways and for all sorts of reasons. Allegations of detrimental reliance require judges to decide which of these changes of position would be factually disadvantageous to a claimant, should an assurance of ownership subsequently be denied, and to decide which of them were motivated by beliefs arising from that assurance. Not surprisingly, the results arrived at in the reported cases appear to be arbitrary and unrealistic'.

A Lawson, 'The Things We Do for Love: Detrimental Reliance in the Family Home' (1996) 16 Legal Studies 218

Detrimental reliance can take many forms:

**1.** Clearly, financial contributions will qualify but, as already noted, if made at the time the property was purchased then this will give rise to a resulting trust.

**2.** Improvement of the trust property will qualify. In *Eves v Eves* the woman undertook extensive work which even involved wielding a sledge hammer weighing 14 lbs, demolishing a shed and preparing the garden for the laying of turf.

**3.** 'In my judgement it must be conduct on which the woman could not reasonably have been expected to embark unless she was to have an interest in the house' (Nourse LJ in *Grant v Edwards*).

## Conclusions on detrimental reliance

> 'Some of the arbitrariness caused by the operation of the detrimental reliance requirement, in this context, would be avoided if the approach advocated by Browne-Wilkinson VC in *Grant v Edwards* [1986] were adopted. He believed that acts which could easily be attributed to love and affection, such as setting up house together or having a baby, should be regarded as capable of amounting to detrimental reliance requirement. What is needed is an entirely new method for the determination of the property rights of unmarried couples. It should, perhaps, also be used to determine such rights as between people standing in other relationships to one another, e.g. parents and children, who disagree about the ownership of a home they used to share'.
>
> A Lawson, 'The Things we do for Love: Detrimental Reliance in the
> Family Home' (1996) 16 Legal Studies 218

## ACTIVITY

Assuming there is evidence of express common intention, could any of the following be considered to be detrimental reliance?

**1.** Sally moves in with John and decorates all the bedrooms in her spare time.

**2.** Sally moves in with Carl and later in the year gives birth to twins and stays at home to care for them and uses her savings to buy them clothes and curtains for their new bedroom.

**3.** Sally moves in with Sam and contributes £3,000 towards the purchase price of the property.

**4.** Sally moves in with Paul and pays all the household bills. This allows Paul to pay the mortgage.

**5.** Sally moves in with Alex and pays for a new kitchen and conservatory to be built on to the existing house.

## 3. The legal owner denied rights of the claimant

Finally, a constructive trust cannot be imposed unless there is evidence that the conscience of the legal owner is affected. In Lord Diplock's words in *Gissing v Gissing*: 'a constructive trust will arise only where an owner has so conducted himself that it would be inequitable to allow him to deny to the claimant a beneficial interest in the land'.

## 5.5.4 Quantification of the shares in a constructive trust

### Comparison with a resulting trust

> 'The distinction between constructive trusts and resulting trusts remains crucial when determining beneficial interests. Peter Gibson LJ referred the court back to the judgment of the House of Lords in *Lloyds Bank v Rosset* [1991] 1 AC 107 in which Lord Bridge restated the requirements for establishing a constructive trust: a common intention as to beneficial ownership plus an act of detriment on the part of the claimant in reliance on that common intention as to beneficial intention, such as a financial contribution. Where the courts cannot detect a common intention, a resulting trust may be inferred from financial contribution towards the acquisition of the property, but the resulting trust will only apply where there is no finding of a common intention'.
>
> A Dunn, 'Whipping Up Resulting Trusts and Constructive Trusts' [1997] Conv 467

The shares in a resulting trust are assessed according to the contributions made to the initial purchase price. The courts do not have a discretion to decide how to apportion the shares. In a constructive trust the courts try to assess contributions according to the intentions of the parties.

## APPLYING THE LAW

Alison and Kit decide to set up home together. They find a small cottage in the Yorkshire Dales valued at £120,000 and they both contribute towards the purchase, with Alison contributing £20,000. The house is registered in Kit's name. Over a romantic dinner one evening Kit says to Alison 'Everything we own, we share equally' and she agrees. Her share will therefore be 50 per cent even though this will be well in excess of the actual amount that she has contributed

This means that there will only be a half-share split if there is evidence of the common intention of the parties leading to the assumption that they intended the property to be divided into half shares.

The following cases look closely at the way the courts quantify the shares where the property is held on constructive trust.

## CASE EXAMPLE

### *Midland Bank v Cooke* [1995] 4 All ER 562

This case has already been discussed in connection with resulting trusts. The contribution of the wife was a mere 6.74 per cent which came from a wedding present of the husband's parents towards the deposit on the property which became their matrimonial home. It was assumed that this was a case of resulting trust but the judgment of Waite LJ shows that he based his calculations on the parties' common intention about the share so he attributed to the parties 'an intention to share beneficial ownership equally, explicitly because such a conclusion was mirrored in the past pattern of their shared endeavour, their family life and their mutual commitment'.

The courts also considered quantification in *Drake v Whipp* [1996] 1 FLR 826 and the Court of Appeal found that where there was evidence of the parties' common intention as to the shares of each party then this would be the basis of apportionment of the shares; but where the parties had no clear intention then the courts were free to take a broad approach to quantification of the shares. So matters such as conduct would become relevant. The courts were then free to look at direct and non-direct financial contributions and also indirect contributions such as housework. These matters would not be relevant in looking at whether there was a constructive trust at all.

## CASE EXAMPLE

### *Drake v Whipp* [1996] 1 FLR 826

The claimant had contributed 40 per cent of the total purchase price and had made a small financial contribution of £13,000 towards the cost of conversion of a barn but she had made an additional contribution of about £30,000 in labour on the actual conversion. The court found that there was unchallenged evidence of a common understanding between the parties that they would share the property beneficially; the only question then was: in what shares would they own the property? The courts held in this case that the woman was entitled to a one-third share of the property.

The court can rarely depart from the agreement once it has found that such an agreement exists.

# CASE EXAMPLE

### *Mortgage Corporation Ltd v Shaire* [2000] 1 **FLR** 973

Neuberger J said that such a departure can be made 'only if there is very good reason for doing so'. Such a reason might be either 'subsequent renegotiation' or 'subsequent conduct' which is inconsistent with what was agreed so as to point to some variation or cancellation of that agreement.

## KEY FACTS

### Quantification in constructive trusts

1. If there is evidence of common intention then the shares will be in accordance with that agreement.

2. The court will quantify the shares according to the agreement unless there are exceptional reasons for departing from it.

3. If there is no agreement about exact shares but evidence of a common intention to share then the courts can look at many different factors.

4. The courts can apportion the property according to these other factors rather than according to the size of the actual contribution.

## ACTIVITY

Consider the following facts:

Lizzie, a law student, and John, an estate agent, decide to get married. John's parents say they will help them towards the cost of buying a home. They give them a cheque for £13,500. Lizzie and John find the perfect house, which costs £130,000, and they move in. After 18 months the marriage breaks down and they split up and Lizzie claims a share in the property.

How much can she claim?

# Further reading

Battersby, G, 'How not to judge the quantum (and Priority) of a share in the family home' (1996) 8 CFLQ 261.

Dunn, A, 'Whipping up Resulting Trusts and Constructive Trusts' [1997] Conv 467.

Ferguson, P, 'Constructive trusts – a Note of Caution' (1993) 109 LQR 114.

Hayton, D J, 'Equitable Rights of Cohabitees' [1990] Conv 370.

Lawson, A, 'The Things We Do for Love: Detrimental Reliance in the Family Home' (1996) 16 Legal Studies 218.

O'Hagan, P, 'Quantifying Interests under Resulting Trusts' (1997) 60 MLR 420.

Wragg, D, 'Constructive Trusts and the Unmarried Couple' [1996] Fam Law 298.

# chapter 6

# LICENCES ■

## 6.1 The nature of a licence

### Definition

A licence is simply permission given by the owner of land to a person to do something or to go on the land which would otherwise be a trespass, for example permission given to a neighbour's child to recover a football from your garden; the right of a hotel guest to occupy a room; and the right to enter a cinema to watch a film. There is no doubt that the ownership of the land remains with the owner but it is subject to the licensee's rights which, once granted, cannot be denied. However, it does not grant any rights in the land itself. The landowner can later withdraw that licence.

'A dispensation or licence properly passeth no interest, nor alters or transfers property in any thing but only makes an action lawful, which without it had been unlawful'.

*Thomas v Sorrell* (1673) Vaug H 330

No formalities are required for the creation of a licence. This contrasts with the creation of express rights in land which must be evidenced in writing. So a licence can arise from a written document as well as from the spoken word. It can even arise by implication.

Sometimes a licence is coupled with an interest, in which case the grant of the interest must comply with any formalities necessary for the interest, for example a right to enter someone's land to hunt deer is called a profit à prendre and this type of right can only arise if it has been created by deed.

There are a number of issues to consider in relation to licences:

1. **Is the right claimed a licence or a lease?** This is an important issue because the tenant has a number of significant rights that are often denied to a licensee, for example rights to force the landlord to carry out repairs to the property.
2. **Can the licence bind a third-party purchaser?** Another way of looking at this would be to ask: is a licence a proprietary interest in land? The straightforward answer to that question is 'no' but licences may be binding if they are coupled with other rights.
3. **What rights can a licensee claim against the licensor?** This depends on what type of licence has been granted.

## 6.2 Types of licence

There are four main types of licences :

**1.** bare licences

**2.** licences coupled with an interest

**3.** contractual licences

**4.** estoppel licences.

## 6.2.1 Bare licences

The bare licence is the simplest type of licence. It is permission given to the licensee to enter land belonging to the licensor without the payment of consideration. Any lawful visitor to your house comes with a bare licence.

Permission may be **expressly** given, for example to a guest to a party, or it may be **impliedly** given, for example to the postman delivering mail every day or the right under statute given to a police officer to enter premises under warrant. While the visitor remains within the terms of the invitation, he is a lawful visitor. If he goes beyond the invitation then he becomes a trespasser. For example, if the postman decides to sunbathe in your garden after a tiring morning delivering post, he becomes a trespasser because he has gone beyond the terms of his implied licence.

'When you invite a person into your house you do not invite him to slide down the banisters'.

Scrutton LJ *The Calgarth* [1927] P 93 at 110

CASE EXAMPLE

### *Robson v Hallet* [1967] 2 QB 939

A police sergeant was told to leave by the owner of a house whose son had called the police. The court held that he would not become a trespasser until he had been given time to leave the property which in this case involved going out of the front door, down the steps and through the gate.

# 6.2.2 Licences coupled with an interest

This is a licence that is granted along with the grant of an interest. For example, if you grant someone the right to hunt deer on your land or cut down trees, they must also have the right to go on the land because without such access they will not be able to exercise the right. The interest is called a profit à prendre and can exist as a proprietary right in land if it is created correctly.

CASE EXAMPLE

**_Hurst v Picture Theatres Ltd_ [1915] 1 KB 1**

Hurst was watching a film in a cinema, having bought a ticket. The defendant evicted him for breach of contract because he mistakenly thought that he had entered without paying, and requested him to leave. The claimant then bought an action for assault and false imprisonment. His action was based on his having a lawful right to be there and he based this on his ticket which was accepted by the Court of Appeal who held that he had a licence coupled with an interest:

'the right to go upon the premises, was only something granted him, namely the right to see. He could not see the performance unless he went into the building. His right to go into the building was something given to him in order to enable him to have the benefit of that which had been granted to him namely the right to hear the opera, or see the theatrical performance, or see the moving pictures as was the case here'.

Buckley LJ

Types of interest which can be coupled with the licence:

**1.** the right to see a film at the cinema (_Hurst v Picture Theatres Ltd_)

**2.** the right to attend a creditors' meeting (_Vaughan v Hampson_ [1875] 33 LT 15)

**3.** the right to take away game or timber (_James Jones & Sons Ltd v Earl of Tankerville_ [1909] 2 Ch 440).

CASE EXAMPLE

**_Vaughan v Hampson_ [1875] 33 LT 15**

In this case a solicitor successfully claimed that he had a right to be on premises when he attended a general meeting acting for a creditor which had been held by the debtor. He had been forcibly ejected and the Court of Appeal found this to be an assault because he had a right to be on the premises, coupled with his interest in attending the meeting.

# CASE EXAMPLE

**Hounslow LBC v Twickenham Garden Developments Ltd [1971] Ch 233**

This case considered whether the right of a contractor to do works on land constituted an interest.

> 'If for this purpose "interest" is not confined to an interest in land or in chattels on the land, what does it extend to? If a right to attend a creditors' meeting or to see a cinema performance suffices to constitute an interest, can it be said that the right and duty to do works on land falls short of being an interest? I cannot see why it should. Yet if this be so, it is not so easy to see any fair stopping place in what amounts to an interest, short of any legitimate reason for being on the land'.

Megarry J

The important thing to remember is that this type of licence cannot be revoked until the interest itself has come to an end.

'A licence coupled with an interest is irrevocable so long as the term of the grant of the ancillary interest continues'.

Slade LJ in *Patel v Patel* (1983) unreported, AC

This could affect a third party purchasing land because, as the interest can be in the form of a profit à prendre the purchaser may buy subject to that right and the third party would be bound to allow them to come on to the land to exercise their rights.

## 6.2.3 Contractual licences

A contractual licence is a licence granted in exchange for valuable consideration.

Types of contractual licence:

**1.** a ticket for the theatre or cinema

**2.** the right to park your car in a multi-storey car park

**3.** the right of members to play golf at their golf club

**4.** the right of a lodger to live on the land owned by the licensor.

## The 'contractual terms'

The rules concerning contractual licences lie in the rules of contract as well as the rules of land law. There must be an intention to create legal relations. In informal arrangements between families this may cause difficulties as parties to a relationship do not 'enter into legal relations'. In some cases the courts will imply a contract and its terms.

ASE EXAMPLE

**Tanner v Tanner [1975] 1 WLR 1347**

A married man entered into a relationship with another woman and the woman had twins. The woman left a rent-controlled flat and they went to live together in a house purchased in the name of the man. In fact, he never lived there and after three years he asked her to leave so that he could sell the house. The Court of Appeal found that she had an implied contract and held that she had an irrevocable contractual licence to occupy the house.

So, the terms can be agreed either expressly or impliedly. Some terms will be implied by the courts in the same way that the courts will imply a term into the agreement, for example a right to quiet enjoyment for licensees of residential premises.

If the terms are broken then a right to sue will arise. If the terms provide for the termination of the licence upon notice then the notice must be reasonable. This will vary according to the circumstances of the case.

ASE EXAMPLE

**Winter Garden Theatre (London) Ltd v Millennium Products Ltd [1948] AC 173**

In this case the licensee had a right to produce plays in the licensor's theatre for six months, with options to renew. The licensee exercised his right to renew several times until eventually the defendant revoked the licence. The House of Lords held that the contract was revocable but that reasonable notice of revocation of the licence would have to be given and in these circumstances that would be one month.

At one time the contractual licence was revocable at will by the licensor, even while the contract was in force.

CASE EXAMPLE

> **Wood v Leadbitter** (1845) 13 M & W 838
>
> The licensee sued the defendant who had evicted him from Doncaster racecourse. He had bought a ticket to enter and the defendant used reasonable force to evict him. The court held that the licence could be revoked at will and the defendant was entitled to use reasonable force to eject the licensee. The licensee was not protected under his contractual licence from being evicted at will by the licensor.

In more recent cases such as *Hurst v Picture Theatres* it was accepted that it would be a breach of contract to revoke the contract before it had been fulfilled. It was also accepted in *Hounslow LBC v Twickenham Garden Developments* that the right to carry out building works gave the contractors a contractual right. When they had got behind with their schedule then it was held that they could not be sued for trespass when they remained on the land, having been given a notice to quit by the claimants. These cases suggest that a contract cannot be revocable at will.

**Rule:** If a licence has been given for a **particular purpose** there is no right to revoke it while the purpose exists and the licensee remains within the terms of the licence. This only applies to the contracting parties and it would not bind successive owners because the contractual licence does not grant proprietary rights. A licensee of residential premises has no rights under the contractual licence that would be binding on a third-party purchaser.

## 6.2.4 Estoppel licences

A licence by estoppel is a licence that arises under the doctrine of proprietary estoppel.

Estoppel is based on the principle that if a person acts to his detriment in reliance on the belief or promise that they will get rights in land owned by another, the court will uphold their claim.

Under *Taylor Fashions Ltd v Liverpool Victoria Trustees Co Ltd* [1982] QB 133 there are **three** elements in estoppel:

**1.** a **promise** is made

**2.** the claimant **relies** on that promise

**3.** the claimant acts to his **detriment**.

These rules will be considered in detail in Chapter 7.

Under 1. the claimant must prove that a promise or assurance of rights in the land has been made to him. If the claimant is successful in claiming estoppel then the court has a wide discretion in granting rights to the claimant. The right granted will vary according to the circumstances of each case. In some cases the court grants a licence which may be combined with some other right which will make it binding on a third party.

## ASE EXAMPLE

**In Re Sharpe [1980] 1 WLR 219**

An aunt lent her nephew £12,000 in order to buy a house. The aunt was promised a right to remain in the house for the rest of her life. The nephew went bankrupt and his trustee in bankruptcy ordered the aunt to leave. The court found that she had a right to remain in the house, based on an estoppel, and she was granted a licence that was irrevocable during her lifetime.

## CASE EXAMPLE

**Greasley v Cooke [1980] 1 WLR 1306**

In this case Cooke was employed as a maid in Greasley's house. Greasley's son, Kenneth, and Cooke formed a relationship. Greasley died and Cooke continued to perform household duties in the house, including caring for a mentally ill sister of Kenneth, but for no payment although she continued to live in the property and was assured by Kenneth and his brother that she could live in the property rent-free for as long as she liked. The Court of Appeal held that she had a right to live in the property rent-free, based on an estoppel licence.

## ACTIVITY

Consider the following and decide whether a licence is created in each case. If you decide that there is a licence, what type of licence is it?:

1. You are asleep at home. You are awoken in the night by a policeman who shows you a warrant to enter your premises and to look for stolen goods.

2. You visit the Barbican Theatre in London to see *As You Like It*. At the interval you go to the bar to have a drink. Accidentally, you lose your ticket and find someone sitting in you seat. When you challenge the manager, he asks you to leave believing you have not paid to enter.

**3.** You park your car in a multi-storey car park, paying for a monthly season ticket.

**4.** For 10 years you have tended the garden of your employer, an elderly man aged 91, who has promised you the right to go on living in the flat above the garage for the rest of your life. On his death, his son asks you to leave.

**5.** Every year for five years you collect a Christmas tree from the wood owned by your neighbours. This year they challenged you as you went onto their land but you prove that you have always had the right to take the Christmas tree from their land.

# 6.3 The creation of licences

## 6.3.1 Bare licences

A bare licence may be expressly granted and need not adhere to any formalities. It can be impliedly granted, for example to people delivering goods to the premises.

## 6.3.2 Licences coupled with an interest

This type of licence is dependant on the type of interest granted and so if the interest requires any formalities then these must be complied with in order for the licence to be valid. A profit à prendre can be created either by deed or through prescription. Prescription arises from long use of the right.

## APPLYING THE LAW

□□□

A profit à prendre must be created by a deed. If you are granted the right to cut down timber in a neighbouring wood owned by the defendant then that must be granted by deed. If there was no deed then the grant would be invalid and if you tried to enter the wood to cut down timber you would be a trespasser. If you merely had the right to take away felled timber then that would not require a deed and entry to take away the timber would not be a trespass.

□□□

## 6.3.3 Contractual licences

A contractual licence depends on whether there is a valid contract. The terms of the licence are governed by the terms of the contract. Formalities will be governed by the type of contract.

## APPLYING THE LAW

The ticket allowing you to attend a theatre production also allows you to enter the theatre. Once the production is over, you are allowed a reasonable time to leave but after a reasonable time has passed then you become a trespasser.

### Contrast between a contractual licence and a tenancy

The contrast between a right to occupy land under a licence and a right to occupy land under a tenancy highlights the effect of a contractual tenancy. The contractual licence does not confer an interest in land so it does not have to follow the usual formalities, ie evidence in writing in accordance with s 2 of the Law of Property (Miscellaneous Provisions) Act 1989 when conveying an interest in land. The rights of the licensee will depend on the express terms of the contract. However, some terms may be implied into the contract, in particular where the land let is as residential premises.

> **Smith v Nottinghamshire CC, The Times, 13th November 1981**
>
> The Court of Appeal upheld the claim of a number of students who claimed that their right to quiet enjoyment had been challenged when workmen carrying out repairs in the halls of residence made excess noise. This was upheld even though they were only contractual licensees of the premises. The students had entered into an agreement with the university as licensors that they should be able to work in their rooms without undue disturbance.

## 6.3.4 Estoppel licences

The creation of an estoppel licence only arises where the court believes that it would be unconscionable for the owner to deny an interest and this depends on the proof of the three elements of estoppel, namely: the assurance; reliance on that assurance; and proof of acting to your detriment.

## 6.4 The effect of licences on third parties

### 6.4.1 Bare licences

A bare licence is purely personal to the licensee and will not be binding on a purchaser from the licensor, even where he has notice of the licence.

## 6.4.2 Licences coupled with an interest

Where a licence is coupled with an interest it will be binding on a third-party purchaser of land but only where he buys the land subject to that proprietary interest.

---

# APPLYING THE LAW    ☐☐☐

If Alex buys a house which has a wood adjoining it and he is aware that his neighbour James has the right to shoot in the wood and take away any game, Alex cannot deny James the right to come onto his land when he moves into the property.

☐☐☐

---

## 6.4.3 Contractual licences

Licences have always been regarded as purely personal rights and so will only be binding on the licensor. The licensee may be liable to claim damages, if the licence is denied to the licensee. The effect of this was that a third-party purchaser would not be bound by a licence when they bought land, even where they had notice of the rights of the licensee.

# CASE EXAMPLE

### *King v David Allen & Sons Billposting Ltd* **[1916] 2 AC 54**

In this case the defendant had contracted to give the claimant the right to put up posters on some of the walls in a cinema owned by the defendant. The licence was to last for four years. Before the contract had expired, the cinema was sold. It was held that the purchasers took free of the rights of the claimant, who could only sue for breach of contract.

For a while this position was reversed, so that it was possible to claim that the licence **did** create an interest in land.

Lord Denning found in *Errington v Errington & Woods* [1952] 1 KB 290 that contractual licences could be binding on successors in title. In that case a daughter-in-law had been allowed to remain in property which her mother-in-law had inherited from her father-in-law. The mother-in-law had sought to evict the daughter-in-law but the court held that her rights were good against the whole world, with the exception of the *bona fide* purchaser for value without notice of her rights.

Lord Denning continued to champion the rights of the licensee in further cases.

**C**ASE EXAMPLE ──────────────────────────

### *Binions v Evans* [1972] Ch 359

A widow had been given the right to remain in a cottage that her husband had been granted rent-free as part of his job. She had entered an agreement that 'if she kept the cottage in good repair and managed the garden then she could enjoy the property as tenant at will'. The property was subsequently sold to the claimants who bought at a reduced price because they were aware of the rights of the widow. They gave her notice to quit after the purchase. The Court of Appeal upheld her rights to remain in the property although Lord Denning was the only judge who based his decision on a contractual licence.

> 'In my opinion, the defendant, by virtue of the agreement, had an equitable interest in the cottage which the court would protect by granting an injunction against the landlords restraining them from turning her out. When the landlords sold the cottage to a purchaser "subject to" her rights under the agreement, the purchaser took the cottage on a constructive trust to permit the defendant to reside there during her life, or as long as she might desire. The courts will not allow the purchaser to go back on that trust'.

> Lord Denning MR

This approach to contractual licences has been strongly criticised in subsequent cases.

**C**ASE EXAMPLE ──────────────────────────

### *Ashburn Anstalt v Arnold* [1989] Ch 1

The claimants based their claim against third-party purchasers on a contractual licence. Fox LJ categorically denied that a contractual licence can bind purchasers, even where they have notice of the rights, and rejected the law as laid down in *Errington v Errington & Woods*:

> 'A licence in connection with land while entitling the licensee to use the land for the purposes authorised by the licence does not create an estate in the land . . . Before the *Errington* case the law appears to have been well understood. It rested on an important and intelligible distinction between contractual obligations which gave rise to no estate or interest in the land and proprietary rights which by definition, did. The far-reaching statement of principle in *Errington* was not

> supported by authority, not necessary for the decision of the case and *per incuriam* in the sense that it was made without reference to authorities which, if they would not have compelled, would surely have persuaded the court to adopt a different ratio as a response to the problems which had arisen, the *Errington* rule . . . was neither practically necessary nor theoretically convincing'.

The law today will not recognise a contractual licence as a binding interest in land unless it is accompanied by a constructive trust. This will be found by the court where they believe that the conscience of the successor in title is affected so that it would be inequitable to allow him to deny the claimant's interest in the property.

## When will the court find a constructive trust?

In *Binions v Evans* the purchasers bought 'subject to' the widow's rights. This would not have been enough to establish a constructive trust. The **key factor** was that they bought at a reduced price, taking into account the fact that she was in occupation of the premises.

In *Lyus v Prowsa Developments Ltd* [1982] 1 WLR 1044 a development company took over an uncompleted development from a company in liquidation. It purchased expressly subject to the rights of the contractual licensees. This was included as a clause in the contract of sale and the court held that the development company held the property as constructive trustees for the licensees and could not seek to deny their rights after the purchase.

---

### KEY FACTS

**Contractual licences**

1. Contractual licences depend on contractual principles.
2. The licensor will only be bound if a contract can be proved with all the essential features of a contract, for example consideration and an intention to create legal relations.
3. Contractual licences do not give rise to proprietary rights in land even when a third-party purchaser buys with notice and 'subject to' those rights.
4. If the purchaser holds as a constructive trustee then a contractual licence may give rise to a proprietary right in land.
5. A constructive trust is dependent on proof that it would be unconscionable for the owner of the land to deny the rights of the claimant. The fact that the purchaser bought at a reduced price may be sufficient to give rise to a constructive trust in favour of the licensee.

---

## 6.4.4 Estoppel licences

Originally, licences by estoppel developed as rights enforceable only against the licensor and were not therefore capable of binding a successor in title. However, there are several cases which have held that such a right will be binding on the land itself.

This would mean that someone purchasing the land would be bound by the licensee's rights and could not attempt to deny them.

> ## APPLYING THE LAW ☐ ☐ ☐
>
> John purchases Richmond House. He knows that Shirley and Kate have a licence to remain in the two-bedroomed cottage adjoining the house for the rest of Shirley's life. John may be bound by their rights if he had paid a reduced price to the seller of the property.
>
> ☐ ☐ ☐

### Registered land

An estoppel licence is capable of registration in registered land. Under s 116 of the Land Registration Act 2002 estoppel licences are registrable and if properly entered on the Register will be binding on third parties. This has resolved any doubt about whether they will be binding on third-party purchasers.

**'s 116 Proprietary estoppel and mere equities**

It is hereby declared for the avoidance of any doubt that, in relation to registered land, each of the following –

(a) an equity by estoppel, and

(b) a mere equity

has the effect from the time the equity arises as an interest capable of binding successors in title (subject to the rules about the effect of dispositions on priority).'

This means that they will be binding from the time when the innocent party acted to his/her detriment in reliance on the promise. The estoppel requires protection on the Register unless the interest takes effect as an overriding interest by virtue of actual occupation of land.

## Unregistered land

An estoppel licence is subject to the doctrine of notice in unregistered land. It cannot be substantially registered under the Land Charges Act 1972. It will depend on whether the purchaser was aware of the rights of the licensee when he/she purchased the property. The right will only be binding if the purchaser has actual or constructive notice of the licence when he purchased the property.

## CASE EXAMPLE

**Inwards v Baker [1965] 2 WLR 212**

The son of Mr Baker had built a bungalow on his father's land with some financial help from his father. He had lived there for nearly 30 years when proceedings were brought against him by the successors in title of his father who were the children of his father by his second wife. Lord Denning upheld the son's rights to remain:

'All that is necessary is that the licensee should, at the request or with the encouragement of the landlord, have spent the money in the expectation of being allowed to stay there. If so, the court will not allow that expectation to be defeated where it would be inequitable so to do'.

## 6.5 The revocation of a licence

### 6.5.1. Bare licences

A licensor can withdraw a bare licence at any time. This can be done at will, without notice.

> J  '. . . the sergeant had a reasonable time to leave the premises by the most appropriate route for doing so, namely, out of the front door, down the steps and out of the gate, and, provided that he did so with reasonable expedition, he would not be a trespasser while he was doing so'.
>
> Diplock LJ in *Robson v Hallett*

The licensee cannot transfer a bare licence to another as it is a purely personal right against the licensor.

A bare licence can be withdrawn at will. The licensor does not have to give any notice or any reason. Once a licence has been revoked, the licensor must give the licensee a reasonable time to pack up and leave the premises.

A bare licence is always automatically revoked in the following circumstances:

**1.** on the death of the licensor

**2.** when land is sold or disposed of in some other way by the licensor. There has never been any issue as to whether or not the licensee has any interest in the land.

The right to withdraw such a licence at will has been recently reviewed by Jonathan Hill:

> 'Since there are many cases (such as those involving occupational licences) in which it is not practically possible for the licensee to vacate the land immediately on being informed that the licence has been revoked, there is no plausible alternative to the law's recognition of a period of grace in cases involving the termination of a bare licence. There is, of course, no hard and fast rule as to how long the packing-up period should be – as what is reasonable depends on the circumstances. In a case in which a door-to-door salesman is asked by the owner-occupier to leave, a reasonable period would, in most cases, be no more than a few seconds. At the other end of the spectrum, on the termination of a bare licence of residential or commercial premises, a reasonable period would normally be sufficient to allow the licensee to find alternative accommodation and may be as much as a year'.

Jonathan Hill is arguing that although it has long been held that the bare licence can be terminated at will, the law will protect the licensee by upholding his right to a period of grace in which he will be allowed time to leave and this will vary according to the type of property. However, Hill is not convinced that this has a basis in law but feels that it has merely arisen as a result of conflicting case law:

> 'Furthermore, there is no argument of principle in support of the proposition that a licensor should be under obligation to give the licensee a period of notice before revocation of a bare licence is to take effect . . . When bare licences are located in the broader picture of rights in relation to land, the notion that a bare licensee is entitled to a period of notice is illogical. The bare licence's closet analogue is not the contractual licensee, but the rent-free tenancy at will. Given that, as regards a tenancy at will, there is no need for a notice to quit, the law would be incoherent if, in relation to a bare licensee the licensor were under an obligation to give the licensee a reasonable period of notice'.

J Hill, 'The Termination of Bare Licences' [2001] CLJ 89

## 6.5.2 Licences coupled with a grant

A licence coupled with a grant cannot be revoked unless the right or interest itself is withdrawn. The reason for this is that the interest may constitute a proprietary right in land itself, which cannot be withdrawn at will.

## 6.5.3 Contractual licences

Historically, contractual licences were capable of being withdrawn at will. The licensee would have a remedy in damages which would be calculated according to ordinary contractual principles but the right to remain on the premises was not protected. So, in *Wood v Leadbitter* it was held that the racegoer who was ejected from the licensor's racecourse could only claim for damages, as the licensor had the right to exclude him at will.

The more modern approach is to uphold the rights of the licensee to remain on the property for the duration of the contract. Today, according to G P Selvam J:

'A contractual licence is irrevocable except as contemplated by the terms of the contract'.

*Tan Hin Leong v Lee Teck Im* [2000] 3 SLR 85.

If the licensee is deprived of his right to live on the property then the court has a choice of whether or not to grant contractual damages or to grant specific performance of the contract. The change in attitude was championed by Lord Denning and one of the first cases to reflect this was *Errington v Errington & Woods* (1952):

# CASE EXAMPLE

### *Errington v Errington & Woods* [1952] 1 KB 290

This concerned the right of a daughter-in-law to live in property bought by her father-in-law. The father-in-law promised his son and his wife that they could have the property transferred to them if they continued to live in the house and paid all the mortgage instalments. The father died and left all his property to his wife, including this house. The son left his wife and returned to live with his mother. His wife continued to pay the mortgage. The widow brought an action to evict her from the house, on the basis that the daughter-in-law had only a revocable licence. The Court of Appeal refused the action and upheld the right of the daughter-in-law to continue to live in the house, on the undertaking that she would continue to repay the mortgage instalments.

These rights were not rights in law but were rights in equity. The right was 'a contractual right, or at any rate, an equitable right to remain so long as they paid the instalments, which would grow into a good equitable title to the house as soon as the mortgage was paid'.

The decision has been criticised in later cases, in particular *Ashburn Anstalt v Arnold*. A contractual licence can only be binding on third parties if there is evidence of a constructive trust. As mentioned above, the contractual licence in *Binions v Evans* was not binding on the third-party purchasers even though they bought knowing of its existence but the widow's rights were binding because they held as constructive trustees.

A licence is a personal right only and so the licence can be revoked by someone other than the licensor. Such rights do not bind the third-party purchaser.

## 6.5.4 Estoppel licences

Revocation of an estoppel licence will depend on the terms of the licence. The court will usually determine the extent of the rights of the licensee under the estoppel. A licence will not be revocable if the licence is held to be perpetual. If the court holds that a licence can be determined on the occurrence of certain events then that is the only condition by which the licence can be revoked.

## APPLYING THE LAW

Gerald builds a cottage on his grandfather's land and lives there for 10 years. On the death of his grandfather his uncle takes over the land including his cottage. If the court holds that the nephew has an estoppel licence to last as long as he wants to live there, then these rights will be binding on the uncle. If the nephew decides to move, then his licence to remain in the cottage will cease.

# 6.6 Comparison of different types of licence

| | How created | How terminated | Effect on third parties |
|---|---|---|---|
| **Bare licences:** permission to enter someone's land without payment of consideration. | Informally. Can be impliedly created. | Can be withdrawn at will although the licensee usually given time to leave (*Robson v Hallett* (1967)). | Cannot be binding on a third party. |
| **Licences coupled with a grant:** licences granted in order to enjoy an interest on the land. | Dependent on the nature of the interest; if it is a profit à prendre then requires a deed. | Cannot be revoked unless interest is revoked (*Hurst v Picture Theatres Ltd* (1915)). | Will be binding as long as the right to enjoy the interest exists. |

| Contractual licences: licences in exchange for valuable consideration. | Created informally (*Tanner v Tanner* (1975)) unless the contract requires any formalities. | Once could be withdrawn at will (*Wood v Leadbitter* (1845)) but now subject to the terms of the contract. | Third party will not be bound unless there is evidence of a constructive trust (*Binions v Evans* (1972); *Lyus v Prowsa Developments* (1982)). |
| Estoppel licences: licences arising under proprietary estoppel. | Arises informally once the requirements for estoppel are satisfied (*Greasley v Cooke* (1980)). | Depends on the terms of the licence granted by the court. | Can be binding where registered land and the right has been registered. |

# ACTIVITY

Consider the following facts and advise Aunt Martha, Julia and the Runnymede Riders' Society on their rights. Consider on what basis they may claim to be able to continue living in the property.

Felix lived in London but one day he saw the house of his dreams. It was a large property with extensive grounds called Runnymede House. Felix could not afford the property and he saw that one way to raise the money would be to ask his Aunt Martha to help. He offered her a small flat on the ground floor within Runnymede House in return for a financial contribution. She readily agreed and moved in immediately after the purchase had been completed. After moving to Runnymede, Felix met up with an old girlfriend, Felicity, and she moved in to Runnymede House. Felicity loved country life and Felix gave her friend Julia permission to keep four horses in the field next to the house and Julia and Felicity often went riding. They had many friends in the village and the Runnymede Riders' Society asked Felicity and Felix if they could have their monthly meetings at Runnymede House. Felix said he was prepared to let them have use of the library once a month if they brought six bottles of wine and paid the cost of the heating and electricity.

After two years Felicity said she was tired of country life and left Felix, to live in London. Felix decided to sell the property and was offered double the price by Francis although he reduced this when he realised that Aunt Martha was living there.

Francis has moved in and has now given Aunt Martha notice to quit. He has also told Julia that she can no longer keep her horses in the field. The Runnymede Riders' Society arrived last night for their monthly meeting, only to be told by Francis that they would have to find a new venue for their meetings.

# Further reading

Anderson, S, 'Of Licences and Similar Mysteries' (1979) 42 MLR 203.

Battersby, G, 'Informal Transactions in Land, Estoppel and Registration' (1995) 58 MLR 637.

Gray and Gray, 'The Idea of Property in Land' in S Bright and J Dewar (eds) *Land Law: Themes and Perspectives* (Oxford University Press, 1998).

Hill, J, 'The Termination of Bare Licences' [2001] CLJ 89.

Kerbel, T, 'Unreasonable Revocation of a Licence [1996] Conv 63.

Thompson, M P, '"My Home is Not my Castle": *Macclesfield v Parker* [2003] EWHC 1846 [Ch]' [2003] 67 Conv 516.

# PROPRIETARY ESTOPPEL ■

## 7.1 Background to proprietary estoppel

### 7.1.1 Introduction

The transfer of rights in land is subject to a number of strict formalities, in particular the need to have evidence in writing. By way of contrast, the law on proprietary estoppel is a way of establishing informal rights in property. It will generally be considered only where the formalities of transfer of rights in property have been ignored. It often arises in the context of the family home.

**Definition**: a person who has made a representation to another that they have rights in property should not be allowed later to deny those rights where it has been acted upon. The person who relies on the representation must prove that they have acted to their detriment.

There is an overlap with constructive trusts **but** remember

**1.** proprietary estoppel is based on **representations**, whereas

**2.** constructive trusts rely upon **bargains** or **common intention**.

So the importance of this principle in land law is that it allows persons to claim that they have rights where the ordinary formalities associated with the transfer of land have been ignored. However, without formalities to guide us it is particularly important to be clear about when such rights arise.

> J
>
> 'Equity comes in . . . to mitigate the rigours of strict law . . . It will prevent a person insisting on his strict legal rights . . . when it would be inequitable for him to do so having regard to the dealings which have taken place between the parties'.
>
> Denning MR in *Crabb v Arun DC* [1976] 1 Ch 179

# CASE EXAMPLE

**_Crabb v Arun DC_ [1976] 1 Ch 179**

Here, the council had agreed with Crabb that he would have access to some property through the adjacent land owned by it. He intended to sell part of the property which would be inaccessible without this right of way. The council later denied him rights, which resulted in his land becoming landlocked. The court upheld Crabb's claim based on the promise made to him by the council. He had acted on the promise to his detriment by selling the land without reserving rights of access.

The introduction of the Land Registration Act 2002 with its objective of ensuring that as many rights and interests appear on the Register as possible has reinforced the significance of proprietary estoppel as a way of ensuring that informal rights will remain binding on the registered proprietor.

's 116 (a) an equity by estoppel, and
    (b) a mere equity,

has the effect from the time the equity arises as an interest capable of binding successors in title . . .'.

## 7.1.2 Historical background

There are several nineteenth-century cases which show that interests in land could be passed on the basis of **conduct**.

An early example of the operation of the doctrine is:

**C**ASE EXAMPLE

### *Dillwyn v Llewelyn* (1862) 4 De GF & J 517

A son built a house in reliance on an informal memorandum that he would have rights in his father's land. The memorandum did not satisfy the necessary formal requirements but the son's rights were nevertheless upheld, on the basis that he had incurred expenditure in reliance on a promise made to him by his father.

This case was based on the express promise made but estoppel has been held to extend further to include circumstances where there have been dealings between parties which **suggest** that one party has made an assumption and acted on that assumption:

**C**ASE EXAMPLE

### *Ramsden v Dyson* (1866) LR 1 HL 129

A tenant built on his land, believing he would be entitled to a long lease. The House of Lords, by majority, decided he could not claim the lease but the case lays down the following important principle of law: 'if a stranger begins to build on my land supposing it to be his own, and I perceiving his mistake, abstain from setting him right, and leave him to persevere in his error, a court of equity will not allow me afterwards to assert my title to the land on which he had expended money on the supposition that the land was his own' (Lord Cranworth LC).

The formula for the acquisition of such rights was laid down by Fry J in *Willmot v Barber* (1880) 15 Ch D 96. It involved satisfying five requirements, or *probanda*, as they were known.

The *Willmot v Barber probanda*:

**1.** the claimant must have made a mistake about his legal rights

**2.** the claimant must have spent money relying on his mistaken belief

**3.** the defendant must know of his own right which is inconsistent with the right claimed by the claimant

**4.** the defendant must know of the claimant's mistaken belief

**5.** the defendant must have encouraged the claimant when spending money in his mistaken belief, either actively or by abstaining from asserting his legal right.

The leading authority today is *Taylor Fashions Ltd v Liverpool Victoria Trustees Co Ltd* [1982] QB 133.

This case replaced the five *probanda* by three requirements for estoppel to be successful:

- a representation

- reliance on that representation

- detriment.

# ASE EXAMPLE

### *Taylor Fashions Ltd v Liverpool Victoria Trustees Co Ltd* [1982] QB 133

Liverpool Victoria Trustees had purchased land subject to a lease. The tenants had options to renew their leases but had failed to register them, believing that they were not registrable. This rendered them unenforceable. The tenants, however, spent money on the premises, expecting to exercise the options, and no one was aware of the need to register them. They attempted to renew the lease and were challenged by the landlords.

The judge dismissed part of the claim by the tenants because the defendants had not encouraged the tenants to act on the belief that the lease was renewable.

> 'More recent cases indicate . . . that proprietary estoppel . . . requires a very much broader approach which is directed rather at ascertaining whether, in particular individual circumstances, it would be unconscionable for a party to be permitted to deny that which, knowingly, or unknowingly, he has allowed or encouraged another to assume to his detriment than to inquiring whether the circumstances can be fitted within the confines of some preconceived formula serving as a universal yardstick for every form of unconscionable behaviour'.

Oliver J

The distinction here lies in the fact that there does not have to be a mistake about rights and knowledge that the other party has made a mistake about their rights.

However, some recent cases have still relied on the older criteria.

> **Coombes v Smith [1986] 1 WLR 808**
>
> A woman living in a relationship with children claimed the right to be able to continuing living in the property owned by her partner as long as she wished.
>
> 'The second element or requisite is that the plaintiff must have expended money, or otherwise prejudiced himself or acted to his detriment, on the faith of his mistaken belief in his legal rights'.
>
> Deputy Judge Jonathan Parker QC

> **Matharu v Matharu [1994] 2 FLR 597**
>
> A woman's father-in-law tried to recover possession after the breakdown of her marriage and the death of her husband, his son. The daughter-in-law based her claim on her mistaken belief, which was known to her father-in-law, that the house belonged to her husband. She had worked on the house and so acted to her detriment on the basis of this belief. The court upheld her rights on the basis of estoppel, allowing her the right to remain in the property, but it did not grant her any proprietary rights. She was granted a licence to remain in the house 'for her life or such shorter period as she may decide'. This right was granted subject to her agreeing to pay for the outgoings on the property, including the mortgage repayments. The claim was based on establishing all five of the *probanda* under *Willmot v Barber*.

## 7.2 The elements of proprietary estoppel

### 7.2.1 The representation

The claimant must prove that some kind of representation or assurance was made which encouraged him to believe that he would acquire rights over the land.

## Different types of representation

**1.** Representations can be **positive** assurances or

**2. mere silence** leading the claimant to believe that he had rights.

*1. Positive assurances or representations*

The assurance made must be an express promise of positive rights in the land.

## APPLYING THE LAW

Thomas tells his sister Rachael that the field adjoining her house would be a perfect location for a house and he asks her if he can build on her land. She agrees and assures him that the house will be his but the agreement is not recorded in writing as necessary for a transfer of an interest in land. She cannot later try to evict him after the house has been built and rely on the lack of written evidence. He can argue that he has relied on her assurance. The court would uphold his rights on the basis of proprietary estoppel.

The promise made does not have to amount to an enforceable contract. The contract itself could be void.

### *Inwards v Baker* [1965] 2 QB 929

In this case a father encouraged his son to build a bungalow on his land. The son acted on this and built on the land. The son would not be contractually bound to build the bungalow on the father's land. So where the father gave permission and encouragement then this amounted to a representation sufficient to raise estoppel.

If the father had later refused to offer the land before he had started building then the son could not force him to do so. Equally, if the son had gone back on his promise to build on the land he could not be forced to do so.

The representation can be held to be binding on the representor even where it is made within a will.

If a representation is made in a will then it will not necessarily be binding on the representor for the rest of his lifetime. If your grandmother tells you that she is going to leave her house to you in her will, she is not bound to do so. Everyone has the right to change his will any time up until death. However, if you immediately act on your grandmother's promise it may then be held sufficient to raise an estoppel on her death if she has not left her house to you.

### Taylor v Dickens [1998] 3 FCR 455

An old lady had told her gardener that she would leave her estate to him in her will. He relied on this statement and carried on working for her without pay. On her death, she did not leave the property to him. The court did not uphold his claim since she had the right at any time to revoke her will and she had not led him to believe that she would not do so.

J   'Subject to specific statutory exceptions (such as for dependants) the right to decide, and change one's mind as to, the devolution of one's estate is a basic and well understood feature of English law. The law allows one to disappoint the expectations of those who have no more than a moral claim on one's affections, however strong. During the lifetime of the potential testator, that is a risk which anyone seeking to rely on such a representation necessarily faces'.

Carnwath J in *Gillett v Holt* [1998] 3 All ER 917

### Gillett v Holt [1998] 3 All ER 917

Mr Gillett had worked for Mr Holt for over 30 years and had been promised, over a period of years on at least seven occasions, that Mr Holt would leave his farm to him. In the event, they fell out and Mr Holt left his property to someone else whom he had known for a very short period of time. Even though it is open to anyone to change their will up until death, estoppel can always be argued if a representation can be shown and in reponse the claimant has acted to his detriment.

However, it was held in that case that there may be some circumstances where a representation that someone is to inherit property on the death of the representor will be held to be binding.

'In the generality of cases it is no doubt correct [that one should not count one's chickens before they were hatched], and it is notorious that some elderly persons of means derive enjoyment from the possession of a testamentary power, and

> from dropping hints as to their intentions, without any question of an estoppel arising. But in this case Mr Holt's assurances were repeated over a long period, usually before the assembled company on special family occasions, and some of them . . . were completely unambiguous . . . Plainly some of the assurances were to be relied on'.
>
> Robert Walker LJ

The following factors from *Gillett v Holt* (1998) suggest that a representation may be acted on:

- repetition of representations made
- representations made before witnesses
- the nature of the representation was unambiguous.

## Agents

The representation can be made by the agent of the owner of the land where the claim has been made. However, a tenant cannot make a representation on behalf of the landlord.

## Generally worded representations do not raise proprietary estoppel

If a representation is made in very general terms, no estoppel can arise. So if a promise to support someone financially is made then this will not be directly linked to rights in property.

ASE EXAMPLE

**Layton v Martin [1986] 2 FLR 227**

Here, the claimant had been told that she would be provided for by the representor. There was no express reference to rights in land.

The problem with this representation was that it was very general and did not relate directly to the acquisition of rights in the property itself. So it does not matter if the representation is general in terms where the promise is of actual rights in land.

# CASE EXAMPLE

**Pascoe v Turner [1979] 1 WLR 431**

The defendant said to the claimant during their relationship together 'The house is yours and everything in it'. This was a clear representation of rights in the property.

## 2. Mere silence

In *Ramsden v Dyson* (1866) LR 1 HL 129 Lord Cranworth referred to the silence of a landowner in the light of someone building on their land. He suggested that equity would intervene if someone silently allows another to build on his land and does not interfere to prevent that.

## APPLYING THE LAW

Edward and Gerald live next door to each other. Gerald says to Edward: 'You need somewhere to keep your vintage car – it will get very rusty if you leave it outside all winter'. Edward decides to build a shed to house his vintage car and he builds it on some land belonging to Gerald which adjoins his garden. The shed was finished earlier this year and he moved in his vintage car. Gerald has watched it being built and has said nothing about the fact that it is on his land. Gerald has suddenly become less friendly and told Edward last week that he expected him to move the car out as the shed was his property. Has Edward a claim to the shed?

The important point here is that there must be some encouragement from the owner of the property. If the claimant simply moves on to the land and starts to build then the court would never hold that he has rights in the property. This is referred to as a **legitimate expectation of rights** and, even if it is reasonable, the claimant must be encouraged in his belief before the courts will uphold his rights.

The courts are careful not to allow mere silence to be legally significant unless it can be clearly linked to an acceptance or endorsement of rights in property.

## Other jurisdictions

In other jurisdictions the courts have been prepared to grant rights in land in the absence of any representation or assurance. In Australia, the doctrine of unjust enrichment would allow a successful claim based on expenditure incurred where no representation about rights has been made. The Australian courts look at the issue from the point of view of the landowner and see the issue as one of unjust enrichment of the landowner at the expense of the claimant.

# KEY FACTS

### Representations

**1.** A representation can be a positive statement or mere silence.

**2.** There must be some form of encouragement to the claimant that he has acquired rights in the property.

**3.** A representation of future rights under a will can be binding in some circumstances. These will be where the representor shows an intention to be bound.

**4.** A representation can still be binding if it is made by an agent of the owner of the land.

**5.** A tenant cannot make a representation on behalf of his landlord.

# ACTIVITY

Consider the following situations and decide whether they amount to a representation:

1. Mr Wells was getting elderly and when his son Andrew came to visit he told him if he wanted to build a bungalow on the side of the garden where apple trees were growing at present, then he could have the bungalow for himself. Nothing was put into writing. When the bungalow was built, Andrew moved in and lived there for 20 years until Mr Wells died. Mr Wells left no will. Andrew's sisters, to whom he had not spoken for 30 years, contested Andrew's rights over the land.

2. Andrew visited his grandfather and found him to be getting rather infirm. He said he would move in to help him. He spent several weekends decorating the house.

3. Andrew's girlfriend Sue comes to live with him. Andrew tells her she has nothing to worry about as half the house and its contents will be hers from now on. Nothing is put into writing. She carries out repairs amounting to over £3,000 which was about one-quarter of the total capital that she had.

## 7.2.2 Reliance on the representation

The claimant must show that he relied on the representation made to him and changed his position in reliance on that representation. It is going to be more important to establish what constitutes reliance as conveyancing becomes subject to more stringent formalities.

'In the foreseeable future, the scheme of compulsory electronic conveyancing will be introduced. Under s.93 of the Land Registration Act 2002 a disposition will only have effect if made by electronic means and is electronically communicated to the registrar and the relevant registration requirements are met. One does not have to be Mystic Meg to foresee that disputes will arise when parties have failed to comply with these requirements'.

M P Thompson, 'Estoppel: Reliance, Remedy and Priority:
*Campbell v Griffin* [2001] EWCA Civ 990' [2003] 67 Conv 157

Reliance is based on the change of position so there must be a link between the representation made and the change of position.

## APPLYING THE LAW

If an elderly relative promises his niece rights in his house if she will come and live closer to him and the niece acts on this, then this would be evidence of reliance. Contrast the position of the niece who moves closer because her job changes; in this case there is no connection between the promise made and the reliance on that promise or assurance. The niece must show that she genuinely believed that she would gain an interest in the property, if she moved closer.

There is an overlap between reliance and acting to your detriment. Many of the factors that are relevant under this heading will be relevant under the next heading but it is important that the claimant can show that he acted the way he did because he relied on the assurance made.

ASE EXAMPLE

### *Campbell v Griffin* [2001] EWCA Civ 990

Mr Campbell had answered an advertisement and as a result had gone to live with an elderly couple, paying rent. After five years their relationship changed and he became like a son to them. They made promises that he would have a home for life. When they both

died there was no will in existence and Mr Campbell made a claim that he could live in the house for the rest of his life. He produced evidence of ways that he had helped the couple over the years but the court did not place much reliance on this. It found that the expenditure was small and could not be taken as reliance on the assurances which Mr Campbell had been given with regard to the house. However, the court was prepared to uphold his claim in spite of the fact that he had said in evidence that he would have cared for them under any circumstances and even without promises concerning the property.

'This seems sensible and avoids carers who have a close personal relationship with the people being cared for, being in a potentially worse position than those who perform such tasks without the prior existence of such a bond'.

M P Thompson, 'Estoppel: Reliance, Remedy and Priority' [2003] Conv 157

'It is the element of prejudice to the representee which confers a legal significance upon the parties' dealings and renders it unconscionable that the relevant assurance, once given, should be subsequently withdrawn or denied'.

Gray and Gray, *Elements of Land Law* (3rd edn, Butterworths, 2001), p 793

# CASE EXAMPLE

### Re Basham [1986] 1 WLR 1498

The claimant and her husband had cared for her step-father for a period of many years. They had been led to believe by him that his entire estate would be left to them when he died.

# CASE EXAMPLE

### Greasley v Cooke [1980] 1 WLR 1306

In this case the maid, Cooke, had been assured of the right to remain in the property for her lifetime when she started to live with one of the members of the family. She continued to care for the property and also to look after a mentally ill member of the family. Her right to live in the property for her lifetime was upheld.

One issue in this case was whether Cooke could claim estoppel when she had not spent any money on the property. Lord Denning found that she did not need to prove that she

acted on the assurances; it could be assumed that she did so. There was no need to prove that she specifically acted to her detriment as it could be assumed from the fact that she stayed on to care for property without payment when she could go elsewhere to find another job.

> 'No one can say what she would have done if Kenneth and Hedley had not made those statements. It is quite possible that she would have said to herself, "I am not married to Kenneth. I am on my own. What will happen to me if anything happens to him? I had better look out for another job now: rather than stay here where I have no security"'.
>
> Denning MR

## Expenditure of money

In most cases, change of position will be shown by expenditure of money: *Inwards v Baker* and *Dillwyn v Llewelyn*. In both cases the claimants had spent money on improving the land of the defendant by building on that land.

Expenditure of money alone is not enough to raise an estoppel. If the claimant would have acted in this way without the assurance, then estoppel does not arise.

ASE EXAMPLE

### *Coombes v Smith* [1986] 1 WLR 808

The claimant formed a relationship with the defendant and left her husband. A house was bought in the man's name and the intention was that they would live there together but at first only the woman lived there. They had a child but they never lived together in the house. She cared for the child and the house and carried out a number of improvements. The judge found no evidence of an assurance that she would have rights in the property so the acts of detriment could not be linked to any rights in property; the two were unrelated.

> 'The reality is that the plaintiff decided to move . . . because she preferred to have a relationship with, and a child by, the defendant rather than continuing to live with her husband. It seems to me to have been as simple as that. There is no evidence that she left her husband in reliance on the defendant's assurance that he would provide for her if and when their relationship came to and end: the idea of detriment or prejudice is only introduced ex post facto'.
>
> Deputy Judge Jonathan Parker QC

The courts could not find the necessary link between the acts to the claimant's detriment and a promise made by the defendant. The judge saw all the acts such as the care of the child as the 'kind of conduct that you would expect of any woman in the same position'.

Compare this case:

## CASE EXAMPLE

### *Wayling v Jones* (1993) 69 P & CR 170

Here, two men had lived together in a relationship for over 16 years. Jones had promised to leave his business to the claimant Wayling and in reliance he had continued to work for very little pay. When cross-examined, the claimant had admitted that he would still have remained even if he had not been promised a share of the property. However, he also said in court that if Jones had said that he would not have kept his promise then he would have left. The Court of Appeal then found that this was sufficient to show the claimant's detriment in this case.

## CASE EXAMPLE

### *Pascoe v Turner* [1979] 1 WLR 431

This case contrasts with *Coombes v Smith* where the court was not convinced that the claimant could rely on general assurances to imply that she would have rights in the house belonging to the father of her child. In this case the representations were much more specific in relation to the house. However, there is considerable dispute about the way the courts reacted to the two cases.

'Jonathon Parker QC distinguished the case on the grounds that in *Pascoe v Turner* there had been a much clearer express representation that Mrs Turner was to "regard the house as belonging to her," but this alone would not have been sufficient to establish the equity in the absence of reliance. The acts of Mrs Turner, such as moving into the cohabited house, could also have been explained on the basis of her affection for Mr Pascoe rather than any expectation of gaining an interest in the land, but this did not prevent a finding that she was entitled to an equity. In reality the judgment in *Coombes v Smith* seems to draw too categorical a distinction between motives of love and affection and the desire to acquire a proprietary interest. People act with mixed motives, and in many cases where a claim by proprietary estoppel has succeeded it could be said that the claimant was motivated by emotional attachment to a relationship'.

R Pearce and J Stevens, *Land Law* (Sweet & Maxwell, 2000), p 475

## Other forms of reliance

There is no requirement that the reliance has to be confined to improvements on the property. There can be estoppel where there is reliance shown in other ways

The burden of proving detrimental reliance will be on the claimant. However, reliance can always be inferred from the circumstances, such as in *Greasley v Cooke*. In that case working without payment was sufficient to raise an inference, then it was up to the defendant to show that the claimant did not rely on the representation made. The facts of *Gillett v Holt* show that working for the landowner could be sufficient. So, in that case, working on the farm owned by the landowner was enough to establish rights in the land itself.

There are several cases where the claimant sells up his home and moves closer to the defendant and this act can be evidence of reliance on an assurance.

# CASE EXAMPLE

### *Jones (A E) v Jones (F W)* [1977] 1 WLR 438

The step-mother of the claimant tried to force him to pay rent for the use that he made of a house that he had jointly owned with his father, having failed in gaining an order for sale. The son had given up his existing job and home and had moved closer to his father, having been promised the right to live there for the rest of his life. The act of selling up and moving was sufficient evidence of reliance.

# CASE EXAMPLE

### *Riches v Hogben* [1986] 1 Qd R 315

This was an Australian case based on the fact that a son had sold up at a loss and left his job and emigrated to Australia in order to be closer to his mother as she got older. This was held to be sufficient reliance to establish estoppel.

## ACTIVITY

Consider the following factual situations and decide whether the claimants have relied on the representation or not.

1. The Browns have longed to move. One day, Mr Brown's widowed mother says to them: 'If you come and live near me then I will leave you my house'. The Browns move to a cottage near Mrs Brown's house. When she dies some four years later, she leaves her house to a charity in her will. Have the Browns any claim to her house?

2. The Whites want to live nearer Mrs White's father who has very bad arthritis. They move at Easter. He says 'I am so glad you have come to be closer to me. I want you to have my house on my death'. When he dies suddenly later that year, they find that under the will his house is to go to the local branch of the Samaritans. Can the Whites claim his house?

3. The Greens live 200 miles away from Mrs Green's parents. Her mother has a bad hip and her father is nearly blind. Her father asks her if they are prepared to move closer. The Greens sell their house during a slump in house prices. If they had waited until the following spring then they would have made an additional £25,000.

## 7.2.3 Detrimental reliance

The claimant must show that they have suffered some detriment. The court will only award the claimant rights if they can show that the representation has left them unconscionably disadvantaged by his reliance on the relevant representation.

> **J** 'There is no doubt that for proprietary estoppel to arise the person claiming must have incurred expenditure or otherwise have prejudiced himself or acted to his detriment.'
>
> Dunn LJ in *Greasley v Cooke*

Lord Denning held in *Greasley v Cooke* that the burden of proof does not rest with the claimant to show that they have suffered detriment. In that case the maid had relied on the assurances given to her by the brothers that she would have a right to stay in the property. Lord Denning found that the burden of proof was on the brothers to prove that she did not rely on the assurances given.

The courts are asking the question: would it be unfair or unjust if the representor could now go back on the representation made to the claimant?

Detriment will be proved in a number of situations:

**1.** expenditure of money on the land of the representor

**2.** acting to one's detriment, incurring financial loss

**3.** suffering personal detriment by not taking advantage of opportunities or giving up time and effort to care for the representor.

## 1. Expenditure of money

The claimant who starts to improve the land or builds on the land will be held to act to his detriment. The most obvious example would be *Inwards v Baker*, where the son built a bungalow, at his own expense, on his father's land. This is clearly evidence of acting to one's detriment. The law assumes that no one would build on land belonging to someone else unless he genuinely believes that he has rights in the land.

Once a promisee has shown that he did something to his detriment then the burden of proof lies with the promisor to show that such acts were **not** done in reliance upon the promise.

The courts can look at other factors but even where there is detrimental reliance they can still refuse to find that the owner is estopped from denying the claimant's rights. In the following case the court found that there had been detrimental reliance but it still refused to recognise the rights because there were other significant factors to consider.

 ASE EXAMPLE

*Sledmore v Dalby* (1996) 72 P & CR 196

Mr Dalby and his wife had moved into a house owned by his parents-in-law. He had carried out a number of improvements to the house and was led to believe that the house would be given to him and his wife. However, the house was passed to the mother-in-law. After the death of his wife, Dalby continued to live at the property without paying rent. By now he had a job and also a new partner who had her own house and he went to live with her for much of the time. Although the Court of Appeal thought that an equity had been raised in his favour, it also felt that other factors should be considered. It did not think that Dalby should be able to claim his share through proprietary estoppel.

Factors which influenced the Court of Appeal:

**1.** Dalby was now in employment and did not need the rent-free accommodation

**2.** the mother-in-law was elderly and was now in reduced financial circumstances

**3.** the house was in disrepair and needed work carried out which the mother-in-law could not afford

**4.** Mr Dalby's children were all grown up and did not need accommodation for themselves.

When these factors were all assessed, the court found that here it was no longer inequitable to deny the claimant the equity through change of circumstances so it could refuse to give a remedy to the claimant, Mr Dalby.

## 2. Acting to one's detriment, incurring financial loss

This will generally involve expenditure on the land itself. If you believe that a house will be yours one day, then you are going to ensure that the property is in good repair and to maintain a high standard of decoration. The logic of this is that someone would not spend money on improving land unless he genuinely believed that he had rights in that property. You do not simply paint another's house without believing that you will have rights in the land.

Cases such as *Coombes v Smith* show that the claim will be defeated if there are other reasons why you have undertaken the work. So in that case the work carried out could be justified because of the relationship between the parties and not because the woman thought the work on the house would lead to her having rights in the land.

## 3. Suffering other forms of detriment

There may be other forms of detriment suffered by the claimant. In *Crabb v Arun DC* the claimant had sold off part of his land in the belief that he had rights of way over the defendant's land. The fact that he had not reserved himself these rights was held to constitute detriment.

The care of the house and family for no payment in *Greasley v Cooke* constituted detriment since, as the court pointed out, the maid could have left at any time to find another job. Similarly, in *Re Basham* the claimant's husband had given up opportunities to get a better job and also to move but had instead remained to care for the claimant's elderly step-father. This was held to be sufficient detriment although it was not expressly expenditure on the land itself.

Rosalyn Wells has considered the different types of detriment that the Gilletts had suffered in *Gillett v Holt*. In this case representations had been made over a period of time to Mr Gillett by Mr Holt that he would leave his farm to him. She writes:

> 'Robert Walker L.J. who delivered the judgement said that detriment is not a narrow or technical concept and need not consist of the expenditure of money or other quantifiable financial detriment so long as it is substantial. The requirement for detriment must be approached as part of the inquiry as to whether or not the repudiation of the assurances is unconscionable in all the circumstances'.

R Wells, 'The Element of Detriment in Proprietary Estoppel' [2001] 65 Conv 13

In *Gillett v Holt* the following were all held to constitute detriment:

**a  Mr Gillett had continued to work for his employer rather than to pursue opportunities of going into work on his own account.** In the words of the Court of Appeal, he had devoted the best years of his life to working for Mr Holt and his company, showing loyalty and devotion to his business interests. The facts are similar in *Wayling v Jones*, where the claimant had remained working for little more than pocket money because he expected to inherit his partner's business.

**b  Mr Gillett and his family had spent time with his employer, Mr Holt, beyond the normal scope of an employee's duty.** It was accepted that not only had Mr Gillett continued to work for Mr Holt but he had also spent considerable time with him outside his duties as an employee. Mr Gillett and the rest of his family spent time sharing normal family and social activities. This is a rather controversial aspect of detriment since Mr Gillett and the rest of his family undoubtedly also gained advantages from these social activities but the Court of Appeal also accepted that Mr and Mrs Gillett and their sons had provided Mr Holt with a sort of 'surrogate family'. This aspect of detriment has been found in earlier cases. In *Re Basham* it was said that 'the claimant's acts went far beyond what was called for by the natural love and affection for someone to whom she had no blood relationship'.

**c  Loyalty and devotion to the defendant's wishes.** The most important factor here was the sending of the Gilletts' children to boarding school. They had to find the funds to send the second child to boarding school as the first child's fees had been funded by Mr Holt. They did not wish to treat the two children differently. The judge thought that part of the detriment that they had suffered was the subordination of their wishes to those of Mr Holt. The judge found that they had adopted a higher standard of living than they would have envisaged and one higher than was appropriate to their income.

---

## KEY FACTS

### Detrimental reliance

**1.** A representation followed by expenditure on the land will constitute detriment (*Inwards v Baker* (1965)).

**2.** A representation followed by other forms of expenditure which can be linked to the belief that you have rights in the land can also constitute detriment (*Gillett v Holt* (1998)).

**3.** Detriment need not be purely financial in nature but it must be linked to the belief that it will lead to rights in land (*Re Basham* (1986); *Crabb v Arun DC* (1976)).

**4.** Even where detriment has been proved, the claim may be defeated if there are other factors which show it would not be inequitable to do so (*Sledmore v Dalby* (1996)).

**Key features of estoppel**

| Representation | Positive assurance of rights or silence. Can be made within a will, can be made by an agent but not a tenant on behalf of a landlord. | *Inwards v Baker* (1965) (assurance of rights); *Taylor v Dickens* (1998); *Gillett v Holt* (1998); *Pascoe v Turner* (assurance of rights although in general terms) (1979); *Ramsden v Dyson* (1866) (mere silence) |
| --- | --- | --- |
| Reliance | Genuine belief that rights will arise. | *Re Basham* (1986); *Greasley v Cooke* (1980) (provided care without pay); *Inwards v Baker* (1965) (expenditure of money); *Campbell v Griffin* (2001); *Coombes v Smith* (expenditure of money not referable to rights in the property) (1986); *Jones v Jones* (1977) (son sold house and moved closer to father) |
| Detriment | The representation has led to the claimant suffering some detriment. | *Sledmore v Dalby* (1996) (insufficient detriment shown for remedy); *Crabb v Arun DC* (1976) (failure to reserve rights of way over land was detriment); *Greasley v Cooke* (1980) (maid remained in house when could have left at any time); *Re Basham* (1986) (claimant's husband had given up opportunities at work); *Gillett v Holt* (1998) |

# 7.3 Satisfying proprietary estoppel

Once the three elements of proprietary estoppel have been satisfied, the claimant is entitled to a remedy. The court has a discretion as to what kind of remedy to award. The interests have ranged from conveying the freehold to simply awarding an occupational licence or monetary compensation.

> 'When rights are claimed through the medium of estoppel, the relief sought is entirely equitable. This equitable jurisdiction is widely regarded as fluid. Thus Scarman L.J. approvingly described equitable estoppel as being "immensely flexible, yet perfectly clear . . .". With regard to the issue of flexibility, the general academic view of the court's role in an estoppel case is that it has the power to

make such order as the justice of the case demands and this seems to be accepted by the courts themselves. . . . In selecting the appropriate remedy, a court will have regard to various considerations: the nature of the expectation, the extent of reliance, the relative wealth of the parties, the existence of children and so on. Inequitable conduct by either party is then one factor amongst many to be taken into account. Only in the more extreme cases should someone be disentitled to equitable relief as a result of misconduct'.

M P Thompson, 'Estoppel and Clean Hands' [1986] Conv 406

The courts have some restraint on the way they decide to satisfy the claimant. They should grant the remedy that can be said to best satisfy the reasonable expectations of the claimant. If, as in *Pascoe v Turner* the defendant has made a representation that the claimant shall have legal rights in the land then that is the appropriate remedy. However, if the representation falls short of this, then the remedy should be something less than the freehold estate.

# CASE EXAMPLE

### *Parker (9th Earl of Macclesfield) v Parker* [2003] EWHC 1846 [Ch]

The 9th Earl of Macclesfield claimed the right to live in Shirburn Castle which had been in the family since 1716. This was based on proprietary estoppel. Although the claim had been for a right of occupation for life, the judge held that a successful plea of estoppel was limited to the claimant's expectation. He found that the claimant had not expected to get a life interest and therefore he granted the 9th Earl a right to remain in the property until he was given two years' notice.

## Transfer of the legal estate or legal interest in land

This is granted in a limited number of cases and relies on establishing that the assurance or representation promised the transfer of the freehold rights.

In *Dillwyn v Llewelyn* the transfer of freehold ownership was ordered because the father had gone as far as transferring the interest to the son by written memorandum but had not satisfied the formalities because he had failed to execute a deed. The son had acted on the promise by building a house on the land. The only remedy that would satisfy the expectation of the son would be to transfer the freehold to the son.

A similar decision was reached in *Pascoe v Turner* where the courts had a choice of remedies: either to transfer the fee simple or to grant the wife a licence to live in the property for the woman's life. They chose to transfer the freehold because it was felt that that was the only way that the equity

was satisfied. The facts also indicate that the defendant was trying to evict the claimant and if she had only got a licence then he could have tried to sell to a third party and as her rights were personal only he could sell leaving her without any remedy. This shows us that the remedy granted is firmly equity based and the courts have a wide discretion when deciding what remedy to grant.

By way of contrast, when the son built his bungalow in *Inwards v Baker*, there was some doubt as to what sort of interest the son believed that he was to gain. The courts did not transfer the full freehold estate, transferring instead the right for the son to enjoy the bungalow for his lifetime.

The key issue appears to be that there must be an express representation either orally or in writing that the claimant is to receive the freehold. It is only in these cases that the court is prepared to award the transfer of the legal estate. In these cases there is a much higher standard of proof of an assurance of rights in the freehold.

The claim for the transfer of the legal estate was rejected in this recent case:

CASE EXAMPLE

### Jennings v Rice [2003] 1 P & CR 8

A very wealthy widow died, leaving an estate worth over £1.2 million. She had employed a gardener who had worked for many years and in latter years without pay. When her health failed, he began to look after her and continued to do so until she died. During the time he had worked for her she had made a number of promises concerning the property but they were very vague in nature. However, the court found that she had clearly led him to believe that he would inherit all or part of the estate when she died. The Court of Appeal upheld the finding of the judge at first instance who held that he should be entitled to £200,000. It based its decision on the argument put forward on behalf of her estate 'that the task of the court was to achieve justice and to that end any award made must be proportionate to the expectation and the detriment suffered'. The court rejected the claim on behalf of Jennings that he should be entitled to the whole of the estate although that was what he thought he had been promised.

## The right to occupy

In *Inwards v Baker* the son was not granted a freehold estate but a lifetime right to occupy. The problem with this is that the right was one of enjoyment rather than a right of ownership and a chance to sell or deal in the land.

This remedy is based on a licence which may be deemed to be irrevocable and will give the claimant the right to remain in the property rent-free either for life or for a determined period.

So in *Greasley v Cooke* the claimant was granted the right to remain rent-free for the remainder of her life. It was held to be unjust and inequitable for the party making the representation to go back on it.

In *Campbell v Griffin* the court awarded Mr Campbell an interest in the property valued at £35,000 which would take effect as a charge on the property. He would be required to leave the property. The possibility of a lifetime right to occupy the property had been discussed as that was what he had expected and the remedy given usually reflects the expectations of the parties. However, the court considered the interests of the other parties and decided that a lump sum was more appropriate.

The lifetime right to occupy has one possible complication attached to it. This could be seen as giving the claimant a right similar to a tenant for life in a settlement under the Settled Land Act 1925. The tenant for life has all the rights of an owner and the effect was that a tenant for life had the right to sell the land. This was not the intention when the remedy was granted. Settlements can no longer be created in land and have been replaced by trusts of land. They allow for rights of occupation and so do not create the same sort of problems.

## Financial compensation

Monetary compensation has been ordered in several cases. This will be appropriate where the financial detriment is relatively small in relation to the full value of the property, as shown in the case of *Dodsworth v Dodsworth* (1973) 228 EG 1115, or where it would be impossible for the parties to live together because there has been a breakdown in relations.

# CASE EXAMPLE

### *Dodsworth v Dodsworth* (1973) 228 EG 1115

A sister invited her brother and sister-in-law to come and live with her when they returned from Australia. She said they could live in her bungalow for as long as they liked. In reliance on this promise, they set about carrying out improvements to the property which amounted to over £700. On her death, the administrator brought a successful action against them both, requesting that they should leave but ordering that they should be awarded the costs of the improvements to the property.

### Hussey v Palmer [1972] 1 WLR 1286

Here, a mother-in-law paid £607 for an extension to her son's house as he had told her that she could then make her home with him and his wife. The mother and son argued and she was granted a share in the property. In this case the court imposed a constructive trust. It is arguable that her rights arose by virtue of estoppel and she could claim that she had the right to continue to live there. The problem in this case was that it was impossible for both the son and the mother to live there together because of the breakdown of relations.

### CASE EXAMPLE

### Re Sharpe [1980] 1 WLR 219

An aunt claimed the right to remain in a property purchased by her nephew who had been declared bankrupt. She based this right on the large contributions that she had made to the purchase of the property. The house had cost £17,000 and the aunt had contributed £12,000. The court held that she should be awarded her contribution to the purchase but it refused her a right in the property. However, she could remain until the loan was repaid, based on an estoppel licence.

In *Gillett v Holt* the court ordered the transfer of part of the property as well as a sum in monetary compensation.

### Quantification of the compensation

The courts have a choice between simply assessing the value of the improvements themselves or assessing the increase in value of the property itself. The latter option could be much higher than the cost of the improvements themselves. In *Dodsworth v Dodsworth* the court ordered the cost of the improvements rather than the enhanced value of the property.

## Post-judgment misconduct

Can misconduct by the claimant after the representation has been made be sufficient to prevent the equity arising in favour of the claimant?

The leading case on this issue is *Williams v Staite* [1979] Ch 291. The defendants had been given rights to occupy two cottages indefinitely. The cottages were bought by the claimant who challenged the defendants' right to enjoy the cottages because they had used a paddock which they

knew was not their own and had even erected a stable on it. The claimant had been granted an injunction to prevent the defendants from using the paddock. The claimant then sought an order trying to regain possession of the cottage. His argument was that the defendants had lost their entitlement because of their inequitable conduct.

'Excessive user or bad behaviour towards the legal owner cannot bring an equity to an end or forfeit it. It may give rise to an action for damages for trespass or nuisance or to injunctions to restrain such behaviour, but I can see no ground on which the equity, once established, can be forfeited'.

Goff LJ

In this case the judge held that the rights had been acquired prior to the behaviour complained of and so the defendants' rights in the property could not be challenged as they had already crystallised

However, if the rights have not yet been acquired under estoppel then misconduct of the claimant may become a relevant factor. Consider the facts of the following case.

Compare *Brynowen Estates v Bourne* (1981) 131 NLJ 1212. In this case the claimant had sought a declaration from the courts that she had rights in a caravan park, based on proprietary estoppel. The court found that she was unable to claim such a right because before she had established such a right there was evidence that she had behaved in a most objectionable way herself. She had persistently sworn and made obscene gestures at visitors to the caravan park. This was held by the court to prevent any rights arising in favour of the claimant.

## Other remedies

The courts can combine remedies so that they order the transfer of land to the claimant but they can also order the claimant to compensate the defendant.

# ASE EXAMPLE

### *Lim Teng Huan v Ang Swee Chuan* [1992] 1 WLR 113

Two parties each had an interest in land because it had been conveyed jointly into the names of their fathers. One party (the defendant) decided to build on the land and he drafted an agreement whereby the defendant claimed the whole of the land in exchange for a transfer to the claimant of some land that he anticipated getting from the government. The house was completed and the defendant went into occupation without

any complaint from the claimant. Later, the two argued and the claimant then claimed a half share of the property.

The court held that the defendant was entitled to the whole of the property but that the claimant was also entitled to a sum by way of compensation.

'The doctrine of proprietary estoppel mitigates the harshness this caused to the defendant. Its operation is, however, much more uncertain than a simple case of enforcing an otherwise void contract. Equity is at its most innovative and flexible in cases of this kind and the void agreement is only to be taken into account in deciding how to satisfy the equity. In the circumstances, financial compensation to the defendant for the preparatory and building works while allowing the claimant to share the whole property is clearly impracticable and could create further disputes. To order an immediate sale of the whole property and to divide the balance of the proceeds of sale between them after deducting the increase in value attributable to the defendant's works is equally not equitable . . . The decision that the claimant should convey his half share to the defendant on condition that the defendant pay the claimant compensation for the value of the land as a site excluding the increase in value attributable to the preparatory work seems justifiable in the circumstances'.

S H Goo, 'Satisfying Proprietary Estoppel' (1993) Conv 173

The court has also been prepared to grant an easement by way of remedy where it has been appropriate.

# CASE EXAMPLE

### *E R Ives Investment Ltd v High* [1967] 2 QB 379

The claimant had been granted an easement arising through estoppel where he had resurfaced part of the land owned by his neighbour and he had been assured that he would have a right of way.

## KEY FACTS

### Remedies

1. The court has complete discretion in awarding a remedy.

2. The remedy should be one which as nearly as possible fulfils the parties reasonable expectations raised by the representation given.

3. The grant of the freehold should only be made where that has been assured by the representor.

4. If monetary compensation is awarded it should be either the equivalent sum spent or equivalent to the increase in value.

5. Misconduct by the claimant may result in the loss of rights.

6. Remedies may be combined so the defendant can be ordered to pay money to the claimant in exchange for rights in the property.

### Remedies that can be awarded in proprietary estoppel

| | | |
|---|---|---|
| **Lifetime right to occupy** | May satisfy the equity but limited rights as no right to sell the property. | *Re Basham* (1986); *Inwards v Baker* (1965); *Greasley v Cooke* (1980) |
| **Monetary compensation** | Appropriate where financial detriment is fairly small and the lifetime right to occupy is inappropriate on the facts. | *Dodsworth v Dodsworth* (1973); *Campbell v Griffin* (2001); *Hussey v Palmer* (1972); *Re Sharpe* (1980) |
| **Transfer of the legal estate** | Must be promise of transfer of legal estate; requires a high standard of proof. | *Pascoe v Turner* (1979); *Dillwyn v Llewellyn* (1862) |
| **No remedy where there has been misconduct** | Rights will be upheld where the misconduct took place after the rights had been acquired. | *Williams v Staite* (1979); *Brynowen Estates v Bourne* (1981) |

## 7.4 Loss of rights under proprietary estoppel

### Lack of clean hands

The remedies in equity are subject to the claimant behaving in an equitable manner. If the defendant can prove lack of clean hands then the rights will be defeated. In *Williams v Staite* there was ample evidence that the claimants were guilty of misconduct in the way they had started to build on the land when they knew they had no permission to do so. They also persisted when an injunction had been expressly granted against them. However, this behaviour was not relevant because it all occurred after the rights had been declared in their favour.

The argument would be that as the remedy is based on unconscionability, then it would cease to be unconscionable if the claimant himself has acted unconscionably.

### Delay

Equitable remedies are also defeated where there is evidence of delay in bringing the action. This could be argued where the claimant has delayed in bringing his claim to the courts, however it is likely that in many cases there is bound to be delay because the claimant is enjoying undisturbed rights in land.

## APPLYING THE LAW

Freddie lives in Yorkshire and his elderly father, Jim, lives in Surrey. Jim is getting less and less mobile and recently twisted his ankle badly when he fell down on the path outside his front door. He asks Freddie if he would like to come and live in the old family home and to help him out when necessary. Freddie cannot make up his mind but Jim tells him that he will leave him his house in his will on his death if he will come and live with him. Freddie sells his own house and moves in.

At this stage Freddie would not be expected to take any action. If he finds that Jim has left the house to someone else after Jim's death then he should not delay in bringing an action. The house may have been left to a charity which does not want to take possession.

## 7.5 The effect of any previous benefit acquired by the claimant

Where the claimant has derived some benefit from the land then the defendant can claim that there is no reason to grant a remedy in addition. In *Inwards v Baker* the son had lived for a long period of time on his father's land without paying rent and this constituted a considerable advantage for him.

There is an argument that this alone would be sufficient to satisfy the claim. In *Gillett v Holt* [2001] Ch 210 the defendant had given the claimant a number of benefits such as help with the school fees for the claimant's son and other help with such things as pension contributions.

> 'There are a number of authorities in which the court has considered that the benefits received by the claimant have reduced the detriment to such an extent that it is insufficient to support the claim in proprietary estoppel. In other cases the court finds that although an equity has arisen it would not be appropriate to award any remedy in view of the reciprocal benefits received. In each of these categories the claimant is unsuccessful because he has not persuaded the court that it would be unconscionable for the promisor to be allowed to resile from his promises. For the Court of Appeal to dismiss the High Court's approach as too narrow is mistaken because it has thrown into doubt the use of the concept of advantage and disadvantage. It is essential that the court should make an approximate assessment of the extent of the detriment suffered by the claimant. Furthermore the concept of advantage and disadvantage is an important one which allows the court considerable lee way in the exercise of its discretion. It is significant that the courts seem only to refer to reciprocal benefits in those cases which are in fact unsuccessful.
>
> In the context of the case the expenditure on schooling was detrimental in the sense the Gilletts had adopted a higher standard of living which might not otherwise have been appropriate to their income had Mr Holt not made promises of future testamentary benefits'.

R Wells, 'The Element of Detriment in Proprietary Estoppel' [2001] 65 Conv 13

In *Watts v Storey* (1983) 134 NLJ 631 the claimant had moved from Leeds, giving up a protected tenancy, to live with his grandmother. His claim for rights in her house based on proprietary estoppel were refused because he had not proved that he had suffered detriment as he had received benefits from making use of rent-free accommodation provided by his grandmother and Slade LJ held that on balance he had not suffered any detriment in financial or material terms.

# ACTIVITY

In what circumstances will the following benefits conferred on the claimant prevent estoppel from arising?

1. The defendant allows the claimant to live in the property rent-free.
2. The defendant's son is friendly with the claimant's son and he promises to pay for his school fees at an expensive public school. The claimant has two other sons.

3. The defendant allows the claimant who worked for him on his farm to join him on several social activities such as joining expensive shoots and going to game fairs.

4. The defendant allowed the claimant to live in property rent free while the claimant cared for the defendant's elderly mother. The claimant did not receive any payment for the care that she provided.

# 7.6 The proprietary nature of a claim to proprietary estoppel

## Personal or proprietary rights?

You may remember that personal rights only take effect as rights against the landowner but proprietary rights will be binding against a third party.

If the court finds that the claimant has rights in land based on equitable estoppel then those rights will be upheld. However, the problem is whether the rights are proprietary in nature and will then be binding on a purchaser.

If the court in a case such as *Greasley v Cooke* grants the maid a right to live in the property for her lifetime, would that bind a third party purchaser if the legal owner tries to sell the legal title? If the right is seen as a licence only, then the nature of a licence is that it is not a proprietary right so it will be personal only.

Winn LJ said in *E R Ives Investment Ltd v High*: 'Estoppels arising from representations made by owners of land that rights exist affecting their land will, unless in form they are limited to the duration of the interest of the representor, bind successors in title'.

## APPLYING THE LAW

☐ ☐ ☐

Gemma Smith has worked for Mrs Brown for many years and when Mrs Brown becomes seriously ill she stays on living in the house without payment and is treated as one of the family. She cares for the youngest child living at home and looks after the house. The brother of Mrs Brown tries to evict her after Mrs Brown's death but Gemma can bring evidence that Mrs Brown promised her the right to live in the house on several occasions before she died. The court will uphold her rights but they may not be binding on a third party.

☐ ☐ ☐

The Land Registration Act 2002 has clarified the position with regard to the nature of estoppel and has accepted that rights arising under proprietary estoppel were proprietary in nature and therefore were capable of binding third parties. Under s 116 of the 2002 Act it is provided:

's 116 It is hereby declared for the avoidance of doubt that, in relation to registered land, each of the following –

(a) an equity by estoppel, and

(b) a mere equity

has the effect from the time the equity arises as an interest capable of binding successors in title (subject to the rules about the effect of dispositions on priority).'

Rights in registered land will need to be registered unless the claimant has a right which can be claimed as an overriding interest.

The decision of *Lloyd v Dugdale* [2001] EWCA Civ 1754 has now clarified any doubt that there may have been surrounding the nature of rights under estoppel.

'Now that *Lloyd v Dugdale* has confirmed – in advance of section 116 lRA 2002 – that estoppel rights are proprietary, and that they can bind a purchaser of registered land as an interest that overrides through actual occupation, the path is clear and well lit for a claimant seeking to impeach the registered title that is to be so carefully protected under the LRA 2002'.

M Dixon, 'Proprietary Estoppel, Third Parties and Constructive Trusts. A Taste for the Future?
*Lloyd v Dugdale* [2001] EWCA Civ 1754' [2002] Conv 584

## Can rights arising under proprietary estoppel be overreached?

**Revision note:** overreaching is the transfer of rights in land from the land itself to the purchase monies. So the claimant would no longer have the right to live in the property but a right to a sum of money.

Rights under proprietary estoppel are subject to overreaching so if the remedy takes the form of an equitable estate then such an estate can be overreached where the purchaser pays the purchase money to two trustees. Some rights arising under estoppel cannot be overreached, such as an easement or a lease.

This still leaves the issue of the status of estoppel in unregistered land. This is still subject to notice.

The effect is that third parties can be bound by these rights.

# CASE EXAMPLE

### *Re Sharpe* [1980] 1 WLR 219

The aunt's rights were held to be binding on the trustee in bankruptcy. She had contributed to the purchase of property by her nephew and the court had granted her a lifetime right to live in the property rather than a right to a share in the property itself. Since these rights were binding, the trustee in bankruptcy was unable to sell to a third party.

# CASE EXAMPLE

### *Voyce v Voyce* (1991) 62 P & CR 290

The rights of one brother who had lived in his mother's house which had been promised to him over many years were held to be binding on his other brother who had received the legal title by way of gift. The rights under estoppel therefore were binding on a third-party donee.

It seems that this type of right can bind the legal owner so long as they have notice of the right, even before the court has granted the remedy.

# ACTIVITY

Consider this situation and discuss whether there could be a successful claim for proprietary estoppel. If there is a claim for estoppel, what would be the appropriate remedy?

Jack Jones bought Laurel Villa 10 years ago and became the registered owner. He travelled around the country and did not like to leave the property empty. He was visiting his cousin Winnie when she told him that her lease had come to an end. He asked her if she would like to come and live in his house. He told her that she could live there rent-free so long as she carried out repairs on the property and kept 'a bit of an eye on things' while he was away. She moved in and immediately started to work on the property, putting in double glazing because it was so cold in the house. This was quite expensive and cost her over £2,000. She also spent money on replacing the bathroom upstairs. Jack was away when she carried out this work and when he came home he said to her 'Keep caring for the house and you can do anything that you want with the property'. Last week he was away on business and he was involved in a fatal accident. Winnie wants to know if she can still remain in the house.

# Further reading

Adams, J E, 'Is Equitable Estoppel a Wasting Asset?' [1997] Conv 458.

Battersby, G, 'Informal transactions in Land, Estoppel and Registration' (1995) 58 MLR 637.

Cooke, E, 'Reliance and Estoppel' (1995) 111 LQR 389.

Davis, C J, 'Proprietary Estoppel: Future interests and Future Property' [1996] Conv 193.

Dixon, M, 'Proprietary Estoppel, Third Parties and Constructive Trusts. A Taste for the Future?: *Lloyd v Dugdale* [2001] EWCA Civ 1754' [2002] Conv 584.

Garner, S, 'The Remedial Discretion in Proprietary Estoppel' (1999) 115 LQR 438.

Goo, S H, 'Satisfying Proprietary Estoppel' [1993] Conv 173.

Haley, M, 'The Flexibility of Estoppel: *Jennings v Rice* [2003] P & CR 8' [2003] 67 Conv.

Jones, S, 'Proprietary Estoppel – Satisfying the Equity' (1992) NLJ (March) 320.

Moriarty, S, 'Licences and Land Law: Legal Principles and Public Policies' (1984) 100 LQR 376.

Thompson, M P, 'Estoppel and Clean Hands' [1986] Conv 406.

Thompson, M P, 'Estoppel: A Return to Principle' [2001] 65 Conv 78.

Thompson, M P, 'Estoppel: Reliance, Remedy and Priority: *Campbell v Griffin* [2001] EWCA Civ 990' [2003] 67 Conv 157.

Thompson, M P, 'My Home is not my Castle' [2003] 67 Conv 516.

Wells, R, 'Restrictive Approach to Proprietary Estoppel in the testamentary Context' [1999] Conv 463.

Wells, R, 'The Element of Detriment in Proprietary Estoppel' [2001] 65 Conv 13.

**chapter 8** CO-OWNERSHIP

## 8.1 The nature of co-ownership

Land is rarely owned by one single owner; it is much more likely that several different people will have an interest in a piece of land. One important factor is that the bulk of property ownership today is ownership of the family home. When property is owned by more than one person it is referred to as 'concurrent ownership'.

When two or more people own an interest in land it becomes subject to **co-ownership**. Co-ownership can only take place behind a trust of land, under the Trusts of Land and Appointment of Trustees Act 1996.

- **Legal title:** There will be co-ownership of the legal title if there is more than one owner of the land in law.

- **Equitable interests:** Co-owners in equity share the equitable ownership of the land behind a trust.

## 8.2 Types of co-ownership

English law recognises two different types of co-ownership:

- the joint tenancy

- tenancy in common.

Where land is co-owned in a joint tenancy, the co-owners are described as **joint tenant**s and where land is co-owned in a tenancy in common they are described as **tenants in common**.

## 8.3 A joint tenancy

There are **three** aspects to a joint tenancy:

1. the main feature of a joint tenancy is that the co-owners are each entitled to the whole of the co-owned land. However, they do not own shares of the land

2. the other feature of the joint tenancy is the 'right of survivorship'

3. there can only be a joint tenancy if 'the four unities' are present.

## APPLYING THE LAW

Duncan and Deirdre are the joint tenants of Lilac Cottage. It is not appropriate to speak of them each owning a half of the cottage. If their friend Jackie comes to visit and they tell her that they are joint tenants, she may say 'Who really owns the cottage?'. The proper answer is that Duncan owns the whole of the cottage and Deirdre owns the whole of the cottage at the same time. There is no part that they do not completely own but there is also no part they own to the exclusion of the other.

## APPLYING THE LAW

Susie, Sally, Vicki and Stuart are all students at the University of Thameshire. They decide that rather than rent property they will all join together to buy a terraced house with four bedrooms at 45 Grange Road. They buy as joint tenants. Although there are four of them, they all own the whole of the house and even though they each have a separate bedroom, no one can claim one of the bedrooms as his or her own. The fact that they each have a separate bedroom that they call their own is just a matter of convenience.

## 8.3.1 The 'four unities'

A joint tenancy will only exist if the four unities are present. If any of these is missing, then there cannot be a joint tenancy of the land.

### 'Unity of possession'

All of the joint tenants must be equally entitled to possess the whole of the co-owned land. One joint tenant cannot exclude another from any part of the land.

## APPLYING THE LAW

In the example above, Sally cannot exclude Susie from her bedroom. If it was possible to do so then it cannot be a joint tenancy.

'Between joint tenants the concept of internal physical boundaries and the consequent idea of trespass have no meaning, except in the sense that any ouster or interference with another's rights over the co-owned whole constitutes an actionable trespass'.

Gray and Gray, *Elements of Land Law* (3rd edn, Butterworths, 2001), p 831

Unity of possession will be displaced in some circumstances, such as an ouster order granted under the Family Law Act 1996 requiring one party to leave the premises.

## 'Unity of interest'

Each of the joint tenants must have the same interest in extent, nature and duration in the land. For example, there cannot be a joint tenancy between a person who has a freehold interest in the land and someone who has a leasehold interest.

## APPLYING THE LAW

If one of the students, Stuart, purchases the property outright then he will own the freehold and if the others rent rooms in the property they will all have leasehold interests. In his case there cannot be a joint tenancy with the other students as there is no unity of interest.

Once property is owned as a joint tenancy at law, any attempt to deal in the title must be with the agreement of all the joint owners. So if there is a sale of the property or a mortgage is executed over the land it will only be effective if everyone agrees. If one person tries to mortgage his share then it may effect the share in equity but not at law.

## APPLYING THE LAW

Susie, Sally and Vicki buy a flat together as joint tenants. Sally is short of money and she attempts to mortgage the property on her own by forging the signatures of the other two owners. This would not affect the co-ownership at law but it would affect her ownership in equity. She cannot mortgage the flat without the others' agreement. The same would apply if she tried to sell the land.

## 'Unity of title'

The joint tenants must derive their title to the land from the same document or alternatively where they have acquired title under adverse possession.

> ## APPLYING THE LAW
>
> The purchase of 45 Grange Road would be by one conveyance or transfer which all four students, Susie, Sally Vicki and Stuart, would sign. They would then derive title from this conveyance or transfer rather than from four separate documents.
>
> The four may have acquired the property through adverse possession which means that they would have taken possession of someone else's land and stayed for 12 years. If they had satisfied the conditions necessary for adverse possession under the pre-2002 rules then they could claim that they were entitled to be registered as joint owners. They would have unity of title as it would derive from the act of adverse possession.

## 'Unity of time'

The interests of all the joint tenants must vest at the same time.

> ## APPLYING THE LAW
>
> Property is left to Deirdre's mother for her lifetime and then to Duncan and Deirdre. There is no unity of time between all three because Deirdre and Duncan do not receive the title until after the death of Deirdre's mother but there is unity of time between Duncan and Deirdre.

# 8.3.2 Survivorship

The key practical difference between a joint tenancy and a tenancy in common is that the principle of survivorship operates between joint tenants. This means that when one joint tenant dies, any interest held by that joint tenant will automatically pass to the remaining joint tenants.

> 'It has been said that the right of survivorship (or *IUS ACCRESCENDI*) is the "grand and distinguishing" incident of joint tenancy. On the death of any one joint tenant the entire co-owned estate "survives to" the remaining joint tenant or tenants. Ultimately, in the manner of the medieval tontine, the surviving joint

tenant becomes the sole owner – the winner takes all. This concentration of ownership was elegantly described by Blackstone . . . *When two or more persons are seised of a joint estate . . . the entire tenancy upon the decease of any of them remains to the survivors, and at length to the last survivor . . . The interest of two joint-tenants is not only equal or similar, but also is one and the same. One has not originally a distinct moiety from the other . . . but . . . each . . . has a concurrent interest in the whole; and therefore, on the death of his companion, the sole interest in the whole remains to the survivor'.*

Gray and Gray, *Elements of Land Law* (3rd edn, Butterworths, 2001), p 824

## APPLYING THE LAW

Duncan and Deirdre own Lilac Cottage as joint tenants. If Duncan has an accident and dies, his share in Lilac Cottage under the joint tenancy will pass automatically to Deirdre. Deirdre then becomes absolute owner. This will apply irrespective of any provision in his will, if there is one, or a provision under the intestacy rules. The effect on Deirdre is that she can sell the property immediately if she wishes.

The joint tenant who dies cannot therefore leave any interest in the land by will nor will his or her interest pass under the rules of intestacy. This is because in the example above both Deirdre and Duncan are joint owners of the cottage but they do not 'own' anything that they can specifically say is his or her own. This means that they could not then leave specific property or a specific share to anyone.

In the other example, if Sally and Susie are involved in a fatal accident both their shares in 45 Grange Road will pass to the survivors, Vicki and Stuart. It would be irrelevant that Susie had made a will leaving all her property to the NSPCC because this part of the will would not take effect. Her share passes immediately on death and before the will takes effect.

Survivorship in practice:

### 1. Simplifies probate

On death the estate vests in the survivors of the joint tenants. There is no need to vest the property in the survivor as the survivor is recognised in law as owning the title. This is far simpler and saves on costs. The effect is that the joint tenants can ignore jointly owned property in their will, indeed for many, who have few assets, the jointly held home is probably the main asset. The principle of survivorship will apply whether they have made a valid will or not.

### 2. Simplifies purchases from joint tenants

As there is just one title which is vested in several co-owners only one title needs to be investigated by a purchaser. If the title of every co-owner needed to be investigated then it would be time-consuming and there would be a risk of many more problems arising.

Historically, land could be subject to several different types of legal estate. This meant that in any sale of the land the property would be potentially complicated because there would be a series of titles to investigate. This was simplified by s 1 of the Law of Property Act 1925 which provided that there could only be two legal estates in land: the freehold and the leasehold.

### 3. Gives effect to the wishes of the majority on succession

Many couples fail to make provision by will for their property on their death but if asked would want the co-owner to benefit. The co-owner may be a spouse or a partner. The right of survivorship reflects this wish.

## APPLYING THE LAW

Tony and Guy live together. They have each contributed to the purchase of a house and own the legal estate as joint tenants. Tony has a fatal heart attack. On his death Guy will automatically get ownership at law of the whole of the property. Although the law may say that his relatives should inherit if he dies intestate, this does not include the house as it is jointly owned and it passes through the right of survivorship immediately on death.

# 8.3.3 Severance

Joint tenants can effectively separate their equitable interest from that of the other joint tenants by means of severance. Their interest is then converted into a tenancy in common and the principle of survivorship will no longer operate.

In *Bedson v Bedson* [1965] 2 QB 666 Lord Denning put forward the suggestion that where spouses hold as beneficial joint tenants they cannot sever their interests so as to convert them into tenancies in common but this has not been followed in subsequent decisions and the views of Russell LJ, the dissenting judge in that case, have been followed:

'I am unable to accept the legal proposition of Lord Denning MR that when husband and wife are joint tenants of the legal estate in the matrimonial home and also beneficial joint tenants in respect of it, neither can, so long as one is in possession, sell his or her beneficial interest therein or otherwise sever the beneficial joint tenancy'.

Where a joint tenant does sever his share in equity, he will be entitled to a proportionate share of the property, depending upon the number of joint tenants. There can never be severance in law of the legal estate.

## APPLYING THE LAW

If Deirdre severs her share from Duncan then she will be entitled to a half share and she can deal in that. She can make a will leaving that share to her sister and that will be operative on her death. Duncan will receive only a half share of the value of the property.

## APPLYING THE LAW

In the example, where the property was owned by Susie, Sally, Vicki and Stuart, if Susie wants to sever her share then she can do so. There are rules as to how this will be done but if Susie and Sally had a fatal accident then on their death Susie's share would pass under her will to the NSPCC whereas Sally's share would pass to the other joint tenants because she had not severed it during her lifetime.

## KEY FACTS

**Joint tenancies**

**1.** No single owner can claim they own a separate share.

**2.** A joint tenancy cannot arise unless the four unities are present: possession, interest, title and time.

**3.** The right of survivorship will operate in a joint tenancy.

**4.** It is possible to sever a joint tenancy in equity.

**5.** The effect of severance is such that the interest in equity will constitute a separate share.

# 8.4 Tenancy in common

In contrast to joint tenants, tenants in common are said to own an undivided share in land. This means that they actually have notional shares of the ownership of the land. They cannot claim any specific physical division of the land into specific areas to represent a separate share. Just as in the case of a joint tenancy, the students cannot say of their bedrooms 'this is mine'.

However, the law will recognise shares which can be dealt with during one's lifetime or on death. The tenant in common can sell his share or mortgage his share and, most significantly, leave it to someone in their will, and that provision will be effective. The shares of the tenants in common may be equal or unequal. Duncan can argue that his share represents two-thirds and Deirdre has a share representing one-third.

## 8.4.1 The 'four unities'

The four unities must be present before a joint tenancy can exist **but** it is only necessary for there to be unity of possession between the tenants in the case of a tenancy in common. So, unlike in a joint tenancy, there does not also have to be unity of interest, or of title or of time.

In practice this means that each joint tenant must be entitled to possession of the whole. So if we refer back to the four students who purchase property together, no one student can claim that they 'own' their bedroom and they could be forced to allow others into their room if they so wish. If Sally decided she did not like the other students, and in particular, Stuart, she could not prevent him from entering her room. She could not successfully bring an action for trespass.

If they were tenants in a relationship of landlord and tenant then their room would be for them alone. They would have a legal estate in the land and it would be exclusive to them, which means they could keep others out including the landlord.

## APPLYING THE LAW

Sally and Stuart take separate leases of 20 Hill Road, Oxford. They may take them at the same time but they are each tenants and they each have a separate legal estate in their part of the land. This will allow them to keep the other out from their part of the property and they can be said to own a separate share of the land.

## 8.4.2 Survivorship

**APPLYING THE LAW**

If Duncan and Deirdre held as tenants in common from the start then you could argue that they always held their shares separately and when one dies then their share would pass under the terms of his or her will or on intestacy and it would not automatically pass to the survivor.

# 8.5 Creation of co-ownership in land

## 8.5.1 The legal title

We have already seen that a person may acquire the legal title to land by means of a conveyance of the title to him followed by registration as the registered proprietor. If the legal title is registered in the name of more than one person then co-ownership of the legal title will arise.

### The legal estate can only exist as a joint tenancy

Under the Law of Property Act 1925:

 's 1(6) A legal estate is not capable of subsisting or of being created in an undivided share in land'.

Under this section it is impossible for there to be a tenancy in common of the legal title of land. So co-ownership of the legal title must be in the form of a joint tenancy.

## The legal estate cannot be severed

Under the Law of Property Act 1925:

**S** 's 36(2) No severance of a joint tenancy of a legal estate, so as to create a tenancy in common in land, shall be permissible, whether by operation of law or otherwise, but this subsection does not affect the right of a joint tenant to release his interest to the other joint tenants, or the right to sever a joint tenant in an equitable interest whether or not the legal estate is vested in the joint tenants'.

Under this section a joint tenancy of the legal title cannot be severed so there can never be a tenancy in common of the legal title.

## There is a limit as to how many people can own the legal title at law

No more than four persons can hold the legal estate. Under the Law of Property Act 1925:

**S** 's 34(2) Where, after the commencement of this Act, land is expressed to be conveyed to any persons in undivided shares and those persons are of full age, the conveyance shall (notwithstanding anything to the contrary in this Act) operate as if the land had been expressed to be conveyed to the grantees, or, if there are more than four grantees, to the four first named in the conveyance, as joint tenants [in trust for the persons interested in the land]'.

This section provides that a maximum of four persons can be joint tenants of the legal title. If the legal title is conveyed to more than four people then it is the first four named on the conveyance who are *sui juris* and will become the joint tenants of the legal title. Anyone suffering from a disability in the eyes of the law is not *sui juris*, for example if they are under 18 or mentally incapable.

## APPLYING THE LAW

Five students – Sarah, Tara, Una, Vera and Wanda – jointly buy a house in Salisbury. Tara is only 17 and therefore cannot hold the legal title to land. Sarah, Una, Vera and Wanda will jointly hold the legal estate. They will hold the equitable estate on trust for themselves and Tara. Tara will get an interest in equity only.

## 8.5.2 Co-ownership in equity

In equity the title can be held either as a joint tenancy or as a tenancy in common. This contrasts with the legal tenancy which can only be held jointly.

### Solving the question: is it a joint tenancy or a tenancy in common?

1. **Intentions of the parties**: the parties may expressly state on the conveyance of the property whether the co-ownership is a joint tenancy or a tenancy in common; any words used which suggest severance will indicate a tenancy in common. Thus there will be a tenancy in common if the conveyance includes such expressions as '**to be divided amongst**', '**equally**' and even '**to be divided equally**'. The reason that this will imply a tenancy in common is because the law sees any suggestion of a share as implying a division between the owners.

Where there is an express statement in the conveyance as to how the shares are to be held that will be conclusive. In *Goodman v Gallant* [1986] Fam 106 the conveyance stated that the property was to be held 'upon trusts to sell . . . as joint tenants'. This was conclusive and it was irrelevant whether the contributions were unequal or whether there were other factors which would suggest a tenancy in common.

The law can imply either a joint tenancy or a tenancy in common. The law will favour a joint tenancy since equity follows the law but there might be some special reason why a tenancy in common may be implied.

2. **Unequal contributions to the purchase price**: where parties have contributed unequally to the purchase price of land, it is implied that there is a tenancy in common. The shares will be proportionate to the size of their contributions. Of course, if they contributed equally, the presumption will be that there was a joint tenancy.

3. **Loan on mortgage**: where money is loaned by two or more mortgagees the interest that they take in the property will be held as tenants in common.

4. **Business partnerships**: where land has been purchased by persons as business partners the assumption is that they would not have wanted their relationship to be determined by survivorship, which is inappropriate in the business context. In this kind of relationship a tenancy in common will be implied. A joint tenancy would be inappropriate to a business relationship.

5. **Individual business tenants**: it will also apply where businessmen have taken a lease of premises together but for their individual purposes.

# CASE EXAMPLE

### *Malayan Credit Ltd v Jack Chia-MPH Ltd* [1986] AC 549 (PC)

Here, two business tenants took a lease. The terms were that they would jointly rent office space for five years. They paid rent and service charges in certain agreed proportions. The lease did not contain any words of severance. The court held that since they took the lease in the course of a partnership, they took as tenants in common.

> 'The argument is that, in the absence of an express agreement, persons who take as joint tenants at law hold as tenants in common in equity only in three classes of case:
>
> **first**, where they have provided the purchase money in unequal shares; in this case they hold the beneficial interest in similar shares;
>
> **secondly**, where the grant consists of a security for a loan and the grantees were equal or unequal contributors to the loan; again they would hold the beneficial interest in the same shares; and
>
> **thirdly**, where they are partners and the subject matter of the grant is partnership property'.
>
> Lord Brightman

He found in this case that there could be a tenancy in common for the following reasons:

1. the lease was clearly taken to serve the separate commercial interest of the defendant and the claimant

2. prior to the grant of the lease the parties had settled between themselves what space they would respectively occupy when the lease came to be granted. This was roughly 62 per cent to the defendant and 38 per cent to the claimant

3. prior to the grant of the lease, the parties had made meticulous measurements of their respective allotted areas, and divided their liability for the rent and service charge in unequal shares in accordance with the respective areas that they would occupy

4. prior to the grant of the lease, the claimant was invoiced for its due share of the deposit. After the grant of the leases, the defendant and the claimant paid the stamp duty and the survey fees in the same unequal shares

5. as from the grant of the lease, the rent and the service charges were paid in the same unequal shares.

**Deciding whether there is a joint tenancy or a tenancy in common**

## KEY FACTS

|  | Joint tenancy | Tenancy in common |
|---|---|---|
| What is expressly or impliedly included in the conveyance? | The law favours a joint tenancy since equity follows the law. A statement in the agreement will be conclusive. | A tenancy in common will not be implied where the agreement is silent. |
| Are the contributions to the purchase price equal or unequal? | Equal contributions. | Unequal contributions. |
| Are the co-owners business partners? | Usually family arrangements. | Business partners. |
| Are the co-owners mortgagees? | If the agreement states it is a joint tenancy then it is irrelevant that there are two or more mortgagees. | Two or more mortgagees. |
| Are the parties individual business tenants? | Must be expressly stated to be a joint tenancy. | If business tenants take a lease together in the course of a business. |

It is clear from the above that if the agreement states how the parties are to hold the property then it will be conclusive and other evidence is irrelevant but if the agreement is silent then the other factors will be material to the decision.

## ACTIVITY

Consider the following and decide whether the parties hold the land as joint tenants or as tenants in common:

1. Gillian purchased Holly Lodge with her two friends, Kim and Keith. The house cost £300,000 and they each contributed £100,000.

2. Gillian purchased Holly Lodge with her two friends, Kim and Keith. The house cost £150,000 and Gillian contributed £70,000 while the others contributed £40,000 each. The conveyance read 'The purchasers declare that they hold Holly Lodge as beneficial joint tenants'.

3. Kim and Keith are business partners in a small business as IT consultants. They buy a terraced house, 2 Microchip Road, Hendon, as their business premises.

4. Bella and Isabel lend money to Kim and Keith to purchase 2 Microchip Road, Hendon.

5. Gillian, Kim and Keith buy Grange Farm for £400,000 and Gillian contributes £200,000. Kim contributes £120,000 leaving Keith to contribute the remaining £80,000.

# 8.6 Methods of severance of a joint tenancy

## 8.6.1 Meaning of 'severance'

It is possible for a joint tenant in equity to sever the tenancy, which means dividing the interest, and he will then become a tenant in common of his share. This does not affect the other joint tenants if there are more than one. Their shares will continue to be held under a joint tenancy.

### What is the effect of this?

The interest will no longer be subject to the right of survivorship. The benefits that arise under the right of survivorship will be lost.

## APPLYING THE LAW

Frederick buys a house with his friends, Francis and Felix. They buy jointly in equal shares and it is held that they are joint tenants. Frederick has made a will leaving all his property, real and personal, to his sister Elsie. As the will cannot sever an interest, if something happens to Frederick and he dies, his share will automatically pass to Francis and Felix, not to Elsie.

Compare these facts:

## APPLYING THE LAW

Four friends – George, Gerald, Gregory and Gary – buy Wintry Lodge as joint tenants. George severs his interest and now holds as a tenant in common. Gerald, Gregory and Gary continue to hold as joint tenants. If Gary has an accident and dies, his share will pass to Gerald and Gregory but not to George as he holds as a tenant in common and cannot benefit from the principle of survivorship.

## 8.6.2 Methods of severance under statute

Severance by written notice under the Law of Property Act 1925:

's 36(2) . . . no severance of a joint tenancy of a legal estate, so as to create a tenancy in common in land, shall be permissible, whether by operation of law or otherwise, but this subsection does not affect the right of a joint tenant to release his interest to the other joint tenants, or the right to sever a joint tenancy in an equitable interest whether or not the legal estate is vested in the joint tenants . . . if any tenant desires to sever the joint tenancy in equity, he shall give to the other joint tenants a notice in writing of such desire or do such other acts or things as would, in the case of personal estate, have been effectual to sever the tenancy in equity'.

One key feature is the need to give written notice to all the other joint tenants. This method is entirely unilateral, which means the joint tenant does not require the consent of the other joint tenants. The written notice does not need to be signed. The notice does not need to be in any particular form.

## APPLYING THE LAW

George, Gerald, Gregory and Gary, four law students, buy Wintry Lodge. They purchase as joint tenants. George decides that law is not for him and wishes to leave Wintry Lodge and go travelling. He can write to Gerald, Gregory and Gary and that would be sufficient for him to sever his interest. If Gary says 'I am not happy about you leaving and I won't agree to you severing your interest' George can ignore this and it would not affect the severance of his equitable share.

The Law of Property Act 1925 covers what constitutes proper service by post for the purposes of s 36(2):

's 196(1) Any notice required or authorised by this Act to be served or given by this Act shall be in writing. . . .

(3) Any notice required or authorised by this Act to be served shall be sufficiently served if it is left at the last-known place of abode or business in the United Kingdom of the lessee, lessor, mortgagee, mortgagor, or other person to be served, or, in the case of a notice required or authorised to be served on a lessee or mortgagor is affixed or left for him on the land or any house or building comprised in the lease or mortgage . . .

(4) Any notice required or authorised by this Act to be served shall also be sufficiently served, if it is sent by post in a registered letter addressed to the lessee, lessor, mortgagee, mortgagor, or other person to be served, by name, at the aforesaid place of abode or business, office, or counting-house, and if that letter is not returned . . . undelivered; and that service shall be deemed to be made at the time at which the registered letter would in the ordinary course be delivered'.

The main difference between the two sections is that under s 196(3) where ordinary post is used then the notice will be properly served if it is left at one of **two** places: either the last place where the joint tenant was living or the last-known business address of the joint tenant.

Under s 196(4), where registered post is used then the letter should be sent to the last-known business address or home address of the joint tenant.

**Key case** on severance:

## CASE EXAMPLE

### *Kinch v Bullard* [1999] 1 WLR 423

A wife, who was terminally ill, decided to take action to sever the joint tenancy of the matrimonial home where she lived with her husband. The relationship had broken down and she was contemplating divorce proceedings. The solicitors prepared a notice of severance and this was posted by ordinary post. The husband suffered a serious heart attack before he read it and went into hospital. The wife found the letter of severance at the home and decided to destroy it. The husband died a fortnight later without reading the notice. Some five months after that, the wife herself died. The court had to decide whether the issue of proceedings by the wife was sufficient to sever the joint tenancy even though the husband had not had an opportunity to read the notice.

It was held that there had been sufficient severance under s 36(2) of the Law of Property Act 1925, even though the husband had not actually read the notice.

The case for the husband's estate relied on the meaning given to s 196(3) of the Law of Property Act 1925 which held that any notice would be sufficiently served if it was left at the last-known place of abode or business in the United Kingdom of the person to be served. It was applied to the facts of the case as follows:

- the last-known abode of the husband was the matrimonial home

- the notice was left at the house because it was placed in the letter box, even though it was later removed by the wife

- in these circumstances the notice had been duly 'served' in accordance with s 196(3).

'The very purpose of sending a notice is to convey information, with legal consequences, on the addressee: it cannot be right that the sender of a notice can take positive steps to ensure that the notice does not come to the attention of the addressee after it has been statutorily deemed to have been served, and then to fall back on the statute to allege that service has none the less been effected'.

Neuberger J

Neuberger J also suggested that the notice of severance could have been withdrawn at any point preceding its postal delivery if the joint tenant had told the other joint tenant that she wished to do so. So the wife could have prevented service of the written notice if she had gone to the husband and told him that she no longer wished to sever. The letter then would have had no effect. Once a letter is in the postal system, it is very difficult to intercept it.

## Key issues to be considered in relation to severance

There will not be severance if the proposal to sever is merely part of **proposals** during negotiations. So if severance of the legal estate is proposed during negotiations for divorce as one of a number of alternatives in relation to jointly owned property, then the court will not accept that this is sufficient severance to satisfy s 36(2) of the Law of Property Act 1925.

# ASE EXAMPLE

### *Gore & Snell v Carpenter* (1990) P & CR 456

After the marriage between the parties had broken down there were negotiations over a separation agreement. A clause of severance of the property was included with the divorce proposals but it was not separate from the other papers. The husband died during the negotiations over the agreement and the divorce. It was held that there had not been effective severance under s 36 of the 1925 Act and the property vested in the wife by survivorship.

'It is in my judgment, a question of intention and this applies also when it is a question of the fourth possible method of severance, namely the service of a notice under s.36(2) of the Law of Property Act 1925. It is argued for the executors that the proposed separation agreement put forward by Mr Carpenter amounted to such notice. It will be recalled that the paragraph I read expressly refers to severance, but that was only part of the deed and the deed was never accepted. It was put forward by Mr Carpenter, not in isolation but as part of the package of proposals, and was not intended, in my judgment, and therefore did not take effect as a notice under section 36(2)'.

Judge Blackett-Ord

Severance will only be effective if the joint tenant manifests an intention of an **immediate** desire to sever his interest. It would not be sufficient to express an intention to sever sometime in the future.

# CASE EXAMPLE

### *Harris v Goddard* [1983] 1 WLR 1203

The husband and wife jointly owned the matrimonial home. When their relationship broke down the wife issued divorce proceedings which included a request 'for such order with regard to their property as may be just', specifically referring to a transfer of property and settlement of the property. The husband died from injuries he sustained in a car crash before the petition was heard.

There were **opposing arguments** as to whether there had been severance:

1. **Counsel for the executors for the husband** claimed that the joint tenancy had been severed by the service of the petition. The effect would be that half the property would pass with his estate.

2. **Counsel for the wife** argued that there had not been severance and that the husband's share would pass to the wife under the principle of survivorship.

The Court of Appeal held that there had been no severance because the wife had not shown an immediate intention to sever. 'A desire to sever must evince an intention to bring about the wanted result immediately' (Lawton LJ).

Notice must be served on **all** the joint tenants.

**No specific form** is necessary for the notice. The notice can take any form so long as it clearly shows a wish to sever immediately. It can be contained in another document such as an application to court for an order concerning the property.

## CASE EXAMPLE

### *Re Draper's Conveyance* [1969] 1 Ch 486

An application for an order directing the sale of the matrimonial home with the proceeds to be distributed between the parties was held to be a written notice of severance. An order had been made, but had not been executed, when the husband died. It was held that there had been severance and the property was held by the wife on trust for herself and her husband's estate in equal shares.

*Harris v Goddard* and *Re Draper's Conveyance* should be compared. The key issue in these cases was whether there was an immediate desire to sever. Although both cases concerned applications to the court, *Harris v Goddard* did not show an immediate desire to sever the estate, but merely a request for the court to decide the issue, and this was not enough for severance.

**Service** of the notice can be by ordinary post **or** registered post. It will be sufficient to send a notice by registered post to either the other joint tenant's last-known abode or his place of business, even if he does not receive it. However, a notice sent by registered post to either of these addresses will be effective even if it is not delivered, unless it is expressly returned to the sender.

# CASE EXAMPLE

### Re 88 Berkeley Road NW9 [1971] Ch 648

Miss Goodwin and Miss Eldridge lived together at the same address as joint tenants. Miss Goodwin decided to get married and served a notice of severance on Miss Eldridge by sending a registered letter to the address where they lived together. Miss Eldridge was away on holiday when the letter arrived, so Miss Goodwin signed a receipt for her own notice of severance. She died a few weeks later. Miss Eldridge contested that she had never received the notice.

The court decided that service is effective when the letter is sent by registered post, even if the co-owner seeking to sever signs on behalf of the recipient to prove receipt of the notice.

'The decision in *Kinch* echoes the earlier case of *Re 88 Berkeley Road* since it again raises the question of whether or not a written notice of severance from one joint tenant to another had been "given" as required by s 36(2) LPA 1925. This, in turn, requires consideration of what constitutes proper service of a notice under s 196 LPA 1925 – is it sufficient merely to leave it at the premises or must it be established that it was actually received by the addressee? In *Re 88 Berkeley Road* the court held that delivery at the last known address of the other joint tenant constituted service without the need to establish actual receipt. This decision would clearly have disposed of *Kinch* had it not been for the fact that the notice in *Re 88 Berkeley Road* was sent by recorded delivery and came under s 196(4) whereas the notice in *Kinch* went by ordinary first class post and so was covered by s 196(3). In the event Neuberger J refused to distinguish between these two methods of delivery and held that, as in *Re 88 Berkeley Road*, it was sufficient to establish that the notice sent by first class post had been delivered to the addressee's last known place of abode and there was no further necessity to show actual receipt by the addressee . . . A more difficult argument put forward by the defendants was that a notice should not be treated as properly given where it is the actual sender who picks it up and files or destroys it, as opposed, for example, to its having been eaten by the family dog. The judge saw here a possibility of abuse by a joint tenant who might post a notice of severance and then collect it on its arrival at the house thereby ensuring that it never came to the attention of the other joint tenant'.

M Percival, 'Severance by Written Notice – A Matter of Delivery?' [1999] 63 Conv 61

## KEY FACTS

**Severance by written notice**

**1.** Under s 36(2) of the Law of Property Act 1925, notice can be effected by serving notice in writing.

**2.** It is entirely unilateral and does not require consent from the other joint tenants.

**3.** Written notice will only be effective where the severance is to take effect immediately.

**4.** There is no written severance if the proposal to sever is simply part of other proposals and is not mentioned separately.

**5.** The notice must be served on all the joint tenants.

**6.** No specific form is necessary for the written notice.

**7.** Service of the notice can be by registered post or simple post if there is proof that it was actually served at the correct address.

## 8.6.3 Severance at common law under *Williams v Hensman*

J 'A joint tenancy may be severed in three ways: in the first place, an act of any one of the persons interested operating upon his own share may create a severance as to that share. The right of each joint tenant is a right by survivorship only in the event of no severance having taken place of the share which is claimed under the *ius accrescendi*. Each one is at liberty to dispose of his own interest in such manner as to sever it from the joint fund – losing, of course, at the same time, his own right of survivorship. Secondly a joint tenancy may be severed by mutual agreement. And in the third place, there may be severance by any course of dealing sufficient to intimate that the interests of all were mutually treated as constituting a tenancy in common. When the severance depends on an inference of this kind without any express act of severance, it will not suffice to rely on an intention, with respect to the particular share, declared only behind the backs of the other persons interested'

Wood V C in *Williams v Hensman* (1861) 1 J&H 546 (70 ER 802)

*Williams v Hensman* suggests that there are three different ways that a joint tenancy can be severed at common law:

- severance by **conduct**
  (an act of any one of the persons interested operating upon his own share; eg joint tenant transfers his share to a third party; a transfer of the joint tenant's share in the land to another joint tenant)
- severance by **mutual agreement**
  (dependent on all the joint tenants being in agreement)
- severance by **mutual conduct**
  (this involves actual physical division of the land).

## 8.6.4 Severance by conduct

There are several different ways that this can be put into effect:

### An act of one party operating upon his share

The most obvious example would be **sale** of your share. The reason it severs the joint tenancy is because it destroys unity of title and all four unities are essential to a joint tenancy.

## APPLYING THE LAW

Janet, John and Sally purchase No 3 Maiden Lane in London from Mr Rules, when they are students at Thameshire University. Sally's course ends after three years and she sells her share to Kevin. Janet and John each have one more year at university. Kevin will not have the same title as the others as his purchase derives from Sally and the others have purchased from Mr Rules.

Note that the legal title cannot be severed and although Sally has sold her equitable estate she will remain joint tenant of the legal estate. This means that when eventually the property is sold, Sally will have to consent to the sale of the property and Kevin will receive only a share in equity.

The formal commencement of litigation concerning a joint tenancy will be considered as an act operating upon one's share.

# CASE EXAMPLE

### Re Draper's Conveyance [1969] 1 Ch 486

It was held that proceedings prior to the court order such as the serving of the summons and the affidavit in this case could constitute acting on one's share as well as severance under s 36(2) of the 1925 Act. It is important to see that the court order itself did not constitute the act; the order was merely putting into effect the request made to the court under the summons.

Another example of severance under this head would be by mortgaging his share. It will also be severance where the tenant applies to court for an order directing sale of the jointly owned property. The position is the same even if the mortgage itself is fraudulent

# CASE EXAMPLE

### First National Securities v Hegerty [1985] QB 850

A husband fraudulently forged his wife's signature when applying for a mortgage of the family home owned by them as joint tenants. He defaulted on the mortgage instalments but the court held that there had been severance at the time of the application and they then held as tenants in common. The important effect of this was that Mrs Hegerty's share was free of the mortgage.

The position is different where all the joint tenants join together to seek a mortgage over the property. As they are acting together, they will not be held to sever their interests.

## Bankruptcy

A joint tenant's bankruptcy will also sever his interest which will then vest in his trustee in bankruptcy. This means that the trustee in bankruptcy takes over as if he is the owner of the property. It is irrelevant to the issue of severance that this is a hostile and involuntary act.

A difficulty may arise in deciding at what point the bankruptcy actually severs the estate. Consider the following two cases, the result of which depended on whether the Bankruptcy Act 1914 or the Insolvency Act 1986 applied:

ASE EXAMPLE

### Re Dennis (A Bankrupt) [1996] Ch 80

Property was jointly owned by a husband and wife. The husband committed an act of bankruptcy and the case was governed by the Bankruptcy Act 1914. A bankruptcy petition was presented but before the trustee in bankruptcy was appointed, the wife died. The issue was whether the presentation of the petition was sufficient to sever the share of the husband or whether there was only severance at the time of the appointment of the trustee in bankruptcy. Under the doctrine of relation back, the bankruptcy would take effect when the first act of bankruptcy took place. In this case it was before the wife died, so there was severance before her death. The doctrine of survivorship could not take effect.

**C**ASE EXAMPLE

### Re Palmer Dec'd (A Debtor) [1994] Ch 314

Under the Insolvency Act 1986 it was held that an insolvency order does not take effect until there has been an order of bankruptcy from the court. If the debtor who is a joint tenant dies without such an order being made, the whole of the property will vest under the doctrine of survivorship in the other joint tenant.

A gift of the property under a will is not seen as 'acting on one's share'.

If one joint tenant draws up a will and leaves his share to another, that will not be seen as acting on one's share. There will be no severance of the interest and the gift under the will does not take effect on death.

## Transfer by one party to a third party

Here there is an overlap with the previous section. The transfer of one's share to another will constitute an act of severance. This may be by way of gift or sale.

# APPLYING THE LAW

In Figure 8.1, W, X, Y and Z own the title of the property in law and in equity. W decides to sell his share and A agrees to buy. W will remain joint owner of the legal estate but A will now own a share in equity as tenant in common. X, Y and Z continue to own jointly in equity.

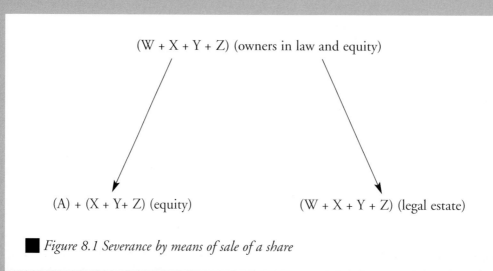

(W + X + Y + Z) (owners in law and equity)

(A) + (X + Y+ Z) (equity)          (W + X + Y + Z) (legal estate)

■ *Figure 8.1 Severance by means of sale of a share*

If Y had an accident and died, his share would now pass to X and Z. A would not receive a share as A holds as a tenant in common.

If they all decide to sell after the death of Y, A will receive a quarter share as A's share will remain the same fraction as when he bought the property. The remaining purchase money will then be shared between X and Z. W will have to take part in the sale.

No decision on the legal estate can be taken without the agreement of W but W no longer has an interest in the equitable interest and will receive nothing back from the sale. W received the purchase price when he sold his interest to A.

If W decides to sell his share and Y says that he would like to buy the share, that is also an act of severance. Although there appear to be the same four unities present, unity of interest will no longer be present.

W + X + Y + Z

↓

(Y) + X + Y + Z

 *Figure 8.2 Severance by transfer of one joint tenant's share to another joint tenant*

In Figure 8.2, Y holds one quarter share as a tenant in common. However, he also holds as a joint tenant with X and Z.

If Z had an accident and died, his share would then pass to X and Y but Y's share as a tenant in common would not be affected.

If X and Y now decide to sell to A, the purchase price will be divided as follows. Y will receive one quarter of the money as tenant in common and then X and Y will receive half of the remaining value. If the house was sold for £200,000 it would work out as follows. Y receives £50,000 and then the remaining £150,000 will be divided equally, giving X and Y £75,000 each.

Y will finally have £125,000 and X will have £75,000.

The law is prepared to consider even the contract for sale as constituting an act of transfer. If the contract for sale is itself specifically enforceable then the contract will be sufficient.

## KEY FACTS

### What constitutes 'acting on one's share'?

1. Sale destroys the four unities necessary for there to be a joint tenancy and severance is then effective for that share.

2. The formal start of litigation will be sufficient for severance.

3. Mortgaging one's share, even where there is no agreement from the other tenant.

4. Bankruptcy will sever but it will depend on whether the Bankruptcy Act 1914 or the Insolvency Act 1986 applies as to when the severance actually takes place.

5. A gift of an interest under a joint tenancy in a will cannot be an act of severance sufficient to sever the joint tenancy.

## 8.6.5 Severance by mutual agreement

If severance relies on mutual agreement then there must be some contact and measure of agreement between the parties. Unlike severance under s 36(2) of the 1925 Act, this cannot be a unilateral act. The key feature here is the fact that the joint tenants act together and so an agreement can be inferred. The courts are not necessarily looking for an agreement that can be specifically enforced.

> **J** 'The significance of an agreement is not that it binds the parties; but that it serves as an indication of a common intention to sever, something which it was indisputably within their power to do'.
>
> Sir John Pennycuick in *Burgess v Rawnsley* [1975] Ch 429

## APPLYING THE LAW

If Cato and Peta, who have lived together for 12 years, decide to sever the joint tenancy, then the fact that they agree orally that one party will buy the other's share may be enough to imply an agreement. If the negotiations cast any doubt on this then there can be no severance under this head. So if Cato tries to persuade Peta to stay and not to sell her share to him, it is doubtful whether there is proper severance by mutual agreement.

The agreement would not be legally enforceable because it would not comply with s 2 of the Law of Property (Miscellaneous Provisions) Act 1989 which requires any contract for the sale of an interest in land (subject to certain very limited exceptions) to be in writing. It would still be effective as severance of the legal estate preventing the doctrine of survivorship from applying.

Severance by mutual agreement was contested in the important case of *Burgess v Rawnsley*.

# CASE EXAMPLE

### *Burgess v Rawnsley* [1975] Ch 429

Mrs Rawnsley met Mr Honick at a scripture rally in Trafalgar Square and, in spite of his rather unprepossessing looks ('he looked like a tramp' said Mrs Rawnsley), they formed a close relationship. Shortly after they met, they jointly purchased the property in which for some time he had been living as a tenant. The relationship did not last and Mrs Rawnsley agreed orally that she would sell her share to him. However, she changed her mind about the price and asked for more money. Mr Honick died before the negotiations were finalised. The court considered whether there had been a severance of the joint tenancy. The main problem was that Mrs Rawnsley had decided not to proceed on the oral agreement.

Arguments on behalf of Mrs Rawnsley:

**1.** no conduct is sufficient to sever a joint tenancy unless it is irrevocable

**2.** the agreement was not in writing

**3.** the agreement was revocable.

Arguments on behalf of Mr Honick's estate:

**1.** an oral agreement is capable of severing a joint tenancy

**2.** even where an agreement is not specifically enforceable, it is capable of severing a joint tenancy

**3.** even where an agreement is subsequently revoked, it is still evidence of 'mutual conduct' under *Williams v Hensman*.

The court upheld the arguments on behalf of Mr Honick's estate, which meant that half the value of the property passed with his estate to his daughter. If there had been no severance then Mrs Rawnsley could have claimed the whole of the property under the doctrine of survivorship.

'I think there was evidence that Mr Honick and Mrs Rawnsley did come to an agreement that he would buy her share for £750. That agreement was not in writing and it was not specifically enforceable. Yet it was sufficient to effect a severance. Even if there was not any firm agreement but only a course of dealing, it clearly evinced an intention by both parties that the property should henceforth be held in common and not jointly'.

Denning MR

In *Gore and Snell v Carpenter* the agreement fell short of mutual agreement because there was no evidence of an agreement, merely agreement in principle. There had been discussions but there had never been agreement. There is a direct contrast between this case and *Burgess v Rawnsley* where there had been agreement that Mrs Rawnsley would sell to Mr Honick but the price was not settled.

J 'Then was there a course of dealing? There were negotiations, as I have said, but negotiations are not the same thing as a course of dealing. A course of dealing is where over the years the parties have dealt with their interests in the property on the footing that they are interests in common and are not joint . . . But in the present case there were simply negotiations between the husband and wife and again there was no finality and there was no mutuality. For severance to be effected by a course of dealing all the joint tenants must be concerned in such a course and in the present case there is no evidence that Mrs Carpenter was committing herself to accepting a tenancy in common prior to the property division which would have been made in the divorce proceedings'.

Judge Blackett-Ord

## Types of agreement that will sever the tenancy

- An agreement that contemplates severance expressly, as in *Burgess v Rawnsley*, will be sufficient even if the exact terms such as price have not been agreed.

- An agreement during divorce proceedings about the division of property in specific terms, for example in equal shares.

## Types of agreement that will not sever the joint tenancy

- An agreement by all the co-owners to sell or lease the property.

- An agreement that does not relate specifically to the ownership of the jointly owned land.

# CASE EXAMPLE

### *Nielson-Jones v Fedden and Others* **[1975] Ch 222**

After separation, the parties entered into negotiations about the ownership of their property. They were in very general terms and included a memorandum agreeing that the husband was to use his entire discretion . . . to . . . sell the matrimonial home and employ the proceeds realised to his new home . . . in order to provide a home . . . for himself to live in. Although the husband had indicated his intention to sever the joint tenancy, he died before that was put into effect. It was held that the husband had nothing more than authority to sell the property on behalf of them both; it did not sever the tenancy.

> 'If, as I have held, the memorandum was not an assignment of Mrs Todd's interest in the proceeds of sale of the house to her husband, can it nevertheless be read as a severance of their joint beneficial interests: an agreement to the effect that each of them thereafter is to be solely entitled to his and her respective one half share in such proceeds? With the best will in the world, I find myself wholly unable to give the memorandum such a construction . . . I think it is in fact rather easier to read the memorandum as an assignment than it is as a severance, so that as I cannot give it the first construction, almost *a fortiori* I cannot give it the second . . . The question then is, can such a declaration – a unilateral declaration – ever be effective to sever a beneficial joint tenancy? It appears to me that in principle there is no conceivable ground for saying that it can. So far as I can see, such a mere unilateral declaration does not in any way shatter any one of the essential unities. Moreover if it did, it would appear that a wholly unconscionable amount of time and trouble has been wasted by conveyancers of old in framing elaborate assignments for the purpose of effecting a severance, when all that was required was a simple declaration'.

Walton J

## 8.6.6 Severance by mutual conduct

Severance may be effected 'by any course of dealing sufficient to intimate that the interests of all were mutually treated as constituting a tenancy in common' (Page-Wood V-C in *Williams v Hensman* (1861)).

The **key feature** here is that there must be a **course of conduct** that shows that the parties intended to treat their shares as separate and distinct. If this leads to an agreement then of course it will fall under 'mutual agreement'.

What amounts to a course of dealing sufficient for severance?

## Long-term assumptions about ownership

The parties may have acted in such a way that although they purchased as joint tenants they have treated their shares as separate and distinct shares.

> **J** 'A course of dealing is where over the years the parties have dealt with their interests in the property on the footing that they are interests in common and are not joint'.
>
> Judge Blackett-Ord in *Gore and Snell v Carpenter* (1990) 60 P & CR

In this case there had been discussions about the ownership of jointly owned property but these had not been acted on and the *status quo* remained until the husband died and there was no evidence that the wife had committed herself to a tenancy in common.

## Mutual wills

It is possible for two people to be bound by the terms of wills where they have been drawn up in identical terms and if they intend them to take effect as mutual wills. The usual terms will be to leave property to each other and then to a third party on the death of the survivor. These mutual wills sever the joint tenancy and the doctrine of survivorship will not apply. This is an exception to the principle that there can be no severance of interests in a joint tenancy under a mutual will.

# APPLYING THE LAW  ☐☐☐

Fred and Tina jointly own Grove Farm where they have lived all their life. They want to leave it to their nephew, Jonathan, and their niece, Jane, jointly on their death. They execute mutual wills leaving the farm to the survivor and then to Jonathan and Jane in equal shares. On Fred's death his share will pass under the will rather than under the doctrine of survivorship and Tina will be bound by the terms on her death. If she sought to deal in the property in any other way, this would not be binding.

☐☐☐

## Physical division of the property

Division of the property into separate units will not necessarily amount to a course of dealing leading to severance of the interests.

# CASE EXAMPLE

### *Greenfield v Greenfield* (1979) 38 P & CR 570

A house had been bought jointly by two married brothers. They then divided it up into two separate maisonettes where each brother lived with his wife. One brother died and his widow claimed to be entitled to his share of the property under his will. She argued that there had been severance through the physical division of the property. The court held that this was insufficient to constitute a 'course of dealing' and the share passed to the other brother under the doctrine of survivorship.

> 'The mere existence of separate maisonettes and of their separate occupation is not inconsistent with the continuation of a joint tenancy. The two can perfectly well exist together. The matter must be considered in the light of the evidence of the actual intentions of the parties'.

Fox J

## Inconclusive negotiations over the property

Where the parties discuss severance but do not come to any conclusions then it could be sufficient evidence of a course of dealing for severance. The law is not conclusive because the judiciary are not in agreement over this.

In *Burgess v Rawnsley* Lord Denning held that the fact that there were discussions constituted severance under this head.

> **J** 'It is sufficient if there is a course of dealing in which one party makes it clear to the other that he desires that their shares should no longer be held jointly but be held in common. I emphasise that it must be made clear to the other party . . . Similarly it is sufficient if both parties enter on a course of dealing which evinces an intention by both of them that their shares shall henceforth be held in common and not jointly'.

This view was not supported by the other judges in the case.

231

> **J** 'I do not doubt myself that where one tenant negotiates with another for some rearrangement of interest, it may be possible to infer from the particular facts a common intention to sever even though the negotiations break down. Whether such inference can be drawn must I think depend upon the particular facts. In the present case the negotiations between Mr Honick and Mrs Rawnsley, if they can be properly described as negotiations at all, fall, it seems to me, far short of warranting an inference. One could not ascribe to joint tenants an intention to sever merely because one offers to buy out the other for £X and the other makes a counter-offer of £Y'.
>
> Sir John Pennycuick

## The commencement of litigation

If one of the parties decides to commence litigation over the shares in the property this will not constitute severance under this head but it could be sufficient under one of the other headings under *Williams v Hensman*, for example 'acting on one's share'.

# ACTIVITY

Consider the following examples and decide whether or not there has been severance of the equitable estate, and explain why.

1. Gillian and Jack jointly own Honeysuckle Cottage. They have been living together for the past 15 years. Recently they have begun to argue and Gillian consults a solicitor about how she can sever the equitable estate of the property since she does not want to press for sale immediately. A letter is delivered to Jack at the property but before he has a chance to read it Gillian intercepts it and destroys it.

2. Gillian, Jack and Helen live together in property which all three of them jointly own. Helen lives on the top floor of the property and converts it into a self-contained flat where she lives on her own.

3. Gillian, Jack, Helen and Kerry buy a house together. Jack wants to emigrate and Kerry orally agrees to buy his share. They drew up an informal agreement but Kerry felt that the price was too high and she telephoned Jack to tell him that. The following day, she was run over and killed by a bus.

4. Gillian and Jack buy a house and move in together. They live happily for 10 years and then their relationship breaks down. Gillian finds out that she has a serious illness and decides to make her will and, not wishing Jack to inherit her estate, she leaves her property to his sister, Greta.

**5.** Helen and Ian got married and lived together for 10 years in Chestnut Villa, a house that they jointly owned. Helen met James at a conference in June and she told Ian that she wanted to split up. In July she contacted a solicitor and he wrote to Ian, telling him that Helen wanted to get the property matters sorted out without any fuss and that included ownership of Chestnut Villa. They agreed some matters but before they were finalised Ian had a fatal car crash and Helen is arguing that the interest in Chestnut Villa has not been severed.

## 8.6.7 Severance by operation of law

### Forfeiture

A further means of severing a joint tenancy arises where one joint tenant kills a fellow joint tenant. This has the effect of severing the joint tenancy and through forfeiture the murderer is prevented from profiting from the unlawful killing.

## APPLYING THE LAW

Ralph and Rosie jointly own a house in Yorkshire. Ralph is a very jealous man and he believes that Rosie is having an affair. Rosie comes home late from work one evening and he threatens her with a kitchen knife and eventually loses his temper and plunges it into her back, thereby killing her. The doctrine of survivorship would result in the property passing to Ralph. The law views this as unfair and imposes severance, allowing Rosie's share to pass under her will, or under the rules of intestacy if there is no will.

The effect, then, is that the legal estate is held on trust for the murderer and the victim's estate as tenants in common. So here, the house in Yorkshire will be held on trust for Ralph and Rosie's estate in equal shares.

The Forfeiture Act 1982 gives the court the power to grant relief against forfeiture in cases of homicide other than murder:

 's 2(1) Where a court determines that the forfeiture rule precluded a person (in this section referred to as "the offender") who has unlawfully killed another from acquiring any interest in property . . . the court may make an order under this section modifying the effect of that rule.

(2) The court shall not make an order under this section modifying the effect of the forfeiture rule in any case unless it is satisfied that, having regard to the conduct of the offender and of the deceased and to such other circumstances as appear to the court to be material, the justice of the case requires the effect of the rule to be modified in that case'.

# CASE EXAMPLE

### *Re K* [1985] Ch 85

In this case the wife was convicted of the manslaughter of her husband. The facts of the case showed that she had been subjected to terrible abuse at his hands. The ordinary rules on joint tenancies would allow her to claim the entire estate but the rules on forfeiture prevented her from doing so and she would only have been able to claim a half-share. The court exercised its discretion and allowed her to claim the husband's half-share of the property and so inherit the entire interest.

The situation can become more complicated if there is more than one tenant involved. There is a suggestion from courts in Australia that the innocent joint tenants should not be deprived of their share of the estate from the victim of the murder or manslaughter.

## APPLYING THE LAW

Rosie and Ralph live with Susie and Geoff. They jointly own Rose Villa. Ralph loses his temper and pushes Rosie against the kitchen window, which gives way, and she falls out on to the road below, suffering fatal injuries. Ralph is found guilty of manslaughter. The court would hold that Rosie's share should be held on trust for Susie and Geoff as joint tenants. Ralph should not be able to benefit from the share.

## Application of constructive trust principles

'Increasingly, the view is taken that the forfeiture imposed on the killer is best justified in terms of the application of an equitable doctrine of constructive trust based on unjust enrichment. In other words, the killer is recognised as taking the entirety by survivorship but is, by reason of his misconduct, subjected to the full rigour of equitable control. He is made to hold the legal estate on a constructive trust for himself and the victim's estate in equal shares.'

Gray and Gray, *Elements of Land Law* (3rd edn, Butterworths, 2001), p 873

# 8.6.8 Possible reform of severance

There is uncertainty over the different methods of severance. It is also felt that it should be possible to sever one's estate by will. For this reason, the question of severance was considered by the Law Commission in 1985. It looked at three options:

**1.** no substantive reform, but the incorporation of all methods of severance into a statutory provision

**2.** the restriction of methods of severance to written notice

**3.** the introduction of severance by will.

Possibly the most radical suggestion is the last point, which would allow severance on death through a provision in the will. This is discussed below.

'This is a radical suggestion, which runs counter to the whole concept of joint tenancy with its right of survivorship. This right is its distinctive feature, and is why equity in general favours the less capricious tenancy in common. Thus the arguments in favour of introducing severance by will must be carefully examined. The working paper mentions that in a matrimonial breakdown a spouse may be anxious to sever but unwilling to serve a notice and thereby aggravate negotiations over, for example, access to the children. The argument has a certain force, but the period during which such considerations hold sway should be quite short . . .

A more persuasive argument is that severance by will would prevent undesired devolution of property. There must be many cases where a beneficial joint tenant leaves his property by will, fondly (and not unreasonably) imagining that thereby the "half-share" in the house will go to his children, his new loved one or whomever . . .

The counter argument is two-fold:

**(i)** it would be unfair to allow severance by will, and;

**(ii)** difficult questions of construction would arise.

The first argument is that a "rogue" beneficial joint tenant could secretly sever by will and then enjoy the possibility of the right of survivorship without any risk to his estate. If he survived his co-tenant, he would take all, and if he pre-deceased, his chosen beneficiaries would inherit his share. The other difficulty with severance by will is a practical one – the construction of the will. The working paper states that severance by will should be specified and explicit: "severance should not be implied by a gift for example, of all the residue to a charity, but a gift of 'my half-share of Blackacre' should be sufficiently explicit to sever" . . . At present, it is sometimes uncertain whether *inter vivos* severance has taken place; the additional possibility of severance by will would no doubt result in still more uncertainty for the survivors and a succession of applications to court.'

L Tee, 'Severance Revisited' [1995] Conv 105

Eight years earlier severance was discussed in a series of articles. The main issue was whether the confirmed use of both joint tenancies and tenancies in common could be justified.

'In his recent article "Beneficial Joint Tenancies: A Case for Abolition?" [[1987] Conv 29] Mr Mark Thompson has reviewed a number of complications that can occur in law where land has been vested in co-owners as beneficial joint tenants. His suggested solution is to leave potential co-owners with just the one form, the tenancy in common, in respect of the beneficial interest in land. He also suggests that until legislation is effected to this end practitioners should urge clients to adopt that form of co-ownership. What he does not seem to make entirely clear is whether spouses and other co-purchasers should adopt a tenancy in equal shares or one according to their contributions, in so far as they may be at the outset calculable.

The mischiefs he envisages as justifying this radical solution are:

**(i)** problems when the marriage or other initial arrangement goes sour;

**(ii)** the uncertainties as to the manner in which severance may be effected;

**(iii)** the special problems arising when one co-owner is responsible for the death of another; and

**(iv)** the unpleasant surprise for severing co-owner that a severance will create equal beneficial shares, not resurrect the original contribution proportions.

Underlying all these mischiefs seems to be a belief that the parties have often, perhaps even usually, opted for joint tenancy without adequate advice. Is there any real evidence that this is so?

Against all this is the clear fact that many people are genuinely attracted to the survival aspects of joint tenancy. Not just married couples in the first romantic flush, wishing to demonstrate the full commitment of their mutual vows, but also unmarried siblings anxious to secure the smooth transmission of ownership as death overtakes each of them in their family home; or the father or mother in business with a child, wishing to effect just such a smooth transmission whether deaths do or do not occur in expected order . . .

The fundamental issue, however, remains whether the current option which is, in this writer's experience, often taken up with enthusiasm by co-owners should be denied them. Is it unarguably the case that the unsuccessful partnerships should dictate the apparatus of the law? If a relationship turns sour enough, why should not an aggrieved co-owner effect a severance? And are not the powers of the court to divide property on a break-down of a marriage sufficient?'

A M Pritchard, 'Beneficial Joint Tenancies: A Riposte' [1987] Conv 273

This article makes out a strong case for the retention of two forms of co-ownership in spite of the obvious difficulties. He argues against the proposition put forward by Mark Thompson that there should be only one form of co-ownership, namely the tenancy in common, because for many the joint tenancy genuinely reflects the wishes of the parties. The conversion of all co-owned property into a tenancy in common would only respond to those relationships which break down or encounter problems.

## 8.7 The rights of co-owners in land

### 8.7.1 The right of occupation of the co-owned land

Co-owners are entitled to occupy the land and they cannot exclude each other from the land or any part of it.

---

## KEY FACTS

1. A co-tenant can never legally exclude another co-tenant from his room and could not bring an action for trespass.

2. A co-owner not in occupation of the land through his own choice does not have an automatic right at common law to receive rent.

3. If a co-owner is excluded then rent will become payable by the co-owner in occupation.

---

## CASE EXAMPLE

**Dennis v Macdonald [1982] Fam 63**

A violent husband forced a wife to leave the family home. The court held that he should pay rent to her since he had remained in occupation.

---

Exclusion does not have to be made through an order of the courts. Exclusion can cover the case where one party leaves the family home after the marriage has broken down.

---

**CASE EXAMPLE**

**Re Pavlou (A Bankrupt) [1993] 1 WLR 1046**

The issue arose as to whether rent should be paid by a wife in sole occupation of property but paying the mortgage instalments and making improvements to the property. The husband had left because the relationship had broken down. Where it is a matrimonial home and the marriage has broken down, the party who leaves the property will in most cases, be regarded as excluded from the family home, so that an occupation rent should be paid by the co-owner who remains. But that is not a rule of law; that is merely a statement of the *prima facie* conclusion to be drawn from the facts.

---

The rent is assessed as if it was an assessment of a fair rent assessed at the Rent Tribunal; half the cost of any repairs carried out by the sole occupier can be set off against the rent paid.

## 8.7.2 The right to claim rent received from the land

If the co-owner lets the property then the rent should be shared between the parties, whether or not a co-owner is in possession. The rights of a co-owner are quantified according to the size of their share in the property.

---

### APPLYING THE LAW  □□□

Rosie and Jim are tenants in common of a terraced house in Tooting which they purchased together. Jim contributed two-thirds of the purchase price and Rosie contributed one-third. Rosie goes abroad for a year and Jim lets part of the property without telling Rosie. He gets £450 per month for letting her room. She demands the whole sum when she returns home and discovers what he has been doing with the property while she has been away.

Can she claim the whole £450?

□□□

---

The co-owner who lets out the property is not under any special duty towards his co-owner so they do not have to obtain the highest rent that they can. They have to account for any rent they actually receive but if it is at undervalue they do not have to account for the shortfall in rent.

## APPLYING THE LAW

Rosie cannot argue that the property could have been let at a much higher rent if Jim had advertised harder to find another tenant. If a co-tenant was held to be a fiduciary (someone under special fiduciary duties) then Jim would be liable to get the highest rent possible and would have to pay the difference to Rosie if he let the property at undervalue.

## What if the profit is the consequence of one co-owner's work or expertise?

> 'For instance, one tenant employs his capital and industry in cultivating the whole of a piece of land, the subject of the tenancy, in a mode in which the money and labour expended greatly exceed the value of the rent or compensation for the mere occupation of the land; in raising hops for example, which is a very hazardous adventure. He takes the whole of the crops: and is he to be accountable for any of the profits in such a case, when it is clear that, if the speculation had been a losing one altogether, he could not have called for a moiety of the losses, as he would have been enabled to do had it not been cultivated by the mutual agreement of the co-tenants?'.
>
> Parke B in *Henderson v Eason* (1851) 17 QB 710

The main points raised in this judgment are that:

1. if one tenant does all the work then the logic is that he should be able to claim the profits

2. if one tenant did all the work and made a loss then the other co-tenant could not be made to pay towards the loss, so why should the co-tenant get the profits?

3. the judge says that he who takes the risk should be able to claim the profit for himself.

## When will the co-tenant have to account for profits made on account of his own work?

The co-tenant will be liable for any profits made that affect the value of the land. The type of case would be where mining has taken place and the land is reduced in value. The co-tenant is quarrying for Fuller's Earth which renders the land 10 per cent less valuable than it was before the work began, so he must account for part of the profit that he has made.

It does not matter that he did not try to prevent the other co-owners from also making a profit from the land.

## 8.7.3 Liability for repairs

### APPLYING THE LAW

Tonia and Tony live together in jointly owned property for 10 years. Tonia meets someone else at work and they fall in love and she leaves Tony. They do not immediately plan to sell the property. Tony throws himself into a programme of DIY to console himself. He puts in a new bathroom and extends the kitchen. The property is now worth £20,000 more than it was before he started.

Can he claim a contribution towards the cost of the work from Tonia? Should he be able to keep all the increase in the value of the property or should he share that with Tonia?

### Improvements

The rule is that there is no right to a contribution towards repairs and improvements from a co-tenant.

### CASE EXAMPLE

**Leigh v Dickeson (1884) 15 QBD 60**

This case lays down the principle that the co-owner has no right to claim a contribution for the cost of repairs. A contribution can be claimed if there is an express or implied agreement that they should share the costs, or the work was requested by the co-tenant. Assessing the value of the contributions depends on whether the value of the property has increased or decreased.

### APPLYING THE LAW

If the co-tenant spends time and money on property but the actual increase in value is less than the costs involved, the co-tenant is limited to a claim on the increase in value of the property. If the property increase in value is far in excess of the value of the improvements, the co-tenant may be able to claim the value of the improvements as well as a share in the increased value of the property.

The right to receive compensation from a co-tenant may be an equity in the property itself which can even bind a third party if they buy with notice of such a right.

# 8.8 Termination of co-ownership

Co-ownership can be ended under the following circumstances:

## Transfer of trust property to purchaser

Once the purchaser buys from the co-owners, the trust of land comes to an end and they cease to be co-owners of land. The rights of the beneficiaries will transfer to the proceeds of sale and the purchaser will be absolute owner.

## Partition of trust property

If the co-owned property is effectively split between the co-owners so each has a legal estate carved out of the property, the co-ownership will come to an end. The property is then split into separate legal estates. This can only be done by deed under s 52 of the Law of Property Act 1925. There is provision for partition under s 7(1) of the Trusts of Land and Appointment of Trustees Act 1996 but it has been rarely used.

## Property in hands of sole owner

Sometimes the joint tenants agree that one co-owner will release his share to the other co-owner. Under the Law of Property Act 1925:

**S** 's 36(2) No severance of a joint tenancy of legal estate, so as to create a tenancy in common in land, shall be permissible, whether by operation of law or otherwise, but this subsection does not affect the right of a joint tenant to release his interest to the other joint tenants'.

## APPLYING THE LAW  □□□

Three students, Sue, Andrew and Chris, share a house in Gloucester as joint tenants. Chris decides to go around the world and although he contributed towards the purchase of the property he says he does not want the responsibility of a house in England. He releases his share to Sue and Andrew. There remains a joint tenancy between Sue and Andrew in law and in equity. This is not a sale but merely a release whereby the co-owner loses all rights to the property.

□□□

## Vesting in a sole owner

If one of two surviving joint tenants dies, leaving a sole survivor, the co-ownership is destroyed. This is the result of the doctrine of survivorship. There was a problem in any sale by a sole owner if the title was unregistered land. The purchaser would not be clear whether there had been severance of the title during the co-ownership.

## Registered land

Rule 172 of the Land Registration Rules 1925 lays down that the Registrar can remove from the Register any names of a joint proprietor who may have died, if the death certificate is produced. The registered owner has the right to deal as absolute owner.

## Unregistered land

If the property has unregistered title and the property vests in a single joint tenant, there is always the chance that there had been severance in the lifetime of the tenant and so the property will pass as if it is a separate share in equity. Until 1964 there could be no conveyance by the sole surviving joint tenant of the co-owned property unless a second trustee was appointed.

Under the Law of Property (Joint Tenants) Act 1964:

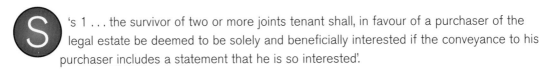 's 1 . . . the survivor of two or more joints tenant shall, in favour of a purchaser of the legal estate be deemed to be solely and beneficially interested if the conveyance to his purchaser includes a statement that he is so interested'.

The section will not apply in **two** circumstances:

1. a memorandum of severance signed by one of the joint tenants has been attached to the conveyance
2. a bankruptcy order made against any of the joint tenants or a petition for such an order has been registered under the Land Charges Act 1925.

It will never apply to registered land.

The effect of s 1(1) of the Law of Property (Joint Tenants) Act 1964 is that the purchaser is allowed to assume that there had not been severance of the legal estate.

# CASE EXAMPLE

**Grindal v Hooper [1999] EGCS 150**

A memorandum of severance had not been annexed to the conveyance as requested but it was effective notice under s 36(2) of the LPA 1925. When the surviving co-owner sold the property there was no memorandum of severance. However, the purchaser knew the owner and was aware of the fact that there had been severance of the interests. The court held that there been severance and the fact that the purchaser had notice was sufficient for him to be fixed with notice. The purchaser was not deemed to be a purchaser in good faith sufficient for him to ignore the rights of the tenant in common.

## Further reading

Hayton, D, 'Joint Tenancies – Severance' (note on *Burgess v Rawnsley* and *Nielson-Jones v Fedden*) [1976] CLJ 20.

Luther, P, '*Williams v Hensman* and the Uses of History' (1995) 15 Legal Studies 219.

Percival, M, 'Severance by Written Notice – A Matter of Delivery?' (note on *Kinch v Bullard*) [1999] 63 Conv 61.

Pritchard, A M, 'Beneficial Joint Tenancies: A Riposte' [1987] Conv 273.

Tee, L, 'Severance Revisited' [1995] Conv 105.

Thompson, M, 'Beneficial Joint Tenancies: A Case for Abolition?' [1987] Conv 29.

Thompson, M, 'A Reply to Professor Pritchard' [1987] Conv 275.

# chapter 9 TRUSTS OF LAND ∎

## 9.1 Introduction

Whenever two or more people have interests in property, be it a house or a piece of land, their interests are held under a trust of land.

The rights could be either **concurrent** or **successive**. Different rules take effect, depending on the nature of the interest.

### Concurrent rights

Where property is purchased by two or more people at the same time, their rights are said to be concurrent.

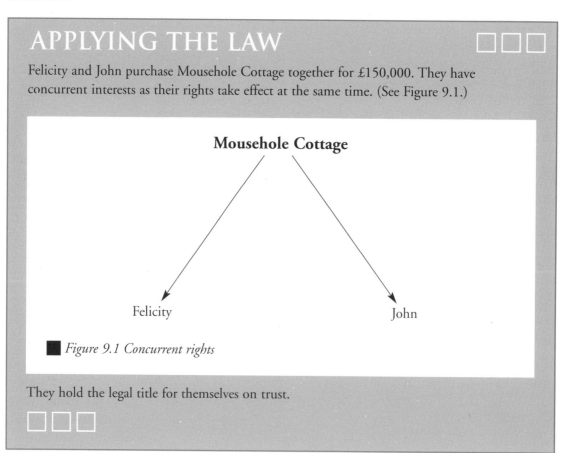

## APPLYING THE LAW ▢▢▢

Felicity and John purchase Mousehole Cottage together for £150,000. They have concurrent interests as their rights take effect at the same time. (See Figure 9.1.)

**Mousehole Cottage**

Felicity                John

∎ *Figure 9.1 Concurrent rights*

They hold the legal title for themselves on trust.

▢▢▢

## Successive interests

Where property is held by one or more persons for their lifetime with the property passing to one or more persons on their death, their rights are said to be successive.

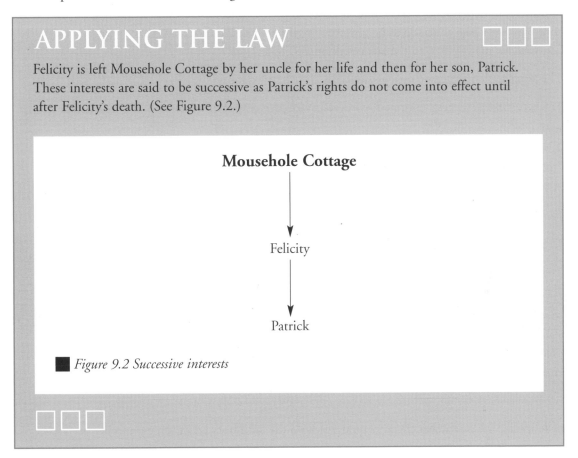

# APPLYING THE LAW

Felicity is left Mousehole Cottage by her uncle for her life and then for her son, Patrick. These interests are said to be successive as Patrick's rights do not come into effect until after Felicity's death. (See Figure 9.2.)

**Mousehole Cottage**

Felicity

Patrick

*Figure 9.2 Successive interests*

# 9.2 The old law

Today, all trusts of land are governed by the Trusts of Land and Appointment of Trustees Act 1996 (usually referred to as 'TOLATA') but it is useful to consider the traditional principles operating under the 1925 legislation which led to the passage of the 1996 Act.

Before TOLATA 1996, where land was co-owned it took effect as either

• a trust for sale or

• a strict settlement.

The trust for sale had many similarities with today's trust of land.

## 9.2.1 The strict settlement

This is a trust comprising land which gave effect to successive interests and is governed by the Settled Land Act 1925. Since 31st December 1996, no new strict settlements can be created. However, any settlements which were in existence at the time TOLATA 1996 was passed were not abolished and these continue to be governed by the Settled Land Act 1925. A significant few will continue for many years, so the law is still of some relevance.

The strict settlement came into existence in two circumstances:

**1.** where limited successive equitable interests were carved out of ownership of a legal estate in land

**2.** where an absolute (as distinct from a limited) interest in land was conferred on a grantee who was subject to some disability, liability or contingency which qualified his capacity or entitlement to hold such an interest.

So **either** it applied where there were people entitled in succession to the property:

### APPLYING THE LAW

Whiteacres 'to June for life remainder to Cecilia remainder to Alice':

June will have a lifetime interest in the property which then passes to Cecilia on her death. Cecilia also has a lifetime interest which will pass to Alice on her death. Alice holds the property absolutely and the settlement will come to an end.

**or** it applied where the beneficiary could not hold the land because of some disability or contingency:

### APPLYING THE LAW

Greenacres 'to Henry absolutely'. Henry is only 12 years old and the law does not allow ownership of a legal estate in land if someone is under the age of 18. The property will be held by trustees until Henry reaches 18.

## KEY FACTS

### Strict settlement

**1.** The person entitled to enjoy the property for their lifetime (called the **tenant for life**) has all the powers of ownership which include the right to sell the property and the power to lease it. He also holds all the powers of management over the property. So the trustees of a strict settlement had a reduced role, although if the tenant for life decided to sell the property he did play the crucial role of receiving the purchase money from the purchaser.

The Settled Land Act 1925 introduced the principle that the tenant for life should be able to sell the land because land was being tied up for too long. Capital was often needed to fund work on the property and the only way that could be raised was by selling some of the land.

**2.** Those who have interests in the property after the death of the tenant for life will have rights transferred from the land itself to the money paid for the land, provided that the purchase money is paid to two trustees. If the money is not paid to two trustees then the rights in the property will not be transferred to rights in the purchase money but will remain as rights in the property itself.

## APPLYING THE LAW

June could sell Whiteacres if she wishes but the money that she received would be held for Cecilia. Cecilia could not prevent her from selling and must be content with her interest in Whiteacres being transferred from the land to the purchase money.

The mechanism which allows the purchaser to buy free from the interests of the beneficiaries is called **overreaching**.

The purchaser must pay the money to at least two trustees of the settlement and then he will buy the land free from any claim from the beneficiaries. Indeed, he need not know anything about the beneficiaries themselves.

## APPLYING THE LAW

Whiteacres is left to June for her life and then to Cecilia and Alice in equal shares. The trustees are Anthony and Andrew. The property is in poor repair and June does not want to live there any more. She decides to sell Whiteacres to Bridget. Bridget must pay the purchase money to Anthony and Andrew. If she does this she will get the title to Whiteacres free from the rights of the beneficiaries Cecilia and Alice.

Compare this situation:

## APPLYING THE LAW

If June decides to sell Whiteacres and the terms of the settlement are the same but there is only one trustee, Anthony, because Andrew has died then Bridget will not receive the property free from the rights of Cecilia and June. They still have rights in Whiteacres itself.

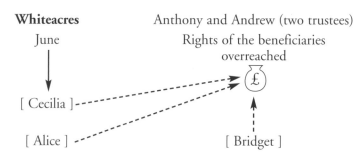

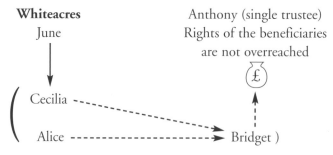

■ *Figure 9.3 Example of overreaching*

## Can strict settlements still exist?

The right to create a strict settlement was abolished by s 2(1) of TOLATA 1996. However, they do still exist because under TOLATA 1996 those settlements that were in existence at the time of the Act were not abolished. The Settled Land Act 1925 will also apply where land within the settlement is resettled on new terms. A strict settlement will continue until it can be said that there is no more land or property within the settlement. If the land is sold but personal property remains in the settlement it is no longer a strict settlement under the Settled Land Act 1925 and it cannot be a trust of land. Under TOLATA 1996:

**S** 's 2(4) . . . Where at any time after the commencement of this Act there is in the case of any settlement which is a settlement for the purposes of the Settled Land Act 1925 no relevant property which is, or is deemed to be, subject to the settlement, the settlement permanently ceases at the time to be a settlement for the purposes of that Act'.

## Mechanics of the strict settlement

If the strict settlement was created during someone's lifetime then two documents were necessary:

1. **a vesting deed**: this was used to pass the legal ownership to the tenant for life. It must name the trustees, the land itself and any extra powers that they had. It may also have included the name of any person who had the power to appoint additional trustees

2. **a trust instrument:** this listed all the beneficial entitlements intended to be held under the trusts of the settlement. It would appoint the trustees of the settlement and any additional powers conferred on the trustees.

The **vesting deed** can be described as a statement of ownership of the tenant for life. This was the document that will be seen by the purchaser. The purchaser could safely ignore the trust instrument and in particular need not consider the rights of the beneficiaries; this is the main purpose of overreaching.

A settlor could choose to settle his land by will which would take effect on his death. Where land was settled by the will of a testator after 1925, the will was treated as the **trust instrument**.

**Comparison of the rights of the tenant for life under a strict settlement and those of the trustees**

| Tenant for life | | Trustees |
|---|---|---|
| Power to sell or exchange the land | Has powers of owner of the settled land. Powers can only be exercised by the tenant for life. Needs the consent of the trustees before sale of the principal mansion house. | Not responsible for the management of the property. |
| Power to grant leases | Length of leases limited to 50 years and must be for the best rent. | If no tenant for life have the power of statutory owner. |
| Power to mortgage the settled land | Can mortgage the settled land but only for specified purposes such as improvements to land. | Have the right to be informed of the exercise of the powers held by the tenant for life. |
| | Powers can be extended by the settlor. | Certain powers of the tenant for life cannot be exercised without the consent of the trustees. |
| | Must inform the trustees when he intends to exercise the powers. | Any purchase money must be paid to the trustees. |

## Conclusion on the difference between the tenant for life's role and the role of the trustees

The role of the trustee compared with that of the tenant for life shows that the trustees have a supervisory role, ensuring that no breach of trust is committed and the tenant for life has a managerial role over the trusts property.

## 9.2.2 The trust for sale

Before 1996 a trust for sale arose in a number of situations under statute:

**1.** Where two or more concurrent interests were held in property they took effect as a trust for sale. It could arise expressly or it could be implied.

## APPLYING THE LAW

Under s 36(1) of the Law of Property Act 1925 a trust for sale would be implied where there was a joint tenancy of the legal estate. It would not matter whether the equitable interests were enjoyed as a joint tenancy or a tenancy in common.

# CASE EXAMPLE

**Bull v Bull [1955] 1 QB 234**

A mother and son jointly purchased property. It gave rise to a resulting trust and as they contributed in unequal contributions their shares in equity were held as tenants in common. Lord Denning considered the status of the trust and held that it took effect as a trust for sale: 'I realise that since 1925 there has been no such thing as a legal tenancy in common: see section 1(6) of the Law of Property Act 1925. All tenancies in common now are equitable only and they take effect behind a trust for sale'.

2. A trust for sale was always imposed where a person died intestate (ie. without making a valid will).

3. The trust for sale was also imposed where interests were successive. Generally, this would only take effect if the settlor expressly stipulated this but the courts were also prepared to imply this into some provisions.

## APPLYING THE LAW

Whiteacres 'to Matthew and Mark to be held on trust for sale for Beverley for life, then to Rashida for life and remainder to Martin'.

## KEY FACTS

### Trusts for sale

1. The trust for sale separated the administrative functions of management and disposition from the beneficial enjoyment of the trust property.

2. The trustees had all the powers of management of the property and the beneficiaries had the right to enjoy the property.

3. The essence of a trust for sale was that it was a 'trust for sale' with the main purpose being that the land should ultimately be sold, rather than enjoyed as property.

4. The trustees had power to postpone sale under s 25 of the Law of Property Act 1925.

5. A trust for sale could not arise unless there was a 'trust', rather than a mere power to sell, the trust for sale was immediate and was not to sell at some future date and the duty to sell the land under the trust was binding.

## CASE EXAMPLE

**Re Mayo [1943] Ch 302**

There was disagreement amongst the trustees about whether or not the trust land should be sold. Two trustees wanted to retain the land and one wanted the land to be sold. In spite of the fact that there was a majority who wanted the land to be retained, the court ordered sale. The court held that under a trust for sale the main purpose was to ensure sale of the land and there would have to be a justifiable reason why the sale should be postponed.

6. Under the doctrine of conversion the rights of a beneficiary under a trust for sale were to be regarded as rights in the proceeds of sale not in the land itself.

## The doctrine of conversion: Why rights in money not rights in land?

Under a trust for sale the trustees had a duty to sell the land, and the doctrine of conversion reflects this principle.

One of the main criticisms of the trust for sale was that the beneficiaries would prefer to have rights in the land and not rights in the proceeds of sale. This was one of the reasons why the law was changed. The law should reflect the **expectations of the parties**.

The doctrine of conversion has been abolished under TOLATA 1996. All trusts for sale in existence on 1st January 1997 were automatically converted into trusts of land. Since 1996 **a trust for sale of land** will take effect as **a trust of land**.

It is still possible to create a trust of land that takes effect as if it is a trust for sale after January 1997 under s 4 of TOLATA 1996.

It is only possible where the trust has been created expressly and the settlor states in the trust instrument that the trust is to be a trust for sale. In this case the trustees will have a duty to sell the trust land immediately but there will be implied into the trust a power for the trustees to postpone sale.

Under s 4 of TOLATA 1996 this power to postpone cannot be excluded even where it is expressly excluded under the trust instrument.

### Why continue to impose a duty to sell?

## APPLYING THE LAW  □□□

Marcus never married. He amassed a sizeable fortune by investing in property and shares before the stock market crashed and he has purchased a large estate in Sussex where he lives. He wants to make provision for his relatives after his death. He wants his five nephews and nieces each to have a share of his property but he does not want them to argue about who is to live in the property after his death. He could leave his property under a trust of land expressly stating that it is a trust for sale of land. However, even if he tries to exclude the trustees' power to postpone the sale he cannot prevent the sale from being postponed by the trustees. The beneficiaries have an automatic right to occupy the property under TOLATA 1996.

□□□

# 9.3 Reform of the law

There were many problems in having two types of trusts of land according to whether the interests were concurrent or successive. There was a certain amount of overlap between the two and the use of the settlement was regarded as outmoded.

## 9.3.1 Criticism of the trust for sale

A trust for sale was implied into many cases of co-ownership. This was impracticable as the whole purpose of purchasing land was not to sell it and the purchasers wanted their rights to be rights in the land, not rights in the capital value.

## APPLYING THE LAW

Rosie and Jim bought Mulberry House in 1994. It cost £200,000 and it took six years for them to save up enough money. They moved in during March 1995. They would hold it on trust for sale for them both. The effect in law is that they had rights in the purchase money rather than rights in the property and they were under a duty to sell the property. The duty to sell could be postponed but it had to be justified. It seemed entirely wrong in cases like this that there would be a duty to sell land which arose as soon as the land was bought. Rosie and Jim had saved up for many years and they bought Mulberry House as a house for them to live in and not as a house to sell.

## 9.3.2 Criticism of the strict settlement

The strict settlement had many drawbacks including the complicated method of creation. Two separate documents – the vesting deed and the trust instrument – had to be used in order to create a strict settlement. There was also a problem in the overlap of function between the tenant for life and the trustees.

> 'The Law Commission in its Report on Transfer of land: Trusts of Land (Law Com No 181) concluded that strict settlements were unnecessarily complex, ill-suited to the conditions of modern property ownership, and were liable to give rise to unforeseen conveyancing complications and should be replaced by an entirely new system applicable to all trusts of land, except existing strict settlements. The recommendations of the Law Commission have led to the enactment of the Trusts of Land and the Appointment of Trustees Act 1996 which came into force 1 January 1997'.

> S H Goo, *Sourcebook on Land Law* (Cavendish, 2002), p 569

Curiously, the settlement has a continued use today which is not necessarily replaced by the trust for land under TOLATA 1996.

> 'It is sad too, and somewhat ironic, that just as the death knell was sounded for the strict settlement, a potential new use for it was arising. Current government policy has it that if you have to go into some kind of care home (nursing, care, etc.) in your old age, your house must be sold and the capital used to pay for such care. True, this will only happen where there is no surviving co-owner of the house, and you are allowed to keep £13,000, but who, if they could, would not prefer to retain the whole of the capital value for their children?

The trust has always been an instrument for legitimate tax avoidance; on the same basis, the strict settlement could have been used to keep the children's inheritance for them. The house could be left to the surviving spouse for life and then to the children absolutely. Whilst in care, the tenant for life would be entitled to the income from the invested capital and this, subject to the statutory allowance, The Department of Social Security could take, but the capital would be secure. It may be argued that the trust of land (or some other form of trust, for example a discretionary trust) would work just as well, but this is not the case: only with a strict settlement could the tenant for life be sure that her wishes or needs in regard to the property could be fulfilled without the need to gain the consent or agreement of others – the trustees and remaindermen in a trust of land, the trustees in a discretionary trust'.

D Chappelle, *Land Law* (5th edn, Longman, 2001), p 171

## ACTIVITY

Consider the reasons why the Trusts of Land and Appointment of Trustees Act 1996 was passed. What improvements to the law of property have been made by the use of the trust of land?

## 9.4 Trusts of land

TOLATA 1996 introduced a new system of trusts for land which combined both strict settlements and trusts for sale and also bare trusts into one type of trust: **the trust of land**. The trust of land covers both successive ownership as well as concurrent ownership. Under the trust of land the trustees have dual powers of either selling or retaining the trust land. The most important feature is that there is no longer a **duty to sell**.

### 9.4.1 Definition of a 'trust of land'

TOLATA 1996 provides that:

s 1(1)(a): 'Trust of land' means any trust of property which consists of or includes land.

s 1(1)(b): 'Trustees of land' means trustees of a trust of land.

's 2 The reference in subsection (1)(a) to a trust –

(a) is to any description of trust (whether express, implied, resulting or constructive) including a trust for sale and a bare trust, and

(b) includes a trust created or arising, before the commencement of this Act'.

## KEY FACTS

### Trusts of land

1. A trust of land covers all trusts of property which consists of or includes land so a trust of personal property which includes some land will be governed by the new Act.

2. A trust of land includes any trust whether it is express, implied, resulting or constructive and includes a trust for sale under the old law and a bare trust.

3. The trustee now has all the powers of absolute owner including the power to sell or retain the land.

4. Trusts of land include trusts such as all trusts for sale, that were in existence when the 1996 Act came into force.

5. Strict settlements that were in existence when the 1996 Act was passed continue to exist as settlements and are not converted into trusts of land.

6. The doctrine of conversion has been abolished in relation to trusts for sale of land. Rights of the beneficiaries do not automatically attach to the proceeds of sale but are rights in the land itself.

## ACTIVITY

Consider the following examples and explain whether they give rise to a trust of land or not:

1. Janice owns a racing stables in Newmarket. She lives in a small flat above the stables and has five horses at the moment all in training. She wants to leave the stables to her friend, Josie.

2. Janice owns five horses in training that she trains. They are in a stable owned by her friend, Josie. She wants to leave them to her cousin, Annie.

3. Lord Rothermere has a flat in London and a large estate in Yorkshire. He holds them under a settlement created by his father in 1956. Under the settlement they will pass to his eldest son. Is this a trust of land?

4. Lord Rothermere creates a trust for sale of his flat in York, his estate in Lancashire and his collection of vintage cars in 1995.

# 9.5 Powers and duties of the trustees

## 9.5.1 General

### The trustees have the powers of absolute owner

TOLATA 1996 provides that:

 's 6 For the purposes of exercising their functions as trustees, the trustees of land have in relation to the land subject to the trust all the powers of an absolute owner'.

This means that the trustees can treat the land as if they were the absolute owners; in other words, as if the land were their own. It is possible for these powers to be excluded when the trust is created. The trustees must act together so they must either act unanimously or not at all.

This is in direct contrast with the old law where the rights of trustees were carefully restricted. The powers were so restricted that it made it very difficult for the trustees to deal with the property.

## 9.5.2 Power to buy, lease and mortgage land

Under s 6(3) of TOLATA 1996, as amended by the Trustee Act 2000, the trustees of land have the power to purchase freehold or leasehold land in the United Kingdom (previously only in England and Wales). This is important as it allows the trustees to invest in land either to provide accommodation for the beneficiaries or as an investment or for any other reason.

Under the old law the trustees had very limited power to acquire land unless it was expressly allowed in the trust instrument. They could not acquire land to provide accommodation for the beneficiaries and they could not purchase land if there was no existing land in the settlement. Their general powers to lease land were restricted to leases of under 50 years.

## 9.5.3 Power to partition the land

Under TOLATA 1996:

 's 7 . . . the trustees of land may, where beneficiaries of full age are absolutely entitled in undivided shares to land subject to the trust, partition the land, or any part of it'.

This section allows the trustees to divide the land up between the beneficiaries where the estate is large. It was available to trustees for sale before 1997.

Conditions to be satisfied for partition to take effect:

**1.** the beneficiaries must be of full age

**2.** the beneficiaries must all consent

**3.** the beneficiaries must be absolutely entitled.

This power can be expressly excluded under the trust instrument.

## APPLYING THE LAW

□□□

Claude and Jean-Francois are trustees of a trust comprising a large house on the seafront in Brighton. They hold the land on trust for the beneficiaries, Alexis and Olivier. The house has already been split into two self-contained flats which have been let in the past. If Olivier and Alexis agree, the property can be partitioned which means that it is split into two parts, Olivier will own one flat absolutely and the trustees will have to convey the ownership to him by a separate deed and Alexis will own the other flat absolutely. The trust of land will now be at an end.

□□□

## 9.5.4 Power to force the beneficiaries to take a conveyance of the land

Under TOLATA 1996:

**S** 's 6(2) where in the case of any land subject to a trust of land each of the beneficiaries interested in the land is a person of full age and capacity who is absolutely entitled to the land, the powers conferred on the trustees by subsection (1) include the power to convey the land to the beneficiaries even though they have not required the trustees to do so'.

Conditions to be satisfied before the beneficiaries can be compelled to take a conveyance of the land:

**a** the beneficiaries must be of full age and not under any legal disability

**b** the beneficiaries must be absolutely entitled.

The effect of this is that the trustees will cease to be trustees and the land will be held by the beneficiaries. If there is a sole beneficiary then he will simply become absolute owner but where there are several beneficiaries then they will hold as trustees for themselves. It is not necessary under this section to get the beneficiaries to consent.

## APPLYING THE LAW

Delia and Charles are trustees for their five nephews and nieces. All five are now over 18 and Delia and Charles decide that they would like to cease to have the responsibility of being trustees so they transfer the property to the nephews and nieces. As there are five nephews and nieces, one cannot be a trustee as only four can hold the legal estate under s 36 of the Law of Property Act 1925. The first four named on the conveyance will hold as trustees unless they expressly agree to the contrary.

## 9.5.5 Power to delegate their powers in relation to the land

The trustees have extensive power to delegate any of these functions as a trustee (under TOLATA 1996):

's 9(1) The trustees of land may, by Power of Attorney, delegate to any beneficiary or beneficiaries of full age and beneficially entitled to an interest in possession in land subject to the trust any of their functions as trustees which relate to land

. . .

(3) A power of attorney under subsection (1) shall be given by all the trustees jointly and (unless expressed to be irrevocable and to be given by way of security) may be revoked by any one or more of them; and such a power is revoked by the appointment as a trustee of a person other than those by whom it is given.

(4) Where a beneficiary to whom functions are delegated by a Power of Attorney under subsection (1) ceases to be a person beneficially entitled to an interest in possession in land subject to a trust –

(a) if the functions are delegated to him alone, the power is revoked,

(b) If the functions are delegated to him and to other beneficiaries to be exercised by them jointly (but not separately) the power is revoked if each of the other beneficiaries ceases to be so entitled'.

The trustees' duties in relation to delegation have been amended under the Trustee Delegation Act 1999 and a new s 9A has been inserted into TOLATA 1996:

's 9A (1) The duty of care under section 1 of the Trustee Act 2000 applies to trustees of land in deciding whether to delegate any of their functions under section 9'.

The duty of care under the Trustee Act 2000 is a duty 'to exercise such care and skill as is reasonable in the circumstances'.

**S** 's 9A(6) A trustee of land is not liable for any act or default of the beneficiary, or beneficiaries, unless the trustee fails to comply with the duty of care in deciding to delegate any of the trustees' functions under section 9'.

The Law Commission had recommended that the trustees should be strictly liable for any acts or defaults after delegation but this was rejected probably in order to encourage delegation.

The law draws a distinction between delegation, which can only be a unanimous decision between the trustees, and revocation, which can be carried out by a single trustee. Revocation also occurs when a new trustee is appointed and under s 9(4) when a beneficiary to whom functions are delegated by power of attorney ceases to be beneficially entitled.

The 1999 Act also imposes a duty on the trustees to review the delegation from time to time and to act where they think it is appropriate by revoking the delegation or by giving directions to the beneficiaries.

## KEY FACTS

### Delegation of trustees' functions

1. Delegation under TOLATA 1996 must be by power of attorney.

2. The trustees can delegate to a beneficiary any function if that beneficiary is of full age and is beneficially entitled in possession to possession of an interest in the land.

3. Delegation of function must be done collectively by all the trustees.

4. All the powers held by the trustees under s 6(1) of TOLATA 1996 can be delegated to the beneficiaries.

5. TOLATA 1996 does not allow the settlor to exclude the trustees' power to delegate.

6. The trustees are protected from liability for the defaults of the beneficiaries after delegation, so long as they took reasonable care in deciding to delegate the function.

7. The delegation of functions can be revoked by any one of them and revocation is automatic if a new trustee is appointed or a beneficiary loses beneficial entitlement.

## 9.5.6 Duty to consult the beneficiaries

Under s 11 of TOLATA 1996 the trustees have a duty to consult the beneficiaries:

 's 11(1) The trustees of land shall in the exercise of any function relating to land subject to the trust:

(a) so far is practicable, consult the beneficiaries of full age and beneficially entitled to an interest in possession in the land,

(b) so far as consistent with the general interest of the trust, give effect to the wishes of those beneficiaries, or (in case of dispute) of the majority (according to the value of their combined interests)'.

The trustees have no absolute duty, so they only need to consult where it is practicable. This means that where the beneficiaries cannot easily be contacted then the trustees have no obligation to seek them out. They do not have any obligation to act on the beneficiaries' suggestions or comments unless it is 'consistent with the general interest of the trust'. It is unclear whether the beneficiaries could control the trustees' decisions and what would be considered to be in the general interest of the trust.

# 9.6 Rights of the beneficiaries of a trust of land

## 9.6.1 General

The beneficiaries have a number of rights in connection with the land. These include:

- a right to occupy the land and
- a right to be consulted about any sale.

Many of the rights reflect the old law but generally TOLATA 1996 extends the rights of the beneficiaries. The most significant change is that now the beneficiaries are seen as having rights in the property itself rather than rights in the proceeds of sale.

## 9.6.2 The right to occupy the trust property

Where joint tenants occupy land they have rights over the whole of the land which cannot be restricted by each other. Under common law they do not have to pay rent to each other where one of the joint tenants is out of occupation. The courts have only restricted the right of a co-owner to occupy the property in exceptional circumstances.

# CASE EXAMPLE

**Chhokar v Chhokar [1984] FLR 313**

While his wife was in hospital having a baby, the husband sold the matrimonial home to a friend. The wife had an equitable right in the property and was therefore a beneficiary under an implied trust. The purchaser was now owner of the property and should have the right to live there. However, the court refused his right to occupy. If it had upheld his rights there would have been the unfortunate scenario of Mrs Chhokar being forced to live with her husband's friend.

'Why is it that a man who has bought a half-share in a house is told that he cannot live there? That he is a married man is entirely beside the point. If Mrs Chhokar can live there with her husband, why should not Mr Parmar be able to live there with his wife? It cannot, I think be argued that Mr Parmar had no right of occupation. Having a beneficial interest as tenant in common is generally understood to confer a right of occupancy, a view which has been affirmed in a series of cases including decisions of the House of Lords. These cases hold that a beneficial co-tenant, even where there is a trust, enjoys, by reason of that interest, a present right of occupation. Had it not been for that right of occupation, indeed, Mrs Chhokar would not have had any claim to remain in the house after her husband had sold it: she would instead have had to rely on a claim against him for a share in the price he received. It seems, therefore, that the acquisition of a beneficial interest by Mr Parmar should have been enough to confer on him a right of occupation. If the court was denying the existence of any such right, it was wrong'.

R Pearce, 'What Kind of Castle?' [1992] DLJ 153

TOLATA 1996 confers an express right on the beneficiaries to occupy trust property which was denied to the beneficiaries under a trust for sale unless the trust instrument expressly gave them such a right.

 's 12(1) A beneficiary who is entitled to an interest in possession in land subject to a trust of land is entitled by reason of his interest to occupy the land at any time if at that time –

(a) the purposes of the trust include making the land available for his occupation (or for the occupation of beneficiaries of a class of which he is a member or of beneficiaries in general), or

(b) the land is held by the trustees so as to confer on a beneficiary a right to occupy land if it is either unavailable or unsuitable for occupation by him.

(2) Subsection (1) does not confer on a beneficiary a right to occupy land if it is either unavailable or unsuitable for occupation by him

(3) This section is subject to section 13'.

[s 13 allows the trustees to exclude or restrict the right of the beneficiaries to occupy the trust property.]

Under a trust for sale, the beneficiary did not have a right to occupy. He could be given permission to occupy but this was different in effect from the right to occupy. The courts gradually accepted that the beneficiary could expect to be able to occupy the trust land. This was admitted by Lord Denning in *Bull v Bull* but the significance is that the right had to be conferred, it was not a statutory right. Under TOLATA 1996 it is now a statutory right.

## What makes land unavailable or unsuitable for occupation?

'Land is by its very nature almost always available and suitable for some sort of occupation. What then does "unavailable" mean? For example, is land unavailable if it is already occupied by tenants or licensees? Or is it only available if their rights of occupation cannot be terminated? Similar problems arise over "unsuitable". Can land only be unsuitable for occupation by a beneficiary because of its condition, or may his personal circumstances render it unsuitable, quite apart from its condition? Inevitably trustees will form their own judgment as to whether or not land is unavailable or unsuitable for a particular beneficiary who requests occupation. In doing so, they will be carrying out much the same process as trustees carried out before the 1996 Act, when exercising their discretion whether or not to accede to the request of a beneficiary to go into occupation. . . . The crucial difference now is that paragraph (b) of section 12(1) and section 12(2) treat unavailability as objective criteria, depriving a beneficiary of an entitlement that he would otherwise have, and not as considerations for the exercise of a discretion'.

J G Ross Martyn, 'Co-owners and their Entitlement to Occupy their Land before and after the Trusts of Land and Appointment of Trustees Act 1996: Theoretical Doubts are replaced by Practical Difficulties' [1997] Conv 254

## KEY FACTS

### The right of occupation

1. The right is only conferred on beneficiaries with interests in possession.

2. The right is absolute and can only be refused where there are two or more beneficiaries with a claim in the land.

3. It is possible for the trustees to restrict the right to occupy if the property is unsuitable or unavailable for a particular beneficiary.

4. The right to occupy will be conferred if that is the purpose of the trust.

## APPLYING THE LAW

Freda and Harry are trustees of a trust of land created in June 1999. The trust property comprises a bungalow in Sussex and a second-floor flat in London. Under the terms of the trust they hold the legal estate on trust for Jane for life with remainder to Sam in fee simple. Jane will have the right to occupy the property as she has an interest in possession. The right to occupy is denied to Sam until his right comes into possession on Jane's death. If Jane were under a disability which meant that the property was unsuitable for her because it did not have a suitable lift then the right to occupy the flat in London could be denied to her. However, the bungalow in Sussex would be available.

The rights of the beneficiaries to occupy can be limited by s 13 of TOLATA 1996:

 's 13(1) . . . Where two of more beneficiaries are (or apart from this subsection would be) entitled under section 12 to occupy land, the trustees of land may exclude or restrict the entitlement of any one or more (but not all) of them.

(2) Trustees may not . . .

(a) unreasonably exclude any beneficiary's entitlement to occupy land, or

(b) restrict any such entitlement to an unreasonable extent.

(3) The trustees of land may from time to time impose reasonable conditions on any beneficiary in relation to his occupation of land . . .

(5) The conditions which may be imposed on a beneficiary under subsection (3)

include, in particular, conditions requiring him –

(a) to pay any outgoings or expenses in respect of the land, or

(b) to assume any other obligation in relation to the land or to any activity which is or is proposed to be conducted there

(7) The powers conferred on trustees . . . may not be exercised –

(a) so as not to prevent any person who is in occupation of land . . . from continuing to occupy the land,

(b) in a manner likely to result in any such person ceasing to occupy the land,

unless he consents or the court has given approval.'

---

## KEY FACTS

**The exercise of the trustees' powers under s 13 of TOLATA 1996**

**1.** The trustees can exclude the right of the beneficiary to occupy the trust property where there are two or more beneficiaries.

**2.** The trustees cannot exclude or restrict the occupation of all the beneficiaries.

**3.** The right to exclude the beneficiaries from the property must not be exercised unreasonably.

**4.** The trustee can never force a beneficiary already occupying trust land to cease to be in occupation unless he consents or the trustees have taken the issue to court.

**5.** The trustees have the power to impose reasonable terms such as the payment of rent or outgoings on the property.

---

The trustees must take certain factors into account when deciding whether or not to exclude a beneficiary:

**a** What were the intentions of the person(s) who created the trust?

**b** What was the purpose for which the land was held?

**c** What are the individual circumstances and wishes of each beneficiary entitled to occupy the land?

The cases under the previous law may indicate to the court whether the settlor intended the property to be used for the occupation of the beneficiaries or not.

# CASE EXAMPLE

### *Barclay v Barclay* **[1970] 2 QB 677**

One of five beneficiaries under a trust of a bungalow claimed the right to live in the property. The bungalow was left on trust with an instruction for the property to be sold after the death of the settlor and the proceeds to be divided between the five beneficiaries. The beneficiary had been living in the property during the testator's lifetime but the terms of the trust indicated a wish for immediate sale so the proceeds could be distributed between all the members of the family.

One approach used has been apportionment. The property is physically split into two or more parts. It will only be appropriate where the property is large enough to be split in this way.

# CASE EXAMPLE

### *Rodway v Landy* **[2001] Ch 703**

A medical partnership was wound up and the case turned on how the co-owned property should be dealt with. One party claimed immediate sale while the other sought partition so each could claim a separate share of the premises. This was so each could practise from separate parts of the building. The court applied s 13(1) TOLATA 1996: 'Where two or more beneficiaries are (or apart from this subsection would be) entitled under section 12 to occupy land, the trustees of land may exclude or restrict the entitlement of any one or more (but not all) of them'.

It held that the trustees had the power here to divide the property between the partners and so each party would have access to just one part of the property. The trustees had the power to impose the cost of dividing the property on one party alone.

'I do not see why, in relation to a single building which lends itself to physical partition, the trustees could not exclude or restrict one beneficiary's entitlement to occupy one part and at the same time exclude or restrict the other beneficiary's entitlement to occupy the other part. Each part is land subjected to a trust of land and the beneficiaries are entitled to occupy that part until the entitlement of a beneficiary is excluded or restricted by the exercise of the power under s 13'.

Peter Gibson LJ

## 9.6.3 The right to be consulted

 's 11(1)... The trustees of land shall in the exercise of any function relating to land subject to the trust –

(a) so far as practicable, consult the beneficiaries of full age and beneficially entitled to an interest in possession in the land, and

(b) so far as consistent with the general interest of the trust, give effect to the wishes of those beneficiaries, or (in case of dispute) of the majority (according to the value of their combined interests)'.

This section confers a general duty on the trustees to consult with the beneficiaries where they are of full age and are entitled to an interest in possession, before they exercise any function under TOLATA 1996. The importance here is that this provision applies to express trusts.

There was a similar power under the Law of Property Act 1925 (s 26) but it applied to implied trusts and did not automatically apply to express trusts. This is not an absolute duty.

**Key words:** '... so far as is practicable ....'. This means that the trustees would not have to take steps which were disproportionately expensive or complex to try to consult with a beneficiary who was difficult to find.

**Key words:** '... so far as consistent with the general interest of the trust ... give effect to the wishes of those beneficiaries'. This means that they do not have to accept what the beneficiaries say, so long as they actually consult with them. If they choose to ignore their wishes the beneficiaries cannot take the issue to court unless they can contend that the trustees have gone against the general interest of the trust.

The right to consult can be expressly excluded under the trust. It will not apply to any trust for sale created before TOLATA 1996 came into force, unless the settlor is still alive and executes a deed to the effect that it is to apply.

## ACTIVITY

Auntie Margie is trustee with her sister, Auntie Betty. The trust was created in 1998 and the property consists of a large flat in London and three holiday cottages in Deal in Kent. The beneficiaries are their three nephews, Sam, Ben and Guy. The gift is as follows: to Sam, Ben and Guy for life with remainder to Jim. The trustees decide to sell all the property in Kent because they think it is unnecessary to keep these cottages. Sam objects because he likes to spend his holidays there. Can he object?

Would it make any difference if the trust was created in 1995?

## KEY FACTS

### Consultation with the beneficiaries

1. The trustees are under a duty to consult with the beneficiaries but they are not under a duty to follow their wishes.

2. The trustees only have to consult those beneficiaries who are of full age and who have an interest in possession of the land.

3. The duty to consult does not apply to trusts of land created before 1996 (old trusts for sale which were converted under the 1996 Act).

4. The duty to consult can be expressly excluded by the trust instrument itself.

5. The duty to consult can be suspended by order of the court.

## 9.6.4 The right to require that consents be obtained

Under s 10 of TOLATA 1996 the trustees are obliged to gain consents from the beneficiaries where this has been stipulated in the trust instrument. This is a useful device for the settlor to ensure that his wishes are carried out.

There is a further provision in s 8 of TOLATA 1996 that allows the settlor to place further restrictions on the powers of the trustees. This could be in relation to the power to partition the land or just restrict their general powers under s 6 but is most likely to be in connection with s 10 and the requirement that the trustees cannot sell without first obtaining the consent of a named person:

**Exclusion and restriction of powers**

's 8(1) Sections 6 and 7 do not apply in the case of a trust of land created by a disposition in so far as provision to the effect that they do not apply is made by the disposition.

(2) If the disposition creating such a trust makes provision requiring any consent to be obtained to the exercise of any power conferred by section 6 or 7 the power may not be exercised without that consent.

(3) Subsection (1) does not apply in the case of charitable, ecclesiastical or public trusts.

(4) Subsections (1) and (2) have effect subject to any enactment which prohibits or restricts the effect of provision of the description mentioned in them'.

Some argue that these sections re-impose the so-called 'dead hand' of the settlor on the trust.

> 'The provision enshrined in s 8(1) is stated in stark, unqualified terms; the only
> qualification coming *ab extra* in s 8(3) and s 8(4). The effect of s 8(3) is to
> disapply s 8(1) in the case of charitable, ecclesiastical and public trusts. No such
> disapplication applies to provisions made under s 8(2). The natural inference from
> this selective disapplication is that s 8(1) was anticipated to have a radical impact, so
> much so that parliament felt it necessary to limit its effect to private trusts of land.
>
> The overall impression gained from reading s 8(1) is that it is a section clearly
> intended to provide the settlors of private trusts with a powerful new dispositive
> facility as if to reinforce its central importance. The provision which appears in the
> Act as s 8(1) has been promoted by the Parliamentary draftsman from its previous
> position at clause 4(10) of the Law Commission's draft bill which preceded the Act.
>
> The Law Commission itself appears to have anticipated the centrality of s 8(1).
> Having first outlined its proposed scheme under which trustees of land might
> delegate trust powers to the occupying beneficiary, the Commission went on to
> boast that "under the new system, settlors will be able to construct a settlement
> which, while giving an occupying beneficiary powers analogous to those of a
> tenant for life under a strict settlement, also inhibits (if they so wish) that
> beneficiary's powers of disposition . . .
>
> Every conveyancer and property lawyer has been taught at some point that the great
> reforms enacted by the statutory scheme of 1925 facilitated the more liberal use and
> disposition of land. One means by which this liberalisation was achieved was to
> limit the extent to which settlors of trusts of land could restrict the alienation of the
> land by their trustees. It should now be noted that as a result of s 8(1) of the Trusts
> of Land and Appointment of Trustees Act 1996, the settlor is under no such
> limitation. By an appropriate provision in the trust instrument the settlor is able to
> restrict or exclude the trustees' exercise, by means of their statutory powers, of their
> functions as trustees. The deadhand of the settlor has once again taken hold'.

G Watt, 'Escaping Section 8(1) Provisions in "New Style" Trusts of Land' [1997] Conv 263

## The effect on purchasers of the need to require consents

One problem for the purchaser could be that there are several consents to be obtained by the
trustees and there may be disagreement amongst them as to whether or not to give their consent.

Under s 10(1) of TOLATA 1996 the purchaser for value only has to be satisfied that any two of
the named persons have consented. The trustee could always be liable for an action against him by
the beneficiary who has not been consulted so the trustees would be wise to ensure that the
consents of all the beneficiaries have been sought.

Fred and George are trustees of a trust comprising two houses, Nos 2 and 3 Church Road. The trust instrument lays down that they must consult all the beneficiaries before they decide to sell, and get their consent. There are four beneficiaries and three agree but the fourth is on a year-long trip of a lifetime going round the world and is impossible to contact. Fred and George sell No 2 Church Road to Greta. Greta will get the title free of any rights of the beneficiaries but the trustees may be liable for breach of trust if the fourth beneficiary comes home and finds the property sold and says that he would have raised an objection to the sale.

The court has the power under s 10(3) to dispense with the consents which cannot be obtained because someone is away. This contrasts with the need to consult with the beneficiaries under s 11. Under that section the trustees are not under an absolute duty to consult, whereas under s 10 the need to obtain consent is absolute and can only be dispensed with by the court.

The court can also dispense with consent where it is unreasonably withheld.

## 9.6.5 The right to appoint trustees and to remove trustees

TOLATA 1996 expressly confers the right upon beneficiaries of a trust of land to select and also remove trustees. This is against general principles of trusts law where beneficiaries do not generally have this power unless expressly reserved for them by the settlor. These powers apply to trusts of land created after 1997.

 's 19(2) The beneficiaries may give a direction or directions of either or both of the following descriptions –

    (a) a written direction to a trustee or trustees to retire from the trust, and

    (b) a written direction to the trustees or trustee for the time being . . . to appoint by writing to be a trustee or trustees the person or persons specified in the direction'.

Conditions to be satisfied:

**1.** the beneficiaries must be of age and of full legal capacity

**2.** the beneficiaries must act unanimously

**3.** the appointment or removal of a trustee must be carried out in writing by all the trustees

**4.** this power is only given to the beneficiaries where the trust instrument does not nominate someone to carry out the function of nominating a trustee.

This provision gives the beneficiaries considerable control over who should act as trustee since the appointment of a trustee may be instrumental towards ensuring that the views of the beneficiaries are to be acted on. Of course, the major safeguard against this is that the decisions have to be taken unanimously. The issue is not one which can be subject to an application to the court under s 14 of TOLATA 1996.

These provisions apply to all trusts not just trusts of land so they also apply to any settlement which continues to be governed by the Settled Land Act 1925

# 9.7 Resolution by the court of disputes in a trust of land

## APPLYING THE LAW

Trudi, Tony and Jane are trustees of land owned by their parents. The trust includes a large farm called Worley Edge Farm, a cottage by the sea in Cornwall and a house in Basingstoke. The beneficiaries under the trust are Jane's daughter Fifi, who lives abroad; Trudi's two sons, Harry and Max (Max is partially disabled and relies on a wheelchair); and Tony's three daughters, Sue, Tessa and Una. Fifi wants all the property sold and the proceeds divided between the six of them. Max wants to live in the cottage in Cornwall but it is difficult to access in a wheelchair and Una wants to carry on living in the house in Basingstoke where she has been living for the past five years. Harry would like to take control of the farm but he is only 19 and has no experience of farming. Trudi and Jane are not speaking to each other as they are always having rows about who should have the right to live in each property.

There are several problems here and the situation will be difficult to resolve between the three trustees:

1. the trustees are not in agreement and they should act unanimously

2. should the property be sold to satisfy Fifi's claims?

3. should Harry be allowed to farm Worley Edge Farm?

4. can Max live in the cottage in Cornwall?

5. can Una continue to live in the house in Basingstoke?

It is in a situation like this that the intervention of the court is necessary. The trustees must act unanimously and they clearly cannot do so in these circumstances.

The court has always had inherent jurisdiction to intervene in disputes over trusts of land. There was a statutory right under s 30 of the Law of Property Act 1925 to seek resolution of any dispute arising under a trust for sale by taking the matter to court. This has now been replaced by s 14 of TOLATA 1996:

's 14(1) Any person who is a trustee of land or has an interest in property subject to a trust of land may make an application to the court for an order under this section.

(2) On an application for an order under this section the court may make any such order:

(a) relating to the exercise by the trustees of any of their functions (including an order relieving them of any obligation to obtain consent of, or to consult any person in connection with the exercise of any of their functions), or

(b) declaring the nature or extent of a person's interest in property subject to the trust as the court thinks fit.

## 9.7.1 Who can make an application under s 14?

**Key words:** 'Any person who is trustee of land or has an interest in property'. These words suggest that a large number of persons will have sufficient interest to make an application to the court:

**1.** a trustee

**2.** beneficiaries with interests in possession

**3.** beneficiaries with an interest in the remainder

**4.** a mortgagee

**5.** a trustee in bankruptcy of a beneficiary

**6.** (possibly) a creditor with a charge against the property of the beneficiary.

## 9.7.2 Matters to be considered by the court in deciding applications

The court can consider certain matters which are laid down in s 15 of TOLATA 1996 as being relevant to any decision that they take:

### The intentions of the person or persons who created the trust

The intentions of the settlor were relevant in deciding whether to postpone sale under a trust for sale.

## CASE EXAMPLE

### *Barclay v Barclay* [1970] 2 QB 677

The court ordered sale, in spite of the fact that one of the beneficiaries was living in the property, because the testator had expressly left instructions that the property should be sold and the proceeds divided between the beneficiaries.

Sometimes there will be no clear intention expressed in the trust but the intention can be inferred from the overall circumstances.

## The purposes for which the property subject to the trust is held

This was always a significant issue in any decision of the courts under s 30 of the Law of Property Act 1925. The courts looked specifically at the purpose behind the trust for sale and if the purpose had come to an end then the court would not direct that sale should be postponed.

## CASE EXAMPLE

### *Re Buchanan-Wollaston's Conveyance* [1939] Ch 738

Four residents of houses near the sea in Lowestoft, Suffolk, purchased land with the primary purpose of preventing development which would interfere with their view of the sea. They agreed among themselves that they would not sell the land except by unanimous consent. One of the four decided that he wanted to sell his own house and realise his share in the co-owned land. He made an application to court who refused his application for sale of the co-owned land since the main purpose of the trust still existed.

Where the property is purchased to provide a family home then the courts have been reluctant to order sale. *Chhokar v Chhokar* is an example of where the courts have not ordered sale because of the subsisting purpose which was to provide a home for the family. The position is different in case of bankruptcy and the courts will order sale in most cases even where there are children although the sale may be delayed.

## CASE EXAMPLE

### Jones (A E) v Jones (F W) [1977] 1 WLR 438

This case concerned rights of a son who gave up a job to come and live with his father in a house to which he had made a capital contribution. He had been led to believe that he would have a right to live in the property all his life. When his father died his widow tried to sell the property. The court held that the purpose of the original purchase was to provide the son with a home and therefore it would not order sale.

The most difficult decision is where a childless relationship ends and one party wishes to remain in the property while the other party wants the property to be sold. The court will then have to choose between the parties on the basis of other factors.

## CASE EXAMPLE

### Jones v Challenger [1961] 1 QB 176

A couple had purchased property as their matrimonial home. After they split up, the wife sought a sale of the property but the husband wanted to continue to live there. The courts decided that the property had been purchased as a matrimonial home for them both and since they had now divorced the purpose was at an end.

## The welfare of any minor who occupies or might reasonably be expected to occupy the trust land as his home

This section gives effect to the needs of the children of the parties who do not normally have rights in the property and would not have the right to make an application to the court under s 14 of TOLATA 1996.

In *Jones v Challenger* the courts were not prepared to delay sale because the underlying purpose, ie to provide a matrimonial home, had ended. Where there are children then that purpose is seen to subsist.

# CASE EXAMPLE

**Re Evers' Trust, Papps v Evers [1980] 1 WLR 1327**

An application was made to sell property which had been purchased as a matrimonial home. The relationship had broken down but the wife continued to live there with the child of their relationship and two children of the wife's earlier marriage. The husband wanted the house to be sold. The court held that the purpose of the trust would continue until the child reached the age of 18.

'. . . the irresistible inference from these facts is that, as the judge found, they purchased this property as a family home for themselves and the three children. It is difficult to imagine that the mother, then wholly responsible for two children, and partly responsible for the third, would have invested nearly all her capital in the purchase of this property if it was not to be available to her as a home for the children for the indefinite future. It is inconceivable that the father, when he agreed to this joint adventure, could have thought otherwise, or contemplated the possibility of an early sale without the consent of the mother. The underlying purpose of the trust was, therefore to provide a home for all five of them for the indefinite future'.

Ormrod LJ

Ormrod LJ highlighted the inferences that could be drawn in this case from the parties' conduct. These are basic common sense conclusions that can be drawn from the parties' behaviour when purchasing property and the courts are entitled to take them into account.

## The interests of any secured creditors of any beneficiary

The court is here looking at the needs of secured creditors outside an application by the trustee in bankruptcy where different criteria apply. The court should balance their interests against the interests of the co-owner.

## Other matters for the court

These matters are not the only criteria for the court. The needs and preferences of the beneficiaries should also be considered. There is no indication in the legislation as to how much weight is to be placed on each factor.

# CASE EXAMPLE

**Mortgage Corporation v Silkin; Same v Shaire** (2000) 80 P & CR 280

This case gives an indication of how the courts will apply the factors under s 15 of TOLATA 1996. Property was purchased by cohabitees to live in as their home. The woman was held to be entitled to a share of 75 per cent while the man could claim 25 per cent. After his death his share was found to be charged by a loan and forged documents had charged the woman's share also. Although her share was not found to be subject to the mortgage, it was held that there should be an eventual sale of the property but subject to a delay while the woman assessed the options for herself. The court considered the overall effect of s 15:

'To put it at its lowest, it does not seem to me unlikely that the legislature intended to relax its fetters on the way in which the court exercised its discretion in cases such as *Citro* [see below] and *Byrne* and so as to tip the balance somewhat more in favour of families and against banks and other chargees . . . All these factors, to my mind, when taken together point strongly to the conclusion that section 15 has changed the law. As a result of section 15 the court has much greater flexibility than heretofore, as to how it exercises its jurisdiction on an application for an order for sale on facts such as those in *Citro* and *Byrne*'.

Neuberger J

It seems that under s 15 no one factor will be held to take priority over others. According to Neuberger J, the statute had listed the needs of the secured creditor as just one of the factors among others to be considered by the courts. It could not take priority in this case.

## 9.7.3 Disputes likely to come to court

### Occupation of trust property

Where there are several beneficiaries then there are frequently disputes about occupation of the trust property. It may be impossible for all the beneficiaries to occupy at the same time so the trustees will have to give one preference.

### Disputes over sale of trust property

This is a difficult problem which can seldom be resolved without one party feeling that they have been treated unfairly. These disputes will relate to unmarried couples and members of families as above where the Matrimonial Causes Act 1973 does not apply. The court will be guided by the needs of the parties and try to balance them, giving a result that will be the fairest in the circumstances.

## Applications by creditors for sale of the property

These will be initiated by those who have a charge over the property and their needs are listed under s 15 of TOLATA 1996.

## Disputes over the need to consult the beneficiaries

The 1996 Act specifies that the beneficiaries should be consulted but where this is impracticable the need to consult can be dispensed with. However, beneficiaries may challenge in what circumstances it would be impracticable to consult them if they have not been consulted.

The court has a very wide jurisdiction to make orders relating to the trust of land.

# 9.7.4 Applications by the trustee in bankruptcy

The court takes a different approach where there is an application by the trustee in bankruptcy. The court has to make such order as it thinks just, considering a number of factors.

The problem in these cases is that there are **competing claims** between the wife and children who want to retain the property and the creditors who are also keen to realise their asset.

The application may be made by the trustee in bankruptcy under TOLATA 1996 but the issue is governed by matters listed in s 335A of the Insolvency Act 1986.

## KEY FACTS

### Factors to be considered in an application by the trustee in bankruptcy

1. The interests of the bankrupt's creditors.

2. Where the application concerns a dwelling-house which is or has been the home of the bankrupt, his spouse or former spouse, the conduct of the spouse or former spouse in connection with the bankruptcy.

3. The needs and financial resources of the spouse or former spouse.

4. The needs of any children.

5. All the circumstances of the case other than the needs of the bankrupt.

6. If the application is made at least a year after the co-owner has been declared bankrupt then the court must assume that the bankrupt's creditors outweigh all other considerations unless the **circumstances are exceptional**.

## What are 'exceptional' circumstances?

Compare these two cases:

### Re Citro (A Bankrupt) [1991] Ch 142

In this case the trustee in bankruptcy applied for sale of the family home. The wife applied for the sale to be deferred on the basis that the children were young and would be forced to move school in the event of sale. These were not seen as exceptional circumstances under s 335A of the Insolvency Act 1986.

'What then are exceptional circumstances? As the cases show, it is not uncommon for a wife with young children to be faced with eviction in circumstances where the realisation of her beneficial interest will not produce enough to buy a comparable home in the same neighbourhood, or indeed elsewhere. And if she has to move elsewhere, there may be problems over schooling and so forth. Such circumstances while engendering a natural sympathy in all who hear them, cannot be described as exceptional. They are melancholy consequences of debt and improvidence with which every civilised society has been familiar'.

Nourse LJ

### Re Holliday [1981] Ch 405

Property was purchased as the matrimonial home in 1970, after the couple had three children. The wife had filed for divorce and almost immediately after she had applied for ancillary relief the husband had filed his own bankruptcy petition. The wife was without any capital of her own and the court found that she would need £26,000 in order to purchase property of similar quality. The court refused sale because it held that the circumstances in this case were exceptional as the husband had deliberately filed for bankruptcy to thwart the wife's efforts to gain ancillary relief.

'Of course the creditors are entitled to payment as soon as the debtor is in a position to pay them. They are entitled to payment forthwith; they have an unassailable right to be paid out of the assets of the debtor. But in my view, when one of those assets is an undivided share in land in respect of which the debtor's right to an immediate sale is not an absolute right, that is an asset in the bankruptcy which is liable to be affected by the interest of any other party interested in that land, and if there are reasons which seem to the court to be good reasons for saying that the trust for sale of the land should not be immediately enforced, then that is an asset of the bankruptcy which is not immediately available because it cannot be immediately realised for the benefit of the creditors'.

Buckley LJ

The rule in bankruptcy cases was laid down by Nourse LJ in *Re Citro* as follows:

'Where a spouse who has a beneficial interest in the matrimonial home has become bankrupt under debts which cannot be paid without the realisation of that interest, the voice of the creditors will usually prevail over the voice of the other spouse and a sale of the property ordered within a short period. **The voice of the other spouse will only prevail in exceptional circumstances**. No distinction is to be made between a case where the property is still being enjoyed as the matrimonial home and one where it is not'.

It seems that in spite of the decision in *Re Holliday*, it will be very rare for the court to postpone sale. The exceptional circumstances described in s 335A of the Insolvency Act include serious ill-health and specific conversion of the property for a disabled family member. Such exceptional circumstances arose in *Claughton v Charalambour* [1999] 1 FLR 740, where the bankrupt's wife was seriously ill and the property had been specifically converted to her needs. Where bankruptcy does not intervene, the court is entitled to look at the purpose of the original trust. Compare the following cases:

# CASE EXAMPLE

### *Abbey National v Moss* [1993] 1 FLR 307

Property was transferred by a mother into the names of her daughter and herself. The daughter mortgaged her share to the claimant and then failed to maintain the payments. The court held that there was an underlying collateral purpose which was that they should both have the right to live in the property independently of each other. This was not the same as the purchase of property as the matrimonial home.

**C**ASE EXAMPLE

> **Stott v Ratcliffe (1982) 126 Sol Jo 310**
>
> The courts upheld the right of a married man's partner to continue to live in property after his death which had been inherited in part by his former wife. The court refused an order for sale.

# 9.8 The protection of the purchaser

When a purchaser buys land from the trustees he wants to be sure that he purchases free of the rights of the beneficiaries under the trust.

## APPLYING THE LAW

The trustees Alice and Andrew hold property, Willow House, on trust for Jack and Jim. Mr White wishes to buy the house for himself. He does not want to have the worry that Jack and Jim will continue to have rights in the land. Overreaching allows him to buy free from their rights so long as he follows the conditions laid down in the legislation.

The 1925 land law legislation tried to address the potential problems that can arise in this situation by trying to give the rights of each beneficiary protection but also allowing the purchasers to buy free of the rights of the beneficiaries, by introducing overreaching.

## 9.8.1 What does 'overreaching' mean?

1. The purchaser takes the legal estate free from any rights in the land if the correct procedure is followed.

2. The beneficiaries' rights are transferred from the land to the purchase money.

## 9.8.2 How does overreaching protect the purchaser?

1. The purchaser does not have to investigate the trust provisions.

2. The purchaser does not have to check whether the sale is in breach of trust.

## 9.8.3 Conditions necessary for overreaching

Under the Law of Property Act 1925:

's 2(1) . . . A conveyance to a purchaser of a legal estate in land shall overreach any
equitable interest or power affecting that estate, whether or not he has notice
thereof, if − . . .

> (ii) **The conveyance is made by [trustees of land]** and the equitable
> interest or power is at the date of the conveyance capable of being
> overreached by such trustees under the provisions of subsection 2 of this
> section or independently of that subsection, and [the requirements of section
> 27 of this Act respecting the payment of capital money arising on such a
> conveyance] are complied with; . . .
>
> (iv) **The conveyance is made under an order of the court** and the equitable
> interest or power is bound by such order, and any capital money arising from
> the transaction is paid into, or in accordance with the order of, the court'.

### The conveyance must be made by trustees of land

The trustees of the land are the legal owners. All the trustees must join in the sale to pass
ownership to the buyer, for example. If there are four trustees then all four must join in the sale
even though overreaching can take place with only two trustees. A conveyance can include a
mortgage and also a lease. If a sole trustee conveys the land to a purchaser then the rights of the
beneficiaries are not overreached.

**Williams & Glyn's Bank v Boland [1981] AC 487**

A house was registered in the sole name of a husband but the wife had made
contributions which gave her rights in equity in the house. The husband therefore held the
property on trust for them both. He mortgaged the property to the Williams & Glyn's Bank

281

which was treated as a conveyance for the purposes of s 2(1)(ii) of the Law of Property Act 1925. It was held that he was unable to overreach the rights of the wife because he was the sole trustee. Her equitable rights would continue to attach to the land and would not transfer to the proceeds of sale. It gave her the right to continue living in the property.

## The equitable interests must be capable of being overreached

There are some interests in land that are incapable of being overreached. The law draws a distinction between 'general' burdens and 'real' burdens:

### General burdens

The key feature of a general burden is that it is an interest which is readily convertible into monetary terms. The type of rights which can be converted in this way are:

**a** the rights of joint tenants

**b** the rights of tenants in common

**c** the holder of a life interest

**d** the holder of an interest in remainder

**e** the rights behind a bare trust.

## APPLYING THE LAW

If you consider the nature of the rights of tenants in common behind a trust then their rights are to share proportionately to the amount that they put into the property. If Bert and Freda purchase property costing £200,000 and Freda puts in £50,000, if the property is sold and the purchase money is paid to two trustees then Freda's share will be one-quarter of the price received. If the property is now valued at £320,000 she can claim £80,000 as the value of her share.

The holder of a life interest will receive the cash equivalent of the share, which will be the income received from the share if invested. The problem here is assessing how long the person entitled to the share will live. That will have to be calculated on an actuarial basis.

Contrast real burdens which cannot easily be quantified in terms of money. In the words of Robert Walker LJ, these rights 'cannot sensibly shift from the land affected by it to the proceeds of sale' (*Birmingham Midshires Mortgage Services Ltd v Sabherwal* (2000) 80 P & CR 256).

*'Real' burdens*

**a** Estate contracts.

**b** Easements.

**c** Restrictive covenants.

**d** Rights of re-entry.

The key feature here is that these interests were always intended to be rights in the land, for example an easement. If you have a right of way over someone's land the right is only useful if you have the right to cross the land. If that was quantified into rights in money then much would depend on how often you used the right of way and for what purpose. The owner of the land which takes the benefit is probably far more interested in the way such a right enhances his enjoyment in the land.

In registered land these rights may be registrable as burdens on the register and may also be rights capable of taking effect as overriding interests.

## Capital money must be paid over as laid down in the Law of Property Act 1925

The purchaser must pay the money as prescribed under s 27 of the 1925 Act:

's 27 **Purchaser not to be concerned with the trusts of the proceeds of sale which are to be paid to two or more trustees or to a trust corporation**

. . .

(2) . . . the proceeds of sale or other capital money shall not be paid to or applied by the direction of fewer than two persons as [trustees], except where the trustee is a trust corporation, but this subsection does not affect the right of a sole representative as such to give valid receipts for, or direct the application of, proceeds of sale or other capital money . . .'

This section has been strictly applied and it is irrelevant that there is only one trustee or that there is a provision in the trust instrument that expressly lays down that one trustee can receive the proceeds of sale.

The effect of s 27 is that the rights in the land are not overreached.

*Why have two trustees?*

It has always been assumed that having two trustees is much safer for the beneficiaries and that their interests are much better protected. It is less likely that two trustees will misapply the money or take it for their own benefit. Case law suggests that this is incorrect.

# CASE EXAMPLE

### City of London Building Society v Flegg [1988] AC 54

A property was purchased jointly by a husband and wife. Contributions were made by the wife's parents, giving them equitable rights in the property. The husband and wife raised money on mortgage for their own purposes. The mortgage constituted a sale for the purposes of the Law of Property Act 1925 and since there were two trustees the mother- and father-in-law found their rights overreached. Their rights transferred from rights in the property to rights in the purchase money. The problem was that the mortgagees had first claim on the purchase money and there was virtually nothing left after the debt owed by the daughter and son in law had been paid.

# CASE EXAMPLE

### State Bank of India v Sood [1997] Ch 276

The special issue in this case was whether the rights of the beneficiaries could be overreached where no capital monies passed hands so the case did not come strictly within s 27 of the 1925 Act. Here, property was owned by two trustees but occupied by others, all of whom had interests in the property. It was mortgaged to a bank by the trustees. There was no advance of monies because the mortgage was raised as security for debts owed by a company owned by one of the two trustees. The bank tried to enforce their rights when one of the trustees was made bankrupt. Although s 27 of the 1925 Act did not apply, the Court of Appeal held that the principle of overreaching still applied. It can still apply even where no capital monies have actually been paid.

Exceptions to the 'two trustees' rule:

**a** payment to a trust corporation

**b** payment to a sole personal representative.

## 9.8.4 Impact of overreaching on the purchaser

**1.** The purchaser takes the title free from any beneficial rights in the property, even where the beneficiaries are in occupation of the land.

**2.** The trustees are no longer trustees of land but they become trustees of the capital money.

**3.** The purchaser of trust land will not be responsible for applying the trust money.

**4.** Even overriding interests will be overreached if the conditions are complied with; see *City of London Building Society v Flegg*. In that case, once the mortgage money was paid over to the two trustees, the rights of the beneficiaries immediately were transferred to the capital money.

## 9.8.5 The effect of s 16 of the Trusts of Land and Appointment of Trustees Act 1996 on purchasers

There is some possibility that TOLATA 1996 draws a distinction between a conveyance in good faith and one that is carried out *ultra vires*. The result is that overreaching will not occur where a conveyance is not made in good faith. This would result in cases such as *City of London v Flegg* being decided differently today.

'The exclusion of subsections of s.16(2) and s.16(3) of TOLATA from registered land has created a new risk. It is currently assumed that a disposition by two trustees of land allows a purchaser to rely on ss. 2 and 27 of the Act, as explained in *City of London Building Society v Flegg*. *Flegg* established that any overriding interests arising under a trust for sale of land would be overreached and cease to affect the land. This assumption is no longer valid, as explained above.

An explanation of the state of the law after 1996 needs to begin with a consideration of the 1996 Act. The Act clearly operates upon the assumption that overreaching will continue after its passage . . .The only question is, how extensive is overreaching to be? The drafting of s.16(2) and (3) suggests that those provisions are designed to prevent overreaching occurring. Thus the Act does not show any intention to abolish overreaching, but it does show an intention to curtail the operation of overreaching in some situations'.

G Ferris and G Battersby, 'The Impact of the Trusts of Land and Appointment of Trustees Act 1996 on Purchasers of Registered Land' [1998] Conv 168

## Powers and duties of the trustees under TOLATA 1996

| | |
|---|---|
| Trustees have the powers of absolute owner in relation to the trust property and can treat the land as if it were their own | **s 6 of TOLATA 1996** |
| Trustees have the power to partition the trust land if beneficiaries are of full age, all consent and are absolutely entitled | **s 7 of TOLATA 1996** |
| Trustees have power to delegate their functions and will not be liable for defaults of the trustees to comply with the duty of care | **s 9 of TOLATA 1996** |
| Duty to gain consents of the beneficiaries where laid down in the trust instrument | **s 10 of TOLATA 1996** |
| Duty to consult with the beneficiaries of full age where practicable and must give effect to their wishes where consistent with the general interests of the trust | **s 11 of TOLATA** |
| Power to exclude or restrict a beneficiary from their right to occupy under s 12 but not exercise this power unreasonably | **s 13 of TOLATA 1996** |
| Power to make an application to court for an order to declare the interests or in relation to the exercise of their powers under TOLATA 1996. The court shall then consider certain matters laid down in s 15(1) in order to make their decision. | **s 14(1) of TOLATA 1996** |

## Further reading

Harpum, C, 'Overreaching, Trustees' Powers and the Reform of the 1925 Legislation' [1990] CLJ 277.

Harwood, M, 'Gathering Moss – Trusts for Sale' [1996] Family Law 293.

Masseys, W, 'Trusts of Land and Appointment of Trustees Act 1996 and the Family Practitioner' [1997] SJ 1158.

Oldham, O, 'Overreaching where no capital monies arise' [1997] CLJ 494.

Ross Martyn, J G, 'Co-owners and their Entitlement to Occupy Land before and after the Trusts of Land and Appointment of Trustees Act 1996: Theoretical doubts are replaced by Practical Difficulties' [1997] Conv 254.

## chapter 10 EASEMENTS

# 10.1 The characteristics of easements

## 10.1.1 Definition of an 'easement'

Although land may be owned by one person, sometimes others will enjoy rights that they are entitled to exercise over that land. These are known as easements and they consist of a right to use, or restrict the use of, the land of another person in some way, for example a right of way, a right to light and a right to water flowing through your neighbour's land.

A wide range of rights have been held to constitute easements. There is no closed or settled definition of the type of rights that can form the subject-matter of an easement. Instead, there are **four** essential characteristics of easements and if any of these characteristics is missing then the right claimed will not be capable of existing as an easement.

## 10.1.2 The nature of an easement

The main characteristics of an easement are laid down in the following case:

# CASE EXAMPLE

**Re Ellenborough Park [1956] Ch 131**

The owners of Ellenborough Park and surrounding land sold some of the land to property developers. The developers built on the land and sold various plots which included certain rights such as the right to enjoy the land, in particular the pleasure ground (Ellenborough Park), but subject to the payment of a fair and just proportion of the costs, charges and expenses of keeping the ground in good order and condition. The claimant bought the Park and tried to prevent the purchasers of the various plots from enjoying the use of the Park.

'The substantial question in this case, which we briefly indicated, is one of considerable interest and importance . . . if the house owners are now entitled to an enforceable right in respect of the use and enjoyment of Ellenborough Park, that right must have the character and quality for an easement as understood by, and known to our law'.

Evershed MR

## 1. There must be a dominant and a servient tenement

The right must relate to two separate plots of land:

- the **dominant tenement** is the plot of land whose owner enjoys the right constituted as an easement

- the **servient tenement** is the plot of land over which the easement is exercised or the land burdened by the easement. (See Figure 10.1.)

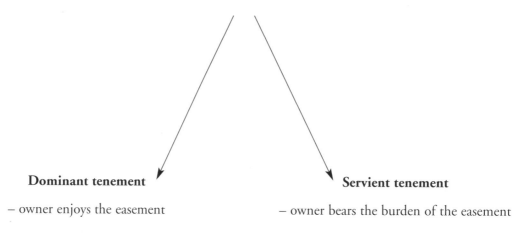

**Dominant tenement**

– owner enjoys the easement

**Servient tenement**

– owner bears the burden of the easement

■ *Figure 10.1 The tenements in an easement*

If the easement is a right of way then it is the land that is crossed that constitutes the servient land.

# APPLYING THE LAW  □ □ □

Hetty lives in Holly Cottage, next door to Rachael in Holly Lodge. Hetty likes to walk her two dogs on the common which adjoins Rachael's garden. She has no access to the common and has to walk to the village and then take the main footpath. This takes about 20 minutes. If she could cross Rachael's land then she could get to the common in about four minutes. If Rachael decides to grant a right to Hetty then her land would be the servient land and Hetty's land would be the dominant land. (See Figure 10.2.)

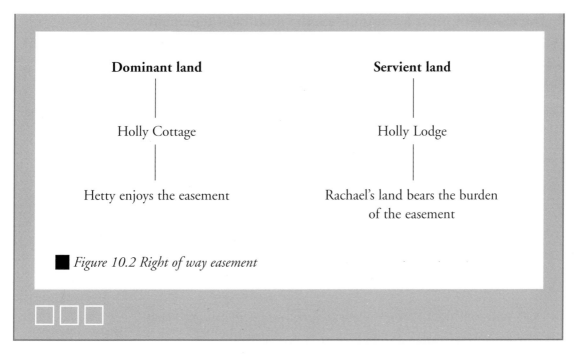

**Figure 10.2 Right of way easement**

This suggests something about the nature of an easement and that is that the right attaches to the **land** and not to a person. In order to have an easement, the owner must have an estate in land. An easement cannot exist independently of the land itself.

A licensee cannot have an easement but a tenant under a lease can have an easement, even against land retained by his landlord. A public right of way is not an easement because there is no dominant tenement.

ASE EXAMPLE

***London & Blenheim Estates Ltd v Ladbroke Retail Parks Ltd*** [1992] 1 WLR 1278

In this case the claimant, who owned a part of a shopping centre, claimed that the right of customers to park on a central car park could exist as an easement. The problem here was that the claimant had not got any interest in land at the time when the easement was first claimed.

'An easement cannot exist as an incorporeal hereditament unless and until there are both a dominant and servient tenement in separate ownership. That never occurred in this case. Before the dominant tenement had been acquired as a dominant tenement the servient tenement had been disposed of. That, as it seems to me is fatal to the creation of the easement'.

Judge Paul Baker QC

289

## 2. The easement must accommodate the dominant tenement

This means that the right must be for the benefit of the land and not merely for the benefit of a person in his personal capacity. If the right can be said to be attached to land then it is assumed that it is for its benefit.

The dominant and servient land do not have to adjoin each other but they should be close enough to establish a connection between the two.

> **J** 'There can be no right of way over land in Kent appurtenant to an estate in Northumberland'.
>
> Byles J in *Bailey v Stephens* (1862) 12 CB NS 91

There are **three key issues** here:

**(i)** Can an easement for **business use** accommodate a dominant tenement?

**(ii)** Can a purely **recreational right** exist as an easement?

**(iii)** Can an easement with **significantly increased use** from that originally granted still exist as an easement?

### (i) Business use

Problems arise where it is claimed that the right is for the benefit of a business. Since the business is run by an individual, it is difficult to argue that the right takes effect as a right which benefits the land rather than the owner.

# CASE EXAMPLE

### *Hill v Tupper* (1863) 2 H & C 121

The claimant had a lease of an area that fronted on to a canal. He was given the sole and exclusive right to put pleasure boats on it. He claimed that this right was infringed when the defendant, who owned a small inn on the canal, also put boats on it. It was held that the right was no more than a licence as it did not enhance the enjoyment of the land but was merely incidental to the business run by the claimant.

> 'It is clear that what the plaintiff was trying to do was to set up, under the guise of an easement, a monopoly which had no normal connection with the ordinary use of the land, but which was merely an independent business enterprise. So, far from the right claimed subserving or accommodating the land, the land was but a convenient incident to the exercise of the right'.
>
> Evershed MR

Compare this case:

 **C**ASE EXAMPLE

### *Moody v Steggles* (1879) 12 Ch D 261

The issue was whether the right to fix a sign advertising a public house on the wall of a neighbouring property could exist as an easement. The question was whether the easement accommodated the land or merely the business use of the land. The court rather generously found that it could take effect as an easement.

> 'the house can only be used by an occupant, and the occupant only uses the house for the business which he pursues, and therefore in some manner (direct or indirect) an easement is more or less connected with the mode in which the occupant of the house uses it'.
>
> Fry J

*(ii) Recreational use*

Historically, it was held that if the right was purely **recreational** it could not accommodate the land.

**C**ASE EXAMPLE

### *Mounsey v Ismay* (1865) 3 H & C 486

The right 'must be a right of utility and benefit, and not one of mere recreation and amusement' (Martin B). In this case the court refused to accept that the right claimed by the freemen and citizens of Carlisle to use land for annual horseracing on Ascension Day could exist as an easement.

## CASE EXAMPLE

### *International Tea Stores Company v Hobbs* [1903] 2 Ch 165

The use of the landlord's gardens for his own enjoyment could not exist as an easement because it was merely the right to walk at will. It did not appear specifically to increase the enjoyment of the land.

The decision in *Re Ellenborough Park* allows the possibility of an easement where it is purely for recreational or leisure purposes. The facts of this case (discussed at section 10.1.2) allowed owners of houses use of an ornamental leisure park which adjoined their houses. It has to be connected with the dominant land. Lord Evershed discussed how the owners could **not** claim an easement if the right was one to enjoy the right to visit a zoological garden free of charge or to go to cricket matches at Lords cricket ground. This is because there is no real connection between the land and the right claimed.

> **J** 'It is not fairly to be described as one of mere recreation or amusement, and is clearly beneficial to the premises to which it is attached'.
>
> Lord Evershed

### *(c) Increased use of the easement*

Once the easement is held to accommodate the land, an increase in the use of the land will not necessarily extinguish the easement.

## CASE EXAMPLE

### *British Railways Board v Glass* [1965] Ch 587

A farmer had the right 'to cross a railway crossing with all manner of cattle'. Many years later, the farmer gave a number of caravan owners the right to use his land. They all used the railway crossing. The number of caravans grew, so the traffic using the line was quite considerable. However, the court held that so long as the nature of the use did not vary, the use of the railway crossing was within the terms of the initial grant.

If the use becomes **excessive** then the right can be challenged.

# CASE EXAMPLE

### *Jelbert v Davis* [1968] 1 All ER 1182

The owner of land had a right of way over a driveway which led to the main road. Later, he developed his land, creating a caravan park for 200 caravans and/or tents. The owner claimed that the caravan users all had a right to use the right of way across the neighbouring land.

'In my opinion a grant in these terms does not authorise an unlimited use of the way . . . It must not be used so as to interfere unreasonably with the use by those other persons, that is, with their use of it as they do now, or as they may do lawfully in the future . . . More generally, the true proposition is that no one of those entitled to the right of way must use it to an extent which is beyond anything which was contemplated at the time of the grant'.

Lord Denning

## 3. The dominant and servient tenements must be owned or occupied by different persons

This means that the dominant and servient land must be either owned or occupied by different persons. It has long been accepted that you cannot have an easement over your own land. It may be possible to have a quasi-easement but that is not binding until it becomes a full easement.

*Can a tenant acquire an easement over the land owned by his landlord?*

A tenant **can** acquire an easement over his landlord's land because although the dominant and servient lands are owned by the same person, they are occupied by different persons. The key feature here is the fact that the land is occupied by different people.

## 4. The easement must be capable of forming the subject-matter of a grant

There are several different aspects to this:

**a** there must be a capable grantor and grantee

**b** the right itself must be sufficiently definite

**c** the right must be in the nature of an easement.

**a** **There must be a capable grantor and grantee:** only a person with a proprietary interest can grant an easement over land. The grantor must be legally capable of making the grant. If a grantor has not got a legal estate in land then he cannot grant a legal easement. The grantee must also be capable of acquiring an easement. This means that it must be granted

293

to a definite person or a definite body of persons. There could be no effective grant to a fluctuating group of persons, such as people living in a village. An easement can be held by either a leaseholder or a freeholder.

**b The right itself must be sufficiently definite:** It must not be too vague and uncertain. It must be clear to the grantee and the grantor the exact nature of the rights. There could not be an easement of a good view or a prospect: *William Aldred's Case* (1610) 9 Co Rep 57. A challenge was made in *Re Ellenborough Park* by the owner of the Park that the right claimed was merely a right to walk at will over another's land. He argued that the right was too vague in nature. However, the judge found that it was quite different from a right to wander at will but a definitive right to enjoy the Park as a garden which benefited the land owned by the original purchasers.

**c The right must be in the nature of an easement**

'The categories of servitudes and easements must alter and expand with the changes that take place in the circumstances of mankind'.

Lord St Leonards in *Dyce v Lady James Hay* (1852) 1 Macq 305

This means that the right must be within the categories of rights already recognised as easements or very similar to such categories. The law recognises that the categories of easements are not closed but nevertheless there must be justification before the courts are prepared to admit a new type of easement.

# CASE EXAMPLE

### *Phipps v Pears* [1965] 1 QB 76

The claimant based his case on an easement of protection against the weather. This was not a positive right but a negative right which prevented the neighbour from enjoying the property in such a way as to interfere with his neighbour's enjoyment of the property. He claimed damages for breach of the easement.

'If we were to stop a man pulling down his house, we would put a brake on desirable improvement. Every man is entitled to pull down his house if he likes. If it exposes your house to the weather, that is your misfortune. It is no wrong on his part'.

Lord Denning

- There must be no positive burden imposed on the servient owner.
- An easement should not involve the expenditure of money by the servient owner.
- The easement should be permissive rather than imposing a burden to act.

## APPLYING THE LAW

Tony lives at 14 Meadow Rise and uses a short-cut through his neighbour Jane's garden. Tony has the dominant tenement and Jane has the servient tenement. The right of way constitutes an easement. Jane must allow Tony to use the right of way and must in no way obstruct his use. If Tony finds the route muddy and uneven, Jane has no obligation to improve the quality of the road. Her duty is to keep the right of way open and to ensure that it is usable.

There are a few examples of easements that do impose a positive burden on the servient owner, for example fencing: this is one exception to the rule. Fencing has been described as 'in the nature of a spurious easement' by Archibald J in *Lawrence v Jenkins* (1873) LR 8 QB 274. It has been upheld as an easement even though it may involve payment of money by the servient owner.

ASE EXAMPLE

### Crow v Wood [1971] 1 QB 77

The court upheld both the right of the servient owner to use his neighbour's property but also the right to impose the burden of keeping the fence in repair.

## The creation of new types of easements

There is a real problem in finding a balance between allowing new easements to keep abreast with developments and not making land impossible to sell because the land has burdensome limits placed upon it.

ASE EXAMPLE

### Hunter v Canary Wharf [1997] AC 655

When the Canary Wharf tower was built, a number of people living in the neighbourhood found that it interfered with their television reception. They claimed that they had an easement in the nature of television reception. The court refused to accept that such a

right could exist. One reason that influenced the judges was that it could impose an immense burden on a person wishing to build on their land. If such a right existed then Lord Hoffmann saw that there was a risk that the landowner could be sued by 'an indeterminate number of claimants and each would claim compensation in relatively modest amount'. In this case he thought that there were sufficient safeguards in the planning system to ensure that the rights of the people were not intentionally interfered with.

## KEY FACTS

### *Re Ellenborough Park* (1956)

**1.** There must be a dominant and a servient tenement.

**2.** The easement must accommodate the dominant tenement.

**3.** The dominant tenement and the servient tenement must be owned or occupied by different people.

**4.** The easement must be capable of forming the subject matter of a grant.

**5.** There must be a capable grantee and grantor.

**6.** The right must be sufficiently definite.

**7.** The right must be in the nature of an easement.

# 10.2 Easements compared with other rights

## Profits à prendre

A profit à prendre allows the grantee to take from the land of his neighbour rather than simply use his neighbour's land. This could include crops, fruit and fish. The person granted a profit is usually granted a licence to enter the land to take advantage of the right.

The main difference from an easement is that a profit can exist **without ownership of land**. So the right can be given to someone just for their own personal benefit.

Profits also differ from easements because they can be enjoyed by several persons at the same time, whereas an easement is enjoyed by a single landowner and those who derive a right from him.

## Licences

There is a direct contrast between easements and licences:

- licences give someone personal permission to enter the land, whereas legal easements give one a proprietary right in the land

- a licence can never bind a third-party purchaser, whereas a properly created legal easement can be binding on third parties

- there is also an important fundamental difference because a licensee can have exclusive enjoyment of the land while the licence lasts, whereas the grantee of an easement only has a right to use the land, not exclusive rights over the land

- licences need not be created formally but easements can usually only exist in law if certain formalities, for example creation by deed, are complied with.

The type of right covered by licences is much more extensive than the right covered by an easement.

## APPLYING THE LAW

You have very little room to park in your drive. Your neighbour, Keith, approaches you and tells you that you can use his drive at any time. This is not a right which attaches to the land. If you sell the land it will only be in limited circumstances that the purchaser could argue that he too had the right to park in Keith's drive.

## Restrictive covenants

Restrictive covenants restrict the owner's enjoyment of their own land:

- there is an overlap between restrictive covenants and easements, in particular negative easements. Some case law has suggested that restrictive covenants are one type of negative easement

- however, the main difference is that restrictive covenants can only exist in equity, whereas easements can exist in law or in equity

- a restrictive covenant can only limit enjoyment of land, whereas an easement can give both positive rights over land and can also restrict use of land in the case of a negative easement

- the subject-matter of an easement is much more restricted than that of a restrictive covenant.

## Public rights

Certain public rights are very similar to easements, such as a public right of way, but they differ because they are not reliant on the members of the public owning land or having rights in land. There is no necessity for an express grant. The grant is not subject to any formalities.

## Natural rights

Natural rights differ from easements because they arise naturally and are not subject to a grant. The main right is the right of support. Until recently it was only a right of support for the land and never a right for any buildings on the land.

CASE EXAMPLE

### *Holbeck Hall Hotel v Scarborough Borough Council* [2000] 2 All ER 705

In this case the court held that the servient owner may have to take steps to provide positive support for a building if he knows that there is a hazard which would affect his neighbour. The claimants owned a hotel which had been severely affected by a landslip. The local authority owned the land subject to the landslip and the claimants argued that they were responsible because they knew that the land had been subject to two landslips in previous years. Although the court upheld the principle that it could be liable, it did not find the local authority liable in this case because it could not have reasonably foreseen the extent of this land slip. The two previous landslips had been on a much smaller scale.

The court found that there was no difference between a nuisance on the land of the servient owner and the withdrawal of support for buildings of your neighbour.

## ACTIVITY

Consider the following and decide what kind of right arises in each case:

1. David agrees with his neighbour, George, that he can run pipes under his land when George builds a second house in his garden.
2. Fred and George move to a small village in the Cotswolds. They discover that they have a right to walk across fields to the neighbouring village.
3. David moves into his new house and his solicitor tells him that he can cut wood on his neighbour's land.

**4.** George has discovered, after checking at the Land Registry, that his neighbour has a duty to keep the fence between them in good repair.

**5.** Fred has just been told by his solicitor that if he buys the house he wants in Kent he will be unable to run a business from the property.

**6.** Gerald is given permission to store some furniture in his friend's garage.

## Easements and other rights compared

| Easements | Profits à prendre | Restrictive covenants | Licences | Public rights | Natural rights |
|-----------|-------------------|-----------------------|----------|---------------|----------------|
| Subject to formalities; can exist in law and equity. | The holder has a proprietary interest in land. | Only exist in equity, never at law, except between the original parties. | Licensees do not gain proprietary rights. | No proprietary rights can be claimed. | Arise automatically and are incidental to ownership. |
| Must own a parcel of land. | No ownership of land necessary. | Ownership of land necessary. | The licensee does not need to own any land. | No ownership of land necessary. | Dependent on the ownership of land. |
| Subject-matter of an easement within strict limits. | Wide range of rights, eg right to fish or cut down timber. | Covers very broad range of rights. | Covers enjoyment of rights to enter and enjoy another's land. | Fairly restricted subject-matter. Mainly covers rights of way. | Fairly narrow in nature, eg right of support and the right to a flow of water. |

# 10.3 General principles of easements

## 1. Must not impose a positive burden on the servient owner

An easement must not impose any expenditure of money or any positive action on the servient owner unless it has been agreed between the parties or constitutes one of the few exceptions, such as fencing (*Crow v Wood*).

## APPLYING THE LAW

Rodney has a right of way over his neighbour Greg's land. The path goes through the orchard at the back. There is no requirement that the right of way is maintained, so long it remains open.

---

# CASE EXAMPLE

### *Duke of Westminster v Guild* [1985] QB 688

It was held that a tenant's right to use drains running through his landlord's premises imposed no duty on the landlord to keep the drains in repair.

The position would be different if there was a deliberate attempt to interfere with the easement. If the right of way could not be used at all because the path was fenced off, then there could be a challenge.

## 2. Must not exclude reasonable alternative user of the servient tenement

**a** The general principle is that the easement must never exclude the grantor from use of his land. Where use is in the nature of exclusive user, it can never exist as an easement.

**b** There are specific types of easement involved here, for example storage and parking.

*Storage*

# CASE EXAMPLE

### *Wright v Macadam* [1949] 2 KB 744

A tenant was allowed to store her coal in a shed on the landlord's land. This was upheld as an easement although, on the facts, the landlord would not have had access to the shed at all.

### Copeland v Greenhalf [1952] 1 Ch 488

The claimant owned an area of land opposite the defendant, who was a wheelwright. The defendant used some land of the claimant to store vehicles belonging to customers. This constituted almost permanent use by the defendant and it was held that it could not constitute an easement.

'I think that the right claimed goes wholly outside any normal idea of an easement that is, the right of the owner or the occupier of a dominant tenement over a servient tenement. This claim . . . really amounts to a claim to a joint user of the land by the defendant. Practically the defendant is claiming the whole beneficial user of the strip of land on the south-east side of the track'.

Upjohn J

### Grigsby v Melville [1973] 1 All ER 385

The claimant had a right to unlimited storage within a cellar beneath his neighbour's property and it was held that this could not be an easement because it was a claim to beneficial ownership.

'A purchaser does not expect to find the vendor continuing to live mole-like beneath his drawing room floor'.

Brightman J

'The case of *Copeland v Greenhalf* [1952] has puzzled students of land law for over forty years. It is usually taken as authority for the proposition that a claim to an easement will fail if it amounts, in effect, to a claim to exclusive possession of the servient land . . . The issue remains alive largely because the central point of *Copeland v Greenhalf* – obscured though it may be by the description of the defendant as a "wheelwright" and the reference to "carts, carriages and other wheeled of wooden or partly wooden construction" – is whether it is possible to have an easement to park a car or other vehicle on someone else's land. Not only did *Copeland v Greenhalf* prove a hard case to analyse and justify, but it has also

been pointed out by both judges and academics that the judgment of Upjohn J ignored at least one apparently contradictory case decided by a superior court namely *Wright v Macadam* [1949] in which the Court of Appeal had accepted that the right to store coal in a coal shed could be a valid legal easement – it has been suggested as a consequence that the case may have been decided *per incuriam* . . .

With the exception of a few problematic phrases . . . the judgment of Upjohn J in *Copeland v Greenhalf* falls four square into the line of cases which simply stated that a claimed right must be sufficiently certain if it was to qualify as an easement . . . All positive easements must involve doing something jointly with the owner of the land, but what was wrong with the defendant's claim in *Copeland v Greenhalf* was that it amounted, in the judge's view, to joint user for any purpose, or at any rate for too wide a range of purposes. On this analysis *Copeland v Greenhalf* is simply applying a well-established rule about certainty'.

P Luther, 'Easements and Exclusive Possession' (1996) 16 Legal Studies 51

Luther shows here that it is possible to have an easement of storage where the owner may be denied use of the property temporarily. The real issue is what the land owner can still do on the land. If there is still space for him to store his goods or to use his land for parking, then the easement can exist, even if some rights are denied to the owner.

## Parking

The right to park can seem like exclusive use of the land. This could mean that the owner of the land is prevented from any use of his own land. Permanent parking is similar to the claim to storage in *Wright v Macadam* and also *Copeland v Greenhalf.*

'If a simple certainty test can distinguish between *Copeland v Greenhalf* and *Wright v Macadam* could it provide a better answer to some of the problems in the modern law than either the "exclusion" approach or the "substantial interference" approach? It may be objected that it is in a sense asking the same, or correlative question. Surely to ask "What can the claimant do?" (the certainty approach) is the same as to ask "What can the servient owner *not* do?" (the exclusion/substantial interference approach)? There is some substance in this argument, and certainly it is possible to imagine cases where it would be difficult to answer one question without answering the other. A line would still have to be drawn in difficult cases. But against this it must be said that to look at the positive characteristics of a claimed right must in many cases be easier than to assess its negative impact on someone else's rights. This latter enquiry must involve a large number of external factors, not least . . . the total size of the servient tenement, the characteristics of its owner and the uses to which he might wish to put his land. It must involve

uncertainty in the definition of rights. So the right to park a car on a small part of large property would probably qualify as an easement, whereas the same activity in a more restricted space might well not qualify'.

P Luther, 'Easements and Exclusive Possession' (1996) 16 Legal Studies 51

The right to park will therefore depend on extent of use and will not be upheld if it effectively deprives the landowner from using his land.

The following may indicate whether or not parking will give rise to an easement:

*   parking limited to certain times of the day
*   parking anywhere in a general area of land.

(*London & Blenheim Estates Ltd v Ladbroke Retail Parks*).

Compare the following cases:

### Batchelor v Marlow [2001] 82 P & CR 36

In this case the claimant sought the exclusive right to park six cars on a verge of land between 8.30 am and 6.30 pm, Monday to Friday. The effect was that the owner of the land would not be able to park at all during those hours and could only use the area at weekends and for a limited time during the evening and at night. The Court of Appeal rejected the claim for an easement as the right claimed was too excessive, making any enjoyment by the owner of the servient land illusory.

## CASE EXAMPLE

### Hair v Gillman (2000) 80 P & CR 108

The claimant argued that he had the right to park his single car on a forecourt which was big enough for four cars. The Court of Appeal upheld his right because it would not interfere with the owner's right to park a car on the forecourt at any time he wished.

> 'The authorities fall between one side or another of an ill-defined line between rights in the nature of an easement and rights in the nature of an exclusive right to use or possess'.

Chadwick LJ

## 10.4 The grant of easements

Easements can be granted in a number of different ways:

**1.** express grant or reservation

**2.** implied grant or reservation

**3.** prescription.

Easements can be created by means of either **grant** or **reservation**.

A **grant** is made when one landowner, A, creates an easement over his land in favour of his neighbour, B.

## APPLYING THE LAW

☐☐☐

Peter lives next door to Henry. Henry wants to use Peter's garden as a short-cut to get to the woods at the back of it. Peter will grant Henry an easement. This must be created formally by a deed, as the right of way is an interest in land. If the documents used were not in the form of a deed then only an equitable easement would be created.

☐☐☐

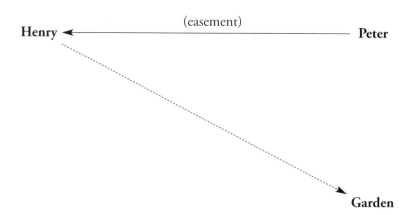

 *Figure 10.3 Creation of an easement by grant*

A **reservation** arises when a landowner transfers part of his land to another but he keeps or reserves himself a right to use part of the land he has sold.

## APPLYING THE LAW

☐☐☐

Peter has a huge garden and he decides to build a house in part of the garden, which he sells to Henry. When the house is sold to Henry, Peter expressly agrees with him that he can continue to use a short-cut which runs from Peter's house through Henry's new garden.

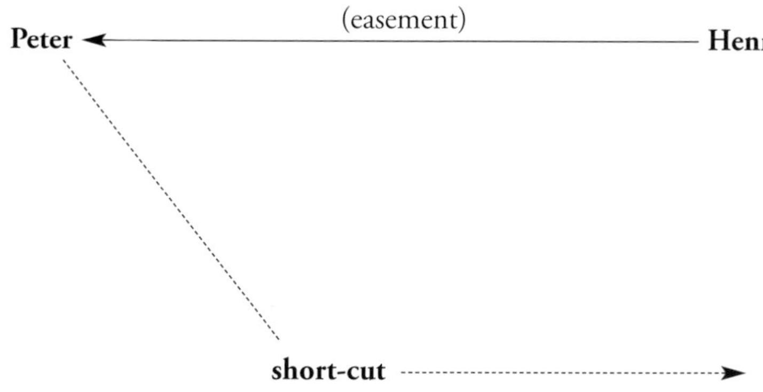

Peter ◄——————— (easement) ———————— Henry

short-cut ----------------------------►

**■** *Figure 10.4 Creation of an easement by reservation*

☐☐☐

The courts have always viewed reservations with suspicion because the vendor is trying to reserve rights over the land he is selling. He is trying to hold something back from the land for himself.

The only circumstances when the courts will imply a reservation are:

* in the case of **necessity** or
* an **intended easement**.

## 10.4.1 Express grant

Two neighbouring landowners can expressly agree about rights to be exercised over the other's land. This may be incorporated into the formal documentation when land is either transferred as freehold or granted as leasehold. Alternatively, it can arise independently of the conveyance of the property.

Occasionally, easements are granted expressly under statute. These are made in favour of some of the privatised utilities that supply essential supplies such as gas or electricity. In these cases the easement will not accommodate the dominant tenement since there will not be a dominant tenement.

## 10.4.2 Implied grant

Sometimes the grant of an easement will be implied or simply inferred in favour of a purchaser of land. These easements will take effect as legal easements. It is important to see that the rights that can be implied into the transfer must be capable of existing as an easement under the conditions in *Re Ellenborough Park*.

Easements by implied grant can arise in the following ways:

1. necessity

2. intended easements

3. the rule in *Wheeldon v Burrows* (1879) 12 Ch D 31

4. s 62 of the Law of Property Act 1925.

## 1. Necessity

Easements of necessity usually arise where the land would be landlocked without the right. The courts will always imply an easement in these circumstances. The land must be genuinely landlocked.

## APPLYING THE LAW

Rodney develops his garden and builds two houses which are bought by Charles and Karina. There is no mention of access in the conveyance but the only way that Charles and Karina can access their land is by using Rodney's drive. The courts will not allow Charles and Karina to be landlocked but will imply into the transfer a right of access over Rodney's land.

The easement of necessity is strictly controlled. The dominant tenement must have no access at all. It is not enough merely to show that there is a route but that it is simply inconvenient or a much longer way round. However, the route must be safe. There is no question of denying such a right where the alternative route would be dangerous, such as along the edge of a cliff. There is no reason why easements of necessity could not arise in the case of access to property for services but it is generally implied in relation to a right of way.

## CASE EXAMPLE

### *Nickerson v Barraclough* [1980] Ch 325

An easement of necessity can only arise on the sale of land where the servient land is genuinely landlocked.

### *The Access to Neighbouring Land Act 1992*

A landowner may not be able to carry out essential repairs to his land without first gaining access to his neighbour's land. Without an easement to enter the neighbouring land, the repairs could not be carried out. Under the Access to Neighbouring Land Act 1992 an access order can be claimed which allows the landowner to claim the right to go on his neighbour's land to carry out the repairs.

### 'Access orders

s 1(1) A person –

    (a) who, for the purpose of carrying out works to any land (the "dominant land"), desires to enter upon any adjoining land (the "servient land"), and

    (b) who needs . . . the consent of some other person to that entry, may make an application to the court for an order . . .

(2) On application under this section, the court shall make an access order if, and only if, it is satisfied –

    (a) that the works are reasonably necessary for the preservation of the whole or any part of the dominant land; and

    (b) that they cannot be carried out, or would be substantially more difficult to carry out, without entry upon the servient land . . .

(3) The court shall not make an access order in any case where it is satisfied that, were it to make such an order –

    (a) the respondent or any other person would suffer interference with, or disturbance of, his use or enjoyment of the servient land, or

    (b) the respondent, or any other person (whether of full age or capacity or not) in occupation of the whole or any part of the servient land, would suffer hardship.

(4) . . . "basic preservation works" means any of the following . . .

    (a) the maintenance, repair or renewal of any part of a building or other structure comprised in, or situate on the dominant land;

    (b) the clearance, repair or renewal of any drain, sewer, pipe or cable so comprised or situate;

    (c) the treatment, cutting back, felling, removal or replacement of any hedge, tree, shrub or other growing thing which is so comprised and which is, or is in danger of becoming, damaged, diseased, dangerous, insecurely rooted or dead;

    (d) the filling in, or clearance, of any ditch so comprised; but this subsection is without prejudice to the generality of the works which may, apart from it, be regarded by the court as reasonably necessary for the preservation of any land . . .

### Terms and conditions of access orders

s 2(1) An access order shall specify –

    (a) the works to the dominant land that may be carried out . . .

(b) the particular area of servient land that may be entered upon by virtue of the order . . .

(c) the date on which, or the period during which, the land may be so entered upon . . .

(3) . . . the terms and conditions which may be imposed under that subsection include provisions with respect to −

(a) the manner in which the specified works are to be carried out;

(b) the days on which, and the hours between which, the work involved may be executed;

(c) the persons who may undertake the carrying out of the specified works or enter upon the servient land or by virtue of the order . . .

### Persons bound by access order, unidentified persons and bar on contracting out

s 4(1) In addition to the respondent, an access order shall, subject to the provisions of the Land Charges Act 1972 and the [Land Registration Act 2002], be binding on −

(a) any of his successors in title to the servient land; and

(b) any person who has an estate or interest in, or right over, the whole or any part of the servient land which was created after the making of the order and who derives his title to that estate, interest or right under the respondent'.

## APPLYING THE LAW

Fred and Dan live next door to each other, with Fred's wall acting as the boundary between the two properties. The two neighbours have argued for years. Fred has no access to part of his roof except by going on to Dan's drive which runs down the side of it. There are no windows along that part of the wall and Fred would really like to put some in. Terrific storms cause several tiles to fall off Fred's roof. If Dan refuses Fred access to mend his roof the alternative is for Fred to apply to court under the Access to Neighbouring Land Act 1992.

*Applying the 1992 Act*

Fred qualifies under s 1 of the 1992 Act as a person wanting to carry out works by entering the servient land.

He can show that the works are reasonably necessary for the preservation of the property. If Fred were to go on the land for the purpose of repairing the roof then that would not interfere with Dan's enjoyment of his land. The work he wants to carry out is included under s 1(4)(a). If he wanted to put new windows in his property he could not use the 1992 Act as that would not be for the preservation of his property.

The order might be very specific under s 2 about its conditions, such as the exact days and hours when the work is to be carried out.

Finally, if Dan moves, then the order will be binding on the purchaser of his property under s 4(1)(a), if properly registered.

## KEY FACTS

### Access to Neighbouring Land Act 1992

**1.** An application may be made where someone needs to go on the land of a neighbour but he will not give his consent for them to do so.

**2.** The court will only make the order if the maintenance works must be carried out.

**3.** The order will only be made if there is no other way of accessing the land to do the work.

**4.** An access order is not an easement over the land; it is only the right to go on the land under the terms of the order.

**5.** An order will be refused where the court thinks that it will be unreasonable because the order will interfere with the landowner's enjoyment of his land.

**6.** Covers a wide variety of works including repair of a building, clearing drains and sewers, cutting back or removing a hedge or tree.

**7.** The order may include conditions such as the timing of the access and who will be responsible for the work.

**8.** The order is capable of registration because although it is not an interest in land it can be binding on a successor in title if it has been correctly registered.

The rule in *Harris v Flower* [1904] 74 LJ Ch 127 prevents exploitation of an easement. If Rodney has built a house in his garden and an easement is implied to allow access to it then it does not give him an automatic right to claim that right of way for a further house.

## CASE EXAMPLE

### *Das v Linden Mews Ltd* [2002] EWCA Civ 590

Two owners of mews houses acquired land near to their houses for parking. They had a right of way over a private road for access to their houses but they also claimed a right of way to gain access to the area for parking. The Court of Appeal held that the claim was for an easement for a separate piece of land rather than an easement to accommodate their dominant tenement. The key issue was whether the use of the area to park was ancillary to the enjoyment of the mews houses or whether there was intrinsic enjoyment in the enjoyment of the area of land itself. It was held that the benefit of access to the garden ground was not for better access to the houses but for the use of the garden ground itself as a car park and so could not exist as an easement.

### *Limitations on easements of necessity*

An easement of necessity will only be implied if there would be no enjoyment of the land at all without such an easement.

## CASE EXAMPLE

### *Union Lighterage Co v London Graving Dock Co* [1902] 2 Ch 557

In this case tie-rods on the claimant's land had held in place the wooden walls of the appellant's dock for over 20 years.

'In my opinion an easement of necessity, such as is referred to, means an easement without which the property retained cannot be used at all, and not one merely necessary to the reasonable enjoyment of that property. In *Wheeldon v Burrows* the lights which were the subject of decision were certainly necessary to the enjoyment of the property retained, which was a workshop, yet there was held to be no reservation of it. So here it may be that the tie-rods which pass through the plaintiff's property are reasonably necessary to the enjoyment of the defendant's dock in its present condition; but the dock is capable of use without them, and I think that there cannot be implied any reservation in respect of them'.

*Stirling J*

## 2. Intended easements

Easements may be implied in favour of a transferee in order to give effect to a common intention of the parties. The law is generally more generous in cases of intended easements than in cases of necessity.

There are two circumstances when an easement of common intention will be implied:

- if it is necessary for the enjoyment of a right that has been expressly granted
- if it can be implied from the circumstances in which the grant was made.

The easements have been described as 'such easements as may be necessary to give effect to the common intention of the parties to a grant of real property, with reference to the manner or purposes in and for which the land granted . . . is to be used . . . It is essential . . . that the parties should intend that the subject matter of the grant . . . should be used in some definite and particular manner' (Lord Parker in *Pwllbach Colliery Company Ltd v Woodman* [1915] AC 634).

ASE EXAMPLE

### *Wong v Beaumont Property Trust Ltd* [1965] 1 QB 173

The claimant had taken over a lease from a tenant with the express purpose of using the premises as a Chinese restaurant. He covenanted to comply with the public health regulations which could only be fulfilled by installing a new ventilation system leading through the upstairs premises retained by the defendant landlord. It became necessary to pass a ventilation shaft through the landlord's property but he refused the access to the tenant.

The Court of Appeal granted the tenant the right on the grounds of necessity. When the tenant took the lease it was clear that it was for use as a restaurant and it was the common intention of the parties that the tenant should have all rights necessary to carry this out.

CASE EXAMPLE

### *Stafford v Lee* (1992) 65 P & CR 172

An area of woodland had been granted by deed of gift. The owners wanted to build a house on the land. They claimed that the builders had the right to use the access to deliver building materials. The owners of the access road claimed that the right of way was limited to the original use of the land, namely as a woodland. As the original grant envisaged that a house was intended on the land, their claim to an easement based on common intention was upheld and the builders were able to deliver materials.

## 3. The rule in *Wheeldon v Burrows* (1879) 12 Ch D 31

This category of implied easements is much more significant than easements of necessity or intended easements. It will only apply to grants of easements and cannot apply to reservations.

The rule will only apply where land is sub-divided into two or more plots.

---

## APPLYING THE LAW

Rodney decides to develop his garden and builds a house for himself in the garden. He usually uses his garden to access the main road by way of a short-cut. The law will imply into the transfer of his old house any right that he exercised in his own favour including the use of the short cut.

---

These rights are usually referred to as quasi-easements. They are then converted by the rule into legal easements

### When does the rule apply?

> **J**  '. . . on the grant by the owner of a tenement of part of that tenement as it is then used and enjoyed there will pass to the grantee all those continuous and apparent easements (by which, I mean quasi-easements), or in other words, all those easements which are necessary to the reasonable enjoyment of the property granted, and which have been and are at the time of the grant used by the owners of the entirety for the benefit of the part granted . . .'.
>
> *Wheeldon v Burrows* (1879) 12 Ch D 31

In order to claim an implied easement under *Wheeldon v Burrows* it is necessary for the quasi-easement to be:

**1.** continuous and apparent

**2.** necessary for the reasonable enjoyment of the property granted and

**3.** in use by the owner at the time of the grant for the benefit of the part granted.

'Continuous and apparent' suggests that the quasi-easement has been enjoyed over a substantial period of time and which is discoverable or detectable on 'a careful inspection by a person ordinarily conversant with the subject'. The purchaser would be able to detect a right of way by a worn path.

Where the conditions are satisfied the rule applies in a wide variety of situations, eg:

**1.** both freehold and leasehold transfer even including a sub-lease

**2.** transfer on sale or a voluntary transfer or a devise

**3.** a legal transfer (eg a sale) or a transfer taking effect in equity (eg a contract to sell the legal estate or a contract to create a lease).

## 4. Easements acquired under s 62 of the Law of Property Act 1925

's 62(1) . . . A Conveyance of land shall be deemed to include . . . all buildings, erections, fixtures, commons, hedges, ditches, fences, ways, waters, watercourses, liberties, privileges, easements, rights, and advantages whatsoever, appertaining or reputed to appertain to the land, or any part thereof, or, at the time of conveyance, demised, occupied, or enjoyed with, or reputed or known as part and parcel of or appurtenant to the land or any part thereof

. . .

(2) . . . A Conveyance of land, having houses or other buildings thereon, shall be deemed to include . . . houses, or other buildings, all outhouses, erections, fixtures, cellars, areas, courts, courtyards, cisterns, sewers, gutters, drains, ways, passages, lights, water-courses, liberties, privileges, easements, rights and advantages whatsoever, appertaining or reputed to appertain to the land, houses or other buildings conveyed, or any part thereof, or, at the time of conveyance, demised, occupied, or enjoyed with, or reputed or known as part or parcel of or appurtenant to, the land , houses, or other buildings conveyed, or any of them, or any part thereof'.

Section 62 contains general words which can imply rights into the conveyance where they have not been specifically mentioned. This has a very dramatic effect on easements since rights which took effect as lesser rights such as licences could later become easements under this section. They would be implied into the conveyance transferring the estate in land and so the law implies that they are created by deed.

## APPLYING THE LAW

Gillian rents a ground-floor flat from her landlord, Craig. He lives on the top two floors but also has a garage and shed and a garden. Gillian has a bicycle and Craig allows her to keep it in the shed in his garden. This is a licence which is enforceable against Craig only. However, if Gillian's lease comes to an end and Craig executes a new lease in her favour but omits to mention the use of the shed for storage of her bicycle, the law will imply an easement in her favour. If Craig sells the house to his friend Angus then Angus will be bound by Gillian's rights. She can carry on storing her bicycle in the shed (as long as the lease lasts). It will now take effect as a legal easement. (See Figure 10.5.)

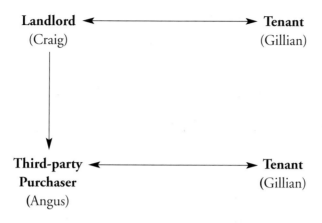

■ *Figure 10.5 Licence taking effect as a legal easement*

## CASE EXAMPLE

**International Tea Stores Co v Hobbs [1903] 2 Ch 165**

A landlord allowed his tenant to use a short-cut across his land. This existed as a licence. The landlord then sold the leased premises to the tenant. Later, it was held that the tenant had the right to use the short-cut as that had now taken effect as an easement which was enforceable against not just the landlord but any third-party purchaser.

### Comparison between s 62 and the rule in *Wheeldon v Burrows*

| **s 62** | Must be prior diversity of occupation. | Must be a conveyance of the property. | No specific requirements but must come within the definition of an easement. | Applies to easements and profits. |
|---|---|---|---|---|
| **Rule in *Wheeldon v Burrows*** | Applies to quasi-easements. | No conveyance is necessary, eg passes with a contract to grant a lease. | Requirements: right must be continuous and apparent right must be reasonably necessary to the enjoyment of the property. | Cannot apply to profits. |

## 10.4.3 Prescription

If a right is exercised over a long period of time then it is possible to claim that the use becomes a legal easement. It is subject to satisfying a number of conditions.

---

### KEY FACTS

**Easements claimed under prescription**

1. The claim is based on a notional grant of the right.

2. It is based on continuous use and although it can still succeed if there is infrequent use, it will fail if the use is separated by several years.

3. The claim cannot succeed if it would be lawful under another rule, for example there could be no easement to use the highway in front of your house if this was already subject to a public right of way.

4. An illegal right cannot be claimed as an easement.

5. The right must be *nec vi, nec clam, nec precario*. The assertion of a right must not be claimed as a result of physical force; the right must be openly exercised; and it must not be based on permission given by the owner of the servient tenement.

6. The claim can only be maintained by one fee simple owner against another fee simple owner. A tenant cannot claim an easement against his landlord by prescription.

7. The right must satisfy the characteristics of an easement as laid down in *Re Ellenborough Park*.

---

Easements can be acquired by prescription under:

a  common law

b  the doctrine of lost modern grant

c  the Prescription Act 1832.

### (a) Common law

The claimant has to show that the easement has been enjoyed not just for a long period of time but since time immemorial. It is extremely difficult to satisfy this test. The law takes that time to start in 1189! As proof of use since 1189 will be virtually impossible, the courts will accept use within living memory.

If the defendant can show that the claimant could not have enjoyed the right at any time since 1189 then the claim would be defeated, for example if there is proof that at any time the land was under common ownership then it would have been impossible to grant an easement and a claim under common law would be defeated.

## CASE EXAMPLE

### *Duke of Norfolk v Arbuthnot* (1880) 5 CPD 390

A claim for the right to light for a church under common law failed because there was proof that the church was built in 1380 and so after 1189.

## APPLYING THE LAW

Rodney lives next door to Graham and is claiming an easement by prescription under common law against him. He can show that he has used a path over Graham's garden for the past 20 years but Graham has evidence that Rodney's house was built in the garden of Rodney's house 50 years ago. In that case there could have been no grant.

### (b) The doctrine of lost modern grant

As it is so difficult to prove that a right has been exercised since 1189, the law has allowed a much easier test to be applied. Claims are based on a legal fiction which suggests that a grant had been made at one time but the grant had been lost. A successful case today would generally show that there had been continuous use for 20 years. It can be any 20-year period. It will not be defeated by evidence that there has been no such grant but it will be defeated if there is evidence that no one could have made the grant, for example there was no one legally competent or again that the land had once been in common ownership.

## CASE EXAMPLE

### *Tehidy Minerals Ltd v Norman* [1971] 2 QB 528

It was held that even where there was evidence that no grant had ever been made, this would not prevent a right from arising under the doctrine.

## (c) The Prescription Act 1832

This Act is popularly known as one of the 'worst drafted Acts' on the statute book. The 1832 Act tried to solve the problems that arise under common law prescription and the doctrine of lost modern grant.

Under the Act, the claimant must satisfy one of two periods of time in order to succeed:

1. the **short period**: 20 years' continuous and uninterrupted use immediately before the claim, 'next before action'. This can be defeated by the defendant if he can prove that the right was based on consent of the owner

2. the **long period**: 40 years' continuous and uninterrupted use immediately before the claim. This claim cannot be defeated even if there is proof that the right was granted with the consent of the landowner, unless the consent was given in writing.

*Rights to light*

The law treats the right to light slightly differently. Under the 1832 Act, 20 years of uninterrupted enjoyment will make the right absolute and indefeasible unless it was by written consent.

---

## KEY FACTS

**The Prescription Act 1832**

1. How long has the right been enjoyed?

2. Has the enjoyment of the right been interrupted and was it immediately before the claim?

3. Has the landowner given consent to the use of the right?

4. In what form was that permission given?

---

**Different ways of acquiring rights under prescription**

| Common law | Doctrine of lost modern grant | Prescription Act 1832 |
|---|---|---|
| Acquired on proof of continuous use 'since time immemorial' (1189). | Continuous use during living memory or for at least 20 years. | Use for either 20 or 40 years immediately before the action is brought. |
| Can be rebutted if there is proof that the right could not have been acquired in 1189. | Rebuttal limited to showing that there was no person legally capable to make the grant. | Rebuttal can be made on proof that written permission was given or in some circumstances oral permission. |
| Takes effect as a legal easement. | Takes effect as a legal easement. | Takes effect as a legal easement. |

# 10.5 Legal and equitable easements

An easement or a profit can be either **legal** or **equitable**.

A legal easement arises when the required formalities have been complied with and it is created for a length of time equivalent to one of the two legal estates that can exist in land:

- a fee simple absolute in possession or
- a term of years absolute in possession.

A legal easement must be created by **deed** under s 52 of the Law of Property Act 1925 because it creates an interest in land.

The deed must comply with s 1 of the Law of Property (Miscellaneous Provisions) Act 1989. If the deed does not comply with the necessary formalities then it will not take effect in law. An easement acquired prescriptively will not have a formal deed but as it is based on a fictitious deed it is still based on a deed. A contract to create a legal easement will take effect but only in equity.

An easement that is implied, for example under s 62 of the 1925 Act, is impliedly created by deed as the easement will be implied into the conveyance. Easements that arise through necessity, common intention and under the rule in *Wheeldon v Burrows* are also implied into the conveyance and will therefore take effect in law.

# ACTIVITY

Consider the following and decide whether they give rise to a legal or equitable easement:

1. Josh wants to use Jaivin's garden as a shortcut to the shops. Jaivin is reluctant to commit himself to an indefinite easement so he grants an easement for Josh's life. Josh pays him £450 for the privilege.

2. Alvin lives next door to Ravi, who is his landlord. Alvin has no parking space in front of his house but he is told by Ravi that he can use his drive to park his car while his lease lasts.

3. Alvin lives next door to Ravi, who is his landlord. Alvin has no parking space in front of his house but Ravi agrees in writing that he will grant him the right to park his car in his drive while the lease lasts.

# 10.6 Extinguishment of easements

There are a limited number of ways that an easement will come to an end:

> J  'A man cannot have an easement over his own land'.
>
> Fry LJ in *Roe v Siddons* (1889) LR 22 QBD 224

## Unity of ownership

If the fee simple of the dominant and servient land is owned by one person, any easements over the servient land will cease. If the fee simple of one piece of land is owned by one person who also owns a lease in the other plot of land, any easements will be suspended rather than extinguished. If the land is later owned by two different people, the easements will revive.

## Release

The owner of the dominant tenement can release his rights over the servient tenement. The release should be carried out by deed. If the release is oral then equity may give this effect if there is evidence in support of the release such as acting to one's detriment.

## CASE EXAMPLE

**Waterlow v Barlow (1886) LR 2 Eq 514**

The dominant owner gave written permission for his neighbour to raise the height of his wall and then tried to claim that his right to light was being affected. There had been an effective release of the easement.

## Abandonment

Once the right has been acquired as a legal easement, failure to make use of the right will not cause the dominant land to lose the right. However, where there has been no use for over 20 years then abandonment can be presumed unless there was no occasion to use the right.

## CASE EXAMPLE

**Benn v Hardinge (1992) 66 P & CR 246**

Non-use for 175 years was not enough to indicate an intention to abandon an easement as there had been no occasion to use the right of way involved because the owner had an alternative means of access to his property.

Compare

## CASE EXAMPLE

**Swan v Sinclair [1924] 1 Ch 254**

The landowner had not used a right of way for 38 years. He assented to building works which would have prevented him permanently from exercising the right of way over his neighbour's land. It was held that the easement had been abandoned.

**Change of circumstances**

# CASE EXAMPLE

***Huckvale v Aegean Hotels Ltd* (1989) P & CR 163**

It was accepted by Slade J that an easement can be extinguished by a change of circumstances because it no longer accommodates the dominant tenement. He thought it would be rare and in that case the right was not lost as there was a chance that it might benefit the dominant land again in the future:

> 'circumstances might have changed so drastically since the date of the original grant of an easement . . . that it would offend common sense and reality for the court to hold that an easement still subsisted. Nevertheless, I think the court could properly so hold only in a very clear case'.

# 10.7 Profits à prendre

## 10.7.1 General

A profit à prendre is created in the same way as an easement and can be either legal or equitable, according to whether it is created for the equivalent of one or two legal estates and according to the required formalities.

## 10.7.2 Types of profits à prendre

**1.** The right to graze cattle on the servient land (profit à pasture).

**2.** The right to fish and take away fish that have been caught (profit à piscary).

**3.** The right to take away and cut down wood (profit à estovers).

---

## KEY FACTS

**The creation of profits à prendre**

**1.** The owner of the servient land can grant a profit à prendre expressly by deed.

**2.** If no deed is used, it will take effect in equity.

**3.** A profit à prendre can arise impliedly but only under s 62 of the Law of Property Act 1925.

**4.** The rule in *Wheeldon v Burrows* does not apply to profits à prendre.

---

> **5.** Profits à prendre can be acquired under the Prescription Act 1832.
>
> **6.** The periods of time to be satisfied are 30 years and 60 years.
>
> **7.** A profit will be lost through release or acquisition of the servient land.

# 10.8 Changes made by the Land Registration Act 2002

The Land Registration Act 2002 has reformed the law on easements in a number of ways. The 2002 Act is discussed in detail in Chapter 3.

## 10.8.1 Overriding interests: equitable easements

One of the main initiatives behind the 2002 Act was to try to limit the number of overriding interests that can exist in land.

### Before the Land Registration Act 2002

Under s 70(1)(a) of the Land Registration Act 1925 (now repealed), legal easements were held to be overriding interests. If the claimant had failed to register a legal interest as a minor interest, it would still be binding on the third-party purchaser.

After *Celsteel Ltd v Alton House Holdings Ltd* [1985] 1 WLR 204 it was held that equitable easements could also have overriding status if they were exercised and enjoyed openly.

### After the Land Registration Act 2002

The 2002 Act has reformed the law so that equitable easements can no longer be overriding under any circumstances.

An equitable easement will only be binding if it has been properly registered. If the land has an unregistered title, it will be lost unless it has been entered in the Land Charges Register. It will then have to be entered on the Register on first registration.

If an equitable easement is created after first registration, it will need to be protected. This is done by entering a burden on the register of title.

## 10.8.2 Overriding interests: legal interests

Legal easements continue to be overriding but in more limited circumstances:

**1.** all legal easements or profits à prendre will take effect as overriding interests against a first registration of title to the land under Schedule 1 to the Land Registration Act 2002

**2.** under Schedule 3 to the Land Registration Act 2002, a limited number of legal easements will continue to be overriding on a subsequent registration of title if they satisfy any of the following conditions:

**(i)** an easement that is within the actual knowledge of the person to whom the disposition is made or

**(ii)** it would have been obvious on a reasonably careful inspection of the land over which the easement or profit is exercisable or

**(iii)** if the easement has been used in the year preceding the disposition.

Under s 27(2)(d) of the 2002 Act, an easement or profit that has been expressly granted must be entered on the Register. It will not take effect at law until it has been entered in this way. It cannot be overriding because it is not yet effective at law and it cannot take effect in equity because equitable interests are no longer overriding. So the only types of easements that will be overriding on a subsequent disposition will be an easement that arises under an implied grant or by prescription.

## APPLYING THE LAW

Windy Hollow and Windy Villa are two neighbouring cottages. Freda is tenant of Windy Hollow and Leila owns Windy Villa. Freda has been given the right to use a short-cut by her neighbour, Leila, who is also her landlord. In December 2003 Freda purchases the freehold of Windy Hollow from Leila. Under s 62 of the 1925 Act, the short-cut becomes a legal easement although it is not expressly mentioned in the conveyance. Leila sells her house to Georgia. Georgia will be bound by Freda's right to use the short-cut if it is obvious when she visits the house. It will also be binding if it has been exercised by Freda during the past year.

There may be some problems over what the courts interpret as reasonably obvious on careful inspection of the land.

> 'Of course, there may be some interpretative difficulties over "obvious on a reasonably careful inspection", especially in relation to long-disused land where the "one year use" clause may not apply'.

M Dixon, 'The Reform of Property Law and the Land Registration Act 2002:
A Risk Assessment' [2003] 67 Conv 136

# ACTIVITY

In 1980 Frank bought a house called Sturdy Manor. He liked to walk on the seashore which was several miles away but he could get to the sea much more quickly by using a short-cut through his neighbour Geraint's land. Geraint ran a small market garden and owned 30 acres of land. Frank could easily get to the sea by the main road but it took much longer. Frank was sent abroad with his job for one year and so did not use the path. When he came back he decided to turn Sturdy Manor into a guest house and he created eight bedrooms. The guests started to use the short-cut to the sea. Geraint decided to sell the market garden to Harry in November 2003. Harry has put up a fence and neither Frank nor his guests have been able to use the path leading to the sea.

Consider whether Frank or his guests can continue to use the short-cut across Harry's land.

# 10.9 Reform of the law on easements and profits

There are many aspects of easements which are unsatisfactory, in particular the law on prescription.

In 1966 the Law Reform Committee reported on *Easements: Acquisition of Easements and Profits by Prescription* (Cmnd 3100). It recommended that prescription should be abolished for both easements and profits. It also recommended that there should be one single period for acquiring rights prescriptively, which would be 12 years. This was not implemented.

The Law Commission report leading up to the 2002 Act (*Land Registration for the 21st Century* (Law Com No 254)) also recommended that the law on prescription should be changed so that both common law prescription and prescription under the doctrine of lost modern grant should be abolished, so that only prescription under the 1832 Act would remain. These proposals were not implemented but other recommended reforms in relation to the overriding nature of easements have been put into effect.

# Further reading

Barnsley, D G, 'Equitable Easements 60 Years on' (1999) 115 LQR 89.

Dixon, M, 'The Reform of Property Law and the Land Registration Act 2002: A Risk Assessment' [2003] 67 Conv 136.

*Gale on Easements* (17th edn, Sweet & Maxwell, 2002).

Harpum, C, 'The Acquisition of Easements' (1992) CLJ 220.

Luther, P, 'Easements and Exclusive Possession' (1996) 16 Legal Studies 51.

Paton, E and Seabourne, G, 'Can't get there from here?: Permissible use of easements after *Das*' [2003] 67 Conv 127.

Tee, L, 'Metamorphoses and s.62 of the Law of Property Act 1925' [1998] Conv 115.

West, J, '*Wheeldon v Burrows* Revisited' [1995] Conv 346.

# chapter 11 RESTRICTIVE COVENANTS ▪▬

Neighbours will often draw up agreements between themselves about the use each makes of his land. These will be personal obligations governed by the rules of contract. Their impact is considerable on the enjoyment of the land and they are quite independent of any rights and obligations which arise under planning law. Land law has long sought a way to make these agreements enforceable against third parties. These agreements often have such a profound effect on the enjoyment of property, unless they are enforceable against successors in title, their value will be limited.

## 11.1 The nature of a restrictive covenant

A covenant is an obligation entered into by deed which usually restricts the use of land for the benefit of another.

## APPLYING THE LAW ☐☐☐

Mr Ford covenants with Miss Carefree not to use his land for business purposes. Miss Carefree can sue if she finds that Mr Ford has set up a printing business in the barn adjoining his house.

☐☐☐

- The agreement is made by deed between the covenantor (who carries the burden) and the covenantee (who carries the benefit).

- As it can be enforced under the law of contract, the rules of privity will apply and this means that the covenant can only be enforced between the original parties and burdens cannot be imposed on third parties.

- As this is a contract, the original parties will continue to be bound even after they have left the property.

Covenants may be either **positive** or **negative** in nature and different rules will apply in each case.

- **Positive covenants**: burdens imposed on the covenantor to carry out a specific act, for example a covenant to repair a wall or to keep property in good repair.

- **Negative covenants**: these prohibit specified kinds of activity or development of the covenantor's land for the benefit of the covenantee's land, for example a covenant against any further development on the land.

# ACTIVITY

Consider the following covenants and decide whether they are positive or negative covenants:

**a** to keep Midsummer Meadow as an open space

**b** to erect a fence along the boundary of Midsummer Meadow

**c** not to divide Midsummer Farm into flats

**d** not to let Midsummer Farm fall into disrepair.

In each case, ask the question 'Would the covenantor have to put his hand into his pocket in order to carry out the covenant?' In other words, does it cost money to comply with the covenant?

Restrictive covenants play a vital role in the development and use of land and rank alongside planning law as a means of regulating its use.

There are a number of questions to consider in relation to covenants: can they be enforced between the original parties and can they be enforced against or by successors in title?

The answers to these questions depend on whether they are enforceable at law or in equity. The enforceability of covenants was extended by equity after the decision of *Tulk v Moxhay* (1843) 2 Ph 773 but the effect was that only negative covenants could be enforced.

**Common law** and **equity** therefore treat covenants and the transfer of the benefits and burdens under them differently.

# 11.2 Covenants at law

The common law rules relating to covenants can be traced far back in history.

# CASE EXAMPLE

**The Prior's case (1368) YB 42 Edw III pl 14**

This was one of the earliest recorded cases, in which it was held that a covenant may be enforceable against the covenantor by the covenantee even where the covenantor owns no land to be benefited. In this case, the covenant was to sing all week in the chapel of the covenantee.

In practice, the covenantor generally owns some land and it is important that the covenantee owns some land to be benefited by the covenant.

# 11.2.1 Enforcement of covenants: special circumstances

There is generally no difficulty in enforcing a covenant between the original parties but there are some special circumstances which extend or restrict the category of person who may enforce the original covenant.

1. **s 56(1) of the Law of Property Act 1925**: this has the effect that a covenant will be enforceable by all persons who are named generically in the covenant, for example if X covenants with Y and all owners for the time being of Blackacre, the unnamed owner will be able to enforce the covenant even though he is not specifically mentioned in the conveyance. This section does not apply to future owners of the land, but only to persons who are in existence and identifiable at the date of the covenant. A person who acquires a benefit under s 56 may then pass it on to his successors in title by annexation or assignment.

2. The **Contracts (Rights of Third Parties) Act 1999** has made extensions to the rights of any third party to enforce a covenant entered into after May 2000. They can now be enforced by anyone for whose benefit a party named in the deed was expressly contracted or was purportedly made for their benefit but they are not expressly referred to by name, for example if X covenants with Y so as to benefit the owners of Blackacre and Greenacre, the owners of the two properties can argue that they have the right to enforce the covenants.

3. The benefit of a covenant which is not exclusively personal may always be assigned in writing as a chose in action under s 136 of the 1925 Act. Notice should be given to the covenantor.

Section 56 creates some special problems. It was considered in *White v Bijou Mansions Ltd* [1937] Ch 610 by Simonds J who said:

> J
>
> 'under section 56 . . . only that person can call it in aid who, although not named as a party to the conveyance or other instrument is yet a person to whom that conveyance or other instrument purports to grant something or with whom some agreement or covenant is purported to be made . . . I interpret [s 56] as a section which can be called in aid only by a person in whose favour the grant purports to be made or with whom the covenant or agreement purports to be made'.

This section was pleaded in the following case:

# CASE EXAMPLE

**_Amstrop Trading Ltd v Harris Distribution_ Ltd [1997] 2 All ER 990**

A superior landlord who had covenanted with a tenant that it would be lawful for the landlord to enter and repair at the cost of the sub-tenant tried to enforce the cost of the repairs against a sub-tenant who refused to pay for them. There was neither privity of contract nor privity of estate between the sub-tenant and the landlord so the landlord tried to use s 56. The judge held that, for s 56 to apply, the covenant must have been made on behalf of the sub-tenant and it clearly had not. This shows that there are clear limits on the extent of s 56.

4. **s 78(1) of the Law of Property Act 1925** provides that a covenant 'relating to' any land of the covenantee is presumptively 'made with the covenantee and his successors in title and the persons deriving title under him or them, and shall have effect as if such successors and other persons were expressed'. This section applies to covenants which relate to (or 'touch and concern') the covenantee's land.

## 11.2.2 The passing of the benefit at law

Property changes hands frequently and so it is important to consider whether the covenant will continue to be binding on purchasers from the covenantee.

## APPLYING THE LAW

If X sells part of Blackacre to Y and Y enters into covenants not to build on the land and also to erect a fence around his plot, the benefit of this covenant may extend to a purchaser, Z, who buys the remaining part of Blackacre from X.

If Y then starts to build a bungalow in the garden of Blackacre, Z can take action against Y. Y is liable both on the positive covenant (to build the fence) and also the negative covenant (not to build on the land).

If Z wants to take action, he must satisfy certain conditions:

### The covenant must 'touch and concern' the land

It must not be purely for the personal benefit of the covenantee, for example it must confer a benefit on you as landowner and not on you as an individual. A right to prevent your neighbour from using his land for business purposes benefits the land. A right to prevent your neighbour from keeping a dog is likely to be seen as a personal benefit and will be unlikely to be upheld as a covenant.

# CASE EXAMPLE

### Smith and Snipes Hall Farm Ltd v River Douglas Catchment Board [1949] 2 KB 500

The covenant by the defendant Catchment Board to improve and keep river banks in repair was held to have 'touched and concerned' the covenantee's land, which was flooded when repair was neglected, because . . . 'it affects the value of the land *per se* and converts it from flooded meadows to land suitable for agriculture'.

In *P & A Swift Investments v Combined English Stores Group* [1989] AC 632 Lord Oliver of Aylmerton laid down a test to discover whether a covenant 'touches and concerns' the land:

1. the covenant must benefit the estate owner for the time being and it would cease to be of benefit to the covenantee if separated from the ownership of the benefited estate

2. the covenant must affect the nature, quality, mode of use or value of the benefited land

3. even where 1 and 2 are satisfied, the covenant will not be regarded as 'touching and concerning the land' if the benefit is in some way expressed to be personal to the covenantee.

# CASE EXAMPLE

### Morrells of Oxford Ltd v Oxford United Football Club Ltd [2001] Ch 459

A covenant that 'the vendors will not at any time hereafter permit any land or building erected thereon within half a mile radius of the land hereby conveyed which is in the ownership of the vendors at the date of this conveyance to be used as a brewery or club or licensed premises' was held to operate as a personal covenant only.

# CASE EXAMPLE

### Hua Chiao Commercial Bank v Chiaphua Industries [1987] AC 99

This case held that a promise by the landlord to return a deposit paid as security for rent at the end of the lease was purely personal and so the successor in title from the landlord had no obligation to return the deposit to the tenant at the end of the lease. This remained the personal responsibility of the original landlord.

## The original covenantee must have a legal estate in the benefited land

This would be either a fee simple absolute in possession (freehold) or a term of years absolute (leasehold) under s 1 of the Law of Property Act 1925.

## The successor in title of the original covenantee must have a legal estate in the benefited land

Until 1926 it was assumed that the successor in title must have the same legal estate in land as the original covenantee. Under s 78 of the 1925 Act, it is held that the legal estate held by the successor in title can be different. So the original covenantee can hold a fee simple absolute but the successor in title can be a leaseholder and still have the right to enforce the covenant at law. On the rare occasions that the covenant in question was made before 1925 then the assignee could not.

In *Smith and Snipes Hall Farm Ltd v River Douglas Catchment Board* the original covenantee sold his land to the first plaintiff who then leased the land to the second plaintiff. Under s 78, both parties were able to enforce the covenant. The court held that the effect of s 78 is that a covenant is enforceable on behalf of not only the original covenantee, but all successors in title and all persons deriving title from such successors.

## The benefit must have been intended to run with the benefited land

The parties must intend that the benefit of the covenant is to run with the land. It had to be shown that the parties to the deed intended the covenant to be enforceable not only by the original covenantee but also by successors in title to the original covenantee.

This caused problems before 1926 because the covenant had to be very specific in its wording in order to allow the benefit to pass to their successors. After 1925, such an intention is assumed by s 78 of the 1925 Act:

 's 78 ... The covenant is deemed to be made with the covenantee and his successors in title and the persons deriving title under him'.

In *Smith and Snipes Hall Farm Ltd v River Douglas Catchment Board* Lord Denning said:

> 'The covenant of the catchment board in this case clearly relates to the land of the covenantees. It was a covenant to do work on the land for the benefit of the land. By the statute therefore, it is deemed to be made, not only with the original owner, but also with the purchasers of the land and their tenants as if they were expressed. Now if they were expressed, it would be clear that the covenant was made for their benefit; and they have sufficient interest to entitle them to enforce it because they have suffered the damage'.

The benefit of both negative and also positive covenants can pass at common law, provided the criteria discussed above are satisfied. In *P & A Swift v Combined English Stores* a covenant was enforceable which concerned the provision of a surety for rent payable under a lease.

# ACTIVITY

Consider the following situations and decide whether the successors of the original covenantee can sue on the running of the covenant at common law:

1. Mr and Mrs Brown purchased Blackacre. The title was registered in Mr Brown's name but Mrs Brown had contributed to the purchase. While Mr Brown is in South America on a two-year contract, their neighbour starts to build industrial units which Mrs Brown believes to be in breach of the covenant not to use the property for business purposes. Can she take action against the neighbour?

2. Mr White acquired a long leasehold of The Laurels in 1923 which he left to his grandson in 1960. The original covenantee, Mr Grey, had purchased The Laurels in 1920. Can Mr White's grandson sue on the covenant not to allow the garden of the property next door to become overgrown?

3. Mr Wong covenanted with Mr Wu not to alter the exterior of any of the buildings which he purchased in 1980. Will the benefit of this covenant run to Mr Wang when he buys the properties from Mr Wang in 2000?

## 11.2.3 The running of the burden at law

The general rule is that the burden of a covenant will never run at common law. So the purchaser from the covenantor will not be bound by any covenants which they agreed with the covenantee.

# APPLYING THE LAW

If Mr Brown covenants with Mr Grey not to let the exterior of his house, Ivy Cottage, fall into disrepair, the burden of this covenant will not run at law. When Mrs Green purchases Ivy Cottage from Mr Brown, she will not become liable for the positive covenant entered into by her predecessor in title, Mr Brown.

Mr Brown himself will remain liable and so Mr Grey could always sue the original covenantor, Mr Brown. Mr Brown will remain liable until the covenant is eventually discharged.

# CASE EXAMPLE

**Austerberry v Corporation of Oldham (1885) 29 Ch D 750**

The claimant's predecessors in title had, along with others, conveyed land to trustees, with the aim of forming a new road. The trustees covenanted that they would make the road and keep it in repair. The cost would be met by levying a toll. The trustees made the road but ultimately ownership of it passed to the Corporation. The Corporation tried to recover the costs of repair from the claimant and the other owners of property fronting the road.

It was held by Cotton LJ that the burden of a covenant cannot run at common law.

The explanation for this can be found in a recent judgment of Lord Templeman.

# CASE EXAMPLE

**Rhone v Stephens [1994] 2 AC 310**

'To enforce a positive covenant would be to enforce a personal obligation against a person who has not covenanted. To enforce negative covenants is only to treat the land as subject to a restriction'.

This case concerned the enforcement of a covenant entered into by a freehold owner agreeing 'to maintain to the reasonable satisfaction of the purchasers and their successors in title such part of the roof as lies above the property conveyed in wind and water tight condition'. Part of the roof of a house extended over an adjoining cottage. The cottage and house ceased to be owned by the same person and the cottage owner sought to enforce the covenant to repair his roof against the owner of the house. However, by this time the house had changed hands and had been bought by the defendant. The House of Lords held that the original covenant to repair, being positive in nature, could not bind the defendant who was the original covenantor's successor in title at common law, under the rule in *Austerberry v Oldham Corporation*.

This is an inconvenient rule, as shown by the facts of *Rhone v Stephens*. It would be very valuable to enforce repairing covenants against your neighbour where properties are divided into two plots but there is some measure of overlap between the properties.

## How can the rule be justified?

We can justify the rule because land may become burdened with endless covenants which then make it difficult to sell freely. It is possible in the future that the rule in *Austerberry v Oldham Corporation* will be reversed. There have been several proposals by the Law Commission to allow the burden of positive covenants to run at law, for example in Law Commission Report No 127 *Transfer of Land: The Law of Positive and Restrictive Covenants* (1984).

> **J** 'Your Lordships were invited to overrule the decision of the Court of Appeal in the *Austerberry* case. To do so would destroy the distinction between law and equity and to convert the rule of equity into a rule of notice. It is plain from the articles, reports and papers to which we were referred that judicial legislation to overrule the *Austerberry* case would create a number of difficulties, anomalies and uncertainties and affect the rights and liabilities of people who have for over 100 years bought and sold land in the knowledge, imparted at an elementary stage to every student of the law of real property, that positive covenants, affecting freehold land are not directly enforceable except against the original covenantor'. Lord Templeman in *Rhone v Stephens*.

## Possible reform: commonhold

Under the Commonhold and Leasehold Reform Act 2002, ownership of land can be held under a commonhold scheme. The land must be specified under a memorandum of commonhold association as land in relation to which the association can exercise certain functions. The commonhold community statement will lay down the rights and duties of each owner of land. Within this statement will be the rules and regulations. The statement will lay down both rights and also duties and these can be both positive and negative. Although it is expected that commonhold will mainly cover blocks of flats, it could also be used for communal ownership of gardens in towns and also the shared ownership of roads and communal gardens; there could be an association of just two members. This Act has recently come into force and it will be interesting to see whether the problems of non-enforceability of positive covenants will be solved by the commonhold. This may be one way forward to allow positive covenants to be enforceable in the future. This is considered in detail in Chapter 15.

# 11.2.4 Methods by which the rule in *Austerberry v Oldham Corporation* can be avoided

- **Chains of indemnity covenants**: the original covenantor will remain liable on the original covenant. In practice, the original covenantor will take out an indemnity covenant with any purchaser in order to protect himself against subsequent breaches of covenant over which he will not have any control. Then, on a later sale, another indemnity covenant will be taken out with the new purchaser. The main disadvantage is that as the chain grows, it is likely that it

may break. The original covenantor may have died or just cannot be found or may have become insolvent and so there is no point in suing. The only remedy is damages, which may not be as appropriate as an injunction or specific performance.

## APPLYING THE LAW

Charlotte covenants with Kate not to allow the garden of her property, Mistletoe Cottage, to become overgrown. Charlotte will remain liable on the covenant even when she moves away from the area. So when Charlotte sells the property to Lydia, as this is a positive covenant, Lydia, will not be liable to Kate. Kate, however, can sue Charlotte although she has now moved away but she in turn can sue Lydia and if Charlotte has taken out an indemnity covenant with Lydia, she must indemnify Charlotte for any damages she has to pay.

- **A long lease**: this may be enlarged into a fee simple under s 153 of the Law of Property Act 1925. It is suggested that this will allow the freehold to be subject to the same covenants as those contained originally in the lease. This is rarely used as it is both cumbersome and artificial.
- **The rule in *Halsall v Brizell*** [1957] Ch 169: this is also known as the doctrine of mutual benefit and burden. This is a useful rule frequently used to enforce positive covenants. If a purchaser takes certain benefits under the conveyance then the purchaser cannot avoid the burdens of an associated covenant.

ASE EXAMPLE

### *Halsall v Brizell* [1957] Ch 169

When an estate was developed, each owner agreed by deed that they would contribute towards the upkeep of certain communally enjoyed benefits including the drive, the sewers and the repair of the sea wall. Since each owner had the right to enjoy the benefits, the court held that they had an obligation to contribute towards their upkeep.

The rule holds that if you have the right to use your neighbour's drive or sewers then you have to bear some of the cost of their upkeep, even where you are not the original covenantor: 'A man cannot take benefit under a deed without subscribing to obligations thereunder'.

In recent cases this rule has been interpreted narrowly. In *Rhone v Stephens* it was held that just because the deed conferred a benefit on a person, it did not mean that all the

burdens imposed by that deed became enforceable. The burden must in some way relate to the benefit conferred. This will be so where the covenantor can make a choice between accepting the benefit and burden or rejecting the benefit and thereby being released from the burden. So in this case the fact that A's roof was supported by B's property did not entitle B to enforce a positive covenant to repair the roof made by A's predecessor in title because he had no choice between accepting and rejecting the burden.

# ASE EXAMPLE

### *Thamesmead Town v Allotey* [2000] 79 P & CR 557

The defendant was relieved of maintenance costs in respect of certain facilities because they were the ones that he did not use and from which, therefore, he derived no benefit. Here, the owners chose not to use pathways and footpaths in a London County Council estate and so escaped an obligation towards their upkeep.

- **Rights of re-entry**: the dominant owner can reserve a right of entry which will become exercisable upon a breach of a positive covenant.

- **The grant of a lease**: the land can always be leased rather than sold and then there is no difficulty in enforcing covenants against successors to the original covenantor.

- **A rent charge**: it is possible to annex a right of entry to a legal rentcharge which is itself a legal interest in the land. In this way positive covenants to repair, even covenants to build and improve the land, can be enforced. The proprietor can enter the land where the covenants have not been observed and make good himself, charging the cost to the landowner. It is an ingenious device but only useful where lawyers can deal with the legal complexities, so making it an expensive option. **Note**: a rentcharge is a right to claim a periodical sum of money from the owner of land which is not dependent on a landlord and tenant relationship.

**Methods by which the rule in *Austerberry v Oldham Corporation* can be avoided**

| Method of avoidance | How it works | Disadvantages |
|---|---|---|
| Chain of indemnity covenants | Dependent on the legal right to sue the original covenantor; depends on each owner taking out a covenant indemnifying them from loss arising from a breach of covenant. | The chain can easily break down; difficult always to locate the original owner; original owner may have become insolvent or have died. |

| A long lease | May be enlarged into a fee simple under s 153 of the LPA 1925. | Rarely used as cumbersome method of ensuring that the covenants are enforced. |
|---|---|---|
| The rule in *Halsall v Brizell* | Known as the doctrine of mutual benefit and burden; if you receive a benefit you must also bear the burden. | Interpreted narrowly so must relate to the benefit conferred, if no benefit can be proved then will be released from obligation: *Thamesmead Town v Allotey*. |
| Rights of re-entry | The dominant owner can reserve a right to re-enter the premises if there is a breach of covenant. | Legalistic and complicated. |
| The grant of a lease | Covenants can always be enforced within a lease and against successors in title. | It is easy to enforce the covenants but it relies on a method which forces you to accept leasehold ownership when you wanted to buy freehold. |
| A rent charge | Can annexe a right of re-entry to a legal rentcharge. | Complex and legalistic. |

There has been considerable criticism of the position of the law on positive covenants since the decision in *Rhone v Stephens*.

'In 1971 the Law Commission described the law on rights appurtenant to land as "illogical, uncertain, incomplete and inflexible" (Law Commission W.P. No 36 Appurtenant Rights (1971) paras 31–35). The incompleteness of the law was specifically attributed to the failure to make provision for the enforcement of the positive covenants relating to freehold land against successors in title to the original covenantor. The decision of the House of Lords in *Rhone v Stephens* [1994] has reaffirmed that incompleteness and has thereby underlined the need to revive the recommendations of the Law Commission and others on land obligations and common hold schemes. . . . Although the enforcement of positive covenants has been recommended in a series of reports over the past thirty years, Lord Templeman regarded it as inappropriate for the courts to overrule the *Austerberry* case, which had provided for the basis for transactions relating to the rights and liabilities of landowners for over 100 years. On the contrary, the potential problems of such judicial legislation together with the experience in relation to the enforcement of positive covenants between landlord and tenant, pointed to the clear need for Parliamentary legislation to deal with consequences . . . Few would

dissent from the view that in appropriate circumstances positive covenants should be capable of enforcement against successors in title to the original covenantor'.

N P Gravells, 'Enforcement of Positive Covenants Affecting Freehold Land' (1994) 110 LQR 346

There continue to be advantages of suing at law rather than in equity and the reform of the rule in *Austerberry v Oldham* remains a continuing necessity.

Advantages of the common law for the enforcement of covenants:

**1.** the claimant can claim damages as of right once the breach of the covenant has been proved

**2.** the covenantor does not need to own land before a case can be brought by the claimant at common law

**3.** the covenant can be either positive or negative to be enforceable at common law.

# 11.3 Covenants in equity

## The benefit

For the benefit of a covenant to run in equity, it is necessary for the covenant to be one that 'touches and concerns' the land. It is also necessary to show that the benefit of the covenant has passed to the covenantee.

There are several ways in which the benefit can pass in equity and the different rules are complicated. The benefit will pass through either:

**1.** annexation

**2.** assignment or

**3.** a building scheme.

## 11.3.1 Annexation

'Annexation is the process by which the benefit of a restrictive covenant is metaphorically "nailed" to a clearly defined area of land belonging to the covenantee, in such a way that the benefit passes with any subsequent transfer of the covenantee's interest in that land'.

Gray and Gray, *Elements of Land Law* (3rd edn, Butterworths, 2001), p 1163.

Annexation can be **express**, **implied or statutory**.

## Express annexation

At common law, the question of annexation rested on the question of intention. The conveyance had to annex the covenant expressly.

For example, the purchaser Myrtle Brown covenants with vendor Pansy Green so that the benefit is annexed to each and every part of the land that the seller retains. The law was fairly strict about the way this was interpreted.

In *Re Ballard's Conveyance* [1937] Ch 473 it was held that there was no express annexation of a covenant which purportedly benefited the whole of an estate of 1,700 acres, although in a more recent decision (*Wrotham Park Estate Co Ltd v Parkside Homes Ltd* [1974] 1 WLR 798) a less strict approach was taken, allowing a covenant to be annexed where it benefits a substantial part of the dominant tenement.

## Implied annexation

It has also been held that a covenant can be **impliedly annexed** from surrounding circumstances but the benefit of the covenant must be clearly referable to a defined piece of land and the parties must have intended that the benefit attach to the land and not to the covenantee personally.

## Statutory annexation

If there are no words of express annexation and the covenant cannot be impliedly annexed then it may be **statutorily annexed** under s 78 of the Law of Property Act 1925.

This section reads as follows:

's 78(1) A covenant relating to any land of the covenantee shall be deemed to be made with the covenantee and his successors in title and the persons deriving title under him or them and shall have the effect as if such successors and other persons were expressed.

For the purposes of this subsection in connection with covenants restrictive of the user of land "successors in title" shall be deemed to include the owners and occupiers for the time being of the land of the covenantee intended to be benefited.

(2) This section applies to covenants made after the commencement of this Act, but the repeal of section 58 of the Conveyancing Act 1881 does not affect the operation of covenants to which that section applied.'

The law is now governed by an interpretation of this section in the following case:

ASE EXAMPLE

### *Federated Homes Ltd v Mill Lodge Properties Ltd* [1980] 1 WLR 594

The case concerned the owners (Mackenzie Hill) of land which was divided into four plots. They obtained planning permission to build 1,250 houses on the site. The owners sold one plot (the 'blue site') to Mill Lodge Properties Ltd.

The conveyance contained the following covenant: 'the purchaser Mill Lodge hereby
covenants with the vendor that . . . in carrying out the development of the land the
purchaser shall not build at a greater density than a total of 300 dwellings so as not to
reduce the number of units which the vendor might eventually erect on the retained land
under the existing planning consent'. It was clear that the covenant was intended to
benefit the 'adjoining or adjacent property retained' by the covenantee, although the terms
of the covenant were not expressly annexed to the remaining plots of land. The owners
sold two of the remaining plots of his land and they eventually came into the hands of the
claimant. Mill Lodge (the covenantor) tried to build more than 300 houses on the 'blue
site' and the question was whether the owners of the adjoining two sites had the benefit
of the covenant which could stop Mill Lodge from building. For one plot there had been
an express assignment of the covenant but for the other plot the conveyance had not
referred to it.

Brightman LJ considered s 78 of the 1925 Act and found three ways of interpreting the
section:

**1.** it was simply a word-saving device aimed at reducing the length of legal documents.
This was rejected

**2.** the section only operated to annex a covenant if the document in some way showed
that the land was intended to have the benefit of it

**3.** the section effected annexation as long as the covenant touched and concerned the
land of the covenantee and this applied whether or not it was apparent from the
document or from surrounding circumstances.

He concluded that if a covenant touched and concerned the land then that covenant will
run with the land for the benefit of his successors in title, persons deriving title under him
or them and other owners and occupiers.

The section will allow covenants to be automatically annexed by virtue of s 78 unless there is a
contrary intention as discussed below. There is no necessity for the successors in title to be even
aware that they have the benefit of such a covenant annexed to their land.

There are **criticisms** of this approach. They centre on the fact that Brightman LJ's decision seems
to run contrary to all the previous decisions on the running of covenants. In particular, how could
a section that had been on the statute book for over 50 years suddenly transform the whole law on
restrictive covenants?

Strong arguments against Brightman LJ's approach were made in the following extract:

> 'Annexation was always considered to be a matter of intention . . . There is not a
> word in any earlier case to suggest that annexation could come about without the

parties intending to bring it about, and the conventional rules had been accepted universally by practitioners until November 1979, whatever the date of the covenant. Further, it was repeatedly held, from *Renals v Cowlishaw* [(1879) LR 11 Ch D 866] onwards, that the presence of words referring to successors of the covenantee was not of itself sufficient to effect annexation. Such words had been added by the Conveyancing Act 1881 s 58 and still did not of themselves effect annexation, but the Court of Appeal concluded in the *Federated Homes* case, that the change of wording between s 58 of the Conveyancing Act 1881, and its successor s 78 of the Law of Property Act 1925, necessarily made this drastic change, a change unsuspected from 1926, when apparently it occurred, until the end of 1979 . . . The Act of 1925 was a consolidating Act and it would be decidedly odd if a change of such far-reaching importance was to be made by such an Act'.

> C H S Preston and G H Newsom, *Preston and Newsom's Restrictive Covenants affecting Freehold Land*
> (9th edn, Sweet & Maxwell, 1998), p 17

Two subsequent cases have restricted the effect of the decision in *Federated Homes v Mill Lodge Properties Ltd*:

1. *Roake v Chadha* [1984] 1 WLR 40: if there is a contrary intention shown in the conveyance expressly restricting the passing of the benefit to successors in title then s 78 will not automatically annex a covenant to land. The wording in this case was that the covenant was expressed 'not to enure for the benefit of any owner or subsequent purchaser of the . . . estate unless the benefit of the covenant shall be expressly assigned'. It was held that the covenant did not relate to the land and was not therefore annexed to it.

2. The conveyance must be construed in the light of all the circumstances: *Sainsbury (J) v Enfield London Borough Council* [1989] 1 WLR 590.

It is also dependent on the landowner owning land before sale which carries the benefit of the covenant and the purchaser must also own land after sale; the covenant cannot be assigned in isolation.

The impact of s 78 in the context of restrictive covenants is even more wide ranging because of the inclusion of mere occupiers within its scope, so that a restrictive covenant may be enforced by a licensee of the dominant tenement.

## ACTIVITY

Consider the main arguments against Lord Brightman's interpretation of s 78 of the 1925 Act in the case of *Federated Homes v Mill Lodge Properties Ltd*.

## 11.3.2 Assignment

The decision of *Federated Homes v Mill Lodge Properties Ltd* has resulted in assignment becoming far less important as a way of transferring the benefit of a covenant to successors in title of the original covenantee.

There may be reasons why the benefit of a covenant has not been annexed to the dominant land, for example the original covenant may provide that the benefit can only be passed by express assignment. In these cases the benefit can still pass to a successor in title if there is an express assignment.

The difference between **annexation** and **assignment** is that **assignment** will only take place when the land is transferred by a person who enjoys the benefit of the land. **Annexation** is effected the moment that the covenant is granted.

At common law, assignment must satisfy s 136 of the 1925 Act.

In equity, these conditions must be satisfied:

**1.** the covenant that is assigned must be capable of benefiting the dominant land

**2.** the dominant land must be 'ascertainable' or 'certain'

**3.** the assignment must have taken place contemporaneously with the transfer of the dominant land so that it is actually part of the transaction.

The effect of assignment is that the assignee is entitled to enforce the covenant against the covenantor or his successors in title if it is restrictive.

## 11.3.3 Building schemes

The benefit of covenants may pass where land is under a building scheme. Every owner of the land carrying the benefit will be able to enforce the covenants if he can show that the benefit runs to him. He will be able to enforce against the other owners who in turn will be able to enforce against him.

### What is a building scheme?

In *Elliston v Reacher* [1908] 2 Ch 374 a building scheme was defined as 'a local law for the area over which it extends and has the practical effect of rendering each purchaser and his successors in title subject to the restrictions and of conferring upon them the benefits of the scheme, as between themselves and all other purchasers and their respective successors in title'.

What this means is that each owner of property within the area gets the right to enforce the individual covenants as covenantees and they themselves are also subject to the covenants as covenantors.

## ACTIVITY

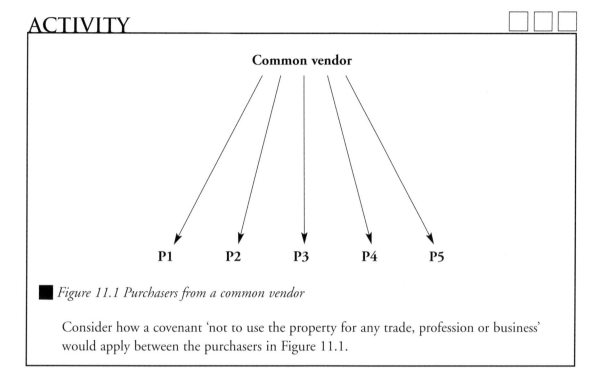

**Figure 11.1 Purchasers from a common vendor**

Consider how a covenant 'not to use the property for any trade, profession or business' would apply between the purchasers in Figure 11.1.

There were **four** requirements laid down in *Elliston v Reacher* before the covenants could be enforced:

**1.** both the claimant and the defendant must have derived title from a common owner

**2.** the common vendor must, prior to the sale of the plots now owned by the claimant and defendant, have laid out a definite scheme of development

**3.** there must have been an intention to impose not only on the purchasers of land within the development, but also on their successors in title, a scheme of mutually enforceable restrictions

**4.** every purchaser must have bought his land in full knowledge of the scheme, and with an intention to be bound by its mutually enforceable restrictions.

These have now been reduced to **two**, as specified in the Law Commission Report *Transfer of Land: Obsolete Restrictive Covenants* (Law Com No 201):

**1.** the area of the scheme must be defined and

**2.** those who purchase from the creator of the scheme do so on the footing that all purchasers shall be mutually bound by, and mutually entitled to enforce, a defined set of restrictions (which may nonetheless vary to some extent between the lots).

The value of building schemes enables restrictive covenants to run which would otherwise be defeated either because one of the essential requirement of running the burden cannot be satisfied when the developers sells the last plot or, having sold the last plot, he has no interest in enforcing the covenants. It also ensures that the benefit of the covenants imposed on other plots will automatically run to all successors of the original purchasers without the need for express annexation or for assignment.

## 11.3.4 The running of the burden in equity

Unlike the common law, a doctrine has developed in equity to permit the passing of the burden of covenants to successors in title. This principle was initially introduced by the decision in *Tulk v Moxhay* (1848) 2 Ph 774.

CASE EXAMPLE

---

**Tulk v Moxhay (1848) 2 Ph 774**

The claimant sold land in Leicester Square to the covenantor who covenanted on behalf of himself, his heirs and assigns to keep the land 'in an open state, uncovered with any buildings, in neat and ornamental order'. The covenantor subsequently sold the land to the defendant who had notice of the covenants. The defendant tried to build on the garden area in the centre of the square and was prevented from doing so.

---

This is now known as 'the rule in *Tulk v Moxhay*' and is subject to **four** conditions:

**1.** the covenant must be negative in nature

**2.** the covenant must benefit the dominant tenement. There must be a dominant and servient tenement and both the covenantor and covenantee must own an estate in his land

**3.** the covenantee must, at the date of the covenant, have owned land benefited by the covenant. The well-known case of *LCC v Allen* [1914] 3 KB 642 illustrates this point. There was a covenant between the Council and a builder who agreed not to build on a certain plot of land but the Council never owned any land to be benefited from the covenant. This requirement would cause difficulties for housing developments but for the special rules for building schemes. The area of land to benefit must also be sufficiently close to the land carrying the burden for the covenant to apply. 'Land at Clapham would be too remote and unable to carry a right to enforce . . . covenants in respect of . . . land at Hampstead' (*Kelly v Barrett* [1924] 2 Ch 379).

**4.** The burden of the covenant must have been intended to run with the land of the covenantor. Since the Law of Property Act 1925, the effect of s 79 is such that it will be assumed that it will be intended that the burden of the covenant will run unless the contrary is expressed. The recent case of *Morrells of Oxford Ltd v Oxford United Football Club Ltd* highlights that a contrary intention can be inferred from the difference in the wording of other covenants in the same deed.

So the burden of a covenant can pass in equity so long as all four requirements of the rule are satisfied and the purchaser has notice of it. The purchaser will have notice if the right has been registered correctly. In **registered** land this would have been a minor interest until the Land Registration Act 2002 but now will take effect as an interest requiring protection on the register and must be entered by way of notice against the title of the covenantor's land. This will usually be by an agreed notice but in the event of a dispute between the parties it may be by way of unilateral notice. In **unregistered** land this must be registered as a Class D II land charge entered on the Land Charges Register at Plymouth.

Note that failure to register will render the covenant unenforceable, even where the purchaser has actual notice. So a purchaser would not be bound where they know about a covenant before buying the property but when they check the Register it has not been registered by the vendor.

# ACTIVITY

Mr Brown owns Hazel Lodge which is a pre-fabricated house built in 1947. It has a large plot of land. He decides to knock down the house and build himself a new house and to split the land into two further plots which he intends to sell. They share a large lawn and each has a right to use it for recreation. Mrs Green buys Plot 1 and Miss Black buys Plot 2 and in each conveyance there are the following covenants:

- not to use the property for any trade, profession or business
- not to allow the garden of the property to become overgrown
- to contribute to the upkeep of the common lawn area.

Miss Black does not like the area and sells to Mr Weird, who runs a business as an acupuncturist from his house. He has let the garden become overgrown because he says he likes wild gardens. He is refusing to contribute to the upkeep of the lawn which is overrun by moles.

Advise Mr Brown as to whether he has any rights against Mr Weird.

# 11.4 Breach of covenants and the consequences

If a covenant is broken then the covenantee or their successors can claim a remedy.

In most cases the burden of the covenant will only run in equity so then the remedy will lie in equity. This means that the remedy will be subject to equitable principles, for example delay will defeat a claim. If the claimant has taken no action for years, the court will not award a remedy.

The remedy is also discretionary and the claimant may still find that even after the case against the defendant has been proved, he is without a remedy.

The court may also grant an order for specific performance in the case of a breach of a positive covenant.

The court generally has a choice of damages or an injunction. It will grant an injunction where the breach has not been carried out.

## Damages or an injunction?

The following questions will be asked:

**1.** Has there been a blatant disregard of the claimant's rights?

**2.** Is the injury to the claimant's legal rights small?

**3.** Can the damage be estimated in money and can it adequately be compensated by a small money payment?

**4.** Will it be oppressive to the defendant to grant an injunction?

# ASE EXAMPLE

### *Wakeham v Wood* (1982) 43 P & CR 40 CA

The defendant had flagrantly breached a covenant against building in a way that would obstruct a view of the sea.

The Court of Appeal granted the plaintiffs a mandatory injunction and Waller LJ expressed the opinion that the value of a view could not be expressed in monetary terms and therefore could not be compensated by a small money payment.

# ACTIVITY

Three years ago, Ophelia purchased a large rectory with several acres of garden. The property had a restrictive covenant created in 1980 in favour of the owners of adjoining properties and their successors in title. The covenant prohibited building in the grounds of the Rectory. Last month, Ophelia obtained planning permission to build a block of flats in the orchard of the Rectory. The owners of the adjoining properties, Gertrude and Polonius, have both threatened to seek an injunction to prevent the building in breach of the covenant. Gertrude is concerned that the building will prevent her house and garden from having sunshine in the afternoon and evening. Her house does not get the benefit of a view of the surrounding countryside

but she is able to enjoy views when she walks 100 metres down the road. This view will be lost when the flats are built.

Can Ophelia build the flats without fear from her neighbours claiming breach of covenant and what remedy will they be likely to get if they successfully sue for breach of covenant?

The courts have frequently been reluctant to grant an injunction for the breach of a covenant and tend towards an award of damages. Cases where an injunction may be awarded are where there is a blatant and calculated disregard of the claimant's rights.

> 'Much of the law on restrictive covenants is concerned with the question whether the benefit and burden have passed to the successors in title of the original parties, the construction of particular covenants and whether the covenant has ceased to be enforceable under the general law or may be discharged under s 84 Law of Property Act 1925. That, however, is only half of the story. Equally important is the question of remedies. When may the plaintiff expect to obtain an injunction (final or interlocutory, prohibitory or mandatory)? When will damages be more appropriate? . . . The injunction is the natural remedy for breach of restrictive covenant and the general expectation is that it will be available. . . . The grant of an injunction is always discretionary, however, in *Baxter v Four Oaks Properties Ltd* [1965] [Ch 816] where the defendant demolished a house, rebuilt it as nine self-contained flats, and intended (innocently, but in breach of a "private residence only" covenant) to sell the flats, an injunction was refused because it would have put the plaintiffs in too strong a bargaining position: the defendant would have been forced to leave it unoccupied or to buy a release, no doubt at a "ransom" price. Damages were awarded instead for the modest loss suffered by the breach.
>
> The fact that the plaintiff did not seek an interlocutory injunction at an earlier stage does not itself prevent the grant of a final injunction, even if mandatory, although clearly it will be more difficult to secure the demolition of a building if the plaintiff could have prevented its erection. In *Wrotham Park Estate Co v Parkside Homes Ltd* damages were awarded in lieu of a mandatory injunction to demolish houses built in breach of covenant . . . the mandatory injunction would involve an "unpardonable waste of much needed houses"'.

> J Martin, 'Remedies for Breach of Restrictive Covenants' [1996] Conv 329

# 11.5 Discharge and modification of restrictive covenants

There is no express limit for a covenant. It will continue to affect land until it is discharged or modified. However, it is clear that covenants will often cease to be relevant and may hinder the landowner's enjoyment of land rather than enhance it. The Law of Property Act 1925 includes special provision to cover such situations.

## 11.5.1 Under s 84 of the Law of Property Act 1925

An application to discharge or modify a restrictive covenant may be made to the Lands Tribunal under s 84 of the 1925 Act. The grounds include that the restrictive covenant impedes some reasonable use of the land and is contrary to the public interest. If the tribunal agrees to discharge or modify the covenant, compensation may be ordered to be paid.

The applicant must bring his case within the following statutory grounds:

1. **Obsolete**: 'that by reason of changes in the character of the property or the neighbourhood or other circumstances of the case . . . the restriction ought to be deemed obsolete'.

2. **Obstruction**: 'that the continued existence thereof would impede [some reasonable user] of the land for public or private purposes . . . or as the case may be, would unless modified so impede such user'.

3. **Agreement**: 'that the persons of full age and capacity for the time being or from time to time entitled to the benefit of the restriction, whether in respect of estates in fee simple or any lesser estates or interests in the property to which the benefit of the restriction is annexed, have agreed, either expressly or by implication, by their acts or omissions, to the same being discharged or modified'.

4. **No injury caused**: 'that the proposed discharge or modification will not injure the persons entitled to the benefit of the restriction.'

The fact that planning permission has already been granted for a development does not mean that the Lands Tribunal will automatically discharge a covenant.

A restrictive covenant cannot be enforced if the character of the neighbourhood has been so altered since the covenant was entered into that it is now of no value to the claimant and it would be inequitable and senseless to enforce it.

A restrictive covenant will automatically be extinguished once the burdened and benefited land come into common ownership and occupation.

An application can be made for both freehold as well as leasehold land if it is a long lease of over 40 years and at least 25 have expired.

Once the terms of a restrictive covenant have been modified or the covenant has been discharged, this must be noted on the Register.

# 11.6 Proposals for reform

'The Law Commission has been working away at the problems posed by restrictive covenants since 1967. In its reports on the Law of Positive and Restrictive Covenants in 1984 it proposed that restrictive covenants should be replaced by a system of land obligation. This obligation would have the characteristics that it would be a new interest in land capable of subsisting as a legal interest so that it bound the person who owned the land from time to time and benefited the owner for the time being of the dominant land. . . . although the current report is entitled "Obsolete Restrictive Covenants" the Law Commission does not limit its recommendations to them. There is no clear distinction between those which are obsolete and those which there are not. They all require to be examined on a conveyance of the property and on title registration. The Registrar has no discretion to omit mention of them whether or not they may be considered obsolete. Application to the Lands Tribunal for discharge or modification is not a practical course of action in most cases and insurance against the possibility of claims is most often an expense which fortunately sees little return'.

H W Wilkinson, 'Nothing to Lose but your Fetters. Obsolete Restrictive Covenants' [1992] Conv 2

## 11.6.1 What are the main problems with the law on restrictive covenants?

The 1984 Law Commission Report on the law of positive and restrictive covenants outlines the main problems with the law at present:

'The burden of a restrictive covenant does not run at all at law, but it does run in equity if certain complicated criteria are met. The benefit by contrast runs at law and in equity but according to rules which are different. These rules are if anything more complicated than the rules about the burden and some of them are particularly technical and hard to grasp; as examples one may cite those about annexation and those about building schemes'.

The thrust of its proposals is that covenants should be replaced by land obligations. These would be subject to rules similar to those applying to easements. The land obligation would take effect in law and would bind successors in title. The important difference would be that after sale the original parties would lose their contractual rights and obligations. This would destroy the present continuing contractual obligation of the original covenantor. Since the original covenantor loses any control over the property it has never made sense to force him to remain liable on the property that he once owned and over which he once entered into a covenant. The new scheme would make no distinction between positive and negative covenants.

# Further reading

Gravells, N P, 'Enforcement of Positive Covenants Affecting Freehold Land' (note on *Rhone v Stephens*) (1994) 110 LQR 346.

Hayton, D, 'Revolution in Restrictive Covenant Law?' (1980) 43 MLR 445.

Martin, J, 'Remedies for Breach of Restrictive Covenants' [1996] Conv 329.

Preston, S and Newsom, G, *Restrictive Covenants affecting Freehold Land* (Sweet & Maxwell, 1998).

Todd, P, 'Annexation after Federated Homes' [1985] Conv 177.

Turano, L, 's.79 Law of Property Act 1925' [2000] Conv 377.

Wilkinson, H W, 'Nothing to Lose but your Fetters. Obsolete Restrictive Covenants' [1992] Conv 2.

# chapter 12 MORTGAGES

## 12.1 Introduction

A mortgage is one of the most important interests in land. In essence, a mortgage is a form of security interest in land which will guarantee the amount of a loan that was made so that the lender has confidence that he will be able to recover his money. Today, mortgages provide a means by which people are able to purchase their homes and raise cash for improvements.

It is rare that a purchaser of property has sufficient capital to finance the purchase from savings. Most people will have to borrow funds but a lender will be unwilling to lend money without a substantial security. The security will ensure that the lender has an asset to claim if the borrower fails to repay the money borrowed.

## APPLYING THE LAW

Darren and Anne wish to purchase a house together. Darren has been given £3,000 from his parents and was left £5,000 by his granny when she died last year. Anne has been saving from her job as a dental hygienist. She has saved £2,200 over three years. Together they have £10,200 which is enough for a deposit on a house but is far too little to purchase property. They see a house – 12 Station Terrace, with two bedrooms and a small garden – for £90,000, which they want to buy. They approach the Helping Hands Building Society which agrees to lend them the money. If Darren and Anne get into financial difficulties the building society can sue them for the outstanding money that it has lent them. The court will find in the lender's favour but it will not be of any practical value because it is unlikely that it will recover any of its money. If the building society has a mortgage over the house in Station Terrace then it can recover its money from any monies received on the sale of the house.

## 12.1.1 Definition of a 'mortgage'

A mortgage is simply a transaction whereby property, either land or personal property, is given as security for the repayment of money borrowed. Normally the security used is real property, in particular a house, but it can also be personal property such as a valuable piece of jewellery.

**Bradley v Carritt [1903] AC 253**

In this case the owner of shares in a tea company mortgaged the shares to raise capital.

## 12.1.2 What is a mortgage?

The borrower, called the **mortgagor**, grants the lender, called the **mortgagee**, a mortgage over his property. The effect of this is that the mortgagee has rights in the property which can be realised if the mortgagor defaults in repayment. If the borrower runs into debt and cannot repay the sum borrowed, the lender can force the sale of the property and recover the sum borrowed from the proceeds of sale.

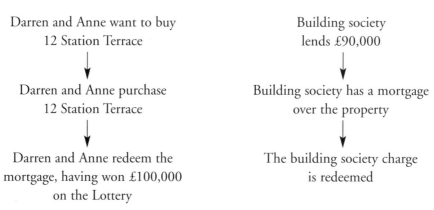

*Figure 12.1 Successful redemption of a mortgage by the mortgagor*

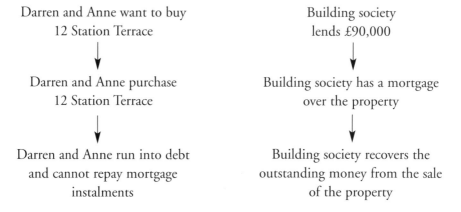

*Figure 12.2 Recovery of sum borrowed under a mortgage*

There is a difference between the mortgagee and the chargee because the mortgagee gains rights in the property whereas the chargee only gets rights against the property. There is a subtle difference between the two.

## The difference between a mortgage and a charge over property

| **A mortgage** | A mortgage is a legal or equitable interest in land granted to the lender as a security for the payment of a debt subject to the borrower's right of redemption |
| --- | --- |
| **A charge** | A charge attaches to the land of the borrower and gives rights over the land but does not convey a legal or equitable interest in the mortgaged land to the chargee. |

'Where one person lends money to another, he may be content to rely on the personal obligation of the borrower to repay the loan. If the borrower fails to repay the loan in accordance with the agreement between the parties, the lender can sue the borrower to recover what is due; and, provided that the borrower remains solvent and has assets at least equal in value to the amount of the loan (and his other liabilities), this right to sue is sufficient protection for the lender. However, if the borrower cannot repay the loan because he is insolvent the lender will become one of the general creditors of the borrower and, along with them, will recover at best only a proportion of the original loan'.

N Gravells, *Land Law: Text and Materials* (Sweet & Maxwell, 1999), p 807

So the true value of the mortgage is the assurance that, in the event of the borrower having no money to repay the loan, there will be an asset which allows you to claim rights over property and which will allow you to realise the full amount that you have loaned.

'The potential consequences for the lender are obvious and, especially where the amount of the loan is substantial . . . a lender will normally refuse to accept the risk of exclusive reliance on the personal obligation of the borrower. Instead he will require the borrower to provide some security for the repayment of the loan. Such security may be personal or real'.

N Gravells, *Land Law: Text and Materials* (Sweet & Maxwell, 1999), p 807

The use of a mortgage also means that someone who needs money, either because they are setting up a new business or simply because they want to buy property, will be more likely to be able to persuade someone to lend them the money.

'Personal security confers on the lender the right to sue a third party if the borrower fails to repay the loan . . . However, such personal security involves similar risks as the personal obligation of the borrower: it is only effective if the third party remains solvent . . . These risks can be avoided by requiring the borrower to provide real security, where the borrower links the obligation to repay the loan to some specific property of his. The advantage of such real security is that, even if the borrower becomes insolvent, the lender, as a secured creditor, will take priority over the general unsecured creditors of the borrower and can demand that the specific property be sold and that the loan be repaid from the proceeds of sale'.

N Gravells, *Land Law: Text and Materials* (2nd edn, Sweet & Maxwell, 1999), p 807

# 12.2 The development of mortgages at common law and in equity

## 12.2.1 Mortgages at common law

The common law did not recognise a mortgage. Lending money at a fixed rate of interest was forbidden. The borrower's rights were not enforceable in common law courts. This often had a disastrous effect on the rights of the borrower. Since it is a fact of commercial life that someone in business will want to borrow money at some stage, other ways of raising capital arose.

The original mortgage took the form of a conveyance. The lender became owner of the property and the borrower did not recover rights in the property until the loan had been repaid. At common law the lender owned the property but the borrower had the chance to recover his property. This had to be on a particular day at a particular time, as stipulated in the contract. This was called the legal right to redeem and was based on the contractual agreement between the parties. If the borrower did not repay the money on the correct day, the property could be claimed by the lender as his own. This could be worth much more than the actual sum owed.

### An example of an early mortgage of land

## APPLYING THE LAW

Edwin wants to raise money on his property, The Old Manor, Broghampton, in Wessex. Felix lends money to Edwin on 12th January 1514. Edwin conveys his interest in The Old Manor House, Broghampton to Felix and he agrees to re-convey the property back to Edwin on 11th January 1534.

On 11th January 1534 Edwin takes the full sum to Felix but he has left the county and has gone away to the North and is nowhere to be found.

> On 12th January 1534 Felix now owns The Old Manor House, Broghampton, without being encumbered by a mortgage in favour of Edwin. Edwin has now been dispossessed of his property and he has lost the chance to redeem the mortgage.
>
> There was no point in Edwin taking the case to the common law courts because his rights would not be recognised. The only chance of recovering his property would have been to take the case to the courts of equity and to ask them to use their discretion to recognise his rights in the property.
>
>

## 12.2.2 Mortgages in equity

### The equity of redemption

The equity of redemption describes the rights that a borrower retains in the property used for the security of the loan. These are rights recognised by equity but not common law. The equity of redemption arises as soon as the mortgage is created.

### The position at common law

Under the common law the lender of capital would become the owner of the borrower's property subject to the mortgage. It gave the lender rights, including the right to sell the property, and the lender was also able to claim any income which arose from the property while the mortgage was in existence. These rights would last until the borrower repaid the mortgage.

Under the common law there was only one day on which repayment could take place and so discharge the mortgage from the land. Repayment had to be on the day laid down in the mortgage deed. This was called the 'legal date of redemption'. If there was a delay, the right to redeem was lost. So if the borrower was just one day late, the land was lost and yet the borrower was still liable for the debt.

Borrowers felt aggrieved by the common law rule, especially when it was not their fault that they were unable to repay the loan because the lender had deliberately made himself unavailable for repayment. The result would be that they lost their property although the amount borrowed might be worth just a fraction of the total value of the property.

## 12.2.3 The equitable right to redeem

What does this mean? The 'equitable right to redeem' allows the borrower to redeem after the legal date for repayment has passed. It is at the heart of the law on mortgages. It meant that any borrower who failed to pay on the legal date for redemption retained the right to redeem. Therefore he could ignore the date set out in the mortgage deed and repay whenever it was convenient, so long as the legal date for redemption under the contract had passed. Equity would uphold the rights of the borrower to have the right to redeem his property at any time on any day.

Initially, this was only allowed in special circumstances:

**1.** the borrower was unable to repay because he had had an accident and physically was unable to repay the money

**2.** the borrower was unable to repay because he had made a mistake about the date of repayment or who was owed the money

**3.** the borrower could prove special hardship.

Later, redemption was allowed in all cases, whatever the circumstances, so long as the debt was repaid by the borrower. The right to redeem was a right in the property so it could be enforced against a third-party purchaser.

## APPLYING THE LAW

Gerald owned Limestone Hall. He needed to borrow some money to fund the marriage of his daughter, Ophelia. He borrowed some money from an acquaintance, Harold, and Limestone Hall was conveyed to Harold. The date for repayment was 10th April 1673. He failed to repay on 10th April but offered to repay on 24th May 1673. Equity recognised Gerald's right to repay on the later date and Gerald could recover his property.

If Harold sold his property to James then the rights of Gerald would be unaffected. Gerald could still redeem the property either on 10th April or later on 24th May since the right to redeem would be seen as an equitable right in the property and James would have been bound so long as he had notice of Gerald's rights.

### The legal right to redeem and the equitable right to redeem compared

| The legal right to redeem | Could only be exercised on the date stipulated in the mortgage deed. | A legal right arising under contract. | Exercisable as of right. | Arises on the legal date for redemption. |
| --- | --- | --- | --- | --- |
| The equitable right to redeem | Could be exercised any time after the stipulated day for repayment. | A right recognised in equity. | Exercised on terms that are considered to be just by the courts of equity. | Arises after the contractual date for redemption has passed. |

The legal date for redemption became less important since the borrower could rely on his rights in equity to allow redemption at any time. Later, the date stipulated as the legal date for redemption was always fixed very early, for example six months after the mortgage. Of course, there was no real expectation that the loan would be repaid on that date. Once this date was passed, the lender had a right to call in the loan and if the money was not forthcoming then he had the right to take proceedings. However, the borrower would not be worried as equity would protect him against a request for repayment on the date agreed in the mortgage deed.

Equity also allowed the borrower the right to any income derived from the property while the lender was in occupation. This reduced the advantage for the lender to occupy the property.

So the nature of a mortgage changed and the borrower would remain in the property and there was no question that the lender would move in to the property. The property was now seen simply as security for the loan.

## What rights arise under the equity of redemption?

The equity of redemption arose as soon as the mortgage was created. It was itself a right in property and it could be dealt with in several ways:

1. it could be conveyed to another
2. it could be leased
3. it could be devised/left to someone by will
4. it could even be mortgaged itself.

---

## KEY FACTS

### The development of mortgages in equity

1. Mortgages were initially not recognised at all by common law.
2. Early mortgages took the form of leases or conveyances of the fee simple to the lender who took possession of the property.
3. At common law, the loan could only be repaid on the specified day, called the legal date for redemption.
4. Failure to repay the loan on the date stipulated in the deed meant that the borrower lost all rights over the property.
5. Equity recognised the rights of the borrower to repay on a later date, called the equity of redemption.
6. Equity gave the borrower an equitable right to redeem which allowed him to redeem after the contractual date for repayment had passed.
7. The right was recognised as an interest in the property itself which could be sold, leased or left to someone by will.

# 12.3 The creation of mortgages

## 12.3.1 Before 1925

Before 1925, a legal mortgage of freehold land was created by conveying the fee simple estate to the lender. This included a covenant for re-conveyance on redemption of the mortgage. The mortgagee then became owner of the mortgaged property. Eventually, equity accepted that the mortgagor retained the right to redeem after the date for repayment had passed.

## 12.3.2 Post-1925

Under s 85 of the Law of Property Act 1925, conveyance and re-conveyance were made impossible. Under the 1925 Act two methods for the creation of mortgages were recognised:

1. a demise for a term of years absolute, subject to a provision for cesser on redemption or

2. a charge by deed expressed to be by way of legal mortgage.

Both types of mortgage had to be created by deed.

1. **demise for a term of years absolute**: this involved creating a long lease, usually for 3,000 years, over the land which would cease as soon as the loan was repaid. The lender would not have the legal estate conveyed to him and the borrower was expressly given the right to remain in the property. The borrower had the right to take further mortgages over the property which meant that there could be several mortgages over one house. The borrower might find it increasingly difficult to persuade anyone to lend him money, on the basis that the rights of a second mortgagee would be secondary to those of a first mortgagee

2. **a charge by deed expressed to be by way of legal mortgage**: this is governed by s 87 of the 1925 Act. Under this form of mortgage there is no conveyance of any estate in the property to the lender. The lender merely gets a charge over the land giving him rights which attach to the property. However, the charge does give the lender rights over the property as if he had an interest in it. The lender has the right to enforce covenants and he is able to create tenancies. This became the main way of creating mortgages and the demise was rarely used.

The advantage of using the legal charge is that it is short and expressed in simple terms.

## 12.3.3 Post-Land Registration Act 2002

Under s 23(1)(a) of the Land Registration Act 2002 the only way that a mortgage of registered land can be created is by registered charge. The law on the creation of mortgages will be substantially affected by the introduction of electronic conveyancing. This is because the mortgage will come into legal effect at the same time as it is created. The present law allows a gap between creation of the mortgage and it taking effect at law. Indeed, under the 2002 Act it will only take effect in law when it is entered on to the title of the registered land.

's 27(1) If a disposition of a registered estate or registered charge is required to be completed by registration, it does not operate at law until the relevant registration requirements are met.

(2) In the case of a registered estate, the following are the dispositions which are required to be completed by registration – . . .

(f) the grant of a legal charge'.

## 12.3.4 Creating equitable mortgages

There are three main ways that an equitable mortgage can be created:

1. A **contract** to create a mortgage: equity will treat a contract to create a mortgage as an enforceable mortgage if it satisfies s 2 of the Law of Property (Miscellaneous Provisions) Act 1989:

's 2 . . . A contract for sale or other disposition of an interest in land can only be made in writing by incorporating all the terms which the parties have expressly agreed in one document or, where contracts are exchanged, in each'.

This means that the contract to create a mortgage must be in writing. **Before 1989** it was possible to have an enforceable equitable mortgage where it was supported by some evidence in writing or there were acts of part-performance.

The document must:

- be in writing
- be signed by both parties
- contain all terms.

The parties may have accidentally created an equitable mortgage because they did not create a legal mortgage by deed or they failed to satisfy the formalities necessary for a deed, such as having the signatures witnessed.

2. An equitable mortgage created by the **deposit of title deeds**: before 1989 it was possible to deposit title deeds in unregistered land with the lender and that would create a mortgage. This method had its merits as it was possible to create a short-term mortgage without having to comply with strict formalities. The intention to create a mortgage had to be proved.

ASE EXAMPLE

### *Russel v Russel* (1783) 1 Bro CC 269

This case upheld the status of this method of creating equitable mortgages. It was assumed that there could also be a mortgage by depositing a land certificate. The 1989 Act should have made this method impossible but there was still some doubt after 1989.

# CASE EXAMPLE

**United Bank of Kuwait v Sahib [1997] Ch 107**

This case makes it clear that this type of mortgage cannot be created unless there is some writing which satisfies s 2 of the 1989 Act, otherwise this will be seen as an attempt to create a mortgage by unwritten contract. The 2002 Act has removed any doubt in relation to registered land because land certificates will no longer be used and without a certificate to deposit it would then be impossible to create mortgages in this way.

**3.** Mortgages of **equitable interests**: the borrower may only have an equitable estate in property because he is an equitable owner behind a trust. In such a case he can only create an equitable mortgage: 'the mortgagor can mortgage only that which he owns'. The mortgage is created by transferring the whole of the interest to the lender with a provision for re-transfer of the interest once the debt has been repaid. There are formalities to be satisfied. The transfer must satisfy s 53(1)(c) of the Law of Property Act 1925 which requires that the transfer should be in writing. Failure to satisfy this requirement will result in the mortgage being void.

## 12.3.5 Equitable charges

An equitable charge is a completely informal way of creating a mortgage over property. There are no specific formalities to satisfy but there must be an **intention** to charge the property with a debt.

# CASE EXAMPLE

**National Provincial and Union Bank of England v Charnley [1924] 1 KB 431**

This case upholds the need for there to be an intention for the property to be so charged for the charge to take effect.

## APPLYING THE LAW ☐☐☐

Charles owes his friend Jamie money. He executes a document saying that if Jamie lends him £15,000, Jamie will get an equitable charge over Charles's house. This does not have the same effect as a legal charge as it will rank lower than any legal charges over the property but it is better than a mere contract where Charles agrees to repay the £15,000 to Jamie on a specified date.

☐☐☐

Because of this uncertainty, it is rare to use an equitable charge in both commercial and domestic mortgages.

# ACTIVITY

In the following examples, are the mortgages either legal or equitable?

1. Kenneth is borrowing £20,000 from his friend, Donald. They draw up a document which creates a charge in favour of Donald over Kenneth's house, Clematis Cottage. Kenneth and Donald both sign the document.

2. Gloria runs a mail order company for dog accessories and wishes to raise money. She borrows money from her sister and the solicitor draws up the terms in a document which Gloria signs. The secretary agrees to sign also.

3. Selina has contributed to the purchase of Trimley House but she is not registered as owner. She wants to raise some cash to fund a trip around the world and she borrows from her friend Sally who signs a document which creates a charge in her favour over Trimley House. Selina's next-door neighbour signs the document.

# 12.4 Protection for the mortgagor

The mortgagor is protected under the law in a number of different ways:

1. the mortgagor retains **an equity of redemption**

2. a mortgage will be set aside if it has been obtained through **undue influence** or **oppression**

3. **no collateral advantages**

4. **the Consumer Credit Act 1974.**

## 12.4.1 The equity of redemption

This describes all the rights of the borrower that arise in the land as soon as the mortgage is executed. It includes the legal rights enforceable in the common law courts as well as the equitable rights arising in equity. It is used to cover not just the right to redeem the mortgage, but also all that bundle of rights protecting the borrower from exploitation by the lender. A mortgage cannot be made irredeemable and it cannot be limited by the terms of the mortgage deed so that it can only be redeemed by certain persons or for a limited time.

> 'the mortgagor is entitled to get his property as free as he gave it, on payment of principal, interest, and costs, and provisions inconsistent with that right cannot be enforced. The equitable rules "once a mortgage always a mortgage", and that the mortgagee cannot impose any "clog or fetter on the equity of redemption" are merely concise statements of the same rules'.

Walker LJ in *Browne v Ryan* [1901] 2 LR 653

361

This principle extends to all types of transactions which can be described as mortgages.

If the right to redeem is merely postponed then the mortgage will be upheld so long as there is still a genuine right to redeem.

## CASE EXAMPLE

### *Knightsbridge Estates Trust Ltd v Byrne* [1939] Ch 441

In this case, redemption of the mortgage was postponed for 40 years. The borrower argued that the period was unreasonable. It was held that so long as the date of redemption is genuine and not a sham, it will be upheld. There were good reasons in the case why the date of redemption was postponed for so long (the rate of interest was reduced and also the repayments were spread over a long period of time to accommodate the borrower). These terms had been negotiated at arm's length and the judge held that there was no requirement for the mortgage to be reasonable.

'But equity does not reform mortgage transactions because they are unreasonable. It is concerned to see two things – one that the essential requirements of a mortgage transaction are observed, and the other that oppressive or unconscionable terms are not enforced. Subject to this, it does not, in our opinion, interfere'.

Sir Wilfred Greene MR

Compare the following case:

## CASE EXAMPLE

### *Fairclough v Swan Brewery Co Ltd* [1912] AC 565

The date for redemption was postponed to six weeks before the end of the mortgage term. The court upheld the claim by the borrower that there could be earlier redemption because the terms made the right to redeem illusory.

The upholding of the right to redeem is applied very strictly by the courts even where, on the facts, it seems to be unfair.

# CASE EXAMPLE

### *Samuel v Jarrah Timber and Wood Paving Corporation Ltd* [1904] AC 323

The mortgagee was given the option to purchase the property of the mortgagor within a year of the date of the loan secured by the mortgage. When the mortgagee sought to exercise this option, the mortgagor challenged on the basis that the term excluded the mortgagor's equity of redemption.

The House of Lords declared the term to be illegal and void. However, it was reluctant to do so. The agreement was negotiated fairly and at arm's length and the parties were both fully aware of the terms. The court was not able to change the rules but would have liked the opportunity to do so.

> 'Speaking for myself, I should not be sorry if your Lordships could see your way to modify it so as to prevent its being used as a means of evading a fair bargain come between persons dealing at arm's length and negotiating on equal terms. The directors of a trading company in search of financial assistance are certainly in a very different position from that of an impecunious landowner in the toils of a crafty money-lender'.

> Lord Macnaghten

However, the principle persists and continues to be protected by the courts.

# CASE EXAMPLE

### *Lewis v Frank Love Ltd* [1961] 1 WLR 261

An option to purchase the mortgaged property was included in a separate document but it was drawn up contemporaneously with the mortgage deed. The court held there to be a clog or fetter on the equity of redemption and refused to uphold the term. The fact that there were two documents was held to be less important than the fact that it was seen as one single and undivided contract rather than two distinct contracts.

## 12.4.2 A mortgage will be set aside if it has been obtained through undue influence or oppression

A mortgage can be set aside or the terms modified where there is evidence of undue influence or misrepresentation. A borrower can be pressurised by the lender in such a way that the transaction

that he enters is not from his own free will, for example the terms may be particularly favourable to the lender because the borrower is so desperate for money that he is willing to accept very unfavourable terms.

## What constitutes undue influence?

Equity has always sought to protect the weaker of two parties from oppression and from exploitation. In the context of a mortgage, equity will seek to intervene where the mortgage terms are oppressive. There are several important developments in this area.

Undue influence can be in **two different forms**:

1. **actual** undue influence: this means that you could rely on evidence of undue influence or pressure put on the borrower by the lender

2. **presumed** undue influence: this means that the relationship of the parties is one where one party is assumed to be more powerful than the other and so they could easily take advantage of this position to put pressure on the other side in negotiations.

Undue influence was defined in *Bank of Credit and Commerce International SA v Aboody* [1990] 1 QB 923 as follows:

- **class 1: actual undue influence**: this is where the claimant can prove that undue influence was in fact exerted on him. The claimant must prove that undue influence was actually exerted by the wrongdoer. However, there is no necessity to show that the transaction operated to the claimant's manifest disadvantage. This had been the position under the previous law but this requirement was removed by *CIBC Mortgages v Pitt* [1994] 1 AC 200. However, it would add weight to the mortgagor's case if it were shown that the transaction was manifestly disadvantageous to the claimant.

- **class 2: presumed undue influence**: this is where the claimant can show that there was a relationship of trust and confidence between the parties of such a nature that it is fair to presume that the trust and confidence of the claimant were abused. Once the claimant can establish the existence of the relationship of trust and confidence, the burden of proof then shifts to the alleged wrongdoer to rebut the presumption of undue influence, and to prove that the transaction was entered into freely.

There are two further types of presumed undue influence:

- **Class 2A** covers **specific relationships,** for example solicitor and client; medical adviser and patient; and parent and child. It does not cover husband and wife. There may be equality between the parties or there may be inequality. It will depend on the particular relationship

- **Class 2B** covers relationships where undue influence would **not automatically be presumed** from the nature of the relationship itself but may arise because **one party placed so much trust in the other** that the presumption would arise.

These further definitions come from the judgment of Lord Browne-Wilkinson in *Barclays Bank v O'Brien* [1994] 1 AC 180 which is considered in detail below.

## Different types of undue influence

| | | |
|---|---|---|
| Class 1: actual undue influence | Claimant must prove that the wrongdoer actually exerted undue influence. | |
| Class 2: presumed undue influence | Claimant must prove that there was a relationship of trust between the parties. | *BCCI SA v Aboody* (1990) |
| Class 2A: relationships where undue influence is presumed | Relationship is one where undue influence is presumed because of the nature of the relationship itself. Husband and wife are excluded from this group. | *Langton v Langton* [1995] 2 FLR 890 *Allcard v Skinner* (1887) |
| Class 2B: relationships where undue influence is presumed because of a specific relationship between the parties | Relationship itself does not give rise to undue influence but it can apply, depending on the actual relationship. | *Barclays Bank v O'Brien* (1994) *Avon Finance v Bridger* [1985] 2 All ER 281 |

# ACTIVITY

Consider the following transactions and decide whether they are affected by undue influence and, if so, what type of undue influence applies:

1. Mr and Mrs Charlesworth own Langley Ridge, a large house in Hendon. They have one son, Ronald, who lives with them. He runs his own business which is a specialist travel firm. Recently it has run into difficulties. He needs to raise some cash quickly and he asks his parents to stand surety for his debts. The mortgage company will only do so if it gets a charge over his parent's house; he tells his parents that the house is safe from the mortgage company.

2. Freddy Spendthrift persuades his partner, Alice Thrifty, to allow him to use her property as surety for a loan that he takes out with Barclays Bank. She does not want to do so but he says if she does not agree he will leave her, so, reluctantly she agrees to what he asks.

In recent years there have been **two** landmark decisions which have clarified the law on what constitutes undue influence in a mortgage transaction.

ASE EXAMPLE

### *Barclays Bank plc v O'Brien* [1994] 1 AC 180

Mrs O'Brien signed a legal charge over the co-owned matrimonial home as security for her husband's debts. The bank did not explain the contents of the mortgage documents to her when they were signed and did not advise her to obtain independent legal advice and she did not read the documents before signing them. Mrs O'Brien relied on her husband's false representation that the security was limited to £60,000 and covered just a short-term loan for three weeks while the house was re-mortgaged. Once the overdraft exceeded the loan, the bank sought an order for possession of the property. Mrs O'Brien then sought to set aside the mortgage transaction on the ground that she signed the documents under undue influence and misrepresentation. It was held that the mortgage had been obtained either by her husband's misrepresentation or because of his undue influence over her and the court ordered it to be set aside.

Lord Browne-Wilkinson sought to bring the law up to date to show that there remains a need for the concept of undue influence even though there is a greater degree of equality between the sexes. However, it would be outmoded to assume that wives will automatically be put under pressure by their husbands when entering into a transaction involving property:

> 'although the concept of the ignorant wife leaving all financial decisions to the husband is outmoded, the practice does not yet coincide with the ideal. In a substantial proportion of marriages it is still the husband who has the business experience and the wife is willing to follow his advice without bringing a truly independent mind and will to bear on financial decisions. The number of recent cases in this field shows that in practice many wives are still subjected to, and yield to, undue influence by their husbands. Such wives can reasonably look to the law for some protection when their husbands have abused the trust and confidence reposed in them'.

The judge considered the actual position of couples who take out mortgages today to decide whether they are likely to be equal in their understanding and approach to the transaction. Undoubtedly, the wife would have been in a very different position 100 years ago when there was far less equality between men and women. However, he accepted that there are still relationships where there is inequality within a marriage or relationship which made the doctrine still significant even in 1994.

'On the other hand, it is important to keep a sense of balance in approaching these cases. It is easy to allow sympathy for the wife who is threatened with the loss of her home at the suit of a rich bank to obscure an important public interest viz. the need to ensure that the wealth currently tied up in the matrimonial home does not become economically sterile'.

There is another argument against extending the doctrine of undue influence. If the rules are too strict then institutions such as banks will be far less ready to lend money on the security of the matrimonial home and that would have a disastrous effect on those reliant on a loan to finance the purchase of their home.

Lord Browne-Wilkinson divided up those who may bring the doctrine to their aid into two groups:

**1.** wives

**2.** other persons.

## Wives

He concluded that a wife may claim to set aside a transaction in cases where she has been induced to stand as her husband's surety by his undue influence, misrepresentation or some other legal wrong. This right will be enforceable against third parties if either:

* the husband was acting as the third parties' agent or
* the third party had actual or constructive notice of the facts giving rise to her equity.

This part of the judgment presents the most difficult issues as the courts have to decide when constructive notice arises, putting the bank on enquiry.

Lord Browne-Wilkinson considered **two** situations:

**1.** the transaction is not, on the face of it, to the wife's advantage

**2.** there is some substantial risk that the husband has committed some legal or equitable wrong in getting his wife to sign the mortgage deed.

The lender must then take reasonable steps to satisfy himself that the wife's agreement to stand surety has been properly obtained. If this has not been done then the lender will take subject to the borrower's rights.

The judge then decided what constitutes 'reasonable steps'. He thought the lender should not be under a duty to interview the wife to check whether she has been subject to undue influence but instead it should advise her to take independent advice and will have fully discharged its duty if it insists that the wife has an independent meeting with a representative of the creditor.

## Other persons

> 'in my judgement the same principles are applicable to all other cases where there is an emotional relationship between cohabitees. The "tenderness" shown by the law to married women is not based on the marriage ceremony but reflects the underlying risk of one cohabitee exploiting the emotional involvement and trust of the other . . . in a case where the creditor is aware that the surety reposes trust and confidence in the principal debtor in relation to his financial affairs, the creditor is put on inquiry in just the same way as he is in relation to husband and wife'.

There are inherent difficulties with Lord Browne-Wilkinson's judgment:

- when has the lender got constructive notice?
- when will undue influence be found?
- what is the consequence of the lender being put on enquiry?

Some of these difficulties are addressed by a subsequent case:

ASE EXAMPLE

### *Royal Bank of Scotland v Etridge (No 2)* [2001] 3 WLR 102

This case concerned the rights of wives in eight different cases, who had entered into charges over their matrimonial homes. The principal judgment was given by Lord Nicholls.

Overall, the decision reduces the threshold for liability for lenders in a number of ways. Lord Nicholls highlighted several areas when liability may arise.

Summary of the main points raised by Lord Nicholls:

**1.** he accepted that undue influence is covered by a large number of situations wherever there is abuse as well as exploitation of trust and confidence, reliance or dependency reposed in another; there are no longer special categories of relationship; he concluded that the division of cases into Class 2A and Class 2B presumed undue influence was not useful

**2.** an inference of undue influence can arise whatever the relationship

**3.** in some relationships trust and confidence must be proven and in others it is assumed

4. the burden of proof shifts to the other party where trust and confidence or dependency has been reposed in them and also that the transaction cannot readily be explained by their relationship

5. in cases of actual undue influence there is no necessity to prove manifest disadvantage; where undue influence is inferred, then manifest disadvantage must be shown.

Lord Nicholls then considered the core duties that **a bank will owe to the claimant** who enters into a transaction as surety for another:

1. a bank or any financial institution lending money should take steps to ensure that the claimant receives legal advice by asking for the name of the claimant's legal adviser

2. the meeting should contain certain core advice, for example the nature of the liability of someone standing as surety, the fact that their home is at risk and the wife should be urged to take legal advice and the name of the legal adviser should be given to them

3. where the claimant is advised by a solicitor, the legal advice should also contain certain core elements such as the nature of the transaction and its implications and the seriousness of the risk and the fact that the wife has a choice in the matter

4. the lender has a duty to inform the solicitor of any concerns that it has over whether the consent is genuine

5. the legal adviser can act for both the husband and also for the wife

6. the bank will not be acting as the agent of the husband so it is assumed that the advice given is given properly.

'The furthest the bank can be expected to go is to take reasonable steps to satisfy itself that the wife has had brought home to her, in a meaningful way, the practical implications of the proposed transaction. This does not wholly eliminate the risk of undue influence or misrepresentation. But it does mean that a wife enters into a transaction with her eyes open so far as the basic elements of the transaction are concerned'.

Lord Nicholls

The effect of this decision could be that the risks are now carried by the solicitor rather than the lending institution who can discharge liability fairly easily.

## ACTIVITY

Consider the following situations and decide whether or not the claimant can argue undue influence:

1. Iman is married to Abu. They jointly own their home. Abu runs a retail business which has recently run into difficulties and persuades Iman to agree to stand as surety for him. They visit the bank, which agrees to lend the money if the wife agrees to act as surety. No separate advice is given to Iman.

2. In the same situation, would it make any difference if Iman was told to seek legal advice and she visited a solicitor, Iman could speak no English and the solicitor could not speak Urdu?

3. Would it make any difference if Iman and Abu took advice from the same solicitor?

4. Would it make any difference if Iman and Abu visited the bank together? Iman can speak English well. She appears nervous when they visit the bank. The bank tells her to seek independent legal advice

5. In the same situation as in 1. above but Iman is Abu's mother.

## Oppressive interest rates

The courts have jealously guarded their right to strike down any term in a mortgage transaction which operates in an oppressive or unconscionable manner. This has usually been in relation to interest rates.

## CASE EXAMPLE

### *Cityland and Property (Holdings) Ltd v Dabrah* **[1968] Ch 166**

This concerned an arrangement between two individuals. The claimant purchased property from the defendant at a price of £3,500. The claimant paid £600 in cash but the rest was to be raised by a mortgage granted by the defendant. However, the sum that the claimant agreed to repay represented a 57 per cent premium over the sum owed. Goff J held that this was an unlawful premium and used the court's inherent jurisdiction to declare this premium to be unconscionable and oppressive. The court then imposed a different rate of interest.

ASE EXAMPLE

### *Multiservice Bookbinding Ltd v Marden* [1979] Ch 84

In this case the mortgage agreement had included a term that linked the interest rates payable to the rate of exchange between the pound Sterling and the Swiss franc. The amount payable by way of interest had increased so significantly that it now exceeded £133,000, whereas the original loan was for £36,000.

The claimants challenged on two grounds:

1. **public policy:** the claimants argued that it was against public policy to have repayment of interest that was index linked. This was rejected by the court, although in previous cases it had been upheld. The reason the defendants wanted to index-link the repayment of interest was to ensure that inflation would not affect the amount repaid

2. the terms were **unconscionable** and **unreasonable**: Browne-Wilkinson J held that the claimant must show that the bargain was unfair and unconscionable and that it was not enough to simply show that it was unreasonable: 'one of the parties must have imposed the objectionable terms in a morally reprehensible manner . . . in a way which affects his conscience'. The sort of example he cited was of taking advantage of a young, inexperienced or ignorant person or party.

Browne-Wilkinson J did not find that there were unconscionable and unfair terms in this case.

### Why?

1. The company needed the money and the lenders were willing to lend it to them.

2. The company had the opportunity to refuse the terms laid down.

3. They had advice from an independent solicitor.

4. The lender was not a professional money lender.

5. Although the terms were unfair, they were not unconscionable, so the court could not intervene.

> 'The parties made a bargain which the [claimants], who are business men, went into with their eyes open, with the benefit of independent advice, without any compelling necessity to accept a loan on these terms and without any sharp practice by the defendant. I cannot see that there was anything unfair or oppressive or morally reprehensible in such a bargain entered into in such circumstances'.
>
> Browne-Wilkinson J

## 12.4.3 The mortgagor is protected from the mortgagee gaining any collateral advantages

Equity developed other ways of protecting the borrower. If the mortgage deed contained a term which prevented the borrowers from redeeming the mortgage for another reason, this term would be void.

There must be no clog or fetter on the borrower's equity of redemption.

The rights of the lender were to have the return of the loan, the interest and costs; and any attempt to get an extra benefit from the borrower was struck down by the courts.

However, the courts have been less strict on collateral terms in more recent years.

> 'Modern courts have had less occasion (and probably less desire) to apply the same
> censure to mortgage terms and collateral advantages which would have attracted
> the displeasure of judges of an earlier generation. Distaste for the self-serving
> preferences of the grasping mortgagee – once considered more a feature of
> Victorian mortgage deeds than of today's standard form high street mortgage
> transaction – has long ago relaxed into a simple prohibition of those collateral
> advantages which are excessive and oppressive'.

Gray and Gray, *Elements of Land Law* (3rd edn, Butterworth, 2001), p 1384

A collateral advantage which ceased when the mortgage was redeemed could be upheld. As this was simply a term of the contract, this did not affect the right of the borrower to redeem the loan.

**C**ASE EXAMPLE

**Biggs v Hoddinot (1898) 2 Ch 307**

The property subject to the mortgage was a public house. The mortgage deed included a term that the borrowers would buy all their beer from the lenders during the subsistence of the mortgage. The covenant was separate from the term allowing the borrowers to redeem the mortgage.

> 'The mortgage here is a mortgage of a public house for a time certain by
> publicans to a brewer effected in the usual way, and it contains a covenant by the
> mortgagors during the continuance of the security to take all their beer from the
> mortgagee, and a covenant by the mortgagee to supply it. It is contended that
> the covenant by the mortgagors is void in equity. The first objection I have to

make is that it in no way affects the equity of redemption, for it is not stipulated that damages for breach of the covenant shall be covered by the security and redemption takes place quite independently of the covenant; so this is not a case where the right to redeem is affected'.

Chitty LJ

Compare the following case:

### Noakes & Co Ltd v Rice [1902] AC 24

The mortgage included a covenant to purchase beer from the lender even after the mortgage had been redeemed. The court refused to enforce the term after the mortgage had been redeemed, relying on the principle 'once a mortgage, always a mortgage and nothing but a mortgage'. The meaning of that is that the mortgagee shall not make any stipulation which will prevent a mortgagor, who has paid principal, interest and costs, from getting back his mortgaged property in the condition in which he parted with it.

The judge added: 'When the mortgage is paid off the security is at an end, and, as the mortgagee is no longer kept out of his money, the remuneration to him for the use of his money is also at an end' (Lord Davey).

### Bradley v Carritt [1903] AC 253

A similar decision was reached when the lender stipulated that the borrower should continue to use the services of the lender as tea broker even after the sum borrowed had been repaid. The House of Lords held this to be a fetter on the equity of redemption. However, there was a strong dissenting judgment form Lord Lindley:

'I cannot bring myself to believe that it is part of the law of this country that mortgagors and mortgagees cannot make what bargains they like with each other so long as such bargains are not inconsistent with the right of the mortgagor to redeem the property mortgaged by discharging the debt or obligation to secure which the mortgage was effected'.

The reason Lord Lindley dissented was because he thought that there was no connection between the right of the borrower to redeem the mortgage and the right of the lender to enforce the covenant. There was no question in *Bradley v Carritt* that the borrower could not redeem the mortgage on the date stipulated. The term would simply be separate from the mortgage.

The courts later upheld the right to enforce the terms of the collateral agreement even after the mortgage had been repaid.

## CASE EXAMPLE

### *Kreglinger v New Patagonia Meat and Cold Storage Co Ltd* [1914] AC 25

The mortgagor agreed with the mortgagee that for five years their sheep skins would be offered to the mortgagee. When the mortgage was redeemed two years later, the mortgagor claimed that they were no longer bound to sell the skins to the mortgagees. The court upheld the original agreement. The mortgage was seen as a commercial transaction. The parties were negotiating at arm's length and neither party was put under any pressure so in this case there was no necessity for the court to intervene. The important issue was whether the term affected the borrower's right to redeem and whether the collateral agreement was outside the mortgage transaction itself.

Three principles emerge from Lord Parker's judgment in *Kreglinger v New Patagonia Meat and Cold Storage Co Ltd*. A collateral advantage will be struck out in the following circumstances:

**1.** the term is unfair and unconscionable

**2.** the term is in the nature of a penalty clogging the equity of redemption or

**3.** the term is inconsistent with or repugnant to the contractual and equitable right to redeem.

## CASE EXAMPLE

### *Re Petrol Filling Station, Vauxhall Bridge Road, London* (1969) 20 P & CR 1

An agreement that the borrower, who was a garage owner, would purchase petrol from the lender, a petrol company, was held to be enforceable even after the repayment of the debt.

'These decisions make good commercial sense. In both *Kreglinger* and *Vauxhall*, the main purpose of the mortgage was not to make loans. The solus agreement in each case was the commercial advantage which the mortgagee sought, and there was evidence in both cases that the loan was a sweetener to entice the mortgagor to enter into the agreement. To deprive agreements of this kind of their validity would inhibit perfectly reasonable business arrangements between businessmen who understand fully what they are doing'.

R Pearce and J Stevens, *Land Law* (2nd edn, Sweet & Maxwell, 2000), p 416

It is not always as easy to separate the collateral advantage from the terms of the mortgage, as they may appear to be part and parcel of one transaction.

## Modern cases and restraint of trade

The modern cases on collateral advantages are more likely to be challenged on the basis of restraint of trade which is a principle arising out of contract law rather than from the law on mortgages.

The law of contract has long held that an agreement which operates unreasonably in **restraint of trade** will be held to be void on the ground of public policy.

# CASE EXAMPLE

### *Esso Petroleum Co Ltd v Harper's Garage (Stourport) Ltd* [1968] AC 269

Under the terms of the mortgage deed over the borrower's garage the garage agreed to sell only the lender's petrol for 21 years. The mortgage had to be redeemed over a period of 21 years. The court considered whether the term was in restraint of trade and held that it should be struck down because it was excessively long. If it had been for a shorter period of time, such as five years, it would have been upheld.

**Cases on whether collateral advantages can be upheld as part of the terms of a mortgage**

| Case | Decision | Comment |
|------|----------|---------|
| *Biggs v Hoddinott* (1898) | A collateral advantage can be upheld so long as it ends when the mortgage comes to an end. | The lenders could enjoy the additional advantage of the covenant as well as the repayment of the capital and the interest. |
| *Noakes & Co v Rice* (1902) | Any collateral terms in the mortgage deed must come to an end when the mortgage is redeemed, even if the mortgage allows them to continue. | 'once a mortgage, always a mortgage and nothing but a mortgage' (Lord Davey). |

| | | |
|---|---|---|
| *Bradley v Carritt* (1903) | A collateral advantage which continued after the mortgage ended was unenforceable. | In this case there was a strong dissenting judgment from Lord Lindley who thought the term should be upheld. |
| *Kreglinger v New Patagonia Meat and Cold Storage Co Ltd* (1914) | A collateral advantage lasting after the mortgage has been redeemed will be upheld if it is fair and does not clog the equity of redemption and is not inconsistent with the right to redeem the mortgage. | This case marked a turning point in the law on collateral advantages in mortgages because it allowed such terms to continue after the mortgage has been redeemed. |

## 12.4.4 The mortgagor is protected by the Consumer Credit Act 1974

A mortgage may fall within the statutory controls imposed on any credit relationship. The mortgage may be regarded as a regulated credit agreement within the provisions of the Consumer Credit Act 1974. However, most mortgages will be above £25,000 which is the upper limit laid down by the 1974 Act. Certain transactions are exempt under the Act and they include a debtor–creditor agreement secured by a land mortgage. However, the 1974 Act does allow even exempt agreements to be re-opened if they can be defined as **extortionate credit bargains**. So the Act will cover many second mortgages which will be for smaller sums and so under the upper limit.

## APPLYING THE LAW  □□□

Penelope wants to raise £10,000 to put in double glazing on all the bedroom windows in her cottage, Wayfarers' Rest. Her bank is unwilling to lend her the money but the Dubious Money Co is willing to lend her the sum, subject to a very high rate of interest. This transaction will be covered by the 1974 Act.

□□□

The courts are reluctant to intervene and re-open a credit agreement under the 1974 Act unless the terms come within s 138 of the Consumer Credit Act 1974.

 's. 138(1) A credit agreement is extortionate if it –

    (a) requires the debtor or a relative of his to make payments (whether unconditionally, or on certain contingencies) which are grossly exorbitant, or

    (b) otherwise grossly contravenes ordinary principles of fair dealing.

(2) In determining whether a credit bargain is extortionate, regard shall be had to such evidence as is adduced concerning –

    (a) interest rates prevailing at the time it was made,

    (b) the factors mentioned in subsections (3) to (5) and

    (c) any other relevant considerations.

(3) Factors applicable under subsection (2) in relation to the debtor include –

    (a) his age, experience, business capacity and state of health; and

    (b) the degree to which, at the time of making the credit bargain, he was under financial pressure, and the nature of that pressure.

(4) Factors applicable under subsection (2) in relation to the creditor include –

    (a) the degree of risk accepted by him, having regard to the value of any security provided;

    (b) his relationship to the debtor.'

If Penelope brings an action against the Dubious Money Co she must first show that the agreement is within s 138 of the 1974 Act. She must show that the credit bargain is extortionate. It will be extortionate if it requires the debtor or a relative of [Penelope's] to make payments which are grossly exorbitant, or otherwise grossly contravenes ordinary principles of fair dealing. The onus then shifts to the lenders to show that they are not extortionate.

ASE EXAMPLE

### Davies v Directloans Ltd [1986] 1 WLR 823

'Under the Act the test is not whether the creditor has acted in a morally reprehensible manner, but whether one or other of the conditions of section 138(1) is fulfilled, although it may be thought that if either condition is fulfilled there is likely to be something morally reprehensible about the creditor's conduct'.

ASE EXAMPLE

### A Ketley Ltd v Scott [1980] CCLR 37

The defendants had been granted a loan by the claimant company. When they failed to repay, the defendants sought relief from the court, on the basis that the agreement was an extortionate credit agreement. However, although the rate of interest in this case was 48 per cent, it was not held to be extortionate under the Consumer Credit Act 1974.

**Why?**

1. The loan was arranged at very short notice for the completion of the purchase of property in favour of the defendants.

2. The documentation had been signed by the parties in great haste.

3. One of the defendants had not disclosed the fact that they had already charged the property to secure a bank overdraft, which amounted to deceit.

4. The defendants had known what they were doing and were in no way subjected by the claimants to pressure.

See also the **Unfair Terms in Consumer Contracts Regulations 1999**. These apply to unfair terms in contracts concluded between a seller or a supplier and a consumer. The type of term affected will be one that has been drafted in advance and into which the consumer has not had any input. The Regulations hold that a contractual term will be unfair if there is a significant imbalance between the parties' rights and obligations. All the circumstances of the contract will be relevant.

# 12.5 Rights of the mortgagee

The law protects the mortgagee or lender in a number of ways. The law offers the mortgagee protection because people or institutions would not lend money unless they felt they were properly protected. The right to sue on the contract may be of little value if the borrower is in financial difficulties and the mortgagee will want to look to the property to ensure that the money that he has lent is not lost.

It is also important that these rights are not dependent on lengthy and expensive court proceedings.

The rights arise either from the agreement itself or arise under the rules of equity or under statute:

1. the right to sue on the covenant
2. the right to possession
3. the power of sale
4. the right to appoint a receiver
5. the right of foreclosure

## The right to sue on the covenant

The mortgage is a contract of loan between the lender and the borrower so the lender has an action on the borrower's express contractual promise to repay the sum borrowed. This arises as soon as the date fixed for repayment has arrived.

## KEY FACTS

**The right to sue on the covenant**

**1.** The mortgage takes the form of a contractual agreement between the mortgagor and the mortgagee.

**2.** The agreement includes a term that the mortgagor will repay the money lent as well as any interest.

**3.** If the mortgagor fails to repay as agreed on the date stipulated in the contract, he is in breach of covenant.

**4.** The mortgagee can then take action against the mortgagor and the court will order payment. Failure to pay will allow the mortgagee to execute the sum against the property of the mortgagor and it can even lead to bankruptcy proceedings against the mortgagor (*Alliance & Leicester plc v Slayford* [2001] 1 All ER (Comm) 1).

**5.** This is a personal action against the mortgagor and the mortgagee can recover any outstanding sums in this way if the value recovered from sale of the property is less than the sum lent.

## The right to possession

The mortgagee usually has the right to possession of the mortgaged property. This is a right which arises as soon as the mortgage is made and is not dependent on default.

'the right of a mortgagee to possession in the absence of some contract has nothing to do with default on the part of the mortgagor. The mortgagee may go into possession before the ink is dry on the mortgage unless there is something in the contract, express or by implication, whereby he has contracted himself out of that right. He has the right because he has a legal term of years in the property or its statutory equivalent'.

Harman J in *Four-Maids Ltd v Dudley Marshall (Properties) Ltd* [1957] Ch 317

Note that there is the possibility that the mortgage itself may prevent the exercise of the right of possession. In some mortgages the mortgagee agrees not to take action to seek possession unless the mortgagor defaults on repayments or some other obligation. In these cases the mortgagor can rely on s 98 of the Law of Property Act 1925

's 98(1) A mortgagor for the time being entitled to the possession or receipt of the rents and profits of any land, as to which the mortgagee has not given notice of his intention to take possession or to enter into the receipt of the rents and profits thereof, may sue for such possession, or for the recovery of such rent and profits, or to prevent or recover damages in respect of any trespass or other wrong relative thereto'.

This section allows the **borrower** to claim possession rather than the lender.

The lender can exercise his right to take possession so that he can let the property and therefore has the right to receive rents and profits to satisfy the sum owed. Alternatively, the right to take possession is the first step before the exercise of the power of sale. An order for possession can be delayed where the borrower believes that he can obtain a higher price if he sells the property himself.

# CASE EXAMPLE

**Target Home Loans Ltd v Clothier [1994] 1 All ER 439**

'If the view is that the prospects of an early sale for the mortgagees as well as for Mr Clothier are best served by deferring an order for possession then it seems to me that that is a solid reason for making such an order but the deferment should be short'.

Nolan LJ

Where, however, the presence of the borrower would depress the sale or perhaps the borrower would not co-operate in the sale of the property, the possession would not be deferred.

The lender will not have the same right to possession where the property is subject to a lease as there will be tenants in occupation of the property.

*Statutory controls on the right to possession*

The borrower in a 'dwelling house' is protected in certain circumstances against an action for possession. Under s 36 of the Administration of Justice Act 1970 (as amended by s 8 of the Administration of Justice Act 1973) the borrower can apply for possession to be:

**1.** suspended

**2.** adjourned or

**3.** postponed by the court.

## KEY FACTS

1. Is the property a dwelling house? This will depend on whether or not the property is being used as a dwelling house at the time when the order for possession is being sought.

2. The borrowers are entitled under the mortgage deed or by some agreement between them and the lenders either:

   **a** to pay the principal sum by instalments or

   **b** to defer payment of it in whole or in part.

3. There is provision made for earlier payment in the event of any default by the borrower or a demand by the lender.

The court must be satisfied that there is a realistic chance of repayment of certain sums outstanding within a reasonable time. Under the 1973 Act these represent such amounts as the mortgagor would have expected to be required to pay if the mortgage had not contained a default clause rendering the entire mortgage moneys payable in the event of any of the instalments falling into arrears. The 1973 Act prevented a potential problem from arising under the 1970 Act which had clearly not been foreseen by the draftsmen of the legislation. A default clause usually results in the borrower becoming immediately liable for the whole of the sum if he defaults on a repayment of the loan. The 1973 Act held that such clauses could be ignored when considering whether the court has power to delay possession proceedings.

The following case considered what is meant by a 'default clause'.

## CASE EXAMPLE

### Habib Bank Ltd v Tailor [1982] 1 WLR 1218

The claimant had a bank overdraft which was secured by a mortgage against his house. He exceeded the overdraft limit and the bank then called in the loan on the basis that it was a term of the loan that the overdraft was repayable on demand. Mr Habib argued that the demand for repayment in full was similar to a default clause and so his case was within s 8 of the 1973 Act. However, the court held that s 8 was not applicable to this type of loan because here there was no question of the bank having the discretion to defer payment once the bank had demanded payment and as the claimant could not repay the whole sum within a reasonable time, possession should be ordered.

If the borrower were to suddenly become liable for the whole sum, there would never be a realistic chance of repayment.

Exercise of the court's discretion:

**1.** the court cannot grant an open-ended postponement of possession orders. The court must lay down a precise period of time for repayment

**2.** the court has power to delay proceedings to allow the borrower to sell the property himself. The Court of Appeal allowed a four-month adjournment in *Target Homes Loans v Clothier* to give the borrower a chance to sell his property

**3.** applications could be granted under this section even where no sum has become due under the mortgage agreement (*Western Bank v Schindler* [1977] Ch 1)

**4.** The position of the borrower should be looked at realistically to see whether there is a genuine prospect of repayment. *Cheltenham and Gloucester Building Society v Norgan* [1996] 1 All ER 449 laid down guidelines as to how to approach these cases; this resulted in reducing the discretion given to judges in these cases and reduced the prospect of recurring litigation in cases where the borrower had defaulted on a previous occasion. There are many questions for the court to consider but the key issues are:

**(i)** how much of the mortgage term remains?

**(ii)** how much can the borrower reasonably afford to pay both now and in the future?

**(iii)** why has the borrower been unable to pay and how long will this reason last? If the prospect for repayment was not reasonable, as in *Bristol and West Building Society v Ellis* (1996) 73 P & CR 158 (here, at the present rate of repayment it would take 98 years to pay off the arrears), an order for possession should be granted immediately

In *Cheltenham & Gloucester Building Society v Norgan* the court was prepared to reschedule repayments over the whole of the remaining term of the mortgage. This represented a marked contrast with the previous attitude of the courts, which was to reschedule repayments over a very short period of time. Once rescheduled, however, the courts will rarely allow further applications to challenge possession.

**5.** under s 91 of the 1925 Act, the court has the power to direct sale on such terms as it sees fit. It may make the order in spite of opposition from others. Often there will be a dispute between the borrower who may want to sell himself and the lender who may also want to sell the property. In *Palk v Mortgage Services Funding plc* [1993] Ch 330 the lender wanted an immediate sale to prevent incurring a larger debt but the borrower wanted to delay sale until the value of the property rose. The court ordered immediate sale. Compare *Cheltenham & Gloucester plc v Krausz* [1997] 1 All ER 21 where the Court of Appeal held that the lenders could take possession and this right is absolute. If the borrowers seek to delay sale under s 36 then this depends on evidence that they have a reasonable chance of repaying the arrears. If there is no reasonable chance of that the court cannot deny the lenders immediate possession of the property.

## The exercise of the court's discretion under s 36 of the 1970 Administration of Justice Act (s 8 of the 1973 Act)

| | |
|---|---|
| The court has no discretion to postpone proceedings indefinitely. | *Royal Trust Co of Canada v Markham* [1975] 1 WLR 1416 |
| The court has power to delay possession in order for the borrower to negotiate a private sale himself. | *Target Homes Loans v Clothier* (1994) |
| The period for repayment must be 'reasonable'. There must be a realistic chance of the borrower being able to repay arrears. The courts may be prepared to reschedule the payment of mortgage arrears allowing a longer period of time for repayment. | *Cheltenham & Gloucester Building Society v Norgan* (1996) *Bristol & West Building Society v Ellis* (1996) |
| The borrower can apply to the court and the court may exercise their discretion even before any mortgage money has become due although this has not been upheld in every case. | *Western Bank Ltd v Schindler* (1977) |
| The court can order sale in favour of the borrower even where it would not fully discharge the debt under s 91 of the 1925 Act. However the borrower cannot resist an application by the lender for possession under s 36 of the 1970 Act. | *Palk v Mortgage Services Funding plc* (1993) *Cheltenham & Gloucester Building Society v Krausz* (1997) |

## Possession without a court order

ASE EXAMPLE

### *Ropaigealach v Barclays Bank* [2000] 3 WLR 17

Here, the lenders took peaceful possession of the mortgaged property while it was standing empty, undergoing repairs. The house was sold at auction with vacant possession. The Court of Appeal held that the lenders had power to take possession in this way. The right to seek relief under s 36 could, however, only arise where possession is sought by a court action. The lender cannot take action in this way if there is anyone present on the property.

## The power of sale

The power of sale arises in conjunction with the right to possession; this is covered under ss 101–107 of the Law of Property Act 1925. It can only arise if three conditions under s 101 are met:

**1.** the mortgage must be made by deed

**2.** there must be no contrary provisions expressed in that deed and

**3.** the mortgage monies must have become due.

Once **all the three conditions** are met, the power of sale arises. However, the power must also be exercisable and this occurs when any one of the three requirements laid down in s 103 of the 1925 Act is satisfied.

Note there is a difference between the power of sale arising and the power of sale becoming exercisable.

's 103 **Regulation of exercise of power of sale**

A mortgagee shall not exercise the power of sale conferred by this Act unless and until –

(i) notice requiring payment of the mortgage money has been served on the mortgagor or one or more mortgagors, and default has been made in payment of the mortgage money, or of part thereof, for three months after such service; or

(ii) some interest under the mortgage is in arrear and unpaid for two months after becoming due; or

(iii) there has been a breach of some provision contained in the mortgage deed or in this Act, or in an enactment replaced by this Act, and on the part of the mortgagor, or of some person concurring in making the mortgage, to be observed or performed, other than and besides a covenant for payment of the mortgage money or interest thereon'.

Where sale by the lender takes place, the purchaser will gain the legal estate and be entitled to register his title.

Duties of the lender when exercising the power of sale:

*   he owes the lender a duty to take reasonable care to obtain a proper price for the mortgaged property

*   he does not have to :

    **a** wait until the property market improves (*Cuckmere Brick v Mutual Finance Ltd* [1971] Ch 949)

**b** take into account persons other than the borrower, such as beneficiaries under a trust (*Parker-Tweedle v Dunbar Bank plc* [1991] Ch 26)

**c** sell immediately and will not be liable for losses incurred if sale is postponed (*China and South Sea Bank Ltd v Tan Soon Gin* [1990] 1 AC 536)

**d** preserve a business until the sale of the property has taken place (*AIB Finance Ltd v Debtors* [1998] 2 All ER 929).

## The right to appoint a receiver

This is a useful right and is another way of recovering the interest owed on the mortgage. The right to appoint a receiver is often included in the mortgage deed itself. If it is not provided in the mortgage deed then it can be made under s 101 of the 1925 Act. It arises in the same circumstances as the power of sale, ie the mortgage must be made by deed with no provision disallowing the appointment of a receiver and mortgage money must now have become due.

The receiver takes control of the mortgaged property and then sells it or manages it and uses the income from it to repay the loan. The receiver acts as agent of the lender. However, the receiver owes a duty to the borrower to act 'with due diligence'.

ASE EXAMPLE

> **Medforth v Blake [2000] Ch 86**
>
> The receiver owes a duty in equity to the mortgagor and anyone else with an interest in the property to act in good faith.

## The right of foreclosure

> J 'foreclosure actions are almost unheard of today and have been so for many years. Mortgagees prefer to exercise other remedies'.
>
> Sir David Nicholls VC in *Palk v Mortgage Services Funding plc* [1993] Ch 330

Foreclosure allows the mortgagee to enforce his rights to possession of the property. The court can order that he can take over the entire ownership of the property irrespective of the size of the debt.

The Law Commission has recommended that foreclosure should be abolished and replaced with a remedy for the lenders to sell the property to themselves.

## KEY FACTS

### Foreclosure

**1.** This is regarded as a very draconian measure and it is rarely ordered today.

**2.** It can only be ordered by the court and if the court does order foreclosure, the mortgagee is entitled to the whole of the property; and that includes any excess over the actual sum lent and any interest that is outstanding.

**3.** Any mortgagee of property can bring an action for foreclosure: s 91(2) of the Law of Property Act 1925.

**4.** The effect of the action is to make the mortgagee owner of the property in law and in equity.

**5.** The right to foreclose arises any time after the legal right to redeem has been lost.

**6.** The mortgagee loses the right to seek any other order, so foreclosure is not advisable in cases of negative equity as the full loan will not be recoverable.

**7.** There are two steps in a foreclosure order: foreclosure *nisi* and foreclosure absolute. Under foreclosure *nisi* the mortgagor has a period of time to repay the mortgage and if he does so, the mortgage is discharged. The foreclosure absolute destroys the mortgagor's equity of redemption and transfers title to the mortgagee.

**8.** In rare cases a court will re-open a foreclosure order absolute. In *Campbell v Holyland* (1877) 7 Ch D 166 the case was re-opened three months after the foreclosure order had been granted.

**9.** The Law Commission has recommended that foreclosure should be abolished.

## KEY FACTS

### Rights of the mortgagee

| | | | |
|---|---|---|---|
| Action on the covenant in the contract | Arises once there is default on the terms of the agreement. | | *Alliance & Leicester v Slayford* (2001) |
| Possession | Automatically arises when the mortgage is made. | s 36 of the Administration of Justice Act 1970 (s 8 of the Administration of Justice Act 1973) | *Target Home Loans Ltd v Clothier* (1994); *Four-Maids Ltd v Dudley Marshall (Properties) Ltd* (1957); *Cheltenham and Gloucester Building Society v Norgan* (1996) |
| Sale | Arises where the mortgage has been made by deed and the mortgage money has become due. | ss 101 and 103 of the Law of Property Act 1925 | *AIB v Debtors* (1998); *Cuckmere Brick Co v Mutual Finance Ltd* (1971) |
| Appointment of a receiver | Where deed allows it, otherwise deed may imply such a power. | s 101 of the 1925 Act s 109 of the 1925 Act | *Medforth v Blake* (2000) |
| Foreclosure | Only arises by order of the court. | | *Campbell v Holyland* (1877) |

## KEY FACTS

**Rights of an equitable mortgagee under an equitable mortgage:**

1. The mortgagee does not hold the legal estate in land so the equitable mortgagee cannot claim possession of the legal estate.

2. The equitable mortgagee has the right to sue for the outstanding money in the same way as the legal mortgagee.

3. If the equitable mortgage was made by deed then there can be a power of sale once the conditions necessary are present. The property cannot be sold by the mortgagee himself.

4. A receiver can be appointed in the same circumstances as in a legal mortgage.

5. An equitable mortgagee has the power to foreclose.

## ACTIVITY

Charlie and Gracie have lived together for the past five years. They bought their house for £220,000 with the aid of a mortgage provided by Easier Banking in 1998. They both had full-time jobs and they were both able to contribute towards the mortgage repayments. Grace loved to decorate the house and she started to buy expensive fittings and furniture. Gracie left her job in 2001 when she took maternity leave. She unexpectedly had twin boys and has not returned to work. Charlie was made redundant in 2002 and has since found it difficult to repay the mortgage instalments. They are now over £20,000 in arrears and Easier Banking want to repossess the property.

Advise Easier Banking on the steps that they should take in order to repossess the property. Have Easier Banking any other rights that they can exercise?

## 12.6 Priority of mortgages

If the borrower takes out a single mortgage then the question of priority does not arise. The lender has the right to recover the outstanding sum and anything outstanding will belong to the borrower. However, there may be more than one mortgage and there may be insufficient funds to cover the outstanding amount.

The law lays down rules as to who is first in the queue to recover outstanding sums. The rules largely depend on three issues:

**1.** are the mortgages legal or equitable?

**2.** is the title to the land registered or unregistered?

**3.** when were the mortgages registered?

Legal mortgages of registered land depend on the date of registration, whereas equitable mortgages depend on date of creation. Properly registered legal mortgages will take priority over all equitable mortgages created after the date of registration. A mortgage will not take effect in law until it has been registered, so an unregistered legal mortgage will not take priority over a registered legal mortgage whatever the date of creation.

Under s 32 of the Land Registration Act 2002, an equitable charge should be protected by entry of a burden on the register but failure to do so may still allow the earlier charge to take priority because equitable charges have always been treated differently from legal charges and the date of creation has governed their priority.

## Further reading

Andrews, G, 'Undue Influence – Where's the Disadvantage?' [2002] Conv 457.

Capper, D, 'Undue Influence and Unconscionability' (1998) 114 LQR 479.

Dixon, M, 'Combating the mortgagee's right to possession: new hope for the mortgagor in chains?' (1998) 18 Legal Studies 279.

Haley, M, 'Mortgage default: Possession, Relief and Judicial Discretion' (1997) 17 Legal Studies 483.

Thomas, S, 'Mortgages: Possession by Default' [1997] Conv 91.

Thompson, M P, 'Wives Sureties and Banks: *Royal Bank of Scotland v Etridge (No 2)* [2000] 4 AER 449' Conv [2002] 174.

## chapter 13 LEASES ▪

If buying freehold property is impossible or undesirable, taking a lease of property presents a solution. It has many advantages which makes it an attractive alternative to owning property. Leases are used for residential premises as well as for business premises and for shops.

It has the advantage of being a very flexible relationship. The tenant of domestic accommodation is always protected from eviction in the short term and the tenant has a legal estate which allows him to prevent anyone, including the landlord, from entering without his permission for the duration of the lease. However, the landlord is usually in a much stronger position than the tenant and can easily take advantage of him. The law has always tried to protect the tenant from his potentially vulnerable position. This protection does not extend to licensees.

So, the first question to ask in a short-term holding of property is always: is this a tenancy at all?

## 13.1 Characteristics of a lease

Under s 1(1)(b) of the Law of Property Act 1925 a lease or 'a term of years absolute' is a legal estate and is also a proprietary estate in land.

's 1(1) . . . The only estates in land which are capable of subsisting or of being conveyed or created at law are:

(a) An estate in fee simple absolute in possession;

(b) A term of years absolute'.

Under the Land Registration Act 2002, a lease of over seven years now qualifies as a registrable interest and it must be compulsorily registered under s 4 if granted out of an unregistered estate or under s 27 if it is granted out of a registered estate. In line with the rules on registration, it will not take effect at law until it has been properly registered. Failure to register will result in the lease losing its status as a legal estate and it will only qualify as a mere contract to grant a legal lease.

If the lease is for less than seven years, it does not matter how short the lease is in actual length, for example it can be for less than a year, it can be one month but such a lease is still considered to be for a term of years absolute.

A lease has always been difficult to define and there is still no adequate statutory definition even today. For a time there was a shift towards holding the intention of the parties as the real indicator of whether a lease or a licence existed. A lease was a lease if the parties intended it to be so.

Today, we are guided by the characteristics laid down in the following case:

# CASE EXAMPLE

**Street v Mountford [1985] AC 809**

'The traditional view that the grant of exclusive possession for a term at a rent creates a tenancy is consistent with the elevation of a tenancy into an estate in land. The tenant possessing exclusive possession is able to exercise the rights of an owner of land, which is in the real sense his land albeit temporarily and subject to certain restrictions. A tenant armed with exclusive possession can keep out strangers and keep out the landlord unless the landlord is exercising limited rights reserved to him by the tenancy agreement to enter and view and repair'.

Lord Templeman

Lord Templeman suggested that there are three characteristics of a lease:

**1.** exclusive possession

**2.** a determinate period

**3.** for a rent or other consideration.

## 13.1.1 Exclusive possession

There has to be exclusive possession for a lease to exist. Lord Templeman held in *Street v Mountford* that this was the conclusive feature of a lease. This means that the tenant has control over anyone who enters the premises and can exclude everyone, including the landlord. If someone occupying property does not have exclusive possession, they can only claim a licence.

> **J** 'There can be no tenancy unless the occupier enjoys exclusive possession but an occupier who enjoys exclusive possession is not necessarily a tenant. He may be owner in fee simple, a trespasser, a mortgagee in possession, an object of charity or a service occupier'.
>
> Lord Templeman in *Street v Mountford* (1985)

There will be no exclusive possession if:

**1.** the landlord is entitled to **move the occupier** at any time from one room to another. In *Westminister City Council v Clarke* [1992] 2 AC 288 there was held to be no exclusive possession in a council-run hostel for homeless persons who could not claim any particular room. Other rules included the provision that they might have to share with others, they had to be in their rooms by 11.00 pm and they could not have visitors after that time

2. someone merely has **exclusive occupation**, such as a hotel guest or a student in a university hall of residence or a resident in a nursing home (*Abbeyfield (Harpenden) Society Ltd v Woods* [1968] 1 WLR 374); the hotel guest has no right to exclude the hotel staff from the room

3. **services** are provided, such as a housekeeper, the collection of rubbish and the cleaning of windows and also the flats themselves. In *Marcou v De Silvesa* [1986] 52 P & CR 2 the agreement required the landlord to provide services. The court considered whether this would require unlimited access to the premises. The type of services provided by the landlord was very limited, such as the removal of rubbish and laundering of linen, and did not need access to the flat. It is not the provision of services which prevents this from being a tenancy but the fact that the owner can enter at will. In *Huwyler v Ruddy* (1995) 28 HLR 550 services were provided by the claimant's brother for the defendant. They were very limited in nature and rarely took more than 20 minutes each week. However, Peter Gibson LJ found that even when the services were wound down to virtually nothing, the nature of the original contract was that the parties had an agreement for the provision of services and the defendant could claim the resumption of the services if he wished. The agreement was therefore a licence

4. occupation of the premises is based on **employment** if it comes within the definition of a 'service occupancy'. This was defined in *Street v Mountford* as occupancy by a servant of his master's premises in order to perform his duties as a servant. Examples include farm workers and members of the armed forces. It is also accepted that the occupation would be for the better performance of the job

5. **purchasers were let into possession** of the premises prior to completion.

There may be exclusive possession **even if**:

1. the **landlord retains a set of keys**. In *Aslan v Murphy* [1990] 1 WLR 766 the owner retained a set of keys and retained the right of entry at any time he wished. This was seen as a pretence to prevent a tenancy arising. A landlord can retain keys but still have to request entry from the tenant if he wants to gain access

2. there are a number of persons **sharing** the premises. This is because they may jointly occupy the premises. In *Antoniades v Villiers* [1990] 1 AC 417 it was held that there was a joint tenancy even though the owner had asked each of the two joint occupiers, who were an unmarried couple living together, to enter separate agreements with himself and each was described as a licence requiring them to separately undertake to pay half of the rent. There were also clauses reserving the right to the owner to occupy the flat with the couple or to introduce others. The House of Lords held these provisions to be a sham

3. premises are **provided by an employer**, so long as occupation is not required for the better performance of the tenant's job. In *Fachini v Bryson* [1952] 1 TLR 1386 the assistant of an ice-cream manufacturer was allowed to live in a house in return for a sum of money paid weekly and this was found to be a tenancy even though the parties referred to it as a licence; the use of the premises did not improve the carrying out of the employee's duties

4. the landlord does not have an **estate to support a lease**. In *Bruton v London & Quadrant Housing Trust* [1999] 3 WLR 150 the landlord had a mere licence but the landlord still had the right to create a lease in favour of the claimant.

## 13.1.2 A determinate period

### Commencement of the lease

If there is any uncertainty in the period, the tenancy will fail. This means that both the commencement and the duration must both be clear on the face of the lease. Even where the other terms of the lease are clear, such as the details of the rent and the length of the actual term, the lease will fail without a date of commencement (*Say v Smith* (1563) 1 Plowd 269).

### Duration of the lease

The maximum date of duration must be certain at the date of commencement. In *Lace v Chantler* [1944] KB 368 a lease granted 'for the duration of the war' was held void. This was because at the time it was granted no one had any idea how long the war would last and therefore no one had any idea when the lease would come to an end.

Consider the following cases:

# CASE EXAMPLE

---

### *Lace v Chantler* [1944] KB 368

'The question immediately arises whether a tenancy for the duration of the war creates a good leasehold interest. In my opinion, it does not. A term created by a leasehold tenancy agreement must be expressed either with certainty and specifically or by reference to something which can, at the time when the lease takes effect, be looked to as a certain ascertainment of what the term is meant to be. In the present case the term was completely uncertain. It was impossible to say how long the tenancy would last'.

Lord Greene MR

Compare these two cases:

# CASE EXAMPLE

### *Ashburn Anstalt v Arnold* [1989] Ch 1

It was held that a term which allowed the occupiers of a shop to remain there rent-free until they provided the landlord with a quarter's notice was certain because in this case the term could be brought to an end by giving a quarter's notice and this was itself sufficiently certain.

> 'The arrangement could be brought to an end by both parties in circumstances which are free from uncertainty in the sense that there would be doubt whether the determining event had occurred. The vice of the uncertainty in relation to the duration of the term is that the parties do not know where they stand'.

> Fox LJ

The problem with this decision is that there was no way of predicting when the quarter's notice would be given, so it was not possible to predict when the lease was going to end.

# CASE EXAMPLE

### *Prudential Assurance Co Ltd v London Residuary Body* [1992] 2 AC 386

The judgment in this case criticised the result in *Ashburn Anstalt v Arnold*. It concerned the sale of a strip of land fronting a highway to the Council which then leased it back to the owner for a period 'until the land is required by the council for the purposes of widening of the highway'. The Council later assigned the reversion to the first defendants who were a highway authority, and the tenancy was then assigned to the claimants. The question was whether or not the agreement created a lease.

If *Ashburn Anstalt v Arnold* was followed, the term would have been sufficiently certain because the defendants had the right to call for the determination of the lease. However, Lord Templeman overruled the earlier case because he viewed it as uncertain and he maintained that one of the hallmarks of a lease remained certainty of duration. He criticised the state of the law because in the *Prudential* case it produced a result that had not been intended by the parties.

Lord Browne-Wilkinson, who also gave judgment in this case, criticised the rule:

> 'This bizarre outcome results from the application of an ancient and technical rule of law which requires the maximum duration of a term of years to be ascertainable from the outset. No one has produced any satisfactory rationale for the genesis of this rule. No one has been able to point to any useful purpose that it serves at the present day . . . for this house to depart from a rule relating to land law which has been established for many centuries might upset long established titles. I must therefore confine myself to expressing the hope that the Law Commission might look at the subject to see whether there is in fact any good reason now for maintaining a rule which operates to defeat contractually agreed arrangements between the parties'.

> Lord Browne-Wilkinson

The lease may have been saved if the parties had included a maximum duration for the lease but had also included an event which would have allowed an early termination of the lease, for example a lease for 900 years but subject to termination by the landlord when the land was required for road widening. The courts would have accepted the 900 years as the maximum length of time that the lease could have lasted.

The rule today is that the maximum duration of the lease must be clear from the start of the lease.

The decision in *Prudential Assurance* has attracted criticism and support from academic writers. Compare the following views:

> 'The decision of the House of Lords in *Prudential Assurance Co Ltd v London Residuary Body* is welcome for its reassertion that the same certainty rule applies to fixed and to periodic terms. Leases had always required certainty of maximum duration at the outset. The choice by the House of Lords to reaffirm the traditional rule was the safe option in view of the danger of upsetting established titles. Any formal requirement, like that of prospective certainty of term, risks upsetting the intention of contracting parties. On balance, it has been argued, the result was not unjust, but if it was, escape routes were available. No need for reform of the law has been demonstrated'.

> P Sparkes, 'Certainty of Leasehold Terms' (1993) 109 LQR 93

'It may well be that the indeterminate nature of the lease will become a problem over time. This will be where the parties contracted on the joint assumption that the terminating event would occur within a short period and allocated risks on this basis, but in fact the event does not occur. In *Lace*, if the war were still continuing after 50 years but the parties had only thought it would last for a couple of years and had agreed a fixed rent, it would clearly be unfair to the landlord that the tenancy could not be renegotiated. This is a contractual problem, not a property one, and should be met by being able to re-open the bargain. To prescribe the circumstances in which renegotiation would be permissible would be a difficult task, indeed this reflects many of the problems that the courts encounter in economic duress cases, in trying to distinguish those cases in which the contractual modification is sensible and reasonable, and those which are exploitative . . . As Lord Browne-Wilkinson observes in *Prudential Assurance*, the ancient and technical rule of law which requires the maximum duration of a term of years to be ascertainable from the outset is ripe for review . . . To recognise this does not mean that the rule should simply be abandoned. It is being used by the courts to free the landlord from a manifestly disadvantageous contractual arrangement'.

S Bright, 'Uncertainty in Leases – Is it a Vice?' (1993) 13 Legal Studies 38

## Periodic tenancies

This rule is difficult to apply to periodic tenancies because a periodic tenancy has no fixed maximum duration at its inception. The reason that it does not infringe the rule is that the length of the term is determined by the period with reference to which the rent payable is calculated.

For example, if the rent of £350 is paid per month then it will be a monthly tenancy. This will be implied even though it has not been specifically mentioned in the agreement.

So the law sees the periodic tenancy as a series of separate terms which then could be terminated at the end of each term. Each period is certain, so the term itself is certain.

## 13.1.3 For a rent

1. Rent is defined as the consideration paid to the landlord by the lessee in return for the use of the premises.

2. It will usually be in money but it can be in any form including benefits in kind.

3. It has historically been seen as an important feature of the landlord and tenant relationship. In more recent cases it has been accepted that you can have a lease without the payment of rent. In *Ashburn Anstalt v Arnold* Fox LJ stated: 'In the circumstances I conclude that the reservation of a rent is not necessary for the creation of a tenancy. That conclusion involves no departure from Lord Templeman's proposition in *Street v Mountford*

"if exclusive possession at a rent for a term does not constitute a tenancy then the distinction between a contractual tenancy and a contractual licence of land becomes wholly unidentifiable". We are saying only that we do not think that Lord Templeman was stating the quite different proposition that you cannot have a tenancy without a rent.' If rent is paid then it can be seen as an indicator of a lease.

4. In cases where no rent is payable, even where exclusive possession is enjoyed it may suggest a licence. A man was held to be a licensee where he occupied agricultural land under an agreement with the council which allowed him to remain in occupation for the rest of the year without charge, and at his own risk (*Colchester Council v Smith* [1991] Ch 446).

5. If rent is to be payable then it must be certain at the commencement of the lease and the amount payable must be clear at the date for payment.

## Key features indicating a lease or a licence

| Exclusive possession | For a term | At a rent |
| --- | --- | --- |
| No exclusive possession if the landlord is entitled to move the occupiers from room to room (*Westminster City Council v Clarke* (1992)). | There must be no uncertainty in the period of the lease. | Any consideration paid to the landlord. |
| No exclusive possession if merely exclusive occupation such as a hotel guest (*Abbeyfield (Harpenden) Society Ltd v Woods* (1968)). | The maximum date of duration must be certain at the start of the lease (*Lace v Chantler* (1944); *Prudential Assurance Co Ltd v London Residuary Body* (1992)). | Usually money but can be paid in kind. |
| No exclusive possession if services are provided or if the premises are provided as part of an employment contract. | Periodic tenancies are saved as each period is determined by the period for which rent is payable. | It is possible to have a lease without rent (*Ashburn Anstalt v Arnold* (1989)). |
| There will be exclusive possession if the provision of services or retention of a key is a sham (*Aslan v Murphy* (1990)). | | If rent is payable then it must be clearly stated in the terms of the lease. |

# 13.2 The distinction between a lease and licence

This remains a difficult issue but since the decision in *Street v Mountford* there are three main indicators outlined by Lord Templeman which, when applied together, will indicate a lease.

**1.** exclusive possession

**2.** for a fixed or periodic term certain

**3.** in consideration of a premium or period payments.

In *Street v Mountford* the agreement specified that the relationship between the parties was one of licence. Lord Templeman held that the issue would be determined by looking at the true nature of the agreement rather than the name given by the parties in the agreement.

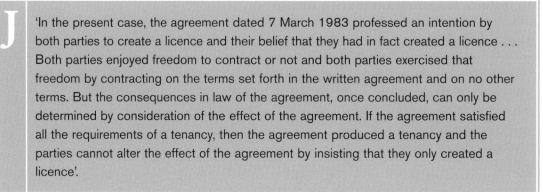

J 'In the present case, the agreement dated 7 March 1983 professed an intention by both parties to create a licence and their belief that they had in fact created a licence . . . Both parties enjoyed freedom to contract or not and both parties exercised that freedom by contracting on the terms set forth in the written agreement and on no other terms. But the consequences in law of the agreement, once concluded, can only be determined by consideration of the effect of the agreement. If the agreement satisfied all the requirements of a tenancy, then the agreement produced a tenancy and the parties cannot alter the effect of the agreement by insisting that they only created a licence'.

In a later case, *Bruton v London & Quadrant Housing Trust* [2000] 1 AC 406, Lord Hoffmann said: 'the fact the parties use language more appropriate to a different kind of agreement, such as a licence, is irrelevant if upon its true construction it has the identifying characteristics of a lease'.

## 13.2.1 The significance of the lease/licence distinction in law

**1.** The tenant can assign his interest in land and the lease is enforceable against the original lessor.

**2.** If the lessor transfers his interest in land, then the lease is capable of binding the transferee. A lease over seven years will be registrable but a lease under seven years will be overriding. A licence is not registrable whatever the length.

**3.** A licensee cannot claim statutory protection for security of tenure under the Landlord and Tenant legislation, for example the Rent Act 1977 or the Landlord and Tenant Act 1954 (business tenants only) although he has some protection under the Housing Act 1985.

**4.** Residential tenants under long leases may have the right to purchase the freehold.

5. Tenants have the right to enforce repairing covenants in the lease unavailable to licensees (Landlord and Tenant Act 1985).

6. The Protection from Eviction Act 1977 will protect licensees in domestic premises from immediate eviction as well as lessees.

# ACTIVITY

Mr Dodgy owns a number of flats in Cedar Mansions and lets them to a number of different people. Consider the following agreements and decide whether they take effect as licences or leases:

1. Lucy and Mary enter into an agreement with Mr Dodgy to occupy a flat in Cedar Mansions. The terms are that they will pay £300 each month. They will have clean sheets and regular cleaning of the premises provided by Mr Dodgy's aunt.

2. Nicki and Owen enter into an agreement with Mr Dodgy to occupy a one-bedroom flat in Cedar Mansions. They are to pay £400 per month. One of the terms included in the agreement was that Mr Dodgy reserves the right to move another person, including Mr Dodgy, into the flat at any time.

3. Mr Dodgy tells his niece Flora that she can have one of the flats for as long as she likes if she pays rent of £350 per month. The agreement is referred to as a lease.

4. Mr Dodgy allows his two nephews, Harry and George, who both work for an independent wine supplier, to live in the flat rent-free but they agree to supply him with two dozen cases of wine each month.

5. Mr and Mrs Bright move into the top-floor flat with their three children. They pay £500 in rent each month. Mr Dodgy retains a spare key and insists he must have constant access because the hot-water boiler for all the flats is in the roof and it is only accessible from the top-floor flat. The agreement is termed a licence.

# 13.3 Types of leases

## 13.3.1 Fixed-term leases

A fixed-term lease is, as the name suggests, a lease where the exact duration is fixed at the outset of the lease. It can be for any period – a week or for 500 years – so long as the period is certain.

# APPLYING THE LAW

To Anthony, a lease for six months of Windy Ridge, rent of £300 to be payable monthly. The lease will automatically determine after six months.

UNLOCKING
LAND
LAW

## 13.3.2 Periodic leases

A periodic tenancy is one that may continue indefinitely. It can last from month to month or from year to year. The length of the tenancy is determined according to the period for which rent is payable. If the period is for less than three years then the periodic tenancy will not require any formalities in spite of the fact that the tenancy may continue for a period well in excess of three years.

> ## APPLYING THE LAW
>
> Tony takes a lease of a flat in Chelsea in July 1995. He is to pay rent of £800 each month. He likes the flat and remains there for many years. He is still there in July 2004. His tenancy has already lasted over nine years. The fact that it was not created by deed does not affect its validity even though it has lasted well in excess of three years.
>
>

Sometimes a periodic tenancy is implied because a property owner accepts rent paid on a periodic basis by a 'tenant at will' (discussed below). A tenant at will is any tenant who occupies with the consent of the owner.

## 13.3.3 Tenancy at will

A tenancy at will arises whenever a tenant, with the consent of the landlord, occupies or continues to occupy premises. The terms will be that the landlord can determine the tenancy whenever he wishes. Rent will usually be payable but will not affect the existence of such a tenancy if it is not payable. However, once rent is paid and accepted on a regular basis then a periodic tenancy will be implied. It has been referred to as:

> 'Not so much an estate as a relationship between landlord and tenant: there is no period for which the tenant is entitled to the land'.

R J Smith, *Property Law Cases and Materials* (2nd edn, Longman, 2003), p 508

The agreement is very informal. Either party can determine at will. It will automatically determine on the death of either party. There is very little difference between the tenancy at will and the licence. The main difference lies in the fact that the tenant at will is able to claim against a stranger in trespass. However, he has no proprietary right in the land.

400

## APPLYING THE LAW

Ellen, an old friend from university, comes to stay while looking for a job in London. You agree that she can stay rent-free. She stays for three months. Her status can be seen as a tenant at will. Ellen has the right to maintain an action in trespass if, while you are away, your daughter's boyfriend decides to use Ellen's room.

The tenancy at will may be expressly granted or it may arise by implication from the act of the parties.

## APPLYING THE LAW

Shelagh rented a flat in Mayfair for three years on a fixed tenancy. She has found a house to buy in Fulham but it will not be available until July and her lease expired in March. The landlord agrees that she can continue to occupy the Mayfair flat on the same terms until July. Her status after March will be as a tenant at will.

## CASE EXAMPLE

### *Javad v Mohammad Aqil* [1991] 1 WLR 1007

The landowner was negotiating for a 10-year lease of premises and allowed the tenants into possession while negotiations were continuing, expecting that an agreement would soon be reached. Although the 'tenant' paid rent, the Court of Appeal held that there was no implied periodic tenancy but merely a tenancy at will.

> 'Where parties are negotiating the terms of a proposed lease, and the prospective tenant is let into possession or permitted to remain in possession in advance of, and in anticipation of, terms being agreed, the fact that the parties have not yet agreed terms will be a factor to be taken into account in ascertaining their intention. It will often be a weighty factor. Frequently in such cases a sum called "rent" is paid at once in accordance with the terms of the

proposed lease: for example, quarterly in advance. But, depending on all the circumstances, parties are not to be supposed thereby to have agreed that the prospective tenant shall be a quarterly tenant. They cannot sensibly be taken to have agreed that he shall have a periodic tenancy, with all the consequences flowing from that'.

Nicholls LJ

A tenancy at will may be brought to an end by conversion into an implied periodic tenancy where rent is paid and accepted on a regular basis.

## APPLYING THE LAW

In the example above, where Shelagh remains in the flat in Mayfair, she may become an implied periodic tenant if the arrangement continues for some time and the rent is payable on a regular basis and accepted by the landlord.

## 13.3.4 Tenancy at sufferance

A tenancy at sufferance will arise where the tenant continues to occupy property but, unlike in a tenancy at will, it is without the consent of the landlord. If the landlord expressly refuses the tenant the right to remain, then the tenant becomes a trespasser subject to the protection afforded by the Protection from Eviction Act 1977.

## CASE EXAMPLE

### *Remon v City of London Real Property Co Ltd* [1921] 1 KB 49

A tenant remained in possession after a valid notice to quit had expired. The tenant claimed to be a tenant at sufferance but the court held that as the landlord had already taken action to endeavour to remove him from the premises, he could not be a tenant at sufferance.

'tenants at sufferance seem to have been confined to persons who held over without the assent or dissent of their landlords, and not to have included persons who held over wrongfully in spite of the active objection of their landlords'.

Scrutton LJ

# 13.3.5 Leases for life

If a lease is granted for someone's lifetime it will be uncertain. Therefore it offends against the rule that the maximum length of a lease must be certain. Under the Law of Property Act 1925:

 's 205(1)(xxvii) . . . a term of years absolute does not include a lease for life or a lease which is determinable on the death of some named person'.

A lease for someone's life may be saved under s 149(6) of the 1925 Act:

 's 149(6) . . . Any lease or underlease at a rent, or in consideration of a fine, for life or for lives or for any term of years determinable with life or lives, or on the marriage of the lessee, or any contract therefore . . . shall take effect as a lease . . . for a term of ninety years determinable after the death or marriage . . . of the original lessee'.

This section only applies where rent is payable. If a lease for life is granted and no rent is payable then it cannot be a legal estate under s 1(1) of the 1925 Act and can only exist in equity under a trust of land as a life interest, if at all.

Where rent is payable then the lease is converted into one of 90 years but will be determinable on the death of the original lessee.

## APPLYING THE LAW

In 1986 Ronald grants a lease to Quentin for his life at a yearly rent of £3,000. On Quentin's death in 2002 there are still over 74 years left to run but Ronald can determine the lease by giving notice to Quentin's successors in title.

# 13.3.6 Perpetually renewable leases

The lease may contain a covenant for the tenant to renew the lease. There is then the prospect that the lease may be indefinitely renewable.

Under s 145 of and Schedule 15 para 5 to the Law of Property Act 1922 such a lease can be automatically converted into a lease for 2,000 years. To many, this seems a very generous provision for a lease which at first sight simply appears to offend the rule against certainty of duration. The provision is subject to quite strict rules. It will only apply if, by the wording, it is shown that the intention of the parties is that it should be perpetually renewable.

## APPLYING THE LAW

Consider this term in a lease letting Greenacres House to Samuel Whitbread and his wife Alice:

'The tenant Samuel Whitbread is entitled to have the lease renewed for a further ten years from the ending of the current term at a rent to be agreed, the lease shall contain the same covenants as in this lease (including an option to renew the lease for a further ten years at the expiry of the term)'.

This would be seen as a perpetually renewable lease and it would be converted into a term of 2,000 years.

## CASE EXAMPLE

### Caerphilly Concrete Products Ltd v Owen [1972] 1 WLR 372

The lease contained the following clause which provided for renewal: ' . . . containing the like covenants and provisos as are herein contained (including an option to renew such lease for the further term of five years at the expiration thereof)'. The court considered whether this was a perpetually renewable lease.

'In the present case the brackets make it abundantly plain that the parties are explaining that "containing the like covenants and provisos" is a phrase intended to embrace an option'.

Russell LJ

'On the other hand, the courts are reluctant to find that leases are perpetually renewable. They will clutch at straws to hold that the option is to be inserted in only the first renewal, resulting in a maximum length of three terms (original and two renewals)'.

R J Smith, *Property Law Cases and Materials* (2nd edn, Longman, 2003), p 388

Compare the following case:

# CASE EXAMPLE

**Marjorie Burnett Ltd v Barclay (1980) 125 Sol Jo 199**

'Here, the second lease would contain a covenant for a further seven years and a rent to be agreed, but the final words, requiring yet another covenant for renewal, could not possibly be included, because they were not part of the covenant for renewal. A point of equal force appeared to be that the notion of a 2000 year term was completely inimical to a lease containing a rent review every seven years'.

Nourse LJ

## 13.3.7 Tenancies by estoppel

A tenancy by estoppel operates where the landlord has no title to the land when a lease is granted. The landlord is trying to do something which in law he is unable to do. However, the tenant believes that he has a legal estate in land, with all the effects of holding a lease, and if the court denied him the lease it would have serious consequences.

'It is a fundamental principle of the common law that a grantor is not entitled to dispute the validity of his own grant and may not therefore disaffirm the title of his grantee'.

*Goodtitle d Edwards v Bailey* (1777) 2 Cowp 597

It makes no difference that the parties were aware that the landlord had a defective title. The doctrine still allows both parties to claim a tenancy by estoppel.

The principle can take effect on both the interest of the tenant and the interest of the landlord.

# CASE EXAMPLE

**Industrial Properties (Barton Hill) Ltd v AEI Ltd [1977] QB 580**

'If a landlord lets a tenant into possession under a lease, then, so long as the tenant remains in possession undisturbed by any adverse claim – then the tenant cannot dispute the landlord's title. Suppose the tenant (not having been disturbed) goes out of possession and the landlord sues the tenant on the covenant for rent or for breach of covenant to repair or to yield up in repair. The tenant cannot say to the landlord: "You are not the true owner of the property"'.

UNLOCKING
LAND
LAW

What the courts are saying here is that the tenant, having paid rent and accepted the terms of the lease, cannot turn around to the landlord and then argue that the agreement was not a tenancy.

The principle has recently been discussed in a landmark decision in the law on landlord and tenant:

# CASE EXAMPLE

### *Bruton v London & Quadrant Housing Trust* [2000] 1 AC 406

The claimant argued that he held a lease from a charitable housing trust. His arguments were based on the fact that he enjoyed exclusive possession. The landlords, however, did not hold the freehold of the property but were merely licensees. They claimed that the claimant could not enjoy the property as a tenant because a lease could not be granted by someone who did not hold a legal estate in land.

The Court of Appeal accepted this argument and held that Bruton held as a licensee because the housing trust could not grant a lease where they did not themselves have a legal estate. The court applied the principle of *nemo dat quod non habet* (no one can grant what they do not own).

The House of Lords rejected this argument. It based its judgment on whether or not the claimant had exclusive possession of the property. There was a significant term in the lease under which the occupier would 'permit the Trust or its Agents, Surveyors or Consultants to enter the property for the purpose of inspecting the state of repair, and cleanliness of the property or for any purpose connected at all reasonable hours of the day'. Lord Hoffmann gave the principal judgment in the case:

> 'There is nothing to suggest the he [Mr Bruton] was to share possession with the trust, the council or anyone else. The trust did not retain such control over the premises as was inconsistent with Mr Bruton having exclusive possession, as was the case in *Westminster City Council v Clarke*. The only rights which it reserved were for itself and the council to enter at certain times and for limited purposes'.

Lord Hoffmann then discussed how a tenancy can arise when the grantor did not have a legal estate in land himself. He looked at the juridical basis for a tenancy by estoppel.

> 'In fact, as the authorities show, it is not the estoppel which creates the tenancy. The estoppel arises when one or other of the parties wants to deny one of the ordinary incidents or obligations of the tenancy on the ground that the landlord had no legal estate. The basis of the estoppel is that having entered into an agreement which constitutes a lease or tenancy, he cannot repudiate that incident or obligation.

406

Thus it is the fact that the agreement between the parties constitutes a tenancy that gives rise to an estoppel and not the other way round. It therefore seems to me that the question of tenancy by estoppel does not arise in this case. The issue is simply whether the agreement is a tenancy. It is not whether either party is entitled to deny some obligation or incident of the tenancy on the ground that the trust had no title'.

The effect of this judgment was that the claimant could enforce repairing covenants under the agreement. These would not have been available if he had been a licensee.

## KEY FACTS

### Different types of lease

| Type of lease | How created | How determined | Key features |
|---|---|---|---|
| Fixed lease | Informally under three years. Only by deed over three years. | Notice to quit formally served. | Must be clear from the outset when it is to determine. |
| Periodic lease | Can be created informally if under three years. | By serving a notice to quit equivalent to the period of rent payment, eg one month for monthly tenancies. | Can last in excess of three years but can be created informally without the need for a deed or even writing. |
| Tenancy at will | A tenant continues in possession after a lease has ended with the consent of the landlord or anyone enters into possession as a tenant but does not gain a proprietary interest. | By converting to an implied periodic tenancy or termination by either party at any time. | Very similar to a licence except that the tenant at will can bring an action for trespass. |

| | | | |
|---|---|---|---|
| Tenancy at sufferance | Arises where the landlord neither assents nor dissents to the presence of the tenant who continues to occupy after his lease has ended. | The landlord denies the tenant's right to be on the premises. | It covers a situation where the tenant simply continues to enjoy the premises. Rarely lasts for any length of time because once the landlord accepts rent it will be converted into an implied periodic tenancy. |
| Lease for life | Any lease that is granted to someone for his lifetime will fail unless can be converted into a 90-year lease under s 149(6) LPA 1925. | Once converted, it can be determined by either party giving at least one month's notice. | Cannot be a legal lease as there is no certain term so will fail unless converted under s 149(6) of LPA 1922. |
| Perpetually renewable lease | A lease which includes a covenant to renew which itself can be renewed. | Unless it has been converted into a 2,000-year lease, under s 145 of LPA 1922 it will determine on the last day of the period of the lease, having allowed one renewal. | These are very strictly construed against allowing conversion into a 2,000-year lease. |
| Estoppel tenancy | A tenancy by estoppel operates where the landlord has no title to the land when the lease is granted. | Can be determined according to the terms of the lease agreed between the parties. | The fact that the court held there to be a tenancy allowed the tenant to enforce significant repairing covenants. These would have been denied to a licensee. |

# 13.4 The creation of a lease

## 13.4.1 Creation of a lease exceeding three years

The grant of a lease for a fixed term of more than three years must be by deed (s 52(1) of the Law of Property Act 1925). This means that it should be signed, sealed and delivered. Further, if the lease is for seven years or more it will not take effect unless it has been registered under the Land Registration Act 2002.

However, a lease can exist where it is for a very short period, even under one year. The formalities for short leases are necessarily much less strict.

## 13.4.2 Creation of a lease for less than three years

A lease for not more than three years may be created by a simple oral or written agreement. However, there are certain requirements that must be satisfied:

- it must take effect in possession
- at the best rent which can be reasonably obtained without taking a fine or premium.

To take effect in possession means that the lease must begin at the date of grant and not at some date in the future. Even if the lease is for less than three years, it must be created by deed if it is to take effect in the future.

# CASE EXAMPLE

**_Long v Tower Hamlets Borough Council_ [1996] 2 All ER 683**

A lease was granted by the council to the claimants. This was confirmed by a letter which was dated 4th September, stating that the lease would take effect on 29th September. The judge held that this could not be a legal lease because it was to take effect in the future. This made it a reversionary lease and it could only have been granted by deed.

## 13.4.3 Contracts to create a lease for more than three years: equitable leases

Circumstances where an equitable lease might arise:

**1.** defects in the grant or transfer of a legal lease

**2.** failure to apply for substantive registration under the Land Registration Act 2002

**3.** a contract to create or transfer a leasehold term

**4.** a grant of a lease by the holder of an equitable estate.

409

Under 3, where the parties have entered into a contract for the grant of a lease for a term of more than three years but no deed is executed to create a legal lease, an equitable lease may arise on the basis of the contract.

- **Before 27th September 1989**: a contract to grant a lease for more than three years had to satisfy s 40 of the 1925 Act; this held that all leases had to be evidenced in writing. The doctrine of part-performance could also apply where there was no evidence in writing. This allowed a tenant who entered into possession on the basis of an oral contract to enjoy an equitable lease even though there was no written evidence of the new contract.
- **After 27th September 1989**: a contract to grant a lease for more than three years must satisfy s 2(1) of the Law of Property (Miscellaneous Provisions) Act 1989. Under this Act, the agreement must be in writing and it must incorporate all the terms the parties have expressly agreed and it must be signed by or on behalf of them. If the contract does not comply with the requirements of s 2(1), then there will be no equitable lease. The doctrine of part-performance no longer applies.

## 13.4.4 The doctrine of *Walsh v Lonsdale*

If the contract to grant a lease satisfies s 2(1) of the 1989 Act, then the lease may be enforceable in equity. The landlord may still be forced to grant the promised lease.

The reason such a lease may be enforceable is on equitable principles: 'equity looks on that as done which ought to be done'. Equity will therefore treat it as if there is a lease in existence. The parties are treated as having a lease in equity from the date of the contract. It depends on whether or not the contract is specifically enforceable.

The doctrine highlights the conflict between equity and common law. The common law would not uphold the lease but equity will allow the lease to be enforceable because it is quite clear what the parties had intended.

The rule was first established in the case of *Walsh v Lonsdale* (1862) 2 De G & J 559. This concerned an agreement for a lease of a mill. It had been executed in writing but not under deed, as required by law. The agreement held that rent was to be paid annually in advance, the actual amount would vary according to the success of the mill. The tenant moved into the mill and started paying rent on a six-monthly basis in arrears. The landlord accepted this for 18 months and then, without notice, demanded rent in advance, which was challenged by the tenant.

**Arguments in *Walsh v Lonsdale* for an equitable or legal lease**

| Equitable lease | Legal lease |
|---|---|
| The act of entering the property and paying rent supported the written agreement. | The tenant had an implied lease because he had possession of the property and paid rent. |
| The agreement was a written agreement not enforceable at law for a lease of seven years with rent payable in advance. | The lease would be an annual tenancy because the rent was paid at six-monthly intervals. |
| The lease would be enforceable in equity under equitable principles. | As rent had been paid and accepted in arrears, the law presumed that it was a term in the legal lease and the landlord could not change to claiming rent in advance. |

The courts applied the Judicature Acts which laid down that in the event of a conflict between equity and common law, equity should prevail. It meant that the lease was declared to be equitable. The landlord had distrained for the outstanding rent and this would have been illegal if the lease had been held to be legal.

(NB Distraining was a form of self-help remedy called distress. It allowed the landlord to come and take goods belonging to the tenant in satisfaction of the rent that was outstanding. This would not have been legal if the tenancy was a legal tenancy as the landlord could not claim the rent in advance in these cases.)

## When will specific performance be available?

Equity will not automatically grant specific performance. Certain conditions must first exist:

**1.** the agreement must be subject to the payment of rent or consideration

**2.** the agreement must be in writing in order to satisfy s 2(1) of the 1989 Act

**3.** the claimant must satisfy the requirement for 'clean hands'. This means that he must not have acted in a fraudulent or otherwise dishonest way. However, where there has been an attempt to rectify a defect such as non-payment of rent then the courts will uphold the right of the claimant.

It has been applied in a recent case:

ASE EXAMPLE

---

**R v Tower Hamlets LBC, ex p Von Goetz [1999] QB 1019**

A written lease for 10 years created an equitable estate. This should have been created by deed but the court held that it created a lease in equity which entitled the claimant to apply for a grant under the Local Government and Housing Act 1989. The council had refused the grant because it was merely an equitable interest.

---

The important factor in this case was that the court could have ordered specific performance of the agreement and forced the defendant to execute a deed to perfect the legal title of the claimant.

### The doctrine of *Walsh v Lonsdale* today

This doctrine applies to a much wider range of issues than merely leases:

**1.** the grant of easements

**2.** the grant of profits

**3.** the grant of a mortgage.

## 13.4.5 Is a *Walsh v Lonsdale* lease as good as a legal lease?

The doctrine of *Walsh v Lonsdale* converts an informal lease into a lease that is enforceable on the same terms as the original agreement.

### Does that mean that an equitable lease is as good as a legal lease?

1. **Effect of equitable leases against third parties**. If Jon grants a lease for five years to Ben in writing but not in the form of a deed then it will be enforceable as an equitable lease. If Jon sells to Sam then Sam will not be bound by the equitable lease unless he has notice of the lease and this depends on whether the lease has been registered. For unregistered land this would be as a Class C(iv) estate contract and for registered land it would be a burden on the register. In registered land it may also take effect as an overriding interest which does not require protection but the tenant must be in occupation of the property. Compare a legal lease which will be binding on any purchaser, and occupation will be irrelevant.

2. **Do the covenants run against the landlord?** If the lease exists in equity only then the rights and duties will not run automatically on assignment of the lease. They will normally run against the landlord on assignment but necessarily to the tenant.

**3.** Informally created rights may take effect in law under s 62 when the land passes under a conveyance. However the section is dependent on a conveyance and there will be no conveyance under an equitable lease. So easements will not automatically pass in equity whereas at common law if the right satisfies the tests necessary for an easement then the right will pass at common law.

**4.** The parties are dependent on the availability of specific performance. As mentioned above, unlike the common remedy of damages, specific performance is only available if certain conditions are satisfied.

# ACTIVITY

Consider the following statement: 'It is often said that an agreement for a lease is as effective as a legal lease'.

Do you agree?

## 13.5 The terms in a lease

Both the landlord and the tenant have obligations under the lease. These may be expressly or impliedly included in the lease, for example if the lease itself is implied such as an implied periodic tenancy then the covenants will be implied into that lease.

There are a number of covenants which are implied into every lease and most leases include a number of express covenants

## 13.5.1 The landlord's covenants

A number of covenants can be implied into the lease both at common law and also under statute.

Implied covenants:

- a covenant to allow the tenant quiet enjoyment
- a covenant that the landlord will not derogate from his grant
- a covenant that the premises are fit for the purpose for which they are let or are habitable.

### A covenant to allow the tenant quiet enjoyment

It is implied in every lease that the landlord shall allow the tenant quiet enjoyment of the premises let.

## KEY FACTS

### Quiet enjoyment

**1.** The tenant is guaranteed the right to enjoy the property without interference from anyone else claiming rights in the land, or anything interfering with enjoyment of the premises, such as allowing the roof to leak, or even allowing other tenants to interfere with enjoyment because they make excessive noise.

**2.** If the tenant can prove that he has been subjected to harassment or to unlawful eviction, this will constitute a breach of quiet enjoyment. The removal of windows and doors in *Lavender v Betts* [1942] 2 All ER 72 was sufficient, as were persistent threats which resulted in the tenant leaving in *Kenny v Preen* [1963] 1 QB 499; interfering with the supply of essential services in *Perera v Vandiyar* [1953] 1 WLR 672, where the landlord was held to be in breach of the covenant when he allowed the gas and electricity supply to be cut off repeatedly. This would now constitute an offence under the Protection from Eviction Act 1977.

**3.** The extent of the covenant: it does not extend to the condition of the property at the start of the lease. In *Southwark LBC v Mills* [1999] 3 WLR 939 the tenants in a block of flats owned by the council complained about the excessive noise from neighbouring flats. It was attributable to the poor quality of the soundproofing rather than the tenants themselves. The House of Lords did not find the Council to be in breach of its covenant for quiet enjoyment because the soundproofing was in place at the start of the tenancy.

**4.** If the breach merely causes inconvenience rather than genuine interference then that will not amount to a breach. In *Browne v Flower* [1911] 1 Ch 219 the tenant complained because an external staircase was erected by the landlord, allowing the tenants to look through the windows of the leased premises, but no breach of quiet enjoyment was found.

**5.** Breaches by third parties: the landlord may be liable to the tenant where the breach is committed by a third party who acts with the authorisation of the landlord but not for anyone acting in excess of the landlord's grant. So the landlord will not be liable for acts of other tenants unless they are acting in an unlawful manner.

**6.** Remedies: it is possible for the tenant to repudiate his lease but it is much more usual for damages or for an injunction to be awarded.

## A covenant that the landlord will not derogate from his grant

The general principle is that you must not take away that which you have given. So the landlord cannot take away from the tenant any rights that have been granted under the lease. There is an overlap with the covenant for quiet enjoyment but under this covenant it is possible to claim a breach where there is no physical interference with the premises.

## KEY FACTS

### Non-derogation from the grant

1. The character of the premises must not be changed by the landlord so that they cannot be used for the purposes of the tenancy. In *Aldin v Latimer Clark Muirhead & Co* [1894] 2 Ch 437 premises had been let to a timber merchant. The premises had a natural flow of air necessary for his business. This came from a neighbouring property also owned by the landlord. When the landlord blocked this up by building on the land it was held to be a derogation from the grant. In *Harmer v Jumbil (Nigeria) Tin Areas Ltd* [1921] 1 Ch 200 the tenant used the leased land to store explosives. Regulations controlling the grant of licences would not allow there to be storage of explosives too close to buildings. This effectively prevented the landlord from building on the other land as it would have resulted in the tenant losing his licence to store explosives if there were buildings too close to the storage site.

2. The tenant cannot claim if the landlord did not know about the tenant's intended use for the land. It must interfere with the use so as to make it impossible to use the land for the purpose at all. If it can be still used for the purpose but it is just more expensive or inconvenient, an injunction is less likely to be granted.

## A covenant that the premises are fit for the purpose that they are let or are habitable

1. There is no general warranty of fitness for purpose. This principle was repeated in *Southwark LBC v Mills*. The general rule is that of *caveat emptor*. ' . . . fraud apart there is no law against letting a tumble down house' Erle J in *Robbins v Jones* (1863) 15 CB (NS) 221).

2. If the premises are furnished, the common law implies a condition of fitness for habitation (*Smith v Marrable* (1843) 11 M & W 5). If the covenant is broken, the tenant has the right to leave immediately, without giving notice to the landlord. The covenant is very limited in scope as it only applies to residential premises at the start of the lease. Only the tenant can sue, which excludes members of his family or visitors.

3. **Duty of care under contract**: the landlord may be liable in contract for breach of an implied term. In *Liverpool City Council v Irwin* [1977] AC 239 a local council was found to be in breach of its contractual duty where it failed to keep certain common areas in a block of flats free from rubbish and debris.

4. **Negligence**: this is wider in ambit as it can bring in liability to members of the tenant family and visitors to the premises.

5. Under s 8 of the Landlord and Tenant Act 1985, if a house is let for human habitation at a low rent then there is an implied condition that it is fit for human habitation at the beginning of the tenancy and an implied undertaking that the landlord will maintain the premises in this condition throughout the tenancy. This rarely applies as the rent must be below £80 per year in London and £52 elsewhere, which has been criticised frequently by the judiciary. It was introduced in 1957. There are other restrictions on the use of the section: it cannot be used where the premises cannot be rendered fit for human habitation at reasonable expense.

6. Under s 11 of the Landlord and Tenant 1985, certain covenants relating to repair and maintenance are impliedly undertaken by the landlord in a lease of a dwelling house for a term of less than seven years. The landlord must keep in repair the structure and exterior of the dwelling house as well as drains, gutterings and external pipes and also maintain the installations of the building, supplying water, gas sanitation, including basins, baths etc and also for space heating and heating water. It is limited in effect. It would not extend to such matters as condensation. In *Quick v Taff Ely BC* [1986] QB 809 it was held that that was caused by faulty design rather than disrepair. 'Disrepair is related to the physical condition of whatever has to be repaired and not to questions of lack of amenity or inefficiency' (Dillon LJ).

*Express covenants*

Most leases will contain a wide range of covenants by the landlord in respect of such matters as repair, insurance, maintenance of the common parts and also allowing the tenant the option for renewal of the terms. In shorter leases the landlord will generally undertake to carry out more structural repairs. In longer leases the responsibility will fall on the shoulders of the tenant.

## 13.5.2 Implied covenants of the tenant

There are a number of obligations implied under law. These are called the 'usual covenants' and include the following:

1. **the tenant's covenant to pay rent**: it is possible to have a tenancy without the payment of rent so this is not implied automatically into every lease but it would usually be implied into most leases

2. **the tenant's covenant to pay rates and other taxes on the premises**: these include any rates or taxes for which the landlord is not responsible

3. **the tenant's liability for damage**: the tenant must not commit voluntary waste which means he must not commit an act or omission which alters the state of the premises. This would include changing the nature of the premises by carrying out internal work such as knocking down walls and taking out windows. The rules vary according to whether it is a weekly, monthly or yearly tenancy. Generally, all tenants must not carry out acts of voluntary waste but some tenants are responsible for permissive waste as well. This includes failing to act when it is clear that the premises are falling into disrepair

4. **a duty to allow the landlord in to view the premises**: the landlord has no automatic right of entry to the tenant's premises but the tenant must allow him to enter at a pre-arranged time if the landlord is under a duty to repair the premises.

The tenant may also have agreed expressly certain covenants in the lease itself:

- payment of rent
- not to assign, sub-let or part with possession.

These covenants can be either:

- absolute: not to sub-let at all or
- qualified: to sub-let only with the consent of the landlord.

The tenant can seek permission from the landlord where there is an absolute covenant against assignment but cannot take action if the landlord refuses. In a qualified covenant the landlord can refuse permission only if the refusal is reasonable: s 19 of the Landlord and Tenant Act 1927.

Section 1 of the Landlord and Tenant Act 1988 ensures that any request from the tenant to assign is dealt with quickly. The landlord has a duty to give consent unless it is reasonable to refuse to do so. The reasons for refusal must be given and if consent is given but subject to conditions then those conditions must be given. The tenant does have the power to create a licence which is often a way around the problem of gaining consent.

The courts regard an objection that is in some way related to the proposed assignee or to the use that he intends to make of the premises as an acceptable reason for withholding consent.

Refusal of consent must not come within the restrictions imposed by any of these statutes:

- s 24 of the Race Relations Act 1976
- s 31 of the Sex Discrimination Act 1975
- ss 22 and 23 of the Disability Discrimination Act 1995.

# ACTIVITY

Consider the following examples and advise whether there has been a breach of covenant by the landlord:

1. Janice has taken the tenancy of a flat in a block of 12 flats called Fabulous Mansions. She likes the flat but has become very annoyed because every night she can hear the television of her neighbours. The block was built in 1972.

2. Kerry has taken a ground-floor flat in Fabulous Mansions. She liked the fact that it was on the ground floor but now she has discovered that it is very damp and frequently there is heavy condensation running down the walls.

3. Lara has another flat in the block. She pays a very low rent. She has recently discovered that the bath has a large crack which had been covered up with Polyfilla.

All three tenants have complained about the frequent build-up of rubbish around the front door. The landlord, Mr Sleasy, has not replied to the complaints but they recently heard him shouting at one of the other tenants, saying that if she did not stop her complaints he would make sure she really did have a cause for complaint. They are now feeling very worried about their position and have come to you for advice.

# 13.6 Determination of leases

## 13.6.1 The effect of determination

When a lease is determined the tenant will no longer have an estate in land. The landlord will be entitled to recover the land immediately and the tenant will no longer have exclusive possession of the property.

If there is a joint tenancy it will be determined if only one tenant gives notice. This is because it has been held that in a joint tenancy there must be agreement between all the parties.

>  'all positive dealings with a joint tenancy require the concurrence of all joint tenants if they are to be effective'.
>
> Bridge LJ in *Hammersmith LBC v Monk* [1992] 1 AC 478

This has been interpreted to mean that if one periodic tenant indicates that he does not want the lease to continue then it will be determined, because a joint tenancy relies on agreement.

## CASE EXAMPLE

### *Hammersmith LBC v Monk* **[1992] 1 AC 478**

A couple took a periodic tenancy of a council flat. After some time, the relationship broke down and the woman moved out. The Council said that it would not re-house her unless she ended the tenancy she already held with it. The House of Lords held that she was able unilaterally to end the tenancy and so the Council could claim back the tenancy and she could be re-housed.

This was a fair decision because if the woman had to get her former partner's agreement he might refuse and she could not exert any pressure on him to do so.

## 13.6.2 Ways of determining a lease

Leases can be brought to an end in a number of different ways. Many of the old common-law means of ending a lease have been affected by the large number of statutory provisions which have been passed to protect tenants. (See Figure 13.1.)

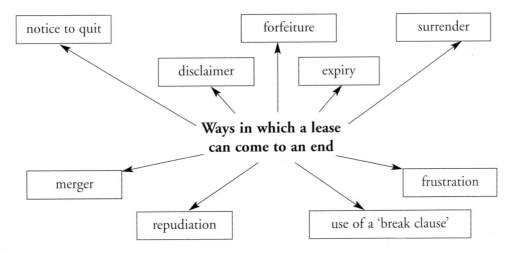

*Figure 13.1 Termination of leases and licences*

There are nine ways in which a lease can come to an end at common law:

**1. notice to quit**: either party can serve on the other a notice to quit which will indicate that they no longer wish the tenancy to continue. Generally, the length of notice required is the same length as the period of the tenancy

## APPLYING THE LAW

Jamil has a periodic tenancy in which he pays rent of £150 every month. If he wishes to end the tenancy he must give the landlord one month's notice and so must the landlord if he wishes to do the same.

2. **forfeiture**: if the tenant is in breach of any covenants in the lease then the landlord may be entitled to forfeit the lease; the landlord has to decide whether the lease is continuing or whether he wishes to treat it as forfeited

3. **surrender**: a lease can be determined by the surrender of the interest of the tenant to his immediate landlord. If the interest is expressly surrendered then it must be contained in a deed in order to comply with s 52(1) of the Law of Property Act 1925. In some cases the law implies surrender by the tenant. An example would be where the tenant gives up possession of the land subject to the tenancy. The doctrine of estoppel would come into operation if the tenant then contested the surrender and claimed to have the property returned to him. However, there must truly be surrender so if there is an uncompleted contract by the tenant to purchase the reversion of the lease but it is not completed there is no surrender by operation of law

4. **disclaimer**: a right to disclaim the lease usually arises under the lease itself or under statute. The most usual examples under statute occur when the trustees in bankruptcy and liquidators of companies disclaim what is termed 'onerous property' which they may have taken over in their role. The tenant would then be released from the tenant's obligations

5. **expiry**: a fixed-term lease or tenancy will automatically end when the term comes to an end

6. **merger**: if the tenant acquires the landlord's freehold interest then the tenancy will immediately come to an end

7. **a 'break clause'**: some leases may contain a clause which allows one party or even both parties to determine the lease on notice before the term expires

8. **frustration**: where frustration operates on the lease it destroys the whole basis of the agreement and so the tenancy comes to an end

9. **repudiation**: if there is a breach by either side that is sufficiently serious then the courts may allow the other party to repudiate the contract.

## 13.7 Remedies of the landlord

If the tenant is in breach of a covenant there are several possible remedies. There is a difference between breach for non-payment of rent and breach of other covenants.

## 13.7.1 Distress

This is available for non-payment of rent and can be enforced without court proceedings. This involves the landlord selling goods belonging to the tenant. The landlord goes onto the premises and takes the equivalent value of goods to the outstanding amount owed in rent. Some items cannot be seized, such as clothes and bedding. The remedy has ancient origins and was once used frequently by landlords. Although it is still in existence it has been criticised recently as representing a serious interference with human rights: 'The ancient . . . self-help remedy of distress involves a serious interference with the right of the tenant under Art 8 of the European Convention on Human Rights to respect for his privacy and home and under Art 1 of the First Protocol to the peaceful enjoyment of his possessions'. (Lightman J in *Fuller v Happy Shopper Markets Ltd* [2001] 1 WLR 1681). The Law Commission has recommended its abolition.

## 13.7.2 Forfeiture

Forfeiture is generally used in connection with non-payment of rent but it can also be used for other breaches of covenant. This is a very important remedy for the landlord. It gives him the right to re-enter the premises and recover the lease. He has two options:

* physical re-entry
* service of proceedings against the tenant.

Today, physical re-entry is not encouraged, even where it is peaceable.

ASE EXAMPLE

### *Billson v Residential Apartments Ltd* [1992] 1 AC 494

A landlord sought forfeiture against tenants who had undertaken works in breach of a repairing covenant in a lease. The landlord had broken into the premises early one morning, changing the locks and leaving notices to the effect that the lease had been forfeited. The House of Lords expressed disapproval of these actions and suggested that it would have been better had he served a writ.

The case suggests that although it is lawful to re-enter the premises, the landlord would be better taking action through the courts.

### When can forfeiture be exercised?

1. It is expressly contained in the lease.
2. It is a condition of the lease that there will be re-entry if the tenant fails to perform his obligations under the lease.

*Waiver*

Once there is breach, the landlord must decide whether to forfeit the lease or treat it as continuing. If he treats it as continuing or waives it, he cannot later attempt to forfeit the lease unless the breach is a continuing breach.

## Procedure

The procedure for forfeiture differs between cases concerning recovery for non-payment of rent and recovery for breach of other covenants.

*Non-payment of rent*

There must firstly be a formal rent demand, although under s 210 of the Common Law Procedure Act 1852 there is no necessity for a rent demand if there are six months' arrears outstanding and the goods on the premises available for distress are less than the amount needed to cover the rent.

The Protection from Eviction Act 1977 prevents forfeiture in the case of residential premises while someone is living at the premises.

Section 166 of the Commonhold and Leasehold Reform Act 2002 prevents forfeiture in the case of a long lease (one exceeding 21 years) of a dwelling against a tenant unless the unpaid amount exceeds the prescribed sum (specified as £500) or it has not been paid for a prescribed period. The section only applies to residential premises. It appears to reduce the availability of forfeiture against tenants in the future.

*Other breaches of covenants*

---

### KEY FACTS

**The s 146 notice**

1. The tenant must be in breach of a covenant other than for non-payment of rent.

2. The tenant must then be given the chance to remedy the breach or to apply for relief from forfeiture.

3. The notice will not be valid unless it specifies the breach.

4. It must require the tenant to remedy the breach if it is capable of being remedied.

5. It must require the tenant to pay compensation for the breach.

---

Under 146 of the Law of Property Act 1925, a notice must be served on the tenant.

Circumstances which do **not** invalidate a s 146 notice:

**1.** If the landlord does not want compensation then if it is left out of the notice that will not invalidate the notice.

## CASE EXAMPLE

### *Rugby School (Governors) v Tannahill* [1935] 1 KB 87

Premises owned by the school had been used for prostitution and it was held that the school did not have to require payment of compensation from the profits made.

**2.** If the breaches cannot be remedied then it will not invalidate the notice if the requirement to remedy them is left out: in *Rugby School (Governors) v Tannahill* it was held that the breach of a negative covenant was incapable of remedy. In this case the covenant was not to use the premises for illegal or immoral purposes. It is not always clear whether a breach can be remedied within a reasonable time.

## CASE EXAMPLE

### *Expert Clothing Service & Sales Ltd v Hillgate House Ltd* [1986] Ch 340

The covenant was to build premises within a limited time. This had not been done but the court held that it was still possible to remedy the breach by performing the covenant out of time. The court drew a distinction between positive covenants and negative covenants and held that it would be rare for positive covenants to be incapable of remedy.

## CASE EXAMPLE

### *Scala House and District Property Co Ltd v Forbes* [1974] QB 575

Where there had been breach of a covenant not to assign or sub-let the premises then it was held to be impossible to remedy such a breach. Russell LJ considered what was the position once the tenant had ceased to be in breach and held that the landlord was still able to pursue forfeiture proceedings and the tenant was able to attempt to seek relief.

Section 168 of the Commonhold and Leasehold Reform Act 2002 provides that in the case of a long lease of a dwelling a landlord may not serve under s 146 of the 1925 Act unless:

**a** the landlord has made an application to the leasehold valuation tribunal for determination of whether the breach of covenant has occurred, unless the issue has been referred to arbitration or the court

**b** the tribunal has decided that a breach has occurred or

**c** the tenant has admitted the breach.

*Breach of repairing covenants*

The Leasehold Property (Repairs) Act 1938 provides relief for tenants who are in breach of the repairing covenants.

---

## KEY FACTS

### The 1938 Act

1. The lease must be a lease for a term of seven years or more, not being an agricultural lease.
2. There are at least three years left to run.
3. The landlord must serve a s 146 notice on the tenant relating to a breach of covenant to keep the premises in repair.
4. The tenant has 28 days to serve a counter-notice.
5. If the tenant serves a counter-notice then the landlord cannot take further proceedings to re-enter the premises without the leave of the court.
6. If the landlord has already carried out the repairs (because he cannot wait for the tenant to act) then the court has no jurisdiction to pursue the tenant for damages. In *SEDAC Investments Ltd v Tanner* [1982] 1 WLR 1342 it was held that where the landlord had already carried out repairs then he lost his right to pursue the tenant under the repairing covenant. However, more recent cases, for example *Jervis v Harris* [1996] Ch 195, have allowed the landlord to claim the cost of the repairs from the tenant, otherwise this would restrict the rights of the landlord.

> 'The short answer to the question is that the tenant's liability to reimburse the landlord for his expenditure on repairs is not a liability in damages for breach of his repairing covenant [at all]. The landlord's claim sounds in debt not damages; and it is not a claim to compensation for breach of the tenant's covenant to repair, but the reimbursement of sums actually spent by the landlord in carrying out repairs himself'.
>
> Millett LJ in *Jervis v Harris*

# Tenants' relief against forfeiture

*Non-payment of rent*

**1.** If the tenant remedies the breach by paying the outstanding rent, the court has the power to reinstate the lease where it is just and equitable to do so.

**2.** The tenant has the power to apply to the court under s 212 of the Common Law Procedure Act 1852 and if all outstanding rent and costs are paid before judgment the tenant is entitled to have the proceedings stayed.

**3.** Under s 138(2) of the County Courts Act 1984 the tenant has the right to have proceedings terminated against him if all the rent arrears and also the costs are paid.

*Other breaches*

Under s 146(2) of the 1925 Act, the tenant is entitled to apply to the court for relief against forfeiture and where he is successful the court will restore the lease.

In *Billson v Residential Apartments Ltd* [1992] 1 AC 494 the court decided that relief would be available in the following circumstances:

| Relief available to a tenant under s 146(2) | Relief denied to a tenant under s 146(2) |
| --- | --- |
| The period prior to possession proceedings. The right to apply for relief arises as soon as the notice is served on the tenant. | Where final judgment has been given and it has not been appealed and is fully executed. |
| Where judgment has been given but has not been executed. | Where the tenant has delayed in seeking relief. |
| In *Billson* the right to relief remains available after the landlord had exercised peaceable re-entry without court order. | |

The court will not grant relief for trivial breaches, for example where there is a covenant against keeping pets and the tenant keeps a hamster in the kitchen, the court is unlikely to grant forfeiture to the landlord even though there has been a breach of a covenant.

# Reform

The Law Commission has proposed reform of the law on forfeiture in 1985 and also in 1994. In its *Report on Forfeiture of Tenancies* (Law Com No 142, 1985) the Commission's main criticisms of the system were that it was unjust and no longer had any coherence:

**1.** the system tried to incorporate two sets of rules – one for non-payment of rent and one for other breaches

2. there was no protection for anyone who derived title from the tenant, such as a sub-tenant or mortgagee

3. there was uncertainty over whether the landlord was going to exercise his discretion and waive the breach

4. there was always the possibility that the court would exercise its discretion and reinstate the lease following forfeiture.

As a result in 1995 a draft Bill was proposed, to contain the following provisions:

1. no distinction to be made between non-payment of rent and other breaches

2. every tenancy would remain in force until the court made a termination order that fixed the date on which the tenancy should end

3. termination would be granted on a wide range of grounds and it would no longer depend on whether there was provision for termination in the lease

4. the court would have the discretion either to grant the termination as requested or to make a remedial order which required the tenant to take remedial action within a timescale.

The Bill met with considerable opposition and has yet to be introduced into Parliament, although there are a number of changes made under the Commonhold and Leasehold Reform Act 2002 which have some impact on forfeiture.

## 13.7.3 Specific performance

The court has power to order specific performance but has shown a reluctance to do so, for example it is unwilling to order specific performance of a covenant to repair.

## 13.7.4 Injunction

The court has the power to grant an injunction but rarely uses it.

## 13.7.5 Damages

Damages may be awarded but only for a breach of a covenant other than non-payment of rent. They are assessed on a contractual basis.

## APPLYING THE LAW ☐☐☐

Mohammed rents a flat in Blackpool. His lease is for five years and includes a clause requiring him to keep the flat in good repair. The landlord has recently visited the flat and has noticed that the windows, which face directly on to the sea, are in a very poor state of repair. Mohammed has refused to undertake the work. He has now been served with a notice to quit and has left. The landlord will be entitled to recover the cost of the work but not in excess of the value of the decrease in the value of the property.

☐☐☐

# 13.8 Enforceability of covenants against third parties on assignment

The enforceability of covenants between the parties has so far depended on the question of what is expressly and what is impliedly covered in the lease. The next issue is whether a third party who receives the property by assignment is able to enforce the covenants against either the original landlord or an assignee.

## 13.8.1 Privity of estate and privity of contract

In leasehold covenants it is important to distinguish between

- privity of estate and
- privity of contract.

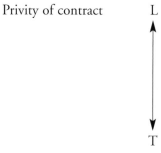

Privity of contract      L

                                       T

■ *Figure 13.2 Privity of contract in a lease*

In Figure 13.2 the landlord (L) has negotiated the lease with the tenant (T) and together they have privity of contract.

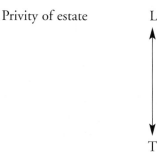

Privity of estate      L

                                       T

■ *Figure 13.3 Privity of estate in a lease*

In Figure 13.3 the landlord (L) has negotiated the lease with the tenant (T) and there is privity of estate as well as privity of contract.

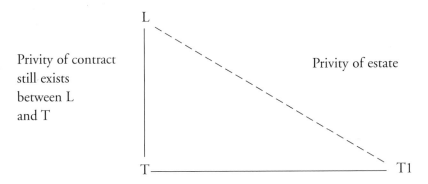

■ *Figure 13.4 Privity on assignment of a lease by the tenant*

In Figure 13.4 the lease has been assigned to T1. T1 now has privity of estate with L but not privity of contract, as he has not negotiated directly with L.

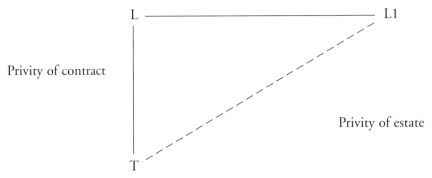

■ *Figure 13.5 Privity of assignment of a lease by the landlord*

In Figure 13.5 there is privity of estate between L1 and T but only privity of contract between L and T.

---

## KEY FACTS

### The nature of privity between a landlord and tenant

**1.** Privity of contract only exists between persons who are parties to a contract.

**2.** Privity of estate exists between the persons who are the current landlord and tenant.

**3.** Privity of estate only lasts while the parties are either landlord or tenant.

**4.** Privity of contract lasts while the parties are bound by the contract, so can last beyond their relationship as landlord and tenant.

It is always possible for a tenant to sub-let to a sub-tenant and there will then be privity of contract and estate between the sub-tenant and the lessee. There is no privity either of contract or of estate between the landlord and the sub-tenant.

There have been some important recent changes in this area of law under the Landlord and Tenant (Covenants) Act 1995. This applies to any tenancy granted after 1st January 1996. The old law applies to tenancies already in existence at that date.

## 13.8.2 The pre-1996 law on assignment of covenants

Before the 1995 Act was passed, the question of whether the benefit or burden of a covenant passed depended on:

**1.** whether there was privity of estate between the parties and

**2.** whether the covenant 'touched and concerned the land'.

The covenant may confer a benefit on one side and a burden on the other side. The law relating to the running of burdens and benefits has already been explored in relation to freehold covenants.

## APPLYING THE LAW

Asif takes a tenancy of Flat 4, Elgin Mansions. He expressly agrees that:

**1.** he will keep the interior of the flat in a good state of repair

**2.** he will not keep a dog

**3.** he will not assign or sub-let without the landlord's permission.

The landlord expressly agrees that he will keep the exterior of the property in a good state of repair and impliedly agrees that

**1.** he will grant the tenant quiet enjoyment, and

**2.** he will not derogate from the grant of the lease.

The landlord takes the burden of keeping the exterior in good repair and the tenant takes the benefit. Under the rules applicable to freehold covenants the burden will not run unless the covenant 'touches and concerns the land'. This is an old rule derived from *Spencer's Case* (1583) 5 Co Rep 16a which holds that the only covenants that can run at common law are those that touch and concern the land.

The test today is one laid down by Lord Oliver in *P & A Swift v Combined English Stores Group plc* [1989] AC 632:

**1.** Could the covenant benefit any owner of an estate in the land, as opposed to the particular original tenant?

**2.** Does the covenant affect the nature, quality, mode of user or value of the land?

**3.** Is the covenant expressed to be personal?

## ACTIVITY

Consider the following covenants and decide whether they 'touch and concern the land':

**1.** covenant by T not to keep a pet at the premises

**2.** covenant by T to keep the property in good repair

**3.** covenant by T to pay rent

**4.** covenant by T not to allow any trees to grow over six feet

**5.** covenant by L to renew the lease

**6.** covenant by L not to open a garage within two miles of the garage leased to T

**7.** covenant by L to ensure that the property is supplied with gas and electricity.

## CASE EXAMPLE

### *P & A Swift v Combined English Stores Group plc* [1989] AC 632

The lessee, A, in this case had in turn granted a sub-lease to B. B was actually connected with C who had entered into a covenant with A concerning the performance of certain covenants by B. When the reversion of the lease was assigned to D there was nothing expressly mentioned about the covenant of C in the assignment. B failed to pay the rent due and went into liquidation. The question was whether the landlord, D, could sue for the outstanding amount. It was held that the covenant undertaken by C was one that touched and concerned the land and could therefore run to D who could in turn enforce it.

If the covenant touches and concerns the land then it can be enforced by the assignee of a lease (T1) **or** they can be enforced against the assignee T1 and either can enforce against the landlord, L.

Under the old law, one of the difficulties was that the original tenant could still be liable under the principles of privity of contract even after he had assigned the lease. This meant that there was always the possibility that the tenant to whom he had assigned would default on the rent and then the original tenant would become liable himself for the outstanding amount.

## The position of the landlord: benefit of covenants

Under s 141 of the 1925 Act, on assignment of the reversion the landlord has the right to sue on all the covenants that have reference to the subject-matter of the lease, in other words covenants that touch and concern the land. This section only applies to leases granted before 1996.

## The position of the landlord: burden of covenants

Under s 142 of the 1925 Act, on assignment of the reversion, the burden of any covenant which has reference to the subject-matter of the lease passes. The burden passes whether or not there is privity of estate. This section only applies to leases granted before 1996.

The law is slightly different for an equitable lease. The benefits and burdens did not automatically run to the tenant since he did not have a legal estate in land.

The right to enforce a covenant may be expressly assigned under an equitable lease but the burden would not and only the original tenant would be liable for a breach of a covenant.

# 13.8.3 The post-1996 law on assignment of covenants

The Landlord and Tenant (Covenants) Act 1995 (LTCA 1995) applies to all leases, whether they are legal or equitable, made after 1st January 1996.

### Main provisions of the 1995 Act

| | |
|---|---|
| The tenant is automatically released from the burden of leasehold covenants on assignment of the tenancy although he may be asked to guarantee performance of the covenant of the next assignee. | s 5 LTCA 1995 |
| The tenant may be asked to enter into an authorised guarantee agreement as a condition to an assignment of the lease. The tenant guarantees the performance of the covenants by the assignee. If the new tenant (T1) himself assigns to T2 the T is released but T1 may have to enter into an authorised guarantee agreement. | s 16 LTCA 1995 |
| The original landlord is not released automatically from the burdens of leasehold covenants but may serve notice for release. | s 8 LTCA 1995 |

| The rule that covenants must touch and concern the land or have reference to the subject-matter of the lease is abolished. | s 2 LTCA 1995 |
|---|---|
| The benefit and burdens of the lease will automatically pass to the assignees of the lease and the reversion unless they are expressed to be personal or held not to be binding on the assignor. | s 7 LTCA 1995<br>s 3 LTCA 1995 |
| The transfer of the benefit of a covenant to an assignee of the landlord does not deprive the assignor of the right to sue in respect of breaches occurring before the assignment. | s 24 LTCA 1995 |

In relation to commercial leases there is an extension to s 19 of the Landlord and Tenant Act 1927 under s 22 of LTCA 1995. This allows a measure of control for the landlord over assignments of the lease by the tenant. The law allows the landlord the right to withhold consent in specified circumstances. The new provisions allow the parties to enter into an agreement specifying the circumstances in which the landlord may withhold consent, for example the landlord can request that the new tenant shall provide certain financial guarantees before the assignment is made.

# ACTIVITY

Consider the following situation:

Some years ago Alison wanted to set up her own business as a beauty consultant. She saw the ideal premises in November 1995 and took a lease for 10 years. The lease contained covenants not to assign or sub-let without the landlord's consent in writing, to keep the premises in good repair and not to use them for illegal or immoral purposes. There was a forfeiture clause.

In 2000 Alison decided that she wanted a change of scene and she assigned the lease to Angela, without gaining the landlord's consent. Angela has been using the premises as an agency for 'escorts for businessmen'. The landlord has recently found this out and when he visited the premises he found that it was in a very poor state of repair.

Please advise the landlord on what can be done about the breaches of covenant.

The Landlord and Tenant Act 1988 introduced a number of changes to assist the tenant seeking permission to assign. The Act requires the landlord to respond to the tenant 'within a reasonable time'. The landlord is required to give reasons for the refusal, in writing. The Act places the burden of proof on the landlord, who must move that his decision was reasonable.

## Further reading

Bright, S, 'Beyond Sham and into Pretence' [1991] 11 OJLS 138.

Bright, S, 'Uncertainty in leases: Is it a vice?' (1993) 13 Legal Studies 38.

Smith, P F, 'What is wrong with Certainty in leases?' [1993] Conv 461.

Smith, P F, 'An Uncertain Shift' [1998] Conv 326.

Walter, P, 'The Landlord and Tenant (Covenants) Act 1995: A Legislative Folly' [1996] Conv 432.

Walton, P, 'Landlord's Distress Past its Sell By Date' [2000] 64 Conv 508.

## chapter 14 ADVERSE POSSESSION

## 14.1 Introduction

Once you have purchased property according to the legal formalities and rules, you are recognised by the law as the legal owner. This should mean that you can be reassured that the only way the legal estate will pass into the hands of another is if you take the initiative by:

**1.** selling the property

**2.** giving the property to another during your lifetime

**3.** leaving it to someone under your will

**4.** mortgaging the property

**5.** creating a legal lease.

So, under 4, if you do not repay the sum borrowed under the mortgage, the mortgagee (the lender) has the right to take possession of the property.

However, that is not the full story as in certain circumstances someone whom we might regard as a mere trespasser with no legal right to be on the property can simply lay claim to rights of possession over your land if they satisfy certain conditions.

### 14.1.1 The Limitation Act 1980

The law has long recognised the rights of others to take over your property if you, as owner, do not assert ownership over a long period of time. We can own personal property such as a valuable painting and leave it in a bank vault for years but it will not undermine ownership. Land is treated differently. It was thought that land is too valuable simply to ignore it.

Therefore the law recognised the rights of others to come and take over the property and if they treated it as their own for a long period of time then they could claim it for themselves. The law refers to those persons as 'squatters'. They are strictly trespassers until they satisfy the conditions required to claim the title.

> **J** 'Those who go to sleep on their claims should not be assisted by the courts in recovering their property'.
>
> *RB Policies at Lloyd's v Butler* [1950] 1 KB 76

Section 15(1) of the Limitation Act 1980 provides that: 'no action shall be brought by any person to recover any land after the expiration of 12 years from the date on which the right of action accrued to him, or if first accrued to some person through whom he claims, to that person'. This means that once 12 years have elapsed the squatter can argue that he now has rights in the property because he has treated it as if it were his own for over 12 years and the paper title owner has not objected.

## 14.1.2 Why allow adverse possession at all?

**1.** It would be very harsh on someone who occupies land for a long period of time and improves it, only to find that his claim cannot be upheld.

**2.** Land should not be withdrawn from the market and removed from general circulation. Land must remain marketable.

**3.** The law should protect defendants from stale claims by landowners.

Martin Dockray argued strongly in favour of upholding adverse possession. One of his arguments was that it helps to encourage better care of natural resources.

> 'It is arguable that it is in the public interest to promote the full use of neglected natural resources and that it is desirable that a fixed time limit should exist to encourage the improvement and development of land which might otherwise lie abandoned or under exploited for many years. For example, someone may have abandoned land many years ago and someone else may have started to use the land – possibly for limited purposes at first – and eventually taken possession of it . . . if the occupant is perpetually barred from dealing with the land as owner, there is a danger that the property will not be utilised to best advantage. This seems highly undesirable'.

M Dockray, 'Why do we need Adverse Possession?' [1985] Conv 272

These arguments are not supported by everyone. Indeed, the doctrine of adverse possession has been criticised by many, including the Law Commission. These criticisms are now reflected in the extensive changes to the law on adverse possession brought about by the Land Registration Act 2002.

## 14.1.3 The Land Registration Act 2002

To allow others to assert claims over your land does not seem fair to the landowner with the paper title who has paid for property and believes that it is still his own. One of the recommendations of the Law Commission (*Land Registration for the 21st Century: A Consultative Document* (Law Com No 254, 1998)) was to modify the rules on adverse possession. As a result, it is far more difficult for anyone to try to claim property of another as their own, simply through long use and enjoyment.

435

Under the Land Registration Act 2002, the paper title owner is better protected from squatters trying to assert rights of ownership over his property. The 'paper title owner' is the owner at law of the property. If it is registered land then he will be registered on the Proprietorship Register at the Land Registry.

The paper title owner has to be notified before the squatter can try to register his rights. This notification then puts the paper title owner on notice that the squatter is trying to gain rights in his land. He will then try to take action to ensure that the squatter is evicted. It is anticipated that there will be far fewer successful claims to adverse possession as a result of the 2002 Act.

## 14.1.4 The meaning of 'adverse possession'

'Adverse possession' means that rights of ownership in land are acquired by simply taking possession of the land. No money passes hands and there is no formal conveyance.

The claimant must satisfy **three** main requirements before the rights are gained in the land:

**1.** he must show that he had **factual possession** of the land

**2.** he must show that he had the necessary **intention** to defeat the interests of the owner

**3.** both factual possession and intention to possess must have been exercised **over a sufficient length of time**.

The THREE elements to prove are:

• factual possession

• intention to possess

• sufficient length of time.

## 14.2 Factual possession

The claimant must take physical possession of the land. Time will only begin to run against the paper title owner from the date that the paper title owner was dispossessed or discontinued possession and the claimant took possession.

> 'In English law, the basis of title to land is possession. Possession of land by itself gives a title to the land good against the whole world except a person with a better right to possession. If X takes possession of A's land, X has a title which will avail against all save A; a title acquired by wrong is still a title. X has a fee simple, and so has A; but all titles are relative, and so although X's fee is good A's is better. If, however, A fails to take steps to recover the land in due time, his claim will be barred by limitation, and X's fee, freed from the superior claims of A's fee, will be good against all the world'.

*Megarry's Manual of the Law of Real Property* (Sweet & Maxwell, 2002), p 548

## 14.2.1 What constitutes factual possession?

There are certain consistent features required in factual possession:

**1.** the claimant must intend to **exclude all others** including the paper title owner

**2.** the claimant must be in factual possession for an **unbroken period of time**

**3.** the factual possession must be **openly exercised**

**4.** the factual possession must be **adverse to the paper title owner**.

### The claimant must intend to exclude all others

Physical control of the property depends on the type of property involved. If it is a very small area of land, then very clear evidence of physical control is necessary. In these cases other evidence is needed. If the adverse possessor puts up signs which attempt to exclude trespassers then the signs will be evidence of factual possession. Fencing constitutes the most conclusive proof of possession and shows an intention to exclude all others but it is not always possible to fence all the boundaries of the area if it is very large.

## CASE EXAMPLE

### *Red House Farms (Thornden) Ltd v Catchpole* [1977] 2 EGLR 125

The area claimed to be adversely possessed was very large and shooting wildfowl was held to be a sufficient act of possession because that was the only purpose for which the land could be used. Fencing would be impossible.

## CASE EXAMPLE

### *Powell v McFarlane* (1979) 38 P & CR 452

A claim for adverse possession was made on behalf of a boy of 14. He had kept a cow, which he named Kashla, on a large open space. The boy used the land as his own in the following ways:

* he cut and took a hay-crop

* he superficially repaired the boundary fences

* he cut back brambles and cut down trees, including a large number of Christmas trees

* he put in his cow and several goats and later more cows to graze

* he put in a rudimentary water supply

* he also did some shooting over the land.

Although there were numerous acts, Slade J thought that the acts themselves were equivocal and could be interpreted as mere temporary use rather than showing an intention to possess. They were not sufficient to support a claim for adverse possession as he thought they did not show that the boy intended to possess the land for himself:

> 'In the case of open land, absolute physical control is normally impracticable, if only because it is generally impossible to secure every part of a boundary so as to prevent intrusion . . . everything must depend on the particular circumstances, but broadly, I think what must be shown as constituting factual possession is that the alleged possessor has been dealing with the land in question as an occupying owner might have been expected to deal with it and that no-one else has done so'.
>
> Slade J

Slade J accepted that the whole area did not need to be fenced but when he analysed the facts in support of factual possession in this case, he found that they could simply establish temporary enjoyment of the property rather than indicate ownership.

# CASE EXAMPLE

### Buckinghamshire County Council v Moran [1990] Ch 623

The land had been acquired by the County Council because it wanted to construct a road diversion. However, although it fenced the land from the road, the boundaries to several properties were left open. The adverse possessor had cultivated a piece of land which belonged to Bucks County Council and which was next to his garden. His successor in title fenced it and also put in a gate which he had both chained and padlocked. This was considered to be very clear evidence of factual possession. The property had been occupied by several different owners each of whom had continued to cultivate the land, and eventually Mr Moran bought it. The County Council wrote one letter to him complaining about the actions taken and disputing the rights of the adverse possessor. The court found that Moran had 'complete and exclusive physical control' of the land belonging to the Council.

## The factual possession must be for an unbroken period of time

If one person dies or sells the property, it is important that there should be no break in the claim to adverse possessory rights over the land.

Adverse possessory rights can be left by will or pass under intestacy; they can also pass with the conveyance of the legal title to the rest of the land.

# CASE EXAMPLE

### *Buckinghamshire County Council v Moran* **[1990] Ch 623**

The property changed hands several times before eventually it came into the lands of Mr Moran; the claim over the additional land passed each time with the purchase. However, there were no breaks in the possession of the property.

If there is any break in the period of possession, the limitation period ceases to run. It does not prevent the limitation period from starting again if the squatter shows the necessary intent.

## APPLYING THE LAW

Ashwin has taken possession of a strip of land which belongs to his neighbour, Imran. The strip borders his garden. He cultivates it for six years and then sells his property to John, who ignores the strip. John then becomes aware that Ashwin has been cultivating it and he starts to work on it. There is nothing to stop him from acquiring rights over the land but time will only run from the time when he restarts the cultivation. The six years of cultivation when the land was owned by Ashwin will not count.

## The factual possession must be openly exercised

It must be possible for the paper title owner to find out about the presence of the squatters and if they deliberately conceal themselves when the paper title owner visits the property then time would not run. If the paper title owner sees squatters in possession then he would be expected to take action to evict them and if he does not then he could not expect the law to protect him.

> 'This requirement of transparency or visibility ensures that the paper title owner is given every opportunity of challenging the possession before it can ripen into an unimpeachable title'.

*Quote this*

Gray and Gray, *Elements of Land Law* (3rd edn, Butterworths, 2001), p 263

It does not matter, however, that the paper title owner is unaware of the fact that the squatter has taken possession. It is just important that it would be clear if the owner visited the property.

## The factual possession must be adverse to the paper title owner

Occupation of the land with the permission of the owner or under some lawful right is not adverse. So where occupation is under a **licence** or even a **lease**, that is not adverse to the owner and the time in occupation cannot be used as evidence of adverse possession.

It is different in those cases where the claimant once had permission to possess the land; he can show that the position has now changed and the possession is now adverse to the owner because the lawful permission has been withdrawn.

## APPLYING THE LAW

Elise and Patience are given a six-month lease of a small cottage on a large estate in Cornwall. Their landlord, Henry, decides to sell to Thomas, who lives for much of the time in Los Angeles. When the lease ends Elise and Patience continue to live in the property and no one claims rent from them. This could be considered to be evidence of adverse possession but only running from the moment when they ceased to be tenants at the end of the six-month lease.

It may also be possible to argue that the terms of the original licence were different from the rights that you are seeking to exercise.

# CASE EXAMPLE

### *Pye (Oxford ) Ltd v Graham* [2001] Ch 804

Pye owned a number of fields adjoining a farm owned by Graham. At first the Grahams used the fields under a written licence given by Pye in 1984. The Grahams requested that those licences be extended in 1986 but the request was not answered. The Grahams continued to use the land from 1986 until 1997 when Mr Graham registered a caution against the property based on his rights under adverse possession. Pye challenged this, arguing that the Grahams had not gained rights under adverse possession. The case was decided in the Grahams' favour by the High Court but the judgment was reversed by the Court of Appeal. The House of Lords upheld the decision of Neuberger J in the High Court and held that the Grahams had established rights over the land.

## KEY FACTS

### *Pye (Oxford) Ltd v Graham*

1. The judgment of the **Court of Appeal**: this was based on the fact that Graham had not got sufficient intention to possess the land. The fact that he had requested further licences suggested that he understood that the land belonged to Pye and therefore he could not use the land without Pye's permission. He admitted that he would have been willing to pay for the use of the land under licence.

2. The **House of Lords** reversed this decision on the basis that the licences were never granted and so the Grahams were in factual possession of the land from 1986. Further, they had sufficient intention because at all times they intended to show an intention to use the land for their own benefit. It was argued on behalf of Pye that the Grahams had been willing to pay for the land and therefore there could be no adverse possession but this was not accepted by the House of Lords. The fact that the land was still used by the squatters proved a continuing intention to treat the land as their own.

Contrast the following case:

# CASE EXAMPLE

### *BP Properties Ltd v Buckler* (1987) 55 P & CR 337

Here, the owner of land granted the squatter a licence to occupy the land. The licence was sent by letter addressed to Mrs Buckler, who was the squatter. The letter was ignored by Mrs Buckler, who continued to live in the property. The question was whether she became a licensee when she ignored the letters that were sent to her.

'The nature of Mrs Buckler's possession after receipt of the letters cannot be decided just by looking at what was locked up in her own mind. It must depend even more, on this aspect of the case, on the position as seen from the standpoint of the person with the paper title . . . The rule that "possession is not adverse if it can be referred to a lawful title" applies even if the person in possession did not know of the lawful title; the lawful title would still preclude the person with the paper title from evicting the person in possession. So far as Mrs Buckler was concerned, even though she did not "accept" the terms of the

letters, BP Properties Ltd would in the absence of any repudiation by her of the two letters, have been bound to treat her as in possession as licensee on the terms of the letters'.

The interesting effect of this is that if BP Properties had wanted to evict Mrs Buckler, it could not do so without first determining her licence, as she was lawfully in the property. She was not a trespasser. In any ordinary case of a squatter then the landowner can simply go to court and claim the land because the squatter is a trespasser.

## The doctrine of implied licence

Before the Limitation Act 1980 was passed it was possible for an owner to use this doctrine to defend claims. The paper title owner could argue that the land was left unused for a period of time but that he had a clear use in mind for the future and so the squatter could not claim rights over the land because he had an 'implied licence' from the owner. The squatter could show clear evidence of both factual possession and an intention to treat the land as his own but the claim would be rejected because the use made by the squatter did not interfere with the future use of the land.

### Leigh v Jack (1879–80) LR 5 Ex D 264

'In order to defeat a title by dispossessing the former owner, acts must be done which are inconsistent with his enjoyment of the soil for the purposes for which he intended to use it: that is not the case here, where the intention of the plaintiff . . . was not either to build upon or cultivate the land, but to devote it at some future time to public purposes'.

Bramwell LJ

### Wallis's Cayton Holiday Camp v Shell-Mex and BP [1975] QB 94

In this case Lord Denning upheld the principle that where the land was occupied by another who had no plans for its immediate use, that occupation could be said to be with licence. This would not be expressly given by the owner.

Under Schedule 1, para 8(4) to the Limitation Act 1980, the doctrine of implied licence has been overturned:

> **S** 'For the purpose of determining whether a person occupying any land is in adverse possession of the land it shall not be assumed by implication of law that his occupation is by permission of the person entitled to the land merely by virtue of the fact that his occupation is not inconsistent with the latter's present or future enjoyment of the land'.

The County Council tried to argue the doctrine of implied licence in *Buckinghamshire County Council v Moran* (1990) but this was rejected.

---

## KEY FACTS

**Factual possession**

1. Acts constituting factual possession will vary according to the type of land.
2. The consistent features of adverse possession are that the claimant must openly exclude all others in a way that is adverse to the paper title owner for an unbroken period of time.
3. Where the area claimed is small then acts constituting factual possession must be very clear.
4. Fencing is very good evidence of factual possession.
5. Some acts, such as grazing animals on open land, are equivocal and may not be sufficient to support a claim for adverse possession.
6. The doctrine of implied licence has been removed by the Limitation Act 1980.
7. The grant of a legal right to be on the land will be contrary to the claim for adverse possession.

---

# 14.3 The intention to possess

The squatter must prove that at all times he had the intention to treat the land as his own.

> **J** '... the intention, in one's own name and on one's own behalf, to exclude the world at large, including the owner with the paper title ... so far as is reasonably practicable and so far as the processes of the law will allow'.
>
> Slade J in *Powell v McFarlane* (1979) 38 P & CR 452

## 14.3.1 Proving intention to possess

The squatter must make it clear to the world that he intends to possess the land. He must show *animus possidendi*. The court will look at the conduct of the claimant and decide whether that is indicative of intention. Of course, it is very easy for the claimant to give evidence that he had the intention to possess the land.

The court needs evidence that the claimant regarded the land as belonging to him.

> J
> 'The position, however, is quite different from a case where the question is whether a trespasser has acquired possession. In such a situation the courts will, in my judgment, require clear and affirmative evidence that the trespasser, claiming that he has acquired possession, not only had the requisite intention to possess, but made such intention clear to the world'.
>
> Slade J in *Powell v McFarlane*

Slade J considered the way that the boy treated the land and decided that his treatment of the land did not prove that he intended to own the land. He was influenced by the boy's age and the fact that he appeared to use the land simply for convenience rather than with the firm intention that the land should become his own. He argued that when the boy got older he was capable of forming such an intention because by then he had started his own business and he treated the land as part of the land for that business.

The squatter need only prove an intention to possess and not necessarily an intention to acquire the property.

## APPLYING THE LAW  ☐☐☐

Richard and Joanna bought a cottage bordering on land owned by the Council. At the back of their property there is no fence or hedge and they can walk straight on to the open land. They have a very small garden and, being keen supporters of the organic movement, they want to grow their own vegetables. They decide to use a strip of land to grow potatoes and other vegetables. Gradually, they take in a further strip of the Council land to extend their vegetable patch. The Council mows the grass of the rest of the land but the strip is ignored. If Richard and Joanna use the strip of land for 12 years then they may have evidence of an intention to possess the land. It is irrelevant that they only wanted to possess the land for the present and did not think about acquiring rights in the property.

☐☐☐

In *J A Pye (Oxford) Ltd v Graham* the House of Lords held that the Grahams had the necessary intention because they showed that they maintained the land and used it as their own along with the rest of their farm property:

> **J** 'there has always both in Roman law and in common law, been a requirement to show an intention to possess in addition to objective acts of physical possession. Such intention may be, and frequently is, deduced from the physical acts themselves. But there is no doubt in my judgment that there are two separate elements in legal possession. So far as English law is concerned intention as a separate element is obviously necessary. Suppose a case where A is found to be in occupation of a locked house. He may be there as a squatter, as an overnight trespasser, or as a friend looking after the house of the paper owner during his absence on holiday. The acts done by A in any given period do not tell you whether there is legal possession. If A is there as a squatter he intends to stay as long as he can for his own benefit: his intention is an intention to possess. But if he only intends to trespass for the night or has expressly agreed to look after the house for his friend he does not have possession. It is not the nature of the acts which A does but the intention with which he does them which determines whether or not he is in possession'.
>
> Lord Browne-Wilkinson

Lord Browne-Wilkinson shows that mere presence on property can have several different implications and does not necessarily mean that someone is there with an intention to possess the property and yet in all cases they may treat the property in the same way.

## 14.3.2 Conduct indicating an intention to possess

Any conduct that indicates a clear intention to possess will be enough. In many cases the evidence establishing an intention to possess will be the same as the evidence that establishes factual possession.

These are some examples of intention to possess:

### Notices

If the squatter moves in and then puts up notices which say 'Keep out – private property' this will be evidence of an intention to possess. However, the notices must be enforced and if the notices are put up but people continue to enter and use the land it will not be evidence of intention to possess.

## APPLYING THE LAW

Russell has started to cultivate an area of land that borders his garden and which is owned by the Council. He plants vegetables and around the boundaries which do not border his property he plants shrubs and bushes. People often walk on the land, believing it to be public property. After 18 months Russell decides to erect two notices at either end of the strip, indicating that it is private property. The next week, he sees a party of walkers on the strip. If he ignores them then the notices cannot be claimed as evidence of factual possession but if he goes out and argues with them and asks them to leave then the notices are very good evidence of factual possession.

### Fences and locked gates

In *Buckinghamshire County Council v Moran* the fact that the squatter had put up fencing and a gate and had then locked the gate was sufficient for the claimant to show an intention of possess. This was also evidence in support of a claim for factual possession. The court was also persuaded by the evidence that the squatter had started to cultivate the land, putting in bulbs and rose bushes.

### Changing the locks

## CASE EXAMPLE

### *Lambeth LBC v Blackburn* [2001] 33 **HLR 74**

If the squatter changes the locks of the property there is clear evidence that he intends to treat it as his own and to exclude the paper title owner from the land.

### Examples of acts disclosing an intention to possess

| | |
|---|---|
| Notices 'Keep out – private property' | |
| Fences and locked gates | *Buckinghamshire County Council v Moran* (1990) |
| Changing the locks | *Lambeth LBC v Blackburn* (2001) |

Some examples of acts disclosing no intention to possess:

## Transient and trivial acts

If the acts are transient, they cannot be sufficient evidence. Most of the acts carried out by the claimant in *Powell v McFarlane* were considered by the courts to be transient.

ASE EXAMPLE

> **Tecbild v Chamberlain (1969) 20 P & CR 633**
>
> The acts relied on were all relatively trivial and included tethering horses and grazing goats and also allowing children to play on the land. Whenever the children and animals were away from the land it would be impossible to know that they had an intention to possess the property.

## Fencing

Even fencing can be equivocal. It is always possible that the intention to own the land is lacking. A fence can be put up to keep the public out and may not be evidence of an intention to possess.

ASE EXAMPLE

> **Fruin v Fruin (1983) Court of Appeal transcript 448**
>
> The claim of the squatter was unsuccessful because, although a fence was erected, it was put up chiefly for the purpose of keeping in a senile member of the family who wandered away from the house from time to time, rather than with the intention of acquiring rights over the land.

## Age of the claimant

Considerable weight was placed on the fact that the claimant was relatively young in *Powell v McFarlane*. This does not mean that a young person, even a child, could not have an intention to possess but it does mean that a much higher standard of proof of intention will be required for a child.

## Equivocal acts

Some acts are equivocal: this means that they could be interpreted in at least two ways. They could be referable to an intention to possess and equally they could be evidence of present enjoyment with no thought about a future intention to possess. Where they have more than one interpretation, the courts are going to require very clear evidence that they are referable to the acquisition of rights to the land.

In *Powell v McFarlane* Slade J decided that the acts carried out by the boy were not sufficiently compelling evidence of his intention to acquire rights in the land rather than just present enjoyment. This view has been subject to criticism since it appears to place a very heavy burden indeed on the adverse possessor.

## ACTIVITY

Calum lives in Durham where he owns a large house and garden. He spends a lot of time in London and abroad as he is a travel writer. His next-door neighbour, Deirdre, uses part of his garden as a vegetable patch.

In the winter the patch lies empty but during the summer she plants all kinds of vegetables. Most years Calum spends Christmas in Durham and usually takes the opportunity to walk around the large garden. He does not notice that some of the land has clearly been tended. He is no gardener and uses contract gardeners to cut the grass once a week in the summer.

Has Deirdre shown sufficient intention to possess the land?

What other acts could also lead the court to think that she has sufficient intention?

**Acts disclosing no intention to possess**

| Acts of the adverse possessor | Case |
| --- | --- |
| Trivial acts such as children playing on the land; occasional grazing of animals. | *Powell v McFarlane* (1979) *Tecbild v Chamberlain* (1969) |
| Fencing without the intention of keeping the public out. | *Fruin v Fruin* (1983) |
| Age of the claimant: the younger the claimant, the harder it is to show intention. | *Powell v McFarlane* (1979) |
| Equivocal acts which can be interpreted in at least two ways cannot easily support an intention to possess. | *Powell v McFarlane* (1979) |

# 14.4 Possession for sufficient length of time

The squatter cannot acquire rights over land until he has occupied the land for a sufficient length of time. The law was earlier governed by the Limitation Act 1980. The Land Registration Act 2002 now applies different periods of time for any land with registered title, so the Limitation Act 1980 is largely redundant except in relation to the relatively small number of properties which continue to have unregistered title.

## 14.4.1 The Limitation Act 1980

's 5 **Time limit for actions founded on simple contract**

An action founded on simple contract shall not be brought after the expiration of six years from the date on which the cause of action accrued'.

This section may apply where land is subject to contract and there has been an exchange of contracts and there is an error on the face of the contract or the landlord is suing for outstanding rent from a tenant.

's 15(1) **Time limit for actions to recover land**

No action shall be brought by any person to recover any land after the expiration of twelve years from the date on which the right of action accrued to him or, if it first accrued to some person through whom he claims, to that person'.

The key issue here is to decide when the right to bring the action arises. There are two conditions to consider:

1. if 12 years have passed, the paper title owner loses his right to recover his land

2. the 12 years runs from the time when the right of action arose. This would be when the paper title owner is dispossessed and the squatter takes possession. The paper title owner could have discontinued use of the land sometime previously but the right of action for the squatter only arises when he takes possession.

## APPLYING THE LAW

Henry owns a large estate in Yorkshire. He works in New York and rarely spends much time there. He has an estate manager who is responsible for the land while he is away. Frank's market garden is on the edge of Henry's estate. Frank may look at Henry's land and form an intention in his mind to acquire rights for himself but that will not be enough. If Frank uses part of Henry's garden for himself then time will run from the day when Frank goes on to the land with the intention to possess it for himself. So the day when he starts to cultivate it will be the day when time begins to run against Henry.

## 14.4.2 The Land Registration Act 2002

This Act radically changes the rules on adverse possession in relation to registered land so that under the Act no period of limitation under s 15 of the Limitation Act 1980 shall run in relation to a registered estate in land.

The 2002 Act effectively abolishes the concept of adverse possession in relation to registered land. The registered title owner can no longer be said to 'lose title' under the rules of adverse possession.

's 96(1) No period of limitation under section 15 of the Limitation Act 1980 . . . shall run against any person, other than a chargee, in relation to an estate in land or rentcharge the title to which is registered'.

Under the 2002 Act there is provision for a squatter to apply to the Registrar to be registered as proprietor of a registered estate if he has been adverse possession of that estate for 10 years.

'Schedule 6, paragraph (1) A person may apply to the registrar to be registered as the proprietor of a registered estate in land if he has been in adverse possession of the estate for the period of ten years ending on the date of the application'.

Proof of adverse possession will be on the established rules. Notification of the application is given to the paper title owner and also others with an interest in the land:

'Schedule 6, paragraph (2) The registrar must give notice of an application under paragraph 1 to:

(a) the proprietor of the estate to which the application relates,

(b) the proprietor of any registered charge on the estate,

(c) where the estate is leasehold, the proprietor of any superior registered estate,

(d) any person who is registered in accordance with rules as a person to be notified under this paragraph, and

(e) such other persons as rules may provide'.

Proof will be on the same basis as the old law:

* evidence of factual possession
* evidence of an intention to possess.

This is the first step in an application for registration of rights. The registered proprietor then has two years to object to the squatter's application. If there is no objection from the registered proprietor during the two years, the squatter's application will be completed.

If the registered proprietor does object, the squatter's application to be registered will be rejected unless one of three exceptions applies:

'Schedule 6, paragraph 5(1) ... the applicant is only entitled to be registered as the new proprietor of the estate if any of the following conditions is met.

(2) The first condition is that –

(a) it would be unconscionable because of an equity by estoppel for the registered proprietor to seek to dispossess the applicant, and

(b) the circumstances are such that the applicant ought to be registered as proprietor

(3) The second condition is that the applicant is for some reason entitled to be registered as the proprietor of the estate.

(4) The third condition is that –

(a) the land to which the application relates is adjacent to land belonging to the applicant,

(b) the exact line of the boundary between the two has not been determined under rules under section 60,

(c) for at least ten years of the period of adverse possession ending on the date of the application, the applicant (or any predecessor in title) reasonably believed that the land to which the application relates belonged to him, and

(d) the estate to which the application relates was registered more than one year prior to the date of the application.'

If any of these three conditions applies then the squatter can apply to be registered but he must still satisfy all the requirements of adverse possession. The 2002 Act has added a further stage to the claim for adverse possession and has given the paper title owner the right to be notified of the claims of the adverse possessor.

**1. Estoppel**: the squatter will rely on the fact that the registered proprietor made a representation to him and he has acted in reliance on that representation to his detriment. Under the rules of estoppel the proprietor is then estopped from going back on his representation. The Registrar could then register the squatter as proprietor but the 2002 Act envisages other forms of relief being given. Under s 110(4) the Registrar is given the power to make any order that the High Court could make in the exercise of its equitable jurisdiction.

**2.** The Registrar may register the applicant if he is entitled to be registered as the proprietor of the estate for some other reason. This covers situations such as where the squatter has rights under intestacy or a valid will of the deceased proprietor.

**3. Boundary disputes**: many of the claims for rights under adverse possession concern boundary disputes. Under the 2002 Act, if the squatter believed the disputed land to be his own for the last 10 years then the squatter is entitled to be registered if he can satisfy the requirements of both factual possession and also an intention to possess.

If any of these conditions applies, the squatter can apply to be registered immediately and so acquire rights in less than 12 years but if none of them applies then the registered proprietor must take action to evict the squatter.

The squatter may make a further application any time over the following two years unless the following conditions apply:

**1.** he is a defendant in proceedings which involve asserting a right to possession of the land

**2.** judgment for possession of the land has been given against him in the last two years or

**3.** he has been evicted from the land pursuant to a judgment for possession.

The 2002 Act is trying to prevent the unnecessary waste of time and money of both the squatter and the paper title owner in repeated applications to be registered as proprietor of the property, most of which will be unsuccessful. However, there is also provision under the Act to allow the adverse possessor to gain rights over the land where justice so permits.

'Schedule 6, paragraph 9 . . . (1) Where a person is registered as the proprietor of an estate in land in pursuance of an application under this Schedule, the title by virtue of adverse possession which he had at the time of the application is extinguished.

(2) Subject to sub-paragraph (3) the registration of a person under this Schedule as the proprietor of an estate in land does not affect the priority of any interest affecting the estate

(3) Subject to sub-paragraph (4) where a person is registered under this schedule as the proprietor of an estate the estate is vested in him free of any registered charge affecting the estate immediately before his registration'.

In any case, if the squatter is then registered as proprietor, he will take the land subject to any interests affecting the estate.

**Steps in acquiring adverse possession rights under the Land Registration Act 2002**

| Step 1 | After 10 years the squatter writes to the Land Registry, applying to be registered as owner of the property. |
|---|---|
| Step 2 | The registered proprietor has two years to object to the squatter's application. |
| Step 3 | **a** If the paper title owner does not object, the squatter is entitled to be registered as owner.<br><br>**b** If the paper title owner objects, the squatter's application is rejected unless one of **three** exceptions applies. |
| Step 4 | The Registrar considers whether the squatter's application comes within one of the following exceptions:<br><br>**a** estoppel<br><br>**b** the squatter is legally entitled to the land<br><br>**c** there is a boundary dispute.<br><br>If the Registrar is satisfied that one of these circumstances exist, then the squatter is entitled to be registered. |
| Step 5 | If the Registrar rejects the squatter's application to be registered, the paper title owner has two years to evict the squatter. If no action is taken then the squatter will have another chance to apply to be registered as proprietor. |

## KEY FACTS

**Adverse possession under the 2002 Act**

**1.** The paper title owner of property will no longer 'lose' title once the period of limitation period has run against him.

**2.** An adverse possessor must apply to become owner of the land.

**3.** The paper title owner has notice of the application.

**4.** The adverse possessor cannot be registered as owner if the paper title owner or anyone else with an interest objects, except in three circumstances.

**5.** The three exceptions are:  **a** estoppel

   **b** the adverse possessor is for some other reason entitled to the land

   **c** a boundary dispute.

**6.** If none of these applies, the registered proprietor has two years to evict the squatter from the land.

**7.** If no action is taken to evict the squatter, he will have the chance to re-apply to be registered.

# 14.5 Adverse possession in tenancies

## 14.5.1 The tenant as the squatter

If the tenant wishes to claim adverse possession against his landlord then time will only run when his lawful right to be there has run its course. So time will only run when the lease has expired and the tenant does not pay rent or acknowledge the landlord's title.

# CASE EXAMPLE

**Hayward v Chaloner [1968] 1 QB 107**

The right to claim adverse possessory rights only arose when the relationship of landlord and tenant ceased. Here, the rector of a parish had been given small holdings. At first he paid rent but later he paid nothing. This was as a result of generosity on the part of the landowner. He claimed that he had the right to acquire rights under adverse possession because he was not there under a lawful agreement.

If the tenant claims adverse possession against other land belonging to the landlord then it will be presumed that he is there lawfully as an extension of his tenancy.

## 14.5.2 Adverse possession against tenants

It is much harder for someone to claim adverse possession against leasehold property than it is against freehold property because the squatter has to claim against both the tenant as well as the freeholder, so they must satisfy two limitation periods. However, there has been doubt as to whether the squatter has the right to remain in the property for the duration of the lease.

The law differs as to whether the title is unregistered or registered.

## Unregistered leases

Once the squatter has taken possession then the question arises whether the tenant still has the right to surrender the lease to the landlord or whether the squatter can claim the right to enjoy the land until the lease ends. The landlord may be concerned as to what the squatter will do with the property while he is in possession.

 **ASE EXAMPLE**

### *Fairweather v St Marylebone Property Co Ltd* [1963] AC 510

A lease had been granted in 1894 for 99 years. Squatters took possession when there were still over 40 years of the lease left to run. The tenant sought to surrender the lease to his landlord in 1959. If the application was unsuccessful the landlord would have to wait until the lease expired in 1993 which was over 30 years away. The House of Lords held the surrender to be effective as the tenant still had a relationship with the landlord and the rights which were extinguished by the Limitation Act were those with the squatter himself. In other words, the tenant still had sufficient interest in the lease to surrender it.

The decision is difficult to justify but it is still upheld in relation to adverse possessory rights against tenants of unregistered land and will be unaffected by the 2002 Act.

## Registered leases

The law is different where the tenancy is in registered land. Once time has run against the tenant, the squatter has the right to be registered as the owner of the leasehold property. This means that once the squatter has registered title, the tenant can no longer surrender the lease as he owns nothing to surrender.

 **ASE EXAMPLE**

### *Spectrum Investments Co v Holmes* [1981] 1 WLR 221

The squatter had applied for registration. He had been in adverse possession for 12 years. The Land Registry registered the squatter with possessory title and that replaced the tenant's title. This was even noted on the landlord's title. After registration had taken place, the tenant tried to surrender his title to the landlord. The judge held that there had been registration of the interest which prevented the tenant from surrendering the tenancy. The squatter had the right to the property until the lease came to an end and the landlord was subject to the squatter's rights as new tenant of the property.

In this case the surrender was attempted by the tenant after the registration had taken place but it was not clear if there could be an effective surrender before registration of the squatter's interests.

## CASE EXAMPLE

**Central London Commercial Estates Ltd v Kato Kagaku Ltd [1998] 4 All ER 948**

Here, the squatter had not yet been registered as owner of the leasehold interest. However, the limitation period had run out and the squatter had the right to apply for registration. The judge held that the tenant had also lost the right to surrender the lease to the landlord. The tenant now held the lease on trust for the squatter.

The law will be different under the 2002 Act as the tenant and the landlord will both have to be notified before there can be an application for registration.

## 14.5.3 Adverse possession against trusts

This is governed by the rule that the trustee's title to trust land is never extinguished by reason of a stranger's adverse possession until the rights of all the trust beneficiaries have been barred.

## KEY FACTS

**Adverse possession against trusts**

1. The trustee can never acquire adverse possessory rights against trust land himself.

2. The beneficiaries cannot acquire adverse possessory rights against each other where the property is co-owned.

3. Where land is held in succession the rights of one beneficiary can be barred, for example the tenant for life, but the rights of the remainderman will not be affected.

4. Under s 15(2) of the Limitation Act 1980 there are two limitation periods which could apply. Recovery by the remainderman could either be six years from when the right fell in, ie when the tenant for life died or the trustees have the right to take action 12 years from when the squatter goes into possession.

# ACTIVITY

> Uncle Edward created a trust over his land. He appoints Babs and Sue as trustees to
> hold his house in the Lake District on trust for Timmy for life with remainder to Ian
> in fee simple absolute. Simon went into adverse possession of the land twelve and a
> half years ago.
>
> Advise Timmy and Ian.
>
> Would it make any difference to your answer if Timmy had died two years before the
> expiry of the limitation period?

# 14.6 The nature of the rights in adverse possession

## 14.6.1 Unregistered land

If adverse possession is successful, the paper title owner is prevented from suing and his title is
effectively extinguished.

Any rights in existence against the title will continue to be effective as the squatter will not be a
*bona fide* purchaser for value of the land.

## 14.6.2 Registered land

Before the 2002 Act the paper title owner was deemed to hold the estate on trust for the squatter
once time had run against him. Under the Act the law is different as the registered title owner does
not lose title just because someone takes possession the land for a fixed period of time (s 96).

> **S** 's 96 . . . no period of limitation under section 15 of the Limitation Act 1980 . . . shall
> run against any person, other than a chargee, in relation to an estate in land or
> rentcharge the title to which is registered'.

The squatter can only successfully obtain rights where he successfully applies to the Registrar for
registration. However, this process is carried out only after the paper title owner has been notified
and has a chance to register any objections to the registration.

# 14.7 Recovery of possession by the paper title owner

In unregistered land and in registered land before the 2002 Act it was very important that
proceedings were initiated before time had run against the paper title owner.

## CASE EXAMPLE

**Mount Carmel Investments v Peter Thurlow Ltd [1988] 1 WLR 1078**

Here, it was held that merely to send a letter demanding return of the property was insufficient to stop time running against the paper title owner. The only way to stop time from running was to start legal proceedings to recover possession.

It is still important that the paper title owner takes action to evict the squatter even when the application to register has been rejected because he has objected. If no action is taken by the owner to evict the squatter, he can reapply to be registered in two years' time.

# 14.8 Adverse possession and the Human Rights Act 1998

The nature of a claim in adverse possession is such that it can be seen to be in contravention of a person's right to peaceful enjoyment of their property under Article 1, Protocol 1 of the European Convention on Human Rights. However, the courts have been reluctant to make a ruling on whether adverse possession does challenge basic human rights.

The courts have had one significant opportunity to rule on the issue of human rights in connection with adverse possession. The issue was raised in *Pye (Oxford) Ltd v Graham* in the Court of Appeal. The House of Lords did not consider the issue in any detail because it decided that the Human Rights Act 1998 did not have retrospective effect and therefore as the claim was brought prior to 2nd October 2000 (when the 1998 Act took effect) then it could not apply to the facts. The judge at first instance and the Court of Appeal did consider the effects of the human rights legislation on adverse possession:

## CASE EXAMPLE

**Pye (Oxford) Ltd v Graham [2001] Ch 804**

'A frequent justification for limitation periods generally is that people should not be able to sit on their rights indefinitely, and that is a proposition to which at least in general nobody could take exception. However, if as in the present case the owner of land has no immediate use for it and is content to let another person trespass on the land for the time being, it is hard to see what principle of justice entitles the trespasser to acquire the land for nothing from the owner simply because he has been permitted to remain there for 12 years. To say that in such circumstances the owner who has sat on his rights should therefore be deprived of his land appears to me to be illogical and disproportionate. Illogical because the only reason that the owner can be said to have sat on his rights is because of the existence of the 12 year limitation period in the first place; if no limitation period existed he would be entitled to claim possession whenever he actually wanted the land'.

Neuberger J, sitting in the High Court

The judge is here challenging the whole justification for adverse possession and arguing that simply because a landowner does not use his land for a period of time it does not then make any difference to the nature of his ownership of the legal title.

'I believe the result is disproportionate because, particularly in a climate of increasing awareness of human rights including the right to enjoy one's own property, it does seem draconian to the owner and a windfall for the squatter that, just because the owner has taken no steps to evict a squatter for 12 years, the owner should lose 25 hectares of land to the squatter with no compensation whatsoever'.

In this part of the judgment, although Neuberger J did not directly rule on the human rights issue, he does suggest that the loss of land through adverse possession presents a direct challenge to the whole principle of the right to enjoy one's own property under human rights legislation.

The Court of Appeal did look at the issue of the impact of the human rights legislation on the facts of the case. The case for Pye was based partly on s 3 of the 1998 Act which holds that legislation must be interpreted in such a way as to be compatible with Convention rights. The court did not think that s 3 applied in this case.

'. . . the parties focused on one point, namely the impact of section 3 of the 1998 Act on the interpretation of the relevant provisions of the 1980 Act . . . My conclusions on the section 3 point are . . . as follows . . . Section 3 does not affect the case. The only Convention right relied on (the protection of property in article 1 of the First Protocol) does not impinge on the relevant provisions of the 1980 Act. Those provisions do not deprive a person of his possessions or interfere with his peaceful enjoyment of them. They deprive a person of his right of access to the courts for the purpose of recovering property if he has delayed the institution of his legal proceedings for 12 years or more after he has been dispossessed of his land by another person who has been in adverse possession of it for at least that period. The extinction of the title of the claimant in those circumstances is not a deprivation of possessions or a confiscatory measure for which the payment of compensation would be appropriate'.

Mummery LJ, in the Court of Appeal

Keene LJ, who also sat in the Court of Appeal, was much stronger in his argument that the human rights legislation did not challenge the claimant's rights in this case:

> 'It has not been suggested in these proceedings that the 12 year limitation period provided for by the English law on actions to recover land is itself incompatible with the Convention. In any event the Strasbourg jurisprudence recognises a margin of appreciation for national legislatures in determining such periods, which exist in most if not all European jurisdictions in some shape or form. There is therefore no reason to conclude that s 15 of the Limitation Act 1980 is incompatible with Convention rights . . . What this demonstrates is that the argument about confiscation or deprivation of property rights without compensation has little to commend it. It was accepted on behalf of the appellants that if this court finds that the respondents had satisfied the requirements of English law as to adverse possession for 12 years, then no breach of the Convention would result . . . To my mind, that means that the arguments based on the Human Rights Act add very little, if anything, to the submissions which relate to the pre-Human Rights Act law. It therefore becomes unnecessary to deal in detail with most of the arguments advanced concerning the interpretation of the Human Rights Act itself and its various provisions'.

Keene LJ, in the Court of Appeal

In the House of Lords Browne-Wilkinson LJ did not consider the human rights issues in the case because under the 1998 Act the case must be initiated after the Act was in force and the case had been brought before the 1998 Act came into force.

## Further reading

Dockray, M, 'Why do we need Adverse Possession?' [1985] Conv 272

Radley-Gardner, O and Harpum, C, 'Adverse Possession and the Intention to Possess – A Reply' [2001] Conv 155.

Rhys, O, 'Adverse Possession, Human Rights and Judicial Heresy' [2002] Conv 470.

Tee, L 'Adverse Possession and the Intention to possess' [2000] Conv 113.

Tee, L, 'Adverse Possession and the Intention to Possess a Rejoiner' [2002] Conv 50.

# chapter 15 COMMONHOLD ■

## 15.1 Introduction

This is a new concept in land. It provides a structure for managing land where property is held for group occupation, such as flats or units on an industrial estate. The problem in the past has been how to manage those areas common to all, for example the road over which everyone passes to his own unit on the industrial estate or the stairs which are used by all the owners in a block of flats. These areas present problems, eg they need maintenance which can be costly and it is not always clear who should be responsible to pay for these costs. The lack of enforceability of positive covenants has made this particularly difficult to address.

The Law Commission considered the issue in 1984 and proposed that there should be a new type of obligation called a **land obligation** which would be enforceable between neighbours.

The essence of its proposals was that there should be two types of obligations:

**1. neighbour obligations** and

**2. development** obligations.

**Neighbour obligations** would be similar to positive and negative covenants between freeholders.

**Development obligations** would be reciprocal obligations within areas of multiple occupation, such as blocks of flats.

These original ideas are incorporated into the new legislation but the proposals made are far more radical and are modelled on concepts used in many countries, in particular North America and Australia. (In North America such properties are known as condominiums.)

The Commonhold and Leasehold Reform Act 2002 lays down a radically new statutory scheme concerning how these areas are to be managed. The basis of the new legislation is that although individuals will own their flats and separate units, the common areas will be owned by what are called **commonhold associations**. Ownership by the commonhold associations will be freehold and there is no provision for combined leasehold and freehold or continued leasehold ownership.

The commonhold association will be a company limited by guarantee that is controlled by the unit holders. It will have several roles, including the administration of the common parts as well as the overseeing of the individual units. The commonhold association will be bound by a community statement. The statement can be changed to adapt to changes in circumstances of the community. The community will be controlled by its members through the commonhold association in general meeting. The directors of the association may be either members elected from their own number or professionals or other outsiders appointed by the members to run the community on behalf of the

association. When a member sells his unit the purchaser will buy into the association. It is always possible to end the association and voluntarily to liquidate the commonhold association. However, there must be a majority in favour of terminating provisions. It is a flexible form of land holding and can be used even where there are only a small number of units, eg three or four flats in a block would qualify.

This is a form of landholding for freehold owners of land and it goes some way towards counteracting the difficulties of enforcing positive rights between owners of freehold land as seen in *Rhone v Stephens* [1994] 2 AC 310.

This will define the roles and duties of the commonhold association and the individual unit-holders. The statements will vary from one unit to another according to their own particular needs.

'A Commonhold is a community of linked freehold estates with mutual interests and obligations. It is a community formed to share facilities and undertake repair and maintenance of common parts. The community of interest (which is a consequence of Commonhold) cannot tolerate other forms of estate within commonhold whether these are standard freehold or pre-existing leasehold. As a consequence, the site of the proposed Commonhold has to be "legally cleared" of existing leasehold interests so that there only remains the freehold fee simple which can then be the basis to establish the Commonhold on the freehold land by what is (essentialy) a second registration of title. The existing freehold title is thereby transformed into a freehold estate in Commonhold land'.

D N Clarke, 'The Enactment of Commonhold – Problems, Principles and Perspectives' [2002] 66 Conv 349

# 15.2 The legislation

In the Commonhold and Leasehold Act 2002:

**'s 1 The definition of commonhold land**

(1) Land is commonhold land if –

(a) the freehold estate in the land is registered as a freehold estate in commonhold land,

(b) the land is specified in the memorandum of association of a commonhold association as land in relation to which the association is to exercise functions, and

(c) a commonhold community statement makes provision for rights and duties of the commonhold association and unit-holders (whether or not the statement has come into force)'.

Initially these three conditions must be satisfied before the 2002 Act will apply. It will not apply where the land has unregistered title. However, under s 2 it is possible to come within the provisions and to register if the applicant purchased with unregistered title and has applied to register, the title now being subject to compulsory registration.

Under s 3(1), an application under s 2 may not be made in respect of a freehold estate in land without the consent of anyone who:

- is the registered proprietor of the freehold estate in the whole or part of the land
- is the registered proprietor of a leasehold estate in the whole or part of the land granted for a term of more than 21 years
- is the registered proprietor of a charge over the whole or part of the land or
- falls within any other class of person which may be prescribed.

It should be noted that there is no possibility of the land being partly held as commonhold and partly held as freehold. This makes it impossible to have a 'flying commonhold'. This would be a commonhold of a group of flats existing above other freehold land. It would not make sense for different rules to apply where property is held in such close proximity. Thus commonhold now allows positive obligations to be enforced within the commonhold.

This section is important because under commonhold all existing charges are extinguished and this must involve agreement from everyone. There may be problems where the development is large or where there are large numbers of long leaseholders. Commonhold cannot exist without reciprocity and so every member must have the same rights and the same duties as everyone else.

's 7 **Registration without unit-holders**

(1) This section applies where –

    (a) a freehold estate in land is registered as a freehold estate in commonhold land in pursuance of an application under section 2 and

    (b) the application is not accompanied by a statement under section 9(1)(b).

(2) On registration

    (a) the applicant shall continue to be registered as the proprietor of the freehold estate in the commonhold land, and;

    (b) The rights and duties conferred and imposed by the commonhold community statement shall not come into force (subject to section 8(2)(b)).

(3) Where after registration a person other than the applicant becomes entitled to be registered as the proprietor of the freehold estate in one or more, but not all, of the commonhold units –

(a) the commonhold association shall be entitled to be registered as the proprietor of the freehold estate in the common parts,

(b) the Registrar shall register the commonhold association in accordance with paragraph (a) (without an application being made)

(c) the right and duties conferred and imposed by the commonhold community statement shall come into force

(d) any lease of the whole or part of the commonhold land shall be extinguished by virtue of this section'.

Section 7 covers new developments. It is envisaged that developers will see the advantages of commonhold and before selling off the parts of the development the developer will incorporate the commonhold association and also prepare the community statement. Once he has done this he will apply for registration of the land as commonhold and for this he will need to support his application with documentation. It is assumed that the developer owns the land because the application must be made by the registered proprietor of the freehold estate.

## APPLYING THE LAW

Bernard owns 'Developments for All'. He purchases a dilapidated house set in four acres of land. He intends to turn it into a number of luxury flats. He decides that he will sell off the flats as commonhold. The first step he must take is to incorporate the commonhold association and prepare the statement and then apply for registration. This precedes any sale of the flats. There then follows a period of transition which is covered in s 8. The developer can still change his mind. If Bernard decides that commonhold will actually reduce the value of the flats then he can change his mind and withdraw from the scheme.

 's 9 **Registration with unit-holders**

This section applies to a freehold estate in commonhold land if –

(a) it is registered as a freehold estate in commonhold land in pursuance of an application under section 2, and

(b) the application is accompanied by a statement by the applicant requesting that this section should apply.

> (2) A statement under subsection (1)(b) must include a list of the commonhold units giving in relation to each one the prescribed details of the proposed initial unitholder or joint unit-holders.
>
> (3) On registration –
>
>> (a) the commonhold association shall be entitled to be registered as the proprietor of the freehold estate in the common parts'.

This section covers registration where there are existing unit-holders and it then allows long leaseholders to have their property converted into commonhold. So here we contrast the situation under s 7, where the developers will not know who is going to form the association, and s 9, where the names of the association holders already exist and a statement covers them all. The commonhold will then come into effect as soon as registration has been completed. The conversion of existing groups of long leaseholders into commonhold will depend on how easy it will be to get everyone's agreement. The application for conversion cannot be made unless everyone involved consents.

## APPLYING THE LAW

Canary Towers is a block of flats with eight long leaseholders. The freehold is owned by Frederick. If they decide to convert then every leaseholder must agree to the conversion as well as Frederick. If one decides he does not want to join the scheme, it cannot be converted.

Under s 7(3)(d) all leases will be converted into commonhold. The effect of this may be that some tenants will actually lose their leases.

## APPLYING THE LAW

Sue owns a long lease of a large mansion flat in Maida Vale. In order to meet some of the rising costs, she lets out her spare bedroom to Carrie who has a sub-lease of one year from Sue. If Sue and the other long leaseholders decide to convert to commonhold, Carrie will lose her rights and her lease will have been extinguished. There are provisions for compensation under s 10 of the 2002 Act and the responsibility for payment will fall on Sue as the most immediate landlord.

465

This presents a challenge to the existing landlord and tenant legislation.

> 'In the case of a developer wishing to refurbish (say) a block of ten flats of which nine are vacant but one of which has a tenant (with some form of security of tenure) it does seem that the developer could proceed to apply (quite properly) for registration of the commonhold ignoring the existence of that tenant who does not need to consent to the registration. The developer would proceed to refurbish the other nine flats. On the sale of the first flat as a commonhold unit, the tenancy is extinguished. Is the developer then able to take possession proceedings to remove the tenant and refurbish the last flat? The 2002 Act is quite clear. The lease is extinguished. A court faced with a claim for possession of such a flat will be forced to consider the relevant earlier legislation providing for security of tenure in the light of the extinguishment of that tenancy under the 2002 Act'.

D N Clarke, 'The Enactment of Commonhold – Problems, Principles and Perspectives' [2002] 66 Conv 349

## The association

The association is dependent on unit-holders and under Schedule 3, para 7 to the 2002 Act a person is entitled to be entered on the register of members once he becomes a unit-holder. Without ownership of a unit, someone is not entitled to become a member of the association. The association takes the form of a private company limited by guarantee.

The management of the association is dealt with under ss 35–36. One key feature is that all members of the association must be given a chance to vote.

## Commonhold community statement

The commonhold community statement is described in s 38. This lays down very specific requirements of the statement. It must make provision:

**a** requiring the directors of the commonhold association to make an annual estimate of the income required to be raised from unit-holders to meet the expenses of the association

**b** enabling the directors of the commonhold association to make estimates from time to time of income required to be raised from unit-holders in addition to the annual estimate.

Section 31 covers the matters covered by the community statement and includes under s 31(5), in particular, a duty –

**a** to pay money

**b** to undertake works

**c** to grant access

**d** to give notice

**e** to refrain from entering into transactions of a specified kind in relation to a commonhold unit

**f** to refrain from using the whole or part of a commonhold unit for a specified purpose or for anything other than a specified purpose.

Other matters covered are to refrain from causing nuisance or annoyance and to refrain from specified behaviour.

The legislation is fairly detailed about the ambit of the statement and the duties that will be covered by commonhold.

## Restrictions on dealing with the commonhold property

There are some restrictions on the way an owner of commonhold can deal with the unit that he owns. The property can be sold in the normal way but the new owner must accept the association and the responsibilities of commonhold. However, there is a restriction on leasing property under s 17 which prevents leases from being created unless they are within the section. This limits leases to the length prescribed by regulations which will be under seven years.

## Termination of commonhold

Commonhold can be brought to an end under ss 43–49 of the 2002 Act. The reasons may be because the commonholders want to be freed from the association or because the property is unsuitable for commonhold.

Under s 43 it is necessary to have the agreement of over 80 per cent of the members of the association. There must be a termination statement and everyone must be in agreement if the application is to go directly to the Registrar. If only 80 per cent agree then the matter must go to the court under s 45.

## Termination by the court

If the association is in debt and unable to meet those debts then an application must be made to the court who can order that another association takes over, called the 'successor commonhold association'.

## 15.3 Summary

Commonhold is a new approach to community property holding. It at last allows freeholders the right to enforce positive obligations among themselves. It has advantages over a landlord taking responsibility for these obligations because the interests of the unit-holders will be identical, whereas the interest of the landlord will never be the same as those of the tenants.

There are a number of disadvantages:

**1.** the unit-holder does not have complete freedom to deal with the unit. The most important restriction is in connection with leases

**2.** there is an expectation that all unit-holders will carry out their duties. This is unlikely to be the case and the 2002 Act does not deal with enforcement adequately

**3.** there is no statutory system for resolution of disputes. There should be a tribunal established with the sole responsibility of dealing with disputes rather than putting the responsibility on to the Lands Tribunal.

> 'Commonhold is not the final answer to the problem of freehold covenants. That awaits the introduction of land obligations, commonhold only solving the problem of positive obligations within the commonhold community. Commonhold is no more than the framework for community living'.

> D N Clarke, 'The Enactment of Commonhold – Problems, Principles and Perspectives' [2002] 66 Conv 349

# ACTIVITY

You are approached by Dan, who is a property developer. He wants to purchase a run-down convalescent home and turn it into luxury flats He asks you what the advantages of adopting commonhold for the flats would be.

Advise Dan.

## Further reading

Clarke, D N, 'The Enactment of Commonhold – Problems: Principles and Perspectives' [2002] 66 Conv 349.

Crabb, L, 'The Commonhold Association As you like it' [1998] 62 Conv 283.

Kenny, P H, 'Commonhold at last?' [2001] 65 Conv 1.

# HOW TO ANSWER
# QUESTIONS ■

When studying law you will be expected to write essays and you will also have to apply the law in legal problems based on scenarios. This appendix gives some hints on the skills you need for both of these.

## Legal problem solving

There are four essential ingredients to answering problem questions. You need to:

**1.** identify the important facts in the questions and from these identify the area of law you need to apply

**2.** define the area of law

**3.** expand your definition, including relevant sections and cases to show that you know and understand the area of law thoroughly

**4.** apply the law to the problem and reach a conclusion.

Consider the following problem:

Jolyon has owned the freehold of a large farm in Hampshire since 1970. Access to the farm is up a track which is about half a mile long and is owned by the farm. There are a number of farm buildings along the track and also a cottage in which, until recently, Eric, Jolyon's son, has lived. Eric decided to try his luck at farming in France and left five years ago. Since then Jolyon has let the cottage to Kenneth and Irene. Kenneth works in London and Irene works from home as a freelance journalist, but her real love is horses. She has her own horse which Jolyon allows her to graze on one of his fields. He has allowed her to use one of the barns as a stable. He has also allowed Kenneth to keep his vintage motorbike collection in an adjoining barn. The cottage has access to a country lane but it is much quicker to get to the nearest town and the station by the track which leads to the main road and Kenneth frequently uses it. Jolyon uses a short-cut across their land because he wants to visit his local pub which is half a mile up the country lane. Kenneth and Irene have not objected to this.

In 1974 Jolyon agreed with Cedric, one of his neighbours, that Cedric could park his car on a piece of rough land on the edge of his land. Cedric often works abroad but whenever he is in England he parks his car on Jolyon's land. If it rains, the land gets heavy and wet, so earlier this year Cedric concreted over the area where he parks his car. Cedric shares Kenneth's interest in vintage motorcycles and they are now very good friends.

Jolyon sold the cottage to Kenneth and Irene in December 2003. He did not seek the assistance of

a solicitor and the conveyance failed to mention the use of the track or the stable.

In January 2004 Jolyon wrote to Kenneth and Irene and asked them to find alternative grazing for the horse. He also asked them to cease using the barns for stabling or storage. This has annoyed them so much that when Jolyon walked across their land for one of his visits to the pub they refused him access.

Kenneth and Irene are now on very poor terms with Jolyon and now he has realised that they are on good terms with Cedric he has asked him to stop parking on his land.

Advise Kenneth and Irene and Cedric.

# Answering the question

## Identifying the facts

This is a complex problem and contains a number of different points each related to easements and profits à prendre. You should start by separating out the main issues and dealing with each in turn.

Kenneth and Irene are claiming several different rights over Jolyon's land:

    (i)   a right of way over his land to get to the main road

    (ii)  a right to use one barn for storage

    (ii)  a right to use another barn as a stable

    (iv)  a right to use the land for grazing purposes.

Jolyon is claiming a right of way over the land of Kenneth and Irene.

Cedric is claiming a right to park his car.

In each case you need to identify whether the right claimed is capable of existing as an easement or a profit à prendre and then you need to identify whether it now attaches to the land either by grant or by reservation, and finally you need to discuss the implications of the Land Registration Act 2002.

We will take each point in turn:

Kenneth and Irene are claiming an easement over Jolyon's land. They will have to show that the right can be an easement and that there has been either an express or an implied grant of such a right. In this part of the question you need to consider the requirements for an easement but as a right of way is not in dispute as constituting an easement it is not worth spending too much time on this.

The requirements for an easement are laid down in *Re Ellenborough Park* [1956] Ch 131 which held that for a valid easement:

    (i)   there must be a dominant and a servient tenement

(ii)   the easement must accommodate the dominant tenement

(iii)   the dominant and servient owners must be different persons and

(iv)   the right must be capable of forming the subject-matter of a grant.

The right satisfies these criteria and constitutes an easement. There are two tenements – one owned by Jolyon and one owned by Kenneth and Irene – and the right improves the enjoyment of Kenneth and Irene's land and it is clearly the type of right which has been accepted as an easement in the past. If there was a new and novel right then it would be useful to discuss this and consider such cases as *Hunter v Canary Wharf* [1997] AC 655.

What is not clear, however, is whether or not this right has been acquired for the benefit of Kenneth and Irene's land.

The right of way may have been in use before it was leased to Kenneth and Irene or used by Eric, presumably under licence. If this can be proved then the right could pass under the rule in *Wheeldon v Burrows* (1879) 12 Ch D 31 which allows quasi-easements to pass where they are continuous, apparent and necessary to the reasonable enjoyment of the land granted and which were at the time of the grant used by the grantor for the benefit of the part granted.

Even if the right was not exercised by Jolyon then it can still pass when Kenneth and Irene purchase the land, under s 62 of the Law of Property Act 1925 which implies into the conveyance all liberties and privileges enjoyed at the time and this would include licences. There must be diversity of occupation under *Sovmots v Secretary for State for the Environment* [1979] AC 144. This suggests that the right of way will be binding on Jolyon.

There will be similar arguments for the storage of the motorbikes and the stabling of the horse, although there will be scope to consider in more detail the requirements of *Re Ellenborough Park*. There is considerable case law on whether storage can constitute an easement. Consider cases such as *Copeland v Greenhalf* [1952] 1 Ch 488 and *Grigsby v Melville* [1973] 1 All ER 385 where the claim failed because it amounted to exclusive user.

Irene may have acquired the right to graze the horse on Jolyon's land. It is possible that this is more than a mere licence and she may have a profit à prendre. This again can be acquired under s 62 of the Law of Property Act 1925. The informal permission granted by Jolyon can become a legal right so long as there is no contrary intention in the conveyance.

Jolyon has been using Kenneth and Irene's land as a short-cut. This is slightly different from the right that they claim over his land. He has leased the land to them so they are now legal owners and if he is to pass over the land legally then he must seek their permission. Until the parties fell out he had a bare licence and they could withdraw that at will. While the relationship was amicable there was no question of this but now they have refused him access and they are entitled to do this. He may have a legal right to continue to use the right of way over the land if he had reserved a right in the conveyance. The conveyance appears not to do so. If it has not been expressly mentioned then it is very difficult to claim that it arises by implication. The courts will construe an

easement arising under an implied reservation very strictly. If he was landlocked and unable to access the main road apart from through Kenneth and Irene's land then an easement of necessity may be implied. However, we are told that he has access from his own land so it is unlikely that he can continue to use their land and he must find another route to the pub.

Cedric's long use of the right to park on Jolyon's land may have given him an easement under prescription. The Prescription Act 1832 will give Cedric rights if he can prove that he has enjoyed the right for 40 years. The right shall be deemed 'absolute and indefeasible unless it shall appear that the same was enjoyed by some consent or agreement expressly given or made for the purpose by deed or writing'. Cedric falls short of this period but may be able to rely on the shorter period under the 1832 Act, which is only 20 years. The problem is that this requires proof that such a right can constitute an easement at all. Rights to park were for some time challenged as not being capable of taking effect as an easement. This is because the courts considered the right to be similar to storage and this sometimes failed where it appeared to be exclusive enjoyment for the claimant which excluded the owner from enjoying his own land. Recent decisions such as *London & Blenheim Estates Ltd v Ladbroke Retail Parks Ltd* [1992] 1 WLR 1278 have made it clear that parking can be an easement if it does not prevent the owner of the land from enjoying his own land. If there is just a single area which Cedric has concreted over then Jolyon may be able to claim that it does not exist as an easement because it denies Jolyon any rights over his own land. Even if it is an easement, Cedric has no right to concrete the area as his right is to park his car; it is a right of *use* and it does not include a right to treat it as his own. Jolyon could claim a mandatory injunction forcing Cedric to remove the concreting from the land. If Cedric is to rely on prescription then he must satisfy the three requirements, namely that the right has been acquired *nec vi*, *nec clam* and *nec precario*. The problem for Cedric is that he has been given the right by Jolyon and so it will be held that he has been using the right with express permission. This will bar his right to claim the right under prescription. If he cannot rely on prescription then Cedric must show that the right has been expressly or impliedly granted to him.

The last point to consider is the need under the Land Registration Act 2002 to register the rights. Under the 2002 Act, easements rely on registration for their effectiveness. Only those legal easements that have been acquired prescriptively or by implied grant can continue to exist as overriding interests. Where an easement passes under s 62 of the Law of Property Act 1925 the easement will be acquired impliedly. Under Schedule 3, para 3 to the 2002 Act an easement will be overriding under only three circumstances:

(a)  the purchaser for valuable consideration actually knows about them

(b)  they are obvious on a reasonably careful inspection of the land

(c)  they have been used in the year preceding the disposition.

In the case of the use of the stable and the short-cut these are in use and known and are also obvious. The same applies to the right to graze the horse on Jolyon's land.

Cedric may argue that he has been expressly granted the right to park on Jolyon's land, in which case the right should be registered if it is to take effect.

You should finish your answer with a conclusion summing up your advice to each of the claimants.

# Legal essay writing

The secret to writing a good essay is to plan carefully what you are going to write. The title must be read carefully and it should be possible to highlight key issues before you start to plan. The essay should have an introductory paragraph and then the main body of the essay should fall into a number of paragraphs each raising a different point. Your essay should end with a conclusion which should sum up the main points you have covered. In an exam this requires careful thought as there is very little time for each part of the process.

Consider the following essay title:

'... The equity arises not from the claimant's expectations alone, but from the combination of expectations, detrimental reliance, and the unconscionableness of allowing the benefactor (or the deceased benefactor's estate) to go back on the assurances'.

Robert Walker LJ in *Jennings v Rice* [2002] EWCA Civ 159

To what extent do you think that this is a valid explanation of the legal basis of proprietary estoppel? How does the court satisfy the equity in cases of proprietary estoppel?

## Answering the question

The key elements in addressing the points in an essay are:

1. setting out certain factual information on the particular area of law, with supporting statutes and cases

2. addressing the actual question set. This involves a critical element. It may be one of a number of different things: a discussion of a development of law; an analysis of case decisions; comment on an area of law; or perhaps the evaluation of the contribution of a case or just the need for reform of an area of law

3. coming to a conclusion by combining both elements.

The first part is easiest to do, but it is important to explain only relevant areas of law. Usually the question will be quite specific on the area required. In the question above, the quotation is fairly broadly based and it requires a discussion of all the three elements mentioned in the quote: expectations, detrimental reliance and unconscionability. The question also considers the remedy that will be awarded by the court in estoppel cases. The court may simply look at the expectations of the claimant or they may look at all the aspects of the case and the quote from Robert Walker LJ suggests that the second approach should be adopted by the court.

The second part involves analysis, criticism, evaluation etc and is much more demanding but needs to be based on the law as set out in the first part. Arguments must be supported by reference to relevant decisions. Where the judges have given different reasons for a decision or where there is a dissenting judgment then the differences need to be explored and discussed.

The third part is to come to a conclusion drawing on the points raised in the essay.

# Putting this into practice

The starting point in this essay question is to look at the different elements of proprietary estoppel.

All claims in proprietary estoppel are based on *expectations*. The other elements will determine whether these are justified or not. There are two situations to consider: X may actively encourage Y to believe that he either has, or will, acquire an interest in X's land. Y then relies upon that expectation and an equity arises in his favour. An obvious case to use here would be *Inwards v Baker* [1965] 2 QB 929 where a father suggested to his son that he might build a bungalow on the father's land when buying other land proved to be very expensive. When the father died, the land was left to someone else. The son was held to have a right to stay in the property indefinitely because the son had an expectation fuelled by his father's active encouragement that he would be able to remain in the property for his lifetime.

The second situation is where the claimant acts upon his expectations of rights in land but there is no active encouragement from the landowner. In such a situation the landowner would be expected actively to discourage the claimant because he is fully aware of the other person's error. The quote from *Ramsden v Dyson* (1866) LR 1 HL 129 could be used here to illustrate this: '. . . If a stranger build upon my land, supposing it to be his own, and, I knowing it to be mine, do not interfere but leave him to go on, equity considers it dishonest in me to remain passive and afterwards to interfere and take the profit . . .'.

Consider the cases on expectations in two groups. The first group covers cases where property has been promised to the claimant during the promisor's lifetime. The second group covers cases where the promisor has made assurances that he will leave property to another on death and then the claimant acts upon that assurance. You could look at cases where the courts refused to uphold the claimant's claim, such as *Taylor v Dickens* [1998] 1 FLR 806. Here, an old lady had promised her gardener rights in her property under her will. When she died, the gardener got nothing. The judge did not grant anything to the gardener. There had been provision in the will but it had since been repealed. In *Gillett v Holt* [2001] Ch 210 the court looked at a similar promise but found in favour of the claimant.

You should try to explain why the court came to a different conclusion.

Historically, the claimant in cases of proprietary estoppel had to establish five *probanda* from the case of *Willmot v Barber* (1880) 15 Ch D 96. More recently, the courts look for just three requirements (which are an assurance; reliance upon the assurance; and the claimant acting to his

detriment), as laid down in *Taylor Fashions Ltd v Liverpool Victoria Trustees Co Ltd* [1982] QB 133.
The quotation in the essay title looks at *expectations* which will arise as a result of the assurance
given. *Taylor Fashions* suggests that assurances can be positive encouragement or mere acquiescence.
An expectation alone can never give rise to rights. This point must be made clear.

The second aspect of estoppel mentioned by Robert Walker LJ is that there is *detrimental reliance*
by the claimant. It must be shown that the claimant has acted in reliance on the expectation – to
his detriment. There is a wealth of case law and it is important that the answer shows how the
court has reacted to different types of detrimental conduct in order to find in favour of the
claimant.

Here is just a short list of the conduct that has successfully supported a claim in estoppel:

(i)   spending money on the extension of a jetty in reliance on a belief that rights under a
      licence would not be revoked: *Plimmer v Mayor of Wellington* (1884) 9 App Cas 699

(ii)  the sale of part of one's land, so leaving another part landlocked, believing that a right of
      way would be granted allowing access: *Crabb v Arun District Council* [1976] 1 Ch 179

(iii) leaving one's job and home to move closer to the promisor: *Jones (A E) v Jones (F W)*
      [1977] 1 WLR 438

(iv)  spending money on improvements to property in reliance on the promise that the property
      would eventually belong to the claimant: *Pascoe v Turner* [1979] 1 WLR 431

(v)   looking after the promisor and members of his family in reliance on a promise that the
      claimant would have rights in property: *Greasley v Cooke* [1980] 1 WLR 1306.

The important point to emphasise is that there is a link between the assurance of rights and the
expectation because, unless there is an assurance, rights cannot arise. In *Pascoe v Turner* the
expectation followed by detriment could not give rise to rights. It was the fact that it had been
preceded by an assurance that allowed a claim. It is the combination that Robert Walker LJ
highlights in the quote and it is important to pick this up when describing the elements of
proprietary estoppel.

In *Coombes v Smith* [1986] 1 WLR 808 the claimant was unsuccessful because she could not show
that her act of leaving her husband and moving in with her lover and having his child could be
attributable to rights in the property. She also worked on the property, as in *Pascoe v Turner*, but
she could not show that that was in reliance on a promise that she was to have rights in the
property.

The other aspect of estoppel is the *unconscionability of the benefactor going back on his assurances*.
This aspect can cause difficulties because there is an element of subjectivity in what constitutes
unconscionable conduct. Unconscionable conduct will inevitably be associated with what
assurances have been given and whether the promisor is aware that the claimant has relied on the
assurances. It is this aspect which has been emphasised in the more recent decisions on proprietary
estoppel, although it has its roots in the decision of *Willmot v Barber*. In *Gillett v Holt* a case also

decided by Robert Walker LJ, it was held that 'the fundamental principle that equity is concerned to prevent unconscionable conduct permeates all the elements of the doctrine'. In that case the court found in favour of Mr Gillett who had worked for Mr Holt for nearly 40 years. He had been given repeated assurances that he would get rights in property and although the court granted him substantially less than his expectations he was still awarded rights in the property. In this part you could criticise the decision of *Taylor v Dickens* because it could be seen as unconscionable for the estate of the benefactor to deny the claimant rights in the property when these had been promised and the claimant had forgone payment in reliance on this promise.

The second part of the question focuses on how the court can satisfy the equity. The courts have complete discretion as to how the claimant's expectations should be satisfied.

Robert Walker LJ's quotation suggests that the remedy the court should award should reflect the expectations of the claimant as well as the degree of detrimental reliance and also whether it would be unconscionable for the benefactor to go back on the assurances made.

The court will try to give effect to the expectations of the claimant and there are cases that you could use to illustrate this. *Pascoe v Turner* is a useful example because there the claimant could prove that she had been promised the fee simple of the property and the courts were prepared to convey that to her. This is unusual and you should show a range of remedies where the courts have awarded different remedies such as monetary compensation or just the right to live in the property for the claimant's lifetime.

*Jennings v Rice* shows how difficult it is for the court to strike a balance between expectations and detriment. Robert Walker LJ discusses how expectations alone can be uncertain, extravagant or out of all proportion to the detriment which the claimant has suffered and in these cases the court can and should recognise that the claimant's equity should be satisfied in another way. It is important here to look at the different approaches taken by the court .

The concluding paragraph should try to draw all aspects of the essay together and to show that proprietary estoppel is made up of different components and that the remedy granted by the court should reflect them all and should not simply satisfy the expectations of the claimant.

# INDEX

Page numbers in italics refer to key facts summaries.

# ADOBE® PHOTOSHOP® LIGHTROOM® 2 FOR DIGITAL PHOTOGRAPHERS ONLY